❖ The Myth of Seneca Falls

Gender and American Culture

COEDITORS
Thadious M. Davis
Mary Kelley

EDITORIAL ADVISORY BOARD
Nancy Cott
Jane Sherron De Hart
John D'Emilio
Linda K. Kerber
Annelise Orleck
Nell Irvin Painter
Janice Radway
Robert Reid-Pharr
Noliwe Rooks
Barbara Sicherman
Cheryl Wall

EMERITA BOARD MEMBERS
Cathy N. Davidson
Sara Evans
Annette Kolodny
Wendy Martin

A complete list of books published in
Gender and American Culture is available
at www.uncpress.unc.edu.

The Myth of Seneca Falls

✢ *Memory and the Women's*
Suffrage Movement, 1848–1898

LISA TETRAULT

The University of North Carolina Press | Chapel Hill

This volume was published with the assistance of the
Greensboro Women's Fund of the University of North Carolina Press.
Founding Contributors: Linda Arnold Carlisle, Sally Schindel Cone,
Anne Faircloth, Bonnie McElveen Hunter, Linda Bullard Jennings,
Janice J. Kerley (in honor of Margaret Supplee Smith), Nancy Rouzer May,
and Betty Hughes Nichols.

The paper in this book meets the guidelines for permanence and
durability of the Committee on Production Guidelines for Book
Longevity of the Council on Library Resources.
The University of North Carolina Press has been a member
of the Green Press Initiative since 2003.

Complete cataloging information for this title is available
from the Library of Congress.

ISBN 978-1-4696-1427-4 (cloth: alk. paper)
ISBN 978-1-4696-1428-1 (ebook)

18 17 16 15 14 5 4 3 2 1

FSC
www.fsc.org

MIX
Paper from
responsible sources
FSC® C013483

For Jeanne Boydston
with love and profound gratitude

Contents

Illustrations

Acknowledgments

It took me a long time to decide I wanted to be a historian. I left the profession several times to test other waters, but each time I found my way back. The reasons are many, and the people who animated my life in that journey are chief among them. I take this opportunity to thank them in print. Although their names appear as simple preface to the many pages to follow, their spirit is present in each and every word.

This project had invaluable financial support that was critical to its realization. For long-term fellowships, I thank the National Endowment for the Humanities, the Massachusetts Historical Society, the Newberry Library, the National Museum of American History at the Smithsonian Institution, the Library of Congress, and the American Historical Association. For short-term funding, I thank the Huntington Library, the American Antiquarian Society, the Sophia Smith Collection, the Wisconsin Historical Society, and the Nantucket Historical Association. Two grants from Carnegie Mellon University, the Berkman Faculty Development Fund and the Falk Research Fund, also aided this project immeasurably. The archivists, staff, librarians, historians, and fellows at each institution played critical roles in the research process and the testing of ideas. Special thanks to Carolyn Brown, Sue Collins, Peter Drummey, Paul Erickson, Lisa Kathleen Grady, James Grossman, Larissa Kennedy, Andrew Marshall, Arthur Patton-Hock, Rosemary Fry Plakas, Mary Lou Reker, Barbara Clark Smith, and Conrad Wright.

I had the good fortune of gifted readers, who read the manuscript, at different stages, in its entirety. For their thoughts, questions, and encouragement, I thank David Blight, the late Jeanne Boydston, Colleen Dunlavy, Paul Eiss, Nan Enstad, Albrecht Funk, Glenda Gilmore, Lori Ginzberg, Linda Gordon, Melanie Gustafson, Nancy Hewitt, Stephen Kantrowitz, Mary Kelley, Lisa Levenstein, David McDowell, Annelise Orleck, Grey Osterud, Roger Rouse, Scott Sandage, Judith Wellman, and an anonymous reviewer for UNC Press. Kathi Kern and Allison Sneider also offered helpful feedback on conference papers. Their collective insights and generosity have made this book immeasurably better. I alone bear responsibility for its continued shortcomings. I found sage guides in my wonderful editors, Mary Kelley and Mark

Simpson-Vos. And I'm grateful for the expertise of the staff at UNC Press—particularly Caitlin Bell-Butterfield and Paul Betz, with the assistance of freelancer Liz Gray—who helped turn my scribblings into an actual book. Russell Kutzman also lent invaluable photographic assistance.

All of us at work in this field owe a tremendous debt to Ann D. Gordon, editor over many decades of the magisterial *Elizabeth Cady Stanton and Susan B. Anthony Papers Project*. Her work has vastly enriched our knowledge about women, history making, and social movements. I also owe a debt of thanks to the incomparable women of the Women's Rights National Historical Park in Seneca Falls, Vivien Rose and Anne Derousie, as well as to Judith Wellman for her support, her scholarship, and her activism. I cherished my days in upstate New York.

The advantage of a long graduate career is that you have the opportunity to build and deepen friendships over many, many years. Judy Houck still keeps me laughing and thinking anew. Lisa Levenstein enriches my life in countless ways. Her enthusiasm for this project kept me going. I am also grateful to her for reading chapters on much shorter timetables than anyone should ever be asked to. Sharmila Rudrappa helped me to heal at a difficult time in my life and has held my hand ever since. As I scribbled, David Ciarlo and Lisa Schreibersdorf kept me company on the other side of the table. Lisa S. also distracted me, bringing invaluable play and adventure into my life, not to mention ongoing humor, faith, and understanding. Other Madison friends supported me in all sorts of imaginative ways. Some even put me up on sojourns away from home. I'm grateful to Cynthia Gill, Colin Haller, Julie Holfeltz, Story Matkin-Rawn, Lisa Nakamura, Joy Newman, Louise Robbins, Lisa Saywell, Ayesha Shariff, and Teri Woods. Teaching with Nancy Worcester and Mariamne Whatley was the highlight of my graduate career. I've learned so much from them about how to be in the world. Thank you as well to Gerda Lerner, who built the program I had the privilege to join, and whose recent death reminds me never to take the existence of this field for granted.

Since leaving Wisconsin, I've had the good fortune to land in all sorts of stimulating places. From my fun-filled days at Hobart and William Smith Colleges, I thank all my colleagues, including Anna Creadick, Kevin Dunn, Nic Sammond, Michael Tinkler, Kanchana Ruwanpura, and John Shovlin. Laura Edwards and Dylan Pennigroth taught me a great deal during my days at the Newberry Library. I then learned more than I could have hoped from the wonderful mix of scholars who made up the Charles Warren Center's Seminar on Politics and Social Movements: Dorothy Sue Cobble, Francoise

Hamlin, Maartje Janse, Albrecht Koschnik, Dan Kryder, Lisa Materson, Timothy McCarthy, Lisa McGirr, Manisha Sinha, and Susan Ware. The invitation to be a part of the Remarque Institute's Kandersteg Seminar joyfully broadened my horizons. I had a cheerful and dedicated research assistant in Dawn Winters, a talented historian in her own right. The footnotes and research herein reveal her skill and care. Abigail Wright also offered valuable research assistance along the way. I have gladly shared the ups and downs of junior faculty life with Allyson Creasman, whose friendship has been invaluable. We too spent many amusing hours across the table from one another, scribbling away. Here in Pittsburgh, I have benefited from the rich environment created by my talented colleagues at Carnegie Mellon University. One deserves special mention. Scott Sandage has read and commented upon more drafts than anyone should ever be expected to. Thanks, Scott.

Amidst the production of this book, I became a parent, which made the writing both harder and easier. Aya reset my priorities, reminded me to put things into perspective, and brought me untold joy. That joy has carried me through this process. Thanks to her for cheerfully enduring my absence. Being returned to her is the best part about finishing this book. The people who cared for my daughter while I cloistered myself away are also due a word of thanks, including the astoundingly talented educators at the Cyert Center for Early Education. My parents, A. Richard Tetrault, Gerry Tetrault, and Mary Ellen Parker have made this all possible. I owe more than I could ever repay to my father, who has sustained me in ways large and small, and who has helped make dreams come true. This book is also for you, dad. My brother will be happy to know that "that paper" is finally done. Thanks especially to David McDowell, whose loving support has been unflagging over a lifetime, and thanks to Cindy McDowell for joining in the fun along the way. Thanks more recently to Pittsburgh friends, who have become cherished parts of my life: Amy Crosson, Paul Eiss, Michal Friedman, Albrecht Funk, Joey Murphy, Lara Putnam, Jessie Ramey, Roger Rouse, Judith Schacter, John Soluri, Shoba Subramanian, Patricia Wright, and John Zimmerman. The chance meeting of Lori Geist has truly made Pittsburgh home. Her friendship and kinship means more than I could ever say.

I dedicate this book to Jeanne Boydston. As a misguided youth, I became curious about U.S. women's history, and I snuck into the back of one of her ginormous lecture courses. I wasn't enrolled. I wasn't even in school. But I never missed a lecture. I was spellbound. At the end of the course, I timidly introduced myself. She was her usual wonderful self about it: open, generous, and inviting. In the ways that accidents often redirect our lives,

I count this one among the most fortunate of my life. Eventually, I began graduate work, with Jeanne as my advisor. I had a long way to go, but she never doubted I could do it. That faith meant more than she could have ever known. I am deeply grateful to have found my way into her orbit, and eventually to myself. Her generous, compassionate blend of creativity, brilliance, and humility amaze me still. Over time, we became family, and then one day, quite suddenly, cancer took her life. Although she did not live to see it, she is present in every page of this book. I miss you, Jeanne.

✢ The Myth of Seneca Falls

Prologue
❖ Getting Acquainted with History

The problem of a beginning is the beginning of a problem.
—UNKNOWN

The Eleventh National Woman's Rights Convention came to order on 10 May 1866. The guns of the Civil War had quieted a year before, and many felt the time had come to revisit unfinished business. The woman's rights movement, which had suspended activity during the bloodiest war in American history, held its first postwar convention in New York City's Church of the Puritans. Lucretia Mott, aged seventy-three and an elder stateswoman of the movement, looked out over the enormous crowd and saw the cause passing into new hands. "It is no loss," she explained to those assembled, "but the proper order of things, that the mothers should depart and give place to the children." The fact that Mott appeared battle scarred, with hoarse voice from a head cold and bruised face from a recent streetcar accident, added poignancy to her remarks. She recalled the long history of women's rights activism that had led to this day. "Young women of America," she urged, "I want you to make yourselves acquainted with the history of the Woman's Rights movement."[1]

Mott highlighted the importance of collective historical memory to the operation of social movements—the central preoccupation of this book. Mott was not alone in urging women to learn their history. After the Civil War, women's rights activists with similar concerns held commemorative conventions, gave speeches on women's rights history, celebrated the accomplishments of pioneering women, held birthday celebrations, observed anniversaries, wrote historical accounts, and more. All of it was instructive. Indeed, activists rebuilt a movement after the disruptions of the Civil War, in no small part, by getting acquainted with history—that is by consciously and unconsciously creating collective memories for the movement. Remembering played a critical role in providing a foundation, justification, and rallying point for rebuilding. Remembering also sustained movement activists over the second half of the nineteenth century, as it became clear that women's rights would not be won anytime soon.

Remembering was a fiercely contentious process, however. It would take the remainder of the century for most white women's rights activists to agree upon a shared history. A shared history they recognized as best representing their collective past—a past used to chart their future. The eventual triumph of one particular story, over any other number of possible stories, was the product of a long-lived contest within and outside the movement. That story was no more "true" than any other. But as a few activists pushed it to the fore, and growing numbers took it to heart, it took on the veneer of truth. As this mythological tale took shape, it did more than simply reflect activists' understanding of the past. It would fundamentally reshape the movement over the second half of the nineteenth century. Put another way, the myth itself became an important actor in the development of nineteenth-century feminism.

That eventually triumphant mythology went something like this: In 1848, Elizabeth Cady Stanton and Lucretia Mott convened the first women's rights meeting the world had ever known, the historic Seneca Falls convention in upstate New York. Here, Stanton famously made the first public demand for women's voting rights. A demand enshrined in that convention's manifesto, the "Declaration of Sentiments." That demand, along with the convention itself, marked the beginning of a women's rights movement. According to this telling, the idea for the convention had arisen far away and years earlier, at the World's Anti-Slavery Convention in London in 1840. British abolitionists had denied seats to U.S. women delegates. Incensed, Mott and Stanton (who first met in London) agreed to hold a protest convention upon their return to the United States. Pulling it off took eight years, when the women finally implemented their long-delayed convention plans. In many accounts, Susan B. Anthony also entered the story, even though she had not been present at the creation associated with 1848. By the turn of the century, this founding myth had become all anyone needed to know about "the history of the Women's Rights movement."[2]

Curiously, when Mott urged young women to learn their history, she did not tell the story we all know, because that story—as a foundational story—did not yet exist in 1866. It was not that Mott favored some other memory. Her historical remarks were notable for the absence of any familiar or cogent story. Mott's movement remained merely a loose collection of events. She made vague allusion to women's rights having begun "more than twenty years since," putting the origin in the early 1840s, or perhaps the 1830s. But then Mott reached back further still. She urged young women to learn their history "from the days of Mary Wollstoncraft [sic]," British woman of letters, who published A Vindication of the Rights of Woman in 1792, the first extended Enlightenment treatise on women's rights. Having gone back to the previous century, Mott treated the 1848 meeting as mere footnote. Surveying the large audience before her in 1866, she could not help but compare it to the relative "handful who met . . . in the first Convention . . . at Seneca Falls." The comparison underscored how the movement had matured, but it hardly cast the 1848 convention as a central event, much less the birthplace of a movement. Later, after praising women literary figures and God's moving grace, Mott recalled women's exclusion from the 1840 World's Anti-Slavery Convention, but she drew no causal connection between it and plans for the 1848 convention. These two events, which would eventually become tightly linked in feminist lore, had no connection at all in Mott's remarks. "I like to allude to these things," she explained by way of closing, "to show what progress we are making." Beyond assessing progress—from small to large numbers, from exclusion to inclusion, from condemnation to acceptance—Mott's remarks followed no particular sequence. Although she urged those assembled to learn their history, she offered them no memorable stories to hold onto—no story at all, in the sense of a linear, unified narrative. Mott's "history" was literally incoherent: without causality or even chronology and without any overarching sense of design. It simply did not cohere into what scholars would call a "master narrative."[3]

Stories are made, not found, and in 1866, the story of Seneca Falls had yet to be made. Even those activists who considered Seneca Falls to be the first U.S. women's rights meeting did not give it the seminal status it would later occupy. Someone, or some collection of people, at some time had to put the story together. And they had to persuade others to accept that story as their own. When, then, did Seneca Falls emerge as a familiar pattern of details, as a recognizable tale, and as nineteenth-century feminism's watershed event? This book locates the origins of the Seneca Falls story in the post–Civil War years, some twenty to thirty years after the actual meeting, arising from the messy, contentious world of post–Civil War politics. It interrogates how the *meeting* at Seneca Falls became the *myth* of Seneca Falls. And it examines the consequences of this development for the women's rights movement.

By tracing that history and its implications, this book tackles one of the still-intractable mythologies of U.S. history and, in the process, offers a new genealogy of American feminism.

Seneca Falls is perhaps the most enduring and long-standing myth ever produced by a U.S. social movement. If schoolchildren learn anything about U.S. women's history, they learn the story of Seneca Falls. The location of the convention is today the site of a national park, the only such park dedicated to women's rights.[4] Given the stature of this story, it is surprising that we do not yet have a history of it. We have many good histories of the meeting, but none of the story.[5] This gap in our knowledge is perhaps less surprising when we consider the internal logic of origins tales themselves. Origins myths work to legitimate and unify the messy contingencies of political struggle, making both the outcome and the story of that struggle seem unmanipulated, if not inevitable. At the same time, an origins story, once dominant, promotes the forgetting of struggles within the struggle, the debates and rivalries within the movement itself. Eventually, several competing narratives give way to a dominant collective memory, and having won, that story appears to tell itself, being self-evidently true. So it has been for over a century with the story of Seneca Falls. That tale has so successfully erased its own contested origins that it has become sacrosanct. It has become "a kind of natural fact, as if it had always been meant to be."[6]

Precisely because of its revered status, questioning this founding myth of feminism—indeed, even to call it a myth—may, at first glance, smack of disrespect. But we might just as easily conclude that querying this story is to finally grant it the respect it deserves. Scholars have taken nearly all the great "myths" of American history seriously enough to investigate and decipher them. In the process, they have given us a much deeper appreciation for such tales and an ability to effectively grapple with and analyze the power dynamics within them. We know, for example, that the civil rights movement did not really begin when Rosa Parks, tired and fed up, spontaneously refused to give up her seat at the front of the bus—a story that obscures the planned and calculated nature of black protest, the scope of white supremacy's operations, and the complexity of Parks herself.[7] And we know that Betty Friedan's 1963 groundbreaking work, *The Feminine Mystique*, did not emerge solely from her discontent as an isolated middle-class housewife—a myth that overlooks Friedan's and other postwar feminists' deep roots in the radical labor movement and the devastating effect of McCarthyism on feminist politics.[8] We tell these canonical stories of American history for the lessons they possess (about the possibilities and limits of the movements they forge), not for their accuracy, which has little correlation to a story's power.[9]

Myth in this context does *not* mean, as it does in popular use, a falsity. Rather, myth means a venerated and celebrated story used to give meaning to the world. The 1848 meeting, so far as we know, was the first meeting explicitly called to demand women's rights in the United States. That is largely undisputed. This does not, however, mean the meeting *began* a movement. That claim—that origins myth—had to be created by people, who infused this event, over other possible events, with a particular kind of meaning. Put another way, an origins myth does not actually pinpoint a beginning so much as it acts as a filter that people use to impose a certain type of meaning onto a complex and contested landscape. Recovering that complex, contested, and contingent world, which the mythology itself has concealed, is one principle aim of this book. To call Seneca Falls a myth, then, is simply to acknowledge that it is an *event* as well as a *story*, and that the two are not one and the same. It draws our attention to the power dynamics *within* the story, rather than calling that story false. In short, it takes the story seriously enough to query it.

Movements can and do begin in many places. One could anchor the beginning of the women's rights movement in the United States in many events—some before, and some after, Seneca Falls. One could begin with the Grimké sisters' practical and theoretical defenses of women as public actors in the 1830s. With black women's resistance to slavery and to the systematic raping of their bodies. With the Lowell Mill textile operatives and their 1834 and 1836 strikes for fair treatment and decent wages. With the early anatomy lectures of Mary Gove Nichols and Paulina Wright (Davis) that helped women claim sovereignty over their bodies. With six women in upstate New York who, in 1846, two years before Seneca Falls (where the first demand for female enfranchisement was supposedly made), petitioned their state constitutional convention for the right to vote. With Lucy Stone's 1847 lecture tour on women's rights. With the first national women's rights convention in Worcester, Massachusetts, in 1850, when local events became coordinated into a larger, national whole. Or on a smaller scale, with the moment any given individual woman chose to enter a life of activism on behalf of her sex. Women's rights had many beginnings. And for much of the early to mid-nineteenth century, people commonly invoked a variety of events when they spoke about the origins of women's rights.[10]

This book, then, is not intended to parse facts versus legends, deciphering whether the Seneca Falls meeting "truly" constitutes the beginning, or arguing for some other "truer" beginning. Although people are nearly universally driven to locate beginnings,[11] we can never really know or fix them.[12] "Every event in history is a beginning, a middle, and an end," historian Lori Ginzberg reminds us; "it just depends on where you pick up the thread and what story you choose to tell."[13] The following pages are dedicated, instead, to understanding how this founding myth was created as well as the politics and lessons it contained. They ask how this story instructed people to act, think, and dream. And they investigate how a story helped transform a movement.

The search for answers to how and why a nineteenth-century women's rights movement came to be rooted in the popular imagination in an ad hoc meeting in upstate New York requires looking in at least two places: heated battles among activists over the direction of a postwar women's rights agenda, and larger battles among Americans over the memory of the Civil War. When the women's suffrage movement regrouped in 1866, it faced difficult challenges. There was external opposition, to be sure. But there was also considerable struggle among women's rights activists. Reform women argued about whether suffrage ought to be *the* postwar women's rights agenda—itself a new idea. And those who thought it should argued passionately over the strategies and goals a postwar women's suffrage movement ought to pursue, a subject that provoked significant dissent. In these intramovement battles, two women, more than any others, used memory to forward their particular political agenda: Elizabeth Cady Stanton and Susan B. Anthony.

Stanton and Anthony met in 1851, and they quickly cemented an abiding friendship that lasted a lifetime. Amelia Bloomer—who, like Stanton, lived in Seneca Falls—had introduced the pair when Anthony visited the area. Anthony lived forty miles north, near Rochester, New York. She was a schoolteacher and the daughter of reform-minded parents. She advocated women's equal wages, temperance, and also abolition. She remained unmarried and never had children. Anthony, as some have commented, was married to her work. Where Stanton was the philosopher, Anthony was the organizer. They complemented one another and did more together than either could have accomplished alone. Throughout the 1850s, Anthony had pushed Stanton, busy with young children, to remain active in reform work. She frequently traveled to Seneca Falls, for example, to lock Stanton in a room to pen an address to an upcoming women's rights convention, taking charge of Stanton's children while their mother worked. At one point, the women had to save Stanton's toddler, who had been thrown into water by his brothers in order to see if the corks they had attached to his body would allow him to float. It was not always a harmonious friendship, but their affection was steadfast, deep, and abiding.[14]

When the pair turned once again to women's rights work after the Civil War, they entered contentious terrain. Battles over the relationship of black men's suffrage and women's suffrage divided activists in an acrimonious split that would last the rest of the century. It produced two competing national women's suffrage organizations, each charting a different path to victory. Many more suffragists organized in different directions on the ground. Meanwhile, other women demanded that postwar activism involve considerably more than demands for the vote—everything from equal wages to control over their bodies to resisting racist violence in the South. And many women had overlapping reform allegiances. For a time, it was not clear what women's rights cause, or what version of suffrage activism, would most successfully vie for women's limited resources. The birth of a divided and chaotic suffrage movement—*within* a rapidly expanding women's movement—left prominent suffragists scrambling to persuade other activists they represented the "true" *version* of women's rights. At the same time, prominent suffragists battled with one another, as well as grassroots suffragists, over which strategy represented the "right" *path* to winning the vote. These contentious intramovement politics motivated Stanton and Anthony to begin creating an origins story in an ongoing effort to unify activists and settle these disputes.

A second context for understanding why Stanton and Anthony made an origins story out of the 1848 meeting was the postwar culture in which they lived. Perhaps at no other time in U.S. history had Americans of all backgrounds argued so vehemently over matters of memory. They argued over how to remember the Civil War in an effort to chart a path forward. The war had settled two things: the South would remain part of the Union, and chattel slavery was over. Much more remained unsettled. How would the South rejoin the Union? Would the terms be harsh or lenient? And would former Confederates be allowed to participate in politics, after the slaughter they had caused? Equally important, and even more vexing (given American racism), was the status of freedpeople. Should they be citizens, and therefore entitled to the benefits and protections citizenship offered? What, if anything, did freedom guarantee? If it guaranteed nothing, was freedom even meaningful? At the heart of the matter was (and is) how to define freedom and, thus, how to define equality—an issue that directly involved the women's movement.[15]

That fierce debate—over competing definitions of freedom—took place in the arena of memory. It was not the only arena, but it was a critical one. Because freedom had no inherent, self-evident meaning, Americans debated its definition by attempting to define the past. Why had the Civil War been fought? Answers to that question, which varied widely, defined different paths forward. Had it been fought, as freedpeople and abolitionists argued, for emancipation? If so, that required a postwar political response that validated the needs of freedpeople and invested freedom with significant weight. Or had it been fought, as white supremacists argued, for valor, honor, and states' rights? If so, that required a postwar political response that elevated the rights of white Confederates over the rights of freedpeople, whose needs were largely erased by such a memory. Or had it been fought for a myriad of other reasons, all of which urged a different political response in the present, and future. Remembering the war became a boom industry, in which Americans argued about how to rebuild the nation. That memory contest consumed the political energies of generations after the war, even those who had not participated in the war, and it was a defining feature of politics for the rest of the century.[16]

Most of these memories were highly masculinist, praising the contributions of men and omitting—indeed, forgetting—the contributions of women. That, in turn, helped marginalize women's demands for equality, demands for their own reconstructed political status, on a national political agenda. It helped cloak the vibrant debates among women about what constituted equality. And it tried to silence women's contributions to and participation in this larger national debate. Determined to be neither erased nor silenced, women entered the memory wars by telling their own versions of history. To enter politics in this era was to enter a conversation about memory. Women, therefore, as one suffragist later put it, began narrating and celebrating history "in our own way."[17] They did this as one way to argue for rights in a climate where history and rights were inextricably interwoven.

No two women did more to create that history than Stanton and Anthony. They were savvy politicians, who increasingly understood—consciously or not—how vital an origins story could be to the operations of activism. Scholars have only just begun to consider how stories operate in social movements, and how stories are, in fact, essential to the life of social movements, instructing activists about what priorities to prize, how to imagine themselves, how to cohere, and how to move forward.[18] Stanton and Anthony learned this lesson about the power of telling stories over the turbulent 1870s, and they learned it better than any of their peers. They built the Seneca Falls mythology piece by piece—sometimes unconsciously, if nevertheless deliberately—to market their particular agenda for women's rights and also to insist upon women's place in national memory. They then worked assiduously to persuade others to listen. Eventually, by century's end, many did. But this was not a given. It required hard, exacting work, and that gathering mythology—along with the leadership of Stanton and Anthony themselves—was always contested. The two are arguably the most important women's historians of the nineteenth century, and overlooking this critical dimension of Stanton's and Anthony's activism discounts the women themselves.[19]

By unraveling the mythology they created, this book presents Stanton and Anthony as we are sometimes unaccustomed to seeing them. A Seneca Falls mythology rings true because we have been reading the end of the story back onto the beginning. A Seneca Falls mythology, which only became dominant at the end of the century, has imposed a sense of order and inevitability onto the whole of nineteenth-century women's rights, onto what was actually a world full of contest and contingency. As a result, Stanton's and Anthony's leadership, and their particular rights vision, has seemed to be a historical constant: "true" from the antebellum era on. We have very little sense of how they became recognized leaders within the movement, and how historical memory played a critical role in that process. Neither do we know much about how suffrage came to dominate a postwar women's rights agenda.

The mythology Stanton and Anthony created has, in turn, sanctified them, so that it can, at times, be uncomfortable to see them as complex political actors, driven by an ambition to lead and animated by the self-assured knowledge that they knew best. That ambition and self-assurance produced undemocratic and domineering behavior at times. In this respect, Stanton and Anthony were no different than male politicians. But ambition and calculation are still traits we have a hard time reconciling with female politicians. At the same time, an expectation that venerated movement activists behave somehow more nobly than ordinary people has added to the challenge of recovering the full complexity of leading activists (particularly these leading women). That expectation, in turn, limits our understanding of the operation of social movements, something that has certainly been true of the suffrage movement.[20]

Given the notoriety of the suffrage movement, it is surprising that we do not have more histories of it.[21] There exist many excellent books that have enhanced our understanding, but woman suffrage continues to be a subject that receives scant attention given the duration and complexity of the movement itself. What scholarship does exist has tended to concentrate on movement origins (1848–60) or on the years leading up to victory (1895–1920), leaving the middle decades of this long movement relatively unexamined. What is more surprising is that the figures most identified with the suffrage movement, Stanton and Anthony, were most active in the very years for which our knowledge is most attenuated, the campaign's middle decades. To date we still do not have a thoroughgoing scholarly biography of Anthony, arguably the most recognizable woman of the nineteenth century (thanks, in part, to the ill-fated dollar coin). The reasons for this are many. Among them are the ways in which the collective memories built by suffragists—including Anthony herself, as well as many others after Anthony's death—have obscured the three-dimensional personality and complicated political world behind those remembrances, collective memories that have had a long, long life.[22]

NOTHING ABOUT THE LITTLE TOWN OF SENECA FALLS suggested it might be the site of the nation's first women's rights convention, save for the fact that Henry Stanton, Elizabeth Cady's new husband, had settled his young family there. Cady Stanton was the precocious daughter of a wealthy New York politician and judge. She had defied her father's wishes and married the nearly penniless Henry Stanton, a scruffy abolitionist, in 1840. Henry had determined that their European honeymoon would start in London, at the World's Anti-Slavery Convention. She was there as a mere spectator, without reform credentials of her own. In fact, it would be many years before Stanton became a committed reformer. In London, Stanton was, as one historian put it, a "political lightweight" in the company of giants.[23] But she experienced a personal conversion there. Meeting Lucretia Mott for the first time, a woman twenty-two years her senior and a towering figure, was life changing for Stanton.[24] Though she herself was not an experienced abolitionist, Stanton felt personally indignant over the exclusion of Mott and other female delegates from the proceedings. After a long and contentious debate that occupied the entire first day's proceedings, male delegates determined women could sit behind a dividing bar and listen, but they would not be seated as formal convention delegates. Stanton also developed a healthy respect for men such as William Lloyd Garrison, who sat behind the bar in solidarity, to protest women's exclusion.[25]

Mott was already a veteran reformer and acknowledged leader in the abolitionist movement. In the 1830s, she had been a founder of biracial organizations such as the Pennsylvania Anti-Slavery Society and the Philadelphia Female Anti-Slavery Society, and she had actively participated in the founding of Garrison's American Anti-Slavery Society. A Quaker minister and ardent abolitionist, she had pioneered new roles for women before the Civil War by speaking and acting publicly at a time when the general sentiment dictated women remain silent and out of the public eye. She lived up to her principles and boycotted slave-produced cotton, sugar, and produce. She was so frugal that she would pack two pages worth of writing onto one piece of paper, filling a page with tightly spaced horizontal lines of text, then giving it a quarter turn and penning a new set of lines on top of and perpendicular to the first. Mott had endured mob attack—both verbal and physical—not just for her abolitionism, a wildly unpopular cause in the North, but also for her women's rights activism.[26]

For Mott, women's exclusion was odious, but familiar. Women abolitionists had fought against social prejudice since their entrance into the movement. The Grimké sisters, Sarah and Angelina, had received resounding criticism for their choice to lecture publicly, to large audiences, against the peculiar institution of slavery. Ministers and others denounced the sisters for defying their expected roles, which dictated that women remain passive and in the private, domestic sphere, away from public politics, which was thought to be an aggressive sport better suited to men. The Grimkés were also criticized for violating the biblical Pauline dictate, in which women were to remain silent. They received equal criticism for speaking to mixed-sex audiences (called "promiscuous" audiences), something considered deeply unacceptable. The sisters fought back and defended their rights as women to be public, political actors. Sarah wrote one of the early theoretical texts defending women's rights: her *Letters on the Equality of the Sexes*, published in 1838. The experience was the same for other women abolitionists, who populated the women's rights movement in significant numbers. Although they had begun as abolitionists, the criticism these women endured transformed them into powerful women's rights advocates. Quickly, the abolitionist movement, founded in the early 1830s, became one that argued for the emancipation of enslaved people while also defending the rights of women. Sometimes opposition came from within the abolitionist movement itself, but American male abolitionists also converted to some degree of support for women's rights.[27]

For Mott, then, the controversy over women's participation in the London

1840 World's Anti-Slavery Convention was nothing new. It was offensive but routine, and not especially threatening. In her diary, she noted pleasantly that first meeting with Stanton but attached no special significance to it. Stanton was a minor figure, while Mott's days in London were filled with adventurous travel and meetings with eminent reformers. Nor did Mott's diary corroborate Stanton's memory that the pair, brimming with indignation, vowed to work together on a women's rights convention upon their return to the United States.[28]

If they made such an agreement, nothing came of it for eight years, during which the two women had little contact. After returning from her honeymoon, Stanton settled into a life of domesticity, birthing children and caring for her growing family. Eventually, Henry settled his family in Seneca Falls, where his wife chafed in domestic confinement. Her native New York State, along with Pennsylvania and New England, were hotbeds of antebellum reform. In the summer of 1848, Mott came from Philadelphia to attend a yearly Quaker meeting and visit her sister. Martha Coffin Wright was expecting a baby and lived in Auburn, New York. Together, the sisters traveled to the area around Seneca Falls on a social visit. Their host, Jane Hunt (of Waterloo), invited a neighbor, Mary Ann McClintock, and Stanton—likely on Mott's suggestion. "What began as a tea party," one historian writes, "turned into something quite different."[29] All the women knew each other through kinship or Quaker networks except Stanton, who nevertheless (so the story goes) poured out her domestic woes to Mott.[30] The group decided to take action. They wrote a notice for the local newspapers announcing "a Convention to discuss the social, civil, and religious condition of woman."[31]

In the eight days between the call and the meeting itself, the women drafted a protest statement—the now-famous Declaration of Sentiments. Stanton outlined ideas for the document, and she called upon Elizabeth McClintock for assistance.[32] The pair, with some help, drafted the meeting's manifesto on a round, mahogany tea table in the McClintock's parlor. Stanton modeled her declaration on the Declaration of Independence. She upended that document, however, by revising its famous line: "We hold these truths to be self-evident, that all men *and women* are created equal."[33] Instead of indicting the King, women went on to indict men for their unequal treatment of women. At the end, they listed a series of demands, or "resolutions." These included women's access to education and the professions, property rights, voting rights, and an end to the sexual double standard. The document would become the centerpiece of the two-day convention.[34]

Lucretia Mott (Courtesy of Special Collections, Fine Arts Library, Harvard University)

On the 19th and 20th of July 1848, the women assembled at the Wesleyan Chapel on the town's main thoroughfare. They were unsure what to expect. To their amazement, roughly 300 people arrived. Because it was considered too scandalous to have a woman as chair, Mott's husband, James, chaired the convention. Stanton read the Declaration of Sentiments, and convention goers debated and voted upon its eleven resolutions. All the resolutions passed unanimously but one: the ninth resolution demanding voting rights. That resolution provoked controversy and nearly failed.[35] Stanton had insisted upon its inclusion in the declaration. Mott thought it ought to be removed. It passed when Frederick Douglass—the escaped slave, abolitionist, and newspaper editor—rose and spoke in its favor.[36] Douglass lived in nearby Rochester. He would become a lifelong supporter of women's rights, and his support for Stanton's resolution proved crucial to its passing. In the end, one hundred women and men signed the document. The convention report then went forward with portions of the Declaration of Sentiments included (notably, the demands, including the ninth for women's voting, were not included).[37]

The 1848 meeting gave Stanton a purpose that lasted until her death in 1902. She gave her first major address on women's rights that fall.[38] She traveled in abolitionist circles, partly because this was where women's rights supporters could be found, but she was always more of a bystander in that cause than an ardent participant. Women's rights consumed her mind. She would struggle over the antebellum years to balance her activism with the demands of her young family. In all, she would have seven children, the last born in 1859. Here, Anthony provided able assistance, helping Stanton carve out time for women's rights work. After meeting in 1851, the pair supported one another's dedication to women's rights. Stanton could not have stayed active in reform during the 1850s without Anthony's help. Anthony not only helped Stanton carve out time to write; she pushed her to do so. Stanton penned the manifestoes and, together, with Anthony's consummate organizing skill, they delivered them.[39]

After the meeting in Seneca Falls, women's rights supporters held more meetings elsewhere. The organizers of Seneca Falls planned a meeting in Rochester, New York, for the following month. (Anthony, who did not meet Stanton until 1851, did not attend this second convention, just as she had not attended the Seneca Falls convention a month earlier.) The Rochester meeting was even more radical in its demands than Seneca Falls had been, and it appointed a woman to chair the proceedings. Soon, women and men convened their own local conventions to protest injustice against women in states including Ohio and Indiana. State and local women's rights organizations also formed. By 1850, agitation was so robust that activists decided to hold the first *national* women's rights convention in Worcester, Massachusetts. It welcomed delegates from women's rights groups around the Northeast and the Midwest. Paulina Wright Davis, who had worked as an abolitionist and a women's health educator, chaired the meeting. After that first national convention in Worcester in 1850, women's rights activists held national meetings annually. Local and state conventions continued to be held as well. Agitation for women's rights was not new in the 1850s. It had occurred in the 1830s and the 1840s as well. Ernestine Rose, for example, had crusaded for married women's property rights, resulting in the expansion of married women's property rights in New York in 1848. And Maria Stewart had lectured on the crippling effects of racism on black women's self-development in the 1830s. What was new was the form that activism took. Conventions now became a staple of women's rights work (as they were for other reform causes), and they helped to propel its growth.[40]

Lucy Stone was a leading figure in this period, and she would do battle with Stanton and Anthony after the Civil War. A Massachusetts native, Stone had deep roots in the abolition and women's rights causes. She had attended Oberlin College (founded by abolitionists), the first school of higher education to admit both women and blacks, and she graduated with honors. In 1847, she became the first woman from Massachusetts to earn a college degree. That same year, she gave her first public speech on women's rights. She then began lecturing on behalf of antislavery, a still-controversial career path for women. She traveled the North speaking to general, and sometimes hostile, audiences about this largely unpopular reform movement. Like other female abolitionists, she defied convention and suffered public attacks for being "unwomanly." In 1848, she felt torn between the two causes, and she arranged with the American Anti-Slavery Society, her employer, to devote weekends to speaking for antislavery, and weekdays to speaking for women's rights. She helped organize the Worcester convention of 1850, and she was a constant presence in all the antebellum national women's rights conventions. Although she vowed, as a very young girl, to never take any man as master, she eventually accepted Henry Blackwell's marriage proposal, and the two married in 1855. She defied convention, however, by rewriting her marriage vows to omit the word "obey" and by keeping her maiden name. (More than a century later, feminists of the 1970s who fought to keep their own names in marriage resurrected Stone's memory and called themselves "Lucy Stoners.") Stone's best friend at Oberlin, Antoinette Brown (Blackwell), the first woman to be ordained as a minister in the United States, married Henry Blackwell's brother and so became Stone's sister-in-law. Henry Blackwell's sister, Elizabeth Blackwell, was the first woman to earn a medical degree in the United States, a degree she received in 1849. Stone was, and would remain throughout the nineteenth century, a prominent, formidable figure in the sprawling feminist-abolitionist coalition.[41]

No one in these years agreed about where the movement had begun. In fact, they spent little time examining the question. Although it would become a major preoccupation among some postwar feminists, the question garnered little fascination in the antebellum decades. Perhaps the only person interested in the matter was Stanton. As early as 1848, she considered authoring a history of women's rights. In 1855, she revived the idea. She wrote Mott for details about the movement, since Stanton herself knew little about activism before her own involvement. Not surprisingly, she drew upon what she did know: her own experience. Stanton suggested the movement had begun in 1840, in London, the site of her own conversion.[42] Mott corrected her, suggesting she reach further back. The movement had begun, Mott wrote, with the formation of the national Anti-Slavery Convention of American Women in 1837.[43]

The 1848 convention came up occasionally, but it certainly did not inspire reverence. When delegates to the 1853 National Women's Rights Convention considered authoring a women's rights declaration, Mott informed them that such a manifesto had already been written in 1848 in Seneca Falls. They resoundingly rejected it.[44] As late as 1861, on the eve of the Civil War, activists did not have a shared, stock origins myth. "It is difficult to tell when or how this idea of human equality first took to itself form and purpose . . . with reference to the inferior position of women," commented one Ohio woman as women suspended annual conventions due to secession.[45] Not even the details of the 1848 convention itself were clear or settled yet. If Mott's 1840 diary made no mention of plans hatched in London for a U.S. women's rights convention, she would later recall a different origin. Mott remembered that she and Stanton had come up with plans for a women's rights convention a year later, in 1841, while strolling the streets of Boston.[46] She would even be unsure when that soon-to-be iconic convention had taken place, asking Stanton: was it in "47 or 8"?[47]

WHEN, THEN, DID SENECA FALLS EMERGE as the main story with a codified, familiar structure? And why? How did the *meeting* at Seneca Falls become the *myth* of Seneca Falls? In what ways did that story, that origins myth, serve as a collective political resource for post–Civil War feminists? And—if stories are actors, essential to mounting resistance campaigns— what type of movement did it help produce? Lastly, how and why did Stanton and Anthony use this story to intervene in broader national memory debates after the Civil War, and with what outcome? These are the central questions of this book. It unravels the tangled skeins of suffragists' collective memories to recover the politics behind this creation legend and its ultimate effects.

Chapter one locates the battle over movement beginnings in the fighting within the antebellum feminist-abolitionist coalition that fractured along painful fault lines immediately following the Civil War. It examines how suffragists responded to the fraught politics of the late 1860s by creating a trial collective memory for the movement. Here, suffragists identified Worcester in 1850, not Seneca Falls in 1848, as the origin of the campaign, revealing how fungible the question of beginnings still was. Chapters two and three explore the sprawling, expanding, and chaotic movement politics over the early 1870s, which left Stanton and Anthony on the defensive more often than they would have liked. So they began tentatively, and then more decisively, sketching out a Seneca Falls origins narrative to try gaining traction in the sprawling postwar movement. Partly because of the eventual triumph of a Seneca Falls origins narrative, which foregrounded woman suffrage and a federal strategy as the pinnacle of a rights agenda, much of the vital debate over what a women's rights agenda should be in the postwar era has been lost—or at least scattered into a host of separate, unconnected stories. Chapters two and three integrate that history back into the story of how a postwar women's suffrage agenda developed and examine how Stanton and Anthony, who faced challenges in every direction, used an increasingly codified Seneca Falls narrative to intervene in that process.

Chapter four examines the politics behind Stanton and Anthony's 1880s production of their massive three-volume *History of Woman Suffrage*. Those magisterial volumes were their most definitive statement of a Seneca Falls origins myth, their most robust intervention in post–Civil War memory politics, and their most righteous insistence that the deeds of women would not go unrecognized or unrewarded by anything less than full citizenship. Here, they used Seneca Falls to lay out an alternative memory of the Civil War, a hitherto unrecognized *suffragist memory*, which defies scholars' efforts to map memory politics of this era as defined by a battle between an emancipationist memory, on the one hand, and a white supremacist memory, on the other. Chapter five argues that the maturation of a Seneca Falls mythology by 1890 helped to fundamentally transform the movement and lift Anthony to the pinnacle of that reorganized movement. After this, it would be harder and harder to see these middle decades without the veil of the collective memories that suffragists built around them. To see through that veil, we must first recover the history of those memories themselves, memories that were born in the immediate, tension-filled aftermath of the American Civil War.

1. Woman's Day in the Negro's Hour
✢ 1865–1870

The newly formed American Equal Rights Association (AERA) appeared doomed before it even got started. At its second annual meeting, in 1867—two years after the Civil War had ended—George T. Downing asked whether those assembled would be willing to support the ballot for black men before women. Lucretia Mott confessed that women "had a right to be a little jealous" of such a development, but she tried not to pick sides. Elizabeth Cady Stanton was unequivocal: "I say, no; I would not trust him [black men] with all my rights; degraded, oppressed himself, he would be . . . despotic." Abby Kelley Foster then piped up. Women had no claim to priority because they were not "in the same civil, social and political status to-day" as black men, who were now "whipped and beaten by thousands, given up to the most horrible outrages, without that protection which his value as property formerly gave him." Stanton disagreed. In her view, if there was to be a question of priority, white women—whom she deemed educated and therefore intelligent—must win out. "The safety of the nation as well as the interests of women," she railed, "demand that we outweigh this incoming tide of ignorance, poverty and vice, with the virtue, wealth and education of the women of the country." To which an outraged and astonished woman shouted, "Shame! shame! shame!"[1]

Tensions over priority—who would vote first, black men or white women—wracked the AERA from its inception. Feminist-abolitionists had organized the AERA a year prior in an effort to jumpstart the women's rights movement, which had suspended operations during the Civil War. What that movement now stood for—in a world where slavery existed no more—sparked intense debate. The AERA was dedicated to the enfranchisement of both black men and all women, in theory. But the practicalities of building a viable campaign around those goals—not widely supported by the general population—proved immediately vexing. Women's and black men's simultaneous enfranchisement seemed politically unrealistic to some. As a result, reformers began arguing among themselves about who should take priority. These clashes intensified over the late 1860s and early 1870s, splitting the feminist-abolitionist coalition into rival factions that lasted for decades.[2]

Disagreements over how to define a postwar rights agenda had a profound and lasting effect upon feminist memory practices. These debates drove some reformers to reach backward in an effort to chart a way forward. Very quickly, women began to make claims about where an antebellum women's movement had begun, and they began to characterize that ostensible beginning in particular ways. Those characterizations generally expressed their hopes for the movement's future. Pinpointing the origins of women's rights would be an elusive target, however. It would be decades before any story won out. Although the stories postwar suffragists created centered on antebellum events, those stories were emphatically about elevating the importance of the vote in a postwar rights agenda as well as navigating the treacherous terrain of postwar politics. Put another way, the story of Seneca Falls was emphatically a post–Civil War story. To locate the roots of a Seneca Falls mythology, and to understand how it operated as both a resource and a strategy, requires looking here, at the late 1860s, where the battle over beginnings began.

✦ The American Equal Rights Association

Quickly, and for complicated reasons, members of the antebellum abolition and women's rights movements, which had overlapping membership, each decided upon the extension of voting rights, or enfranchisement, as the best guarantor of freedom and equality. With slavery ended, questions about the status of formerly enslaved persons consumed postwar politics. Were freedpeople citizens? If so, did they have the same citizenship rights as whites? What did freedom mean? Few people agreed. Freedpeople themselves demanded a host of rights, from land to the right to serve on juries.[3] Many northern abolitionists, however, quickly settled upon voting rights as the innovation most needed, overlooking the broad constellation of freedpeople's demands. Senator Charles Sumner, a leading Radical Republican (meaning those who supported some degree of equal rights for freed persons) argued that the ballot was "the great guarantee and the only sufficient guarantee" of human rights.[4] "The ballot is the one thing needful, without which . . . all other rights will be no better than cobwebs, which the master will break through with impunity. To him who has the ballot all other things shall be given," Sumner thundered.[5] This broader political emphasis on the vote as a "sufficient guarantee" of freedom changed the ways in which some women defined a rights agenda after the Civil War. An antebellum women's rights movement had been about a host of demands, of which the vote was only one. Now, an antebellum women's rights movement shaded into a postwar women's suffrage movement. The women who agreed with this shift in emphasis now called themselves suffragists, and they too began arguing that the vote was women's best guarantee of freedom. But what this new suffrage movement would be—indeed, whether a movement would develop—had yet to be worked out.[6]

The American Equal Rights Association was suffragists' first attempt at organizing on a national scale. Local women's rights organizations and women's suffrage organizations existed in various states, but the AERA was to be national in scope, setting a national agenda—in theory, anyway. It drew many of the same faces that had been arrayed in the antebellum feminist-abolitionist coalition. Lucretia Mott was an important member, as were Elizabeth Cady Stanton, Susan B. Anthony, and Lucy Stone. Henry Blackwell, Stone's husband, was a prominent member, as were other leading abolitionist men such as William Lloyd Garrison, Wendell Philips, Robert Purvis, Frederick Douglass (now the nation's leading African American statesman), and others. Northern black women also played important roles in the AERA. Sojourner Truth and Frances Ellen Watkins Harper, Harriet Purvis, and Sarah Remond were all members. Truth had been formerly enslaved in New York. She became free in the 1820s, and after a revelation from God became an itinerant preacher as well as an antislavery advocate. Harper, Purvis, and Remond were all born free black women, and they hailed from prominent reform families. They were all antislavery as well as women's rights activists. The antebellum women's rights movement had important roots in abolition, and AERA membership showed how important those connections remained after the war.[7]

The relationship between abolitionism and women's rights had always been troubled, however, with some abolitionist men being tepid in their support for women's rights. This tension quickly became evident after the war, when the American Anti-Slavery Society refused to support women's voting rights. In the wake of Union victory, the American Anti-Slavery Society debated its postwar role. Abolition had been won. Was the society's purpose then ended? Many argued it was not, because freed people did not yet enjoy basic civil rights. They committed the organization to a new goal: African American enfranchisement, as a protector of freedom. But many male abolitionists refused to support universal suffrage, meaning voting rights for all—men and women. Members such as Parker Pillsbury and Stephen Foster—husband of the esteemed women's rights and antislavery advocate Abby Kelley Foster—tried to get the American Anti-Slavery Society to endorse universal suffrage over so-called manhood suffrage, but they failed.[8] Wendell Phillips, the American Anti-Slavery Society's president, famously called this the "Negro's Hour."[9] Black voting rights, he insisted, must come first. Women's voting rights would follow at some later, unspecified date—a distant, illusory promise. For understandable reasons, many women, and some men, found this deeply objectionable. The AERA was meant to be the American Anti-Slavery Society's counterpoint, supporting voting rights for all women as well as black men.[10]

As the debate over priority within the AERA and the American Anti-Slavery Society underscored, black women found themselves in a difficult position. The Anti-Slavery Society's support for black voting rights generally meant black male suffrage. Whereas white women in the AERA who demanded women's voting rights generally meant white female suffrage. Northern black men too fell into the trap of assuming black to be male and women to be white, leaving black women struggling for visibility and access.[11] Black women's rights were therefore frequently eclipsed in these postwar discussions. Women such as Harper, Purvis, Remond, Truth, and others fought to keep black women's rights at the forefront of a postwar rights agenda. Harper had urged members of the 1866 AERA founding convention to remember that the rights of black men, black women, and white women were all "bound up together," and that the organization therefore ought to avoid arguments over priority.[12] The battle of Harper and others for recognition—of their existence, their unique needs, and their theoretical contributions to the movement—proved to be particularly difficult and long lived.[13]

All of these tensions came to a head in Kansas in 1867. In that year, the Kansas legislature submitted two referenda to the state's eligible voters (white men): one for black suffrage and one for woman suffrage. Voters in other northern states had already voted down several black suffrage proposals, but this was the first time any state had put the question of woman suffrage to a popular vote.[14] Seeing Kansas as a litmus test, the AERA sent members to canvass the state in order to drum up support. Lucy Stone and her husband Henry Blackwell arrived that spring. Over the summer and fall, the AERA dispatched others to the state. They hoped Kansas might be an opening wedge in the fight for universal suffrage.

When opportunities opened in Kansas, AERA members were still reeling

Frances Ellen Watkins Harper (Courtesy of the Prints & Photographs Division, Library of Congress, LC-USZ62-118946)

from the recent passage of the Fourteenth Amendment, which, for the first time, inserted "male" into the U.S. Constitution. The debates among the feminist-abolitionist coalition over how to define black men's postwar rights wracked the U.S. Congress as well, which struggled to define the legal status of freedpeople. The proposed amendment extended citizenship to African Americans (which had been denied them since the 1857 Dred Scott Supreme Court decision). It also defined citizenship as "male." This threw women's citizenship—long presumed—into question. If women weren't citizens, did they have any legal standing? Were they protected by the U.S. Constitution? Or did they have no legal rights whatsoever? The Fourteenth Amendment raised troubling questions. Instead of opposing its ratification, AERA members turned to Kansas, where they hoped the passage of women's suffrage would settle these questions. If Kansas declared women voters, then they must be citizens.[15]

Leading Republican politicians, however, along with a host of abolitionist men, refused to endorse the woman suffrage referendum in Kansas. This frustrated Stanton and Anthony and prompted them to make a controversial choice. They arrived in Kansas that fall, by which point the chances for either referendum looked grim. With only lackluster support from Republican Party members, the pair decided to team up with a Democrat, the party of the white supremacist South. George Francis Train's entrance into the campaign proved electric. Train supported white women's suffrage but not black suffrage. This put him at odds with the goals of the AERA. An eccentric driven by publicity, Train dressed in patent leather boots, lavender kid gloves, and a blue coat with brass buttons. Train had made a fortune in transportation and railroads. In addition to his wealth, he had grandiose political ambitions, aspiring to the presidency of the United States. His dress was as distinctive as his stage presence. Known for his epigrams, Train let them fly:

> While the muscle and color and wool of the Blacks
> Is the chief stock in trade of your old party hacks,
> My mission to Kansas breaks the White Woman's chains,
> Three cheers then for Virtue and Beauty and Brains.[16]

Because Train supported woman suffrage, unlike many of Stanton's and Anthony's abolitionist colleagues, they found in him a valuable ally. Their choice to align with Train further revealed their willingness to prioritize white women's voting over that of blacks. Anthony began touring Kansas with Train, trying to drum up support for the faltering woman suffrage measure. They spoke from the same platform day after day, as Train lambasted black suffrage and argued for white women's superiority over ostensibly degraded black men. AERA members, including Lucy Stone, who looked on from Boston, were aghast. On Election Day, both measures lost. Kansas would be neither the first state to fully enfranchise women, nor a bellwether in the struggle for black male suffrage. Controversy over why the two measures had lost—the lack of Republican support, the influence of George Francis Train, and other accusations—would be debated within the movement for years to come.[17]

Stone and other AERA allies were further shocked when Stanton and Anthony turned their journey home into a speaking tour with the race-baiting Train. They spoke to audiences along the route from Kansas to New York, denigrating black men and lauding women's suffrage. "Reformers had been so long surfeited with the smell of African," Train railed, "that they had no sense of the white man or woman."[18] Given Train's open opposition to black civil rights, a stated goal of the AERA, Stone and other AERA members were even more astonished to find Stanton and Anthony billing their stops as AERA fundraisers. Train, meanwhile, promised Stanton and Anthony funding for a women's rights newspaper.[19] They were elated. But the content of

Elizabeth Cady Stanton and Susan B. Anthony (The Schlesinger Library, Radcliffe Institute, Harvard University)

their new newspaper, the *Revolution*, which began publication in January of 1868, caused further rifts within the AERA. Train was a contributor, and he and Stanton both advocated educated suffrage in the *Revolution*'s pages.[20] They argued, in short, that only voters who could pass an educational test should be allowed to vote. Many within the AERA felt educated suffrage violated its universal suffrage stand, rendering ineligible most freedpeople (educating enslaved people had been illegal, leaving them without basic literacy). To compound matters, Anthony first tried to run her newspaper from the offices of the AERA, ousting Stone. "Without so much as saying, 'by your leave,'" Stone vented to a coworker, Anthony "literally turned us out. Susan said to us, 'I am the American Equal Rights Association.'"[21] Already, tensions were running high.

GEO. FRANCIS TRAIN
Mrs. E. CADY STANTON,
SUSAN B. ANTHONY

CORINTHIAN HALL,
Monday Eve., Dec. 2d, 1867,
AT 7 1-2 O'CLOCK.

Ticket for lecture by Anthony, Stanton, and Train in Corinthian Hall, 1867 (Susan B. Anthony Papers, Rare Books, Special Collections and Preservation Department, University of Rochester)

The sweeping range of Stanton's pronouncements within the *Revolution*'s pages further enflamed matters. Although Stanton believed the vote was the pinnacle of a rights agenda, she never limited her vision to this goal. Stanton was among the nation's most brilliant intellectuals and a radical thinker (although her radical stands were always limited by her elitism). She was a philosopher at heart. And the *Revolution* gave her a mouthpiece for her political views, views that quickly proved controversial within the movement. Not only did Stanton advocate educated suffrage, she openly advocated women's right to divorce, something considered entirely scandalous among most Americans, a threat to the stability of the family and the nation. When Hester Vaughn, a working-class immigrant, was convicted of infanticide (with no evidence) early in 1868, Stanton rushed to her defense. She used Vaughn's case to illustrate the sexual double standard, the hopelessness of women unable to control their bodies (Vaughn's pregnancy had likely resulted from rape), and the danger of women's economic subordination. Stanton joined a campaign to pardon Vaughn and wrote for the *Revolution* in her defense.[22] Stanton's respectable, white colleagues within the AERA sidestepped the controversial issue. Together with Anthony, Stanton also took a suspicious and sometimes oppositional stance toward the Republican Party. This too proved unwelcome among Stanton's and Anthony's AERA colleagues, most of whom remained loyal to the party of emancipation. Stanton's iconoclasm unsettled many within the AERA, who feared she would bring discredit upon the cause. But Stanton loved ideas, and she followed them to their logical conclusion, regardless of the political fallout. Stanton's work on the *Revolution* also made it clear that she was only marginally at home in the AERA.[23]

By November 1868, a group of anti-Train, pro-Republican suffragists located in the heart of abolition country began a new organization to counter Stanton and Anthony. They called their organization the New England Woman Suffrage Association (NEWSA). A group from within the New England Anti-Slavery Society—including Abby Kelley Foster and her husband, along with Thomas Wentworth Higginson, life-long abolitionist and commander of a regiment of black Union troops—quickly took control of the meeting. Higginson accused Stanton and Anthony, not in attendance, of acting "zealously & constantly" and suggested the new organization "criticize by superior action."[24] The New England Woman Suffrage Association recruited the support of powerful Republican politicians, who were also happy to check Stanton's and Anthony's criticisms of their embattled party. And it moved immediately to build state and local affiliates. Its members also pressed New England state legislatures for action on women's voting. In short, they tried to control the leadership of a fledgling women's suffrage movement.[25]

❖ A Political Firestorm

Soon arguments over a new constitutional amendment, the proposed Fifteenth Amendment, tore apart the already-fragile postwar coalition and left the AERA in tatters. The many constituencies supporting black voting rights—freedpeople, abolitionists, women's rights activists, and radical Republicans—got an unexpected political windfall with the November 1868 elections. The Republican candidate for president, General Ulysses S. Grant, won only a narrow victory, while Democrats took control of the U.S. House of Representatives. That narrow victory along with the loss of the House led even moderate Republicans, still tepid in their support for black voting, to think a federal guarantee for black voting was now necessary. It would, at the very least, boost the numbers of Republican voters and deliver future Republican victories. Before a Republican-controlled Congress left office that March, it hastily moved to consider black voting. Congressmen debated the issue over the early months of 1869, and by February, chances looked slim. Legislators hammered out a last-minute compromise, however, and a Fifteenth Amendment swiftly passed both houses. That amendment banned states from denying voting rights "on account of race, color, or previous condition of servitude," and it gave Congress the power to enforce the provision, something they would do unevenly with the Union troops still stationed in the South. The amendment then moved to the states for ratification, where its chances remained uncertain.[26]

AERA members broke into acrimonious debate about the Fifteenth Amendment at their May 1869 convention. After transacting organizational business, Stanton rose to deliver a major address, an opening salvo in the ensuing fight. "'Manhood suffrage' is national suicide and woman's destruction," she railed. "Remember, the fifteenth amendment takes in a larger population than the 3,000,000 black men on the Southern plantations. It takes in all the foreigners daily landing in our Eastern cities, [and] the Chinese crowding our western shores." "Think of Patrick and Sambo and Hans and Yung Tung, who do not know the difference between a monarchy and a republic, who cannot read the Declaration of Independence or Webster's spelling book, making laws for Lucretia Mott . . . [or] Susan B. Anthony." Ratification, she warned, would further strengthen "the ignorant foreign vote," which "already holds the balance of power in this country by sheer force of numbers," corrupting American democracy by producing elections determined not by reason, but by "impulse or passion, bribery or fraud." Moreover, the amendment, she railed, "creates an antagonism everywhere between educated, refined women and the lower orders of men, especially at the South."[27]

Stephen Foster challenged Stanton's commitment to universal suffrage, the goal of the AERA. The growing opposition to Stanton from within the AERA prevented organizational "harmony," he alleged, and he suggested Stanton retire from leadership. Stanton, in turn, demanded that Foster specify his complaints. Foster obliged and unleashed a litany of objections: the *Revolution*'s recent editorial against the Fifteenth Amendment, Stanton's and Anthony's support for George Francis Train, and Stanton's own declared support for educated suffrage. "Now I put myself on this platform as an enemy of educated suffrage," he continued, "as an enemy of white suffrage, as an enemy of man suffrage, as an enemy of every kind of suffrage except universal suffrage."[28]

As the tumult quelled, Douglass spoke. His voice was quiet, prompting Anthony to deliver an unfriendly jibe about his being inaudible. Douglass played the diplomat. He offered honorifics to Stanton while implicitly criticizing her by disparaging the *Revolution*. He attacked its editorial stands against black suffrage and its use of epithets such as "Sambo." "I must say," he continued, "I do not see how any one can pretend that there is the same urgency in giving the ballot to the woman as to the negro. . . . With us, the matter is a question of life or death. . . . When women, because they are women, are hunted down through the cities of New York and New Orleans; when they are dragged from their houses and hung upon lamp-posts; when their children are torn from their arms, and their brains dashed out upon the pavement; when she is an object of insult and outrage at every turn; when they are in danger of having their homes bur[n]t down over their heads; when their children are not allowed to enter schools, then she will have an urgency to obtain the ballot equal to our own. (Great applause.)" A voice from the audience shouted: "Is that not all true about black women?" "Yes, yes, yes," Douglass rejoined, "but not because she is a woman but because she is black."[29]

Anthony and Stone were then moved to speak. Anthony began: "If you will not give the whole loaf of justice to the entire people, if you are determined to give it, piece by piece, then give it first to women, to the most intelligent & capable of the women at least. . . . When Mr. Douglass tells us today that the cause of black man is so perilous, I tell him that wronged & outraged as they are by this hateful & mean prejudice against color," she continued, "he would not today exchange his sex." Stone praised the Fifteenth Amendment and urged the audience to leave aside questions of priority. "We are lost if we turn away from the middle principle and argue for one class," Stone argued, adding that "the question of priority should never have been introduced into the discussion." She closed by hoping against hope that someone could get them "out of this terrible pit."[30]

The following day, battles continued. Douglass asked permission to present a resolution pledging the association's support for the Fifteenth Amendment. He judged it "preeminent among all political reforms" and said it "should be hailed as a step toward the attainment of the reform sought by this convention—the securing of the ballot for woman."[31] Paulina Wright Davis declared her preference for women's enfranchisement first, arguing that black men would be tyrants. Stanton and Anthony also opposed the resolution. Frances Harper rose in support. "The question of color," she stated, "was far more to her than the question of sex."[32] Pandemonium broke out as Charles Burleigh, a white abolitionist, attempted to speak but was hissed down by the sizeable crowd. Quiet was briefly restored when Anthony begged that the convention "be spared the disgrace of hissing down

Frederick Douglass (Courtesy of the Prints & Photographs Division, Library of Congress, LC-USZ62-15887)

a man!"[33] When Blackwell moved a vote on Douglass's resolution, Stanton suggested the vote be deferred. "All in favor" of deferral, she called, "say Aye!" A small rumble of "ayes" came forth. "All opposed," Stanton rejoined, "say No!" A roaring thunder of noes arose. "The Ayes have it!" Stanton declared. Ripples of laughter and disgust rolled through the crowd in reaction to Stanton's blatant disregard for the actual vote.[34]

The choice was an unenviable one, and the firestorm it generated was about more than race. The Fifteenth Amendment also raised questions about how to achieve social transformation. Should reformers and radicals pursue a piecemeal strategy or try to remake society all at once? Did forestalling one goal equal its loss, as Stanton and Anthony warned? Or could the winning of one goal hasten the winning of other, still-unrealized goals, as Stone, Kelley Foster, Douglass, and others prophesied? No one could foresee the future, so it was impossible to know. But the stakes, no one doubted, were enormous. What came next fueled suffragists' efforts to locate movement origins, something that had not overly preoccupied activists to this point. What came next also decisively influenced the shape those memory projects took.

❖ Which Way Forward? The National and the American Woman Suffrage Associations

Within days, Stanton and Anthony bolted from the AERA and formed a new national organization—the National Woman Suffrage Association. That Saturday evening, two days after the AERA adjourned, Stanton and Anthony held a reception at the Woman's Bureau, a large New York City brownstone that housed the *Revolution*'s offices. Exactly what happened would be the subject of longstanding contention and debate. Stone and Blackwell charged that Stanton and Anthony had called the meeting in secret, waiting until their rivals had left town in order to ensure their exclusion.[35] It was true that no call or announcement had been issued, nothing to announce the plan or welcome interested parties. Stanton and Anthony deflected charges of collusion by claiming the founding of the association had been purely spontaneous, and not even their idea. Western women delegates, who had come East expecting a women's rights convention, had pushed the idea, the pair claimed, expressing "a general dissatisfaction . . . with the name and latitude of debate involved in an 'Equal Rights Association.'" "It was, therefore, decided," Stanton explained, "to organize a National Woman's Suffrage Association."[36] "The purpose of the [new] Association," one newspaper explained, "was . . . a desire to discuss woman suffrage separate and apart from the question of equal rights and manhood suffrage."[37] A lengthy debate about barring male membership lost when put to a vote, while the National Association made the *Revolution* its official organ. The assembled also hastily adopted a constitution and a list of officers and laid plans for pressing women's voting rights.[38]

Stanton and Anthony took an explicit stance against ratification of the Fifteenth Amendment. They ran editorials in the *Revolution* against it. They also took to the lecture circuit to campaign against it.[39] Many of their AERA colleagues—who had spent their lives in the abolitionist movement and who feared for the lives of African Americans being brutally terrorized and murdered in the South—found this opposition odious.

From Stanton's and Anthony's point of view, the Fifteenth Amendment had only one redeeming feature: it set a new constitutional precedent by allowing federal regulation of voting. That right had historically been reserved to the states. State constitutions contained provisions that defined who could qualify as eligible voters. Generally, these provisions specified that voters had to be, among other things, white and male. But the Fifteenth Amendment now declared any provision requiring voters to be "white" un-

Lucy Stone (The Schlesinger Library, Radcliffe Institute, Harvard University)

constitutional. This, Stanton and Anthony argued, had changed the terms of the fight for enfranchisement. Women no longer needed to pursue voting rights at the state level. They could press Congress for a federal amendment.[40]

A Sixteenth Amendment fully enfranchising women was the National Association's principle goal. And its members applauded Congressman George Julian's (R-Ind.) 1869 introduction of a federal amendment to Congress. It read: "The Right of Suffrage in the United States shall be based on citizenship, and shall be regulated by Congress; and all citizens of the United States . . . shall enjoy this right equally without any distinction or discrimination whatever founded on sex." The measure was more than a woman suffrage measure. It nationalized suffrage, making it the province of the federal government, something still uncertain in the wake of the Fifteenth

Amendment. The proposed amendment explicitly enacted a radical revision in how the nation regulated suffrage, something that drew as much, if not more, opposition as its implications for sex. Believing that the amendment properly remade state and federal power, the National Association worked to move the proposal through Congress. The Sixteenth Amendment failed to make Congressional headway, but the strategy generated growing support among suffragists.[41]

The National Association was, at this point, more of a paper tiger than a mass organization. The association began holding weekly meetings in New York City, where it was headquartered and where Stanton now lived.[42] There, members of the National Association struggled both to define a women's rights agenda and to create a constituency. They toyed with aligning with labor activists. And they cast about for ways to forge a postwar coalition that put women's rights at its center. Stone and others were stunned to find the National Association now claiming to represent the cause of women's suffrage. Stanton and Anthony's creation of the National Association was, like the founding of the New England Woman Suffrage Association, a bid for movement leadership, something that continued to be contested and continuously redefined.[43]

Within weeks, the New England Woman Suffrage Association and its allies within the AERA moved to counter.[44] Stone stood at the center of the effort. She and others began corresponding with reformers around the country about the possibility of forming an alternative national women's organization.[45] They stressed the need to support the Fifteenth Amendment as an important piece of a suffrage and civil rights agenda. They also argued that any self-styled national organization should grow out of an open and transparent process.[46] Hoping to check Stanton and Anthony, they soon issued a call for a mass meeting to form an American Woman Suffrage Association. The goal of the new organization, Stone explained in a private letter, was "to unite those who will work steadily to one end, who will not weaken our claim by opposition to the 15th amendment, or by raising side issues. It is especially to unite those who cannot use the methods, and means, which Mrs. Stanton and Susan use, but who" believe that by uniting they "will be more effective than is possible at present."[47] In public, they were a bit more diplomatic, never openly naming Stanton, Anthony, or the Fifteenth Amendment. "Without depreciating the value of associations already existing," read the American Association's public invitation to its founding convention, "it is yet deemed that an organization at once more comprehensive and more widely representative than any of these is urgently called for."[48]

The American Woman Suffrage Association was created in November 1869 at a large convention in Cleveland, Ohio. In contrast to the small gathering that had formed the National Association six months earlier, Stone had reserved a large auditorium, which now filled to capacity. People were forced to stand in the aisles, and the gallery stairs were converted into makeshift seating.[49] In all, roughly 1,000 people attended—some being merely curious onlookers.[50] Leading men in the new organization included abolitionist and Republican stalwarts Thomas Wentworth Higginson and William Lloyd Garrison. The nation's most prominent minister, Henry Ward Beecher, was chosen its president. Other luminaries such as Julia Ward Howe, who had written the "Battle Hymn of the Republic," and Mary Livermore, a moving force in the Midwestern Sanitary Commission, which provided medical care and provisions to the Union Army—both new converts to suffrage—took prominent roles in the new organization. Stone, in turn, chaired the meeting, which carefully avoided any discussion of black suffrage and the divisive Fifteenth Amendment.[51]

The American Association supported a state strategy for winning woman suffrage—the route antebellum reformers had followed. Its officers disagreed that the Fifteenth Amendment had given the federal government the power to appoint voters. The Fifteenth Amendment had been justified by national emergency, but it did not change the balance of federal and state power, they countered. Like many (if not most) Americans, they continued to believe the prerogative to appoint voters rested with the states, as it had since the nation's founding. Anthony attended the Cleveland convention, largely as an onlooker. She tried without success to sway the organization to support a Sixteenth Amendment. This strategic dispute over how to pursue women's voting rights was more than stylistic preference. It represented two very different interpretations of constitutional law, which had larger national repercussions for the appointment and regulation of all voters—something that would soon become evident. The decision of the Wyoming territorial government to fully enfranchise women in 1869 seemed like evidence that a state strategy could and would bear fruit. The decision of the Utah territorial government to do the same the following year offered further encouragement. In both territories, women suddenly exercised full voting rights. The tide, the American Association hoped, was in their favor.[52]

The avoidance of side issues was the keynote of the American Association's new weekly newspaper, the *Woman's Journal*. This was a direct response to the latitude of the *Revolution*. Stone, Livermore, Howe, Higginson, and Garrison edited the *Woman's Journal*, which made its debut in January of 1870.[53] Blackwell explained in the journal's first issue that the American Association sought "to limit the range of discussion to woman suffrage."[54] In this way, its editors hoped to reduce the rancor among reformers that seemed to arise on every score. It also hoped to make the cause reputable in the arena of public opinion by avoiding entanglement with other controversial issues such as divorce. "As advocates of equal rights," Blackwell continued, "we protest loading the good ship of Woman Suffrage with a cargo of irrelevant opinions."[55] Blackwell simultaneously rejected the latitude that had characterized the AERA. That experience taught him that merging several reform goals was ultimately unproductive. The *Journal*'s editors hoped a simpler agenda might help the cause gather momentum. The *Woman's Journal* also avoided endorsement of a Sixteenth Amendment, and its editors pointedly refused to mention the National Association by name.[56]

❖ Tilton's Union

For a brief period, over 1869 and 1870, it was not clear if the organizational split would last. No sooner had Stanton, Anthony, and Stone created their rival organizations than other suffragists began calling for their dissolution. The pressure for unification came from various quarters. Midwestern women denounced the split as divisive, irrelevant, and counterproductive. Many wanted to steer clear of eastern divisions, and they demanded unity from any self-styled national organization.[57] Letters also poured into the *Revolution* denouncing the split.[58] Douglass and Mott too advocated union.[59] Meanwhile, Theodore Tilton—an eastern abolitionist, prominent newspaper editor, and women's rights advocate—began a unification petition drive. (It eventually netted more than 1,000 names.)[60] In March of 1870, he announced that a committee composed of representative members from the National and the American Associations would convene in April at the Fifth Avenue Hotel in New York City to affect a merger.[61]

When Anthony heard of Tilton's plan, she was immediately furious. She opposed unification, and she accused Tilton of knowingly calling the so-called Fifth Avenue Convention for a date when she and Stanton would be away in the Midwest lecturing and thus unable to attend.[62] The *Revolution* denounced the plan as well.[63] For once, the editors of the *Woman's Journal* agreed with their rivals. Its editors also opposed Tilton's unification bid, denouncing it in their pages. They declared that only one national organization existed, the American Association, so there was no need for a merger. The other society, which they declined to name, was no more than a local society, they charged, an exclusive cabal and national in name only.[64] The American Association had extended the olive branch at Cleveland, they reminded readers, inviting everyone to unite, and their rivals had refused to join. If there was division, the American Association bore no responsibility, they explained.[65] The *Revolution* similarly denounced unification plans, while Anthony fired off letters strongly dissuading any collaboration with Tilton, denouncing the plan "as futile" as "overtures to Jeff[erson] Davis and his compeers."[66] Before the April meeting even took place, it appeared doomed.

Tilton nevertheless managed to pull off the meeting, with representatives from each side in attendance. By the time it convened Anthony had changed her tune, largely due to pressure from women of the Midwest, where she was on tour and where everywhere women demand unity. She opposed unification, but she realized that her open opposition was a risky political stand, given the numbers of women who denounced the split.[67] So she directed National Association representatives (Parker Pillsbury, Josephine S. Griffing, and Charlotte Wilbour) to attend the meeting but to concede nothing.[68] The three insisted that any new organization must support a Sixteenth Amendment. In response, representatives from the American Association (Stone, Higginson, and George William Curtis), who claimed to be "volunteers" rather than official representatives, which would have implied an endorsement of the meeting, withdrew. Their withdrawal made the American Association, rather than the National, now appear to be the roadblock to unity. It also took heat off Anthony for appearing to have been the one initially causing division.[69]

After the American Association representatives left the meeting, Tilton, National Association members, and a few neutral parties organized a new society, the Union Woman Suffrage Association. It would mirror the shape and priorities of the National Association. The Union Association was officially launched a month later. In May of 1870, the National and the American Associations both held their annual conventions in New York City, convening on the same day in an explicit challenge to one another. The National Association voted—in a small business meeting, not in a vote of the general membership—to merge into the Union Woman Suffrage Association, with Tilton as president. The Union Association made the Sixteenth Amendment its cornerstone. The American Association, trying to sidestep the Union Association in hopes of marginalizing it, claimed their constitution prevented any vote on unification.[70]

Meanwhile, in conjunction with the American and Union Association meetings, the greatly attenuated AERA met in executive committee. Stone and Blackwell wanted to dissolve it. Tilton, Stanton, and Anthony brought superior numbers with them, however, and insisted the AERA merge into the Union Association. They no doubt hoped this would legitimate the new Union Association, making it seem that old coalitions endorsed the new organization. Anthony and company carried the vote, which Stone and Blackwell saw as rigged.[71] Just weeks before AERA's executive committee met, the American Anti-Slavery Society had met in the same hall where the Union Association now convened and voted to disband. Ratification of the Fifteenth Amendment in March of 1870, they argued, had completed their grand and glorious work.[72] From this point forward, the shape of woman suffrage organizing appeared considerably different than it had immediately after the Civil War in 1866. The organizational split, it became clear, was lasting, and old reform coalitions were now disbanded. The Fourteenth and Fifteenth Amendments became part of the U.S. Constitution. Black men's suffrage had been won. And suffragists hoped they might make women's voting the nation's next great political reform.

✧ Memory and the Second Decade Convention

Quickly, in the face of all these challenges, remembering emerged as an important strategy for inserting women's voting into the national political agenda. Remembering also became central to how some suffragists navigated divisive politics within the movement, divisions that showed no signs of healing. By 1869, Paulina Wright Davis was planning the suffrage movement's first major commemorative event: the 1870 Second Decade Convention. Davis heralded the Second Decade Convention as a celebration of "the twentieth anniversary of the inauguration of the Woman Suffrage movement."[73] Davis, a veteran activist, dated movement origins to 1850. Anniversaries of the 1848 convention in Seneca Falls had passed unnoticed.[74] Suffragists paid them no heed. The first event they used to anchor the movement's beginnings was the 1850 convention in Worcester, Massachusetts. Worcester had been the first national woman suffrage convention, where activists from different states had united into a larger whole. Davis now proposed that they come together again, in a massive show of unity designed to persuade Americans that women's suffrage was not a fringe demand but one made by overwhelming numbers of women. The Second Decade Convention was suffragists' opening salvo in a long contest over memory.

Davis surely proposed the anniversary convention in reaction to larger trends in national memory culture, a culture that marginalized women's rights activists. Following the Civil War, Americans argued vehemently over matters of memory. They argued over how to remember the Civil War in an effort to chart a path forward. In the first years after the Civil War, abolitionists enjoyed a brief period where they successfully competed to define the war's memory. The ratification of the Fifteenth Amendment in March of 1870 was, in some ways, the summit of their ability to impose their Civil War story onto the course of subsequent events. Abolitionists argued that they had effectively persuaded the North of the evils of slavery, and the South, in response, had provoked a war in a desperate attempt to save the institution. "Bitter as the conflict was," it had nevertheless been a noble war, embodying "great principles: freedom and good versus slavery and evil."[75] Blood had been shed, they argued, to cleanse the nation, North and South alike, of that abominable sin. Now, with military victory and the ratification of the Fifteenth Amendment, the nation was being washed clean, and it seemed impossible to abolitionists that such a radical transformation in the political, social, and economic order could ever be forgotten, or reversed. As John Greenleaf Whittier, poet of the abolitionist movement, confidently predicted, Americans would cherish the memories of abolitionists long after "pyramids and monuments shall have crumbled to dust."[76]

White supremacists, on the other hand, offered a different memory of the war, in an effort to argue for a different political settlement after the war. They continued to oppose rights for freedpeople, and so they argued that the war had not been about slavery at all. It had been about honor and country. Each side, they insisted, had fought for the same thing, a defense of white manhood. Both sides represented good; neither was evil. This was a fight among brothers, not enemies. Confederates should therefore be remembered with respect and leniency. They should be allowed to participate in postwar politics and not be banned for treason. At the same time that this memory argued for leniency for white Confederates, it attempted to divert attention away from the collapse of slavery as an essential piece of the war. White supremacists thereby attempted to divert memory away from freedpeople themselves. Emancipation should be forgotten, and freedpeople's strivings forcefully denied.[77]

African Americans, like white abolitionists, made emancipation central to their arguments about how the war ought to be remembered. African Americans busily defined, revised, and retold the story of a slave past, and a black past, in ways that ennobled black people and depicted them as consequently fit for the full entitlements of citizenship. Those entitlements, they argued, should include not just citizenship and the right to vote but land redistribution, freedom of movement, restoration of their families, protection from violence, the right to bear arms, the right to serve on juries, the right to noncoercive labor contracts, and much more. In their view, the Fourteenth and Fifteenth Amendments were only partial steps toward uplifting the race, delivering justice, and rebuilding the nation. Their emancipationist memory of the war and of a black past, along with its inherent political demands, was considerably more complex than that of abolitionists.[78]

Americans articulated (and insisted upon) these competing memories in multiple ways, including commemorative celebrations, which were a tangible part of daily existence after the Civil War. African Americans and abolitionists launched numerous Emancipation Day celebrations, marking that anniversary with events both planned and spontaneous, events that continued for decades after the war. They soon staged celebrations to commemorate the anniversary of the Fifteenth Amendment, too. White supremacists organized lynch mobs to suppress both types of events, and both types of memories. They countered not just with violent repression, but with commemorative celebrations of their own. They erected countless public monuments, large and small, to celebrate the titans of the recent war and to cast Confederate officers into stony immortality. Each monument, and each dedication, argued for white men's heroism. In essence, they argued that ex-Confederates deserved to be remembered honorably, and therefore treated honorably. Confederates and Unionists both dedicated cemeteries to honor the many dead, using those ceremonies to put forth their own arguments about why the dead had given their lives. Confederates and Unionists, black and white, also mounted numerous Veterans Day celebrations to honor the bewildered living. All of them made contrasting arguments about the types of men who had fought and what they had fought for. Americans composed songs to tell stories about the war; they wrote novels to sentimentalize it; and they wrote military memoirs to valorize the living. Freedpeople, too, chronicled their lives in print. Everywhere Americans turned, people launched memory projects to explain why the Civil War had been fought, and what the world, therefore, now ought to look like.[79]

Suffragists launched the Second Decade Convention, in part, to protest the ways in which the history of women's rights activism was marginalized in postwar memory culture and, subsequently, in political culture. Some suffragists became disgruntled with the ways abolitionists' remembrances forgot the contributions of women, who had been integral to the antislavery movement. They saw this forgetting as intimately connected to the refusal of some male abolitionists to support women's voting rights after the war. And they began to disrupt abolitionist anniversary events. Although the American Anti-Slavery Society disbanded in 1870, abolitionists continued to meet periodically, generally to hold reunions and to mark their anniversaries—a chance to celebrate and also defend the political victories they had won. Yet an abolitionist memory, like all memories, involved a fair amount of forgetting. Abolitionists consistently misrepresented—or forgot—the fact that white northerners had only grudgingly supported emancipation as a war aim, and many had never supported it at all. An abolitionist memory neglected the pivotal efforts of enslaved people to free themselves by running away in massive numbers, fleeing to Union Army lines, and making their plight an unavoidable war issue. And as feminist-abolitionists objected, it also forgot women's pivotal role within the abolitionist movement, without which the grand movement surely would have collapsed.[80]

Women had done a fair amount of the legwork for abolition. They were largely responsible for collecting signatures on petitions for the eradication of slavery, which was a massive undertaking, with petitions of all sizes flooding into Congress over the antebellum decades and hampering congressional business. Women wrote some of abolitionism's most famous and incendiary tracts. They were among abolitionism's most famous orators. Their boycotts of slave-made products made an important moral statement. And their fairs and bazaars raised much of the money that sustained northern abolitionism. During the Civil War, northern feminist-abolitionists also abandoned their women's rights work in favor of pressing the federal government to make abolition a Union war aim. Surely they too deserved some of the spotlight celebrating the deeds of abolitionist men. Surely they had shown their political mettle, making them equally worthy of voting rights. Surely they should be remembered. But when abolitionist men organized and held anniversary events, the contributions of women were difficult to see. At an antislavery reunion in Chicago, women seized the floor to ask why more women were not in attendance, angrily accusing organizers of ignoring them. One woman looked out over the crowd, expressing pride in abolitionism's victories but confessing that she felt "sadness mingled with her joy because . . . the meeting . . . was a man's meeting particularly."[81]

The 1870 Second Decade Convention signaled suffragists' intentions to enter the theater of memory and thus compete in this arena of politics. Paulina Wright Davis had been an active participant in the antebellum abolition and women's rights movements. In the 1830s, she worked with Ernestine Rose in New York to secure married women's property rights. (Married women had no legal ability to hold property.) In the 1840s, she studied medicine and gave lectures on anatomy and physiology to women only, helping women claim control over their bodies. In the 1850s, she owned and edited an early women's rights newspaper, the *Una* (1853–55). She had also helped chair and organize the first national women's rights convention in Worcester in 1850. She now planned that event's anniversary celebration for October, the same month that women and men had gathered in Massachusetts twenty years earlier.[82]

Although Davis hoped the anniversary might unite suffragists, it instead began a decades-long contest over movement beginnings. Davis had begun planning the event just as the split in national forces took shape. That organizational split forever shaped the politics of remembering within the suffrage movement, and it influenced how the anniversary took place. Davis's invitation to the Second Decade Convention declared it to be "above all party considerations and personal antagonisms, and this gathering is to be in no way connected with either of our leading Woman Suffrage organizations[;] we hope that the friends of real progress everywhere will come together and unitedly celebrate this twentieth anniversary."[83] But the event had an unmistakable National-turned-Union Association stamp.

Davis, who sided with Stanton and Anthony, announced the event at the May 1870 Union Association convention. And a slate of National Association figures were chosen to help organize it.[84] The leaders of the Union Association evidently then renounced themselves as managers of the anniversary, in order "to divest it in advance of any appearance of being the act of one of the two rival national associations to the exclusion of the other."[85] They recommended management be passed to the "surviving members of the original convention," to enhance the likelihood of neutrality.[86] But surviving members such as Stone and other American Association figures did not get involved. That fall, it appeared the event might not happen at all because Davis fell ill. Stanton stepped in to help with the planning, salvaging the celebration.[87]

On Friday, 20 October 1870, Stanton called the meeting to order and declared that the celebration to commemorate "The Twentieth Anniversary of the Inauguration of the Woman Suffrage Movement" was now in session. They met despite driving rain, gale-force winds, and—dramatically—an earthquake the day prior. "The sky wept, and the earth shook," one newspaper reported, "but nothing daunted the champions of women's freedom."[88] Several competing events in the city that same day drew away potential audience members,[89] but there was a reasonable showing.[90] "The movement in

England, as in America," Stanton instructed those gathered, "may be dated from the first National Convention, held at Worcester."[91]

Stanton then turned the chair over to Davis, who explicitly challenged an abolitionist memory.[92] Davis read a lengthy historical overview of the campaign for women's rights, the culmination of a historical lecture she had been giving at suffrage events throughout 1869.[93] Davis characterized the birth of the suffrage movement as "the greatest movement for humanity ever inaugurated."[94] In so doing she countered abolitionist claims that antislavery had been the greatest movement humanity had ever known. She was already on record opposing black men voting before white women. She now opposed abolitionists' memory claims by arguing that the women's rights movement was more historic than antislavery. Davis excerpted a letter from Garrison, the father of antislavery, to buttress her point: "I doubt whether a more important movement has ever been launched, than this in regard to the equality of the sexes."[95] If woman suffrage was "the greatest movement for humanity ever inaugurated,"[96] then present politics demanded prioritization of sexual equality, not racial justice.

Davis also offered her address, and the anniversary event itself, as a rallying point for rebuilding. The nascent suffrage movement faced a sometimes-hostile political climate, along with internal turmoil, competing allegiances, insufficient resources, and the diluting effect of multiple strategies. There was nothing certain about its survival. Marking a beginning provided a measuring stick, allowing Davis to compare past to present and therefore to judge, by some seemingly objective standard, whether women had cause for encouragement. "Has this work . . . failed," Davis asked, "and become a monument of buried hopes?"[97] No, history proved just the opposite. "In reviewing the past we have only cause for rejoicing . . . and for courage in the future."[98] Davis invoked inevitable victory by invoking the past. She emphasized the "wonderful strides our cause has made . . . , which neither ridicule nor unreason can assail."[99] Davis also made a promise to women considering joining the crusade: they had nothing to fear. Whereas speakers at early conventions "were met with hoots of derision" and required "the services of the police . . . to keep order," audiences now exhibited a "profound respect for the speaker and her subject."[100] Conversion to woman suffrage promised reverence and the chance to participate in something historic, she suggested. "We call young, fresh workers," she continued, "to receive from our hands the sacred cause."[101]

Davis's memory, too, was partial, as all memories are. She chose selectively from the past. An antebellum women's rights movement had numerous priorities, of which the vote was only one, and not always the most important. Yet in Davis's rendition, an antebellum women's rights movement had only one priority: the vote. She made this point by mentioning and highlighting only one of the long list of resolutions, or demands, that had been passed at antebellum women's rights conventions, that for suffrage.[102] This partial memory, too, was instructive. Some veteran workers lamented the turn to suffrage after the Civil War, thinking the movement had given up an important, earlier breadth. Davis treated this change not as a new priority, or a redefinition open to debate, but merely the way it had always been. This helped legitimate the emphasis of the nascent postwar suffrage movement. Davis also used her address to remind politicians and fellow abolitionists that women's disenfranchisement was not new. Women had already been demanding this basic guarantor of freedom for decades, and it was not, therefore, justifiable to postpone those demands. The time to enfranchise women, she emphasized, was now.

However much anniversary organizers strove for neutrality, the event highlighted how profoundly partisan the question of origins now was. In a divided movement, where women marked the start of their movement had important consequences. If suffragists had questions about which organization—or which women—to follow, the event claimed history could answer them. Unlike the partisan politics that produced the split, history appeared to be a neutral judge, rendering unassailable answers. An origins tale, in particular, could do this, since whoever claimed to have been the source of the movement could also claim to be its rightful heir in the present. This is exactly what happened at the Second Decade Convention. After surveying at length women's rights actions in the antebellum decades, Davis claimed the National-turned-Union Association "was the outgrowth of this [earlier] demand for freedom."[103] In other words, she drew a line of succession to Stanton and Anthony and implicitly condemned Stone and her colleagues for being on the wrong side of history. At the commemoration, Anthony also offered a resolution endorsing a Sixteenth Amendment, implying that history moved inexorably toward this strategy, not a state-by-state approach.[104]

Davis extended this logic in her published address. After the Second Decade Convention, she printed her speech under the title *A History of the National Woman's Rights Movement, for Twenty Years*. At roughly twenty-five pages, it was the first extended, published chronicle of the movement.[105] In her account, Davis argued that the National Association carried the mantle of history and thus offered the true path to liberation. To side with Stanton and Anthony and to align behind the vote as the pinnacle of a women's rights agenda was to be on the correct side of history. She defended the National Association by deflecting criticism surrounding the secretive way in which some alleged it had been formed. "Notice was given," she asserted, and the association created "at a large meeting, in which nineteen States were represented." Its formation marked a new "historical era, the influence of which cannot be estimated for years."[106] Davis's characterization of the American Association's ability to lead the charge for the vote, and all that supposedly inhered within in it, was, by contrast, damning. She gave that society one line, charging the American Association had no goal or purpose. "Its work," she wrote, "is yet to be done."[107] With that, she dismissed it. Davis never discussed the causes for division. They were irrelevant in this adjudication. What mattered was who had inherited the past.

The irony was that neither Stanton nor Anthony had attended the 1850 Worcester convention. Anthony did not make her first appearance at a national women's rights convention until 1853.[108] Stanton did not attend any of the 1850s national women's rights conventions. She first appeared at a national women's rights convention in 1860, a full decade later.[109] The pair had been absent from the first national conventions. Their rivals in the American Association, on the other hand, had been present at nearly all the early national conventions.

Yet Stone and other members of the American Association boycotted the Worcester anniversary celebration, although they had been moving influences at the original 1850 convention. They did not even sign the anniversary call.[110] The commemoration failed to unify suffragists, as Davis had originally hoped. Whether Stone and other American Association members were invited to participate in the planning is unclear. But the event went forward without their participation. The decision of Stone, Kelley Foster, Garrison, and others to absent themselves from this inaugural staging of movement memory, to offer no counternarrative, lent further credibility to Davis's claim that the National-turned-Union Association was the legitimate "outgrowth" of this original demand for freedom.

As this inaugural staging of movement memory, the 1848 Seneca Falls convention was visible, but Davis did not highlight it in any particular way. During her historical address from the stage of the anniversary celebration, Davis pointed out that three conventions preceded the 1850 national convention in Worcester: "one at Seneca Falls, one at Ohio, and one at Rochester."[111] Davis pointed out that Stanton had, at Seneca Falls, offered a resolution on the franchise, again reducing the demands made there to this one. But about Seneca Falls, she said no more. The meeting was a passing detail, one in a whole host of early influences. And when she later added to that list the exclusion of women from the 1840 World's Anti-Slavery Convention in London, she made no connection between it and the decision to call the 1848 convention. They were unrelated in her history. Instead, in her account all these early influences led to Worcester, when the movement could be said to have truly begun.[112]

Neither did Stanton discuss the 1848 Seneca Falls convention at the anniversary or in her published writings. She spoke to the 1870 anniversary gathering on marriage and divorce.[113] Two years earlier, in 1868, James Parton had put together a series of biographical sketches of leading women's rights activists, published as *Eminent Women of the Age*. Stanton wrote the short entry titled, "The Woman's Rights Movement and Its Champions in the United States."[114] She referenced the Seneca Falls meeting in her biographical entry on Mott, but she claimed no special significance for that event. She even failed to note that it was the first such convention.[115] Stanton wrote her account before the split in national suffrage forces, and that is evident in the generosity she showed Stone, crediting her with having been "the first speaker who really stirred the nation's heart on the subject of woman's wrongs."[116] Similarly, Theodore Tilton, who authored the biographical sketch of Stanton in Parton's volume, claimed no special significance for the 1848 meeting in Seneca Falls.[117]

If Stanton had backed Davis's 1870 claim that "the movement in England, as in America, may be dated from the first National Convention, held at Worcester," she did not argue that for very long.[118] The newly emergent and evidently lasting split between the National and the American Associations put a new burden on the question of beginnings, and where some suffragists dated their origins began to shift as they fought with one another in the years to come.

2. Movements without Memories
✥ 1870–1873

At the National Woman Suffrage Association's annual 1873 meeting, "a wreath of laurels, interwoven with a silver thread" occupied center stage. The National Association had just been reconstituted, and Stanton and Anthony devoted their 1873 May convention to a celebration of Seneca Falls's twenty-fifth anniversary—to what they were now calling "the 'silver wedding' of the doctrine." Near the wreath and its silver thread sat three original organizers of the 1848 convention: Lucretia Mott, Martha Coffin Wright, and Elizabeth Cady Stanton, who were joined by other leading National Association figures.[1] No longer did Stanton and Anthony insist that the 1850 Worcester convention had begun the movement. They now relocated and antedated the movement's birthplace and time. As events receded and veterans aged, organic memory was both fading and being intentionally remade. The myth of Seneca Falls—in the sense of a venerated story, or collective memory, that gave the movement a particular origin, a particular doctrine, and a particular meaning—first began to cohere here, twenty-five years after the event itself.[2]

The three years preceding the 1873 anniversary convention had been difficult ones for Stanton and Anthony, and those difficulties fueled their efforts to reshape the movement by redefining its ostensible origins. The 1870s saw a new wave of vitality and participation in suffrage organizing, so varied and so widespread that it threatened to overshadow the pair. The movement grew exponentially, its ranks swelled by women with their own agendas, advocacy styles, and senses of history. Although an antebellum origin bolstered a sense of historical continuity between pre- and postwar organizing, the Reconstruction-era suffrage movement was not a mere resumption or continuation of prewar organizing. As the postwar movement splintered, its lack of organizational and individual memory occasioned both creativity and bitterness.

After the Civil War, a new generation of fresh faces and voices took up feminism for the first time, having been radicalized not by the long abolition struggle but rather by their more recent and diverse war work.[3] Through the variety of women's voluntary and paid work supporting the Union and its army, many women developed an understanding of themselves as strong-minded, public citizens.[4] After 1865, they opened new fields of women's rights activism by reinventing it from the ground up. By ignorance or exuberance, some simply took for granted the generation of women who had paved their way, while others expressed open hostility, or a lack of deference, toward movement veterans. This hostility went both ways. In 1869, Stanton accused one group of newcomers of talking "a great deal of nonsense, and . . . hunting after notoriety."[5] Later that year, when a *New York Times* reporter bluntly asked Anthony about rumors that she was an "autocrat," she dismissed the accusations as "efforts of jealous and envious women who have slept while I worked. . . . Now that the movement is a success . . . 'every one is ready to jump aboard the train.'" Revealingly, Anthony complained that "every one [now] thought they had as much right to manage matters as we had." Over the next decade, Anthony and Stanton struggled to respond as more people jumped aboard the women's rights train with their own ideas about where it should be headed.[6]

Such issues had come to a head by 1873, when Anthony felt keenly the need to bring the movement together behind a national-level campaign. For this and other reasons, Stanton and Anthony began to articulate a new origins story for feminism. But to understand why the pair turned to Seneca Falls in particular, as opposed to other plausible beginnings, and how they first began to sketch out an origins story that not only outlived them but took on a life of its own, requires examining on-the-ground movement politics during the 1870s, the goal of this chapter and the next.

✣ A Multiplication of Movements

Seeing the suffrage movement much as Stanton and Anthony eventually depicted it, scholars and popular audiences often refer to a singular, coordinated women's suffrage effort after the Civil War.[7] It was, however, more accurately a collection of movements, goals, strategies, and leaders. Although women sometimes worked in concert, in the 1870s they increasingly worked independently. And they sometimes labored unintentionally at cross-purposes or purposely at odds. Local, state, and regional activism, not to mention rapid westward expansion, weighed against a unitary movement with centralized leadership or control. Stanton and Anthony quite understandably aspired to set the tone and the agenda, but their experienced voices were not always heeded. The chaotic, expanding shape of the movement was exhilarating, producing massive outpourings of diverse support. Initiative and vigor in these years came from the base. The newly created national organizations played important roles, but they frequently found themselves attempting to catch up to local and individual agitation, even struggling to find a place amid the grassroots ferment that exploded after the war.[8]

Perhaps no region inspired more activist women than the Midwest. The Missouri Suffrage Association, one of the first postwar societies, emerged from a convention in St. Louis in 1867.[9] In Dubuque, Iowa, women organized that state's first local society, the Northern Iowa Woman Suffrage Association, in April 1869, and another local group formed in the nearby town of Monticello in October—both before a state suffrage organization was founded in 1870.[10] Chicago activists held several large conventions in 1869 alone, and one group of local activists went on the road for several months, barnstorming all over the region with traveling suffrage conventions.[11] The ubiquity of suffrage ferment prompted one Ohio newspaper to observe in 1869, "the public agitation of the question is [not] confined to State & National conventions, but county conventions are held in all parts of the country."[12]

As far away as California, suffragists held numerous local conventions and meetings in the late 1860s, inspiring larger annual state conventions after January 1870.[13] Places as unexpected as Battle Mountain, Nevada, hosted a woman suffrage convention in July 1870.[14] In a pattern that would repeat itself throughout the remainder of the nineteenth century, the West also enfranchised women in advance of the rest of the nation, first in Wyoming and then in Utah, with future victories also falling west of the Mississippi River.[15]

In the South, no antebellum women's rights movement had taken hold (largely because of the region's complex race and gender dynamics), but women and men raised the issue during the early years of Reconstruction, when former Confederate states dramatically expanded their voter rolls. As early as 1867, a white woman suffrage organization formed in Glendale, Kentucky.[16] A family of African American sisters campaigned actively in South Carolina. Louisa Rollin advocated women's enfranchisement on the floor of the State Assembly in 1869, and Lottie Rollin led a woman suffrage rally at the state capitol two years later.[17] A racially integrated woman's rights convention was held in Columbia in 1870,[18] chaired by one of the Rollin sisters. A year later, a state woman suffrage association formed, with both black and white membership. Conversely, woman suffrage activism in the former Confederacy was sometimes used to support white supremacy. After an 1871 tour through the region, Paulina Wright Davis remarked that opposition to black men's enfranchisement had turned many southern white women and some white men into woman suffrage advocates—but only for white women, who presumably would vote with their husbands to outweigh the black male vote.[19]

In Richmond, Virginia, freedwomen in the former Confederacy also claimed the vote, but did so in ways that bypassed the organized suffrage movement. If the mainstream suffrage movement's vision of voting rights rested on liberal individualism, in which "society is merely an aggregation of individuals, each of whom is ultimately responsible for her/himself," the activism of many freed black women did not. The vote, in their view, was a community possession—to be cast for the mutual benefit of the community, not an individual's self-interest. As one historian has shown, in Richmond and elsewhere, ordinary black women asserted their right to influence how black men cast their ballots, which they claimed as their own. They actively participated in black political meetings, for example, where they sometimes voted and determined community political agendas, which would later be carried out at the polls. Women also showed up at the polls on Election Day and harassed newly enfranchised black men into voting women's collective political will. At the same time, black politicians and political groups agitated for women's voting rights, although they were often not connected to white women's organizing.[20]

The Colored National Labor Convention of 1869, in turn, met in Washington, D.C., and formed a committee on woman suffrage, chaired by a black woman, Mary Ann Shadd Cary.[21] And historian Rosalyn Terborg-Penn has uncovered a hitherto unknown 1870 woman suffrage petition signed by eighteen black women from the D.C. area, each appearing "to be independent woman suffragists." She suggests there are "many more of these women to find in southern cities."[22]

Even in the Northeast, where scholars usually locate suffrage history, a little-known diversity in organizing existed. A German Woman's Rights Convention was held in Roxbury, Massachusetts, in December 1868.[23] In 1872, a convention of German women in New York City debated and endorsed women's right to the ballot.[24] There even existed an active Young Men's Woman Suffrage League in the 1870s; its male membership held regular meetings in New York City.[25] In Boston in 1869, the venerable William Lloyd Garrison marveled at the frequency of state and local suffrage meetings held in the region. Unlike antebellum conventions, which had been controversial, he noted these now-ubiquitous suffrage meetings had aroused "no serious opposition."[26]

Although local and state activists may have been welcome signs to Garrison, whose life's work was more or less done, their numbers, energy, and success sometimes left Stanton and Anthony on the defensive or on the sidelines, even within their own circle. In January 1871, for example, the new suffrage convert Isabella Beecher Hooker—sister of Harriet Beecher Stowe and an ally of Stanton and Anthony—planned the annual meeting of the new Union Woman Suffrage Association. Fearing Stanton's presence would be too controversial, Hooker disinvited her. Anthony was outraged by this slight, but even more so when Stanton quietly decided not to attend. Complaining that "every new convert" wants to "improve upon Christ's methods," Anthony chided Stanton for capitulating, fuming "that you, the pioneer, the originator, the leader, should drop, & say to each of these new converts . . . 'Yes, you may manage. . . . [You]r knowledge, your judgment . . . are all superior to mine.'" Anthony felt that the movement was courting danger while Stanton stood by and watched. Stanton had quickly grown weary of the infighting accompanying organizational politics after the war, and her gradual withdrawal from organizational work alarmed Anthony. "To my mind there was never such suicidal letting go the helm of a ship in a stormy sea as has been that of yours, these last two years." "O! how I have agonized over my utter failure to make you . . . see the importance . . . of standing fast, & holding on to the helm of our good ship," she wrote. "How you can excuse yourself is more than I can understand."[27] For her part, Stanton relished a fight with suffrage opponents but less so with suffragists themselves. "I am between two fires, all the time," she lamented to Martha Coffin Wright. "Some, determined to throw me overboard, & Susan equally determined that I shall stand at mast head, no matter how pitiless the storm."[28]

Stanton and Anthony had a strong claim on movement leadership. Not only gifted thinkers and organizers, they were also rapidly becoming some of the nation's most famous women. They did important work at the federal level and on the ground.[29] But for the moment, there simply was not one "helm" or even one "good ship" of women's rights activism. The groundswell of postwar women's rights in far-flung towns and states made for a vibrant chaos that was not conducive to national leadership or national coordination. Many of the "new converts" were not really converts at all, in the sense of being drawn into existing organizations or strategies. Instead, they pursued their own targets and solutions, and they launched their own organizations, their own plans of attack, and even their own newspapers.[30] They rejected national leadership in favor of grassroots vibrancy and independence. This would frustrate Anthony, in particular. She believed strongly in the need for a coordinated and centralized movement. And her frustration with what she perceived to be the chaos of the immediate postwar years fueled her efforts to unify the movement behind clear leadership. The success of the movement, she believed, depended upon it. But for the time being, women branched out in very direction.

❖ Lecturing Women

The new face of activism was nowhere more evident than on the lecture circuit, where activists built a new type of movement after the war. Women flooded onto the postwar lecture circuit—so much so that one newspaper dubbed it an "invasion." Prominent women had lectured prior to the Civil War, but they did so in much smaller numbers. Lecturing women also shed the negative stigma that had plagued them in the antebellum era. At the same time, the postwar lecture circuit—or the lyceum, as it was called— became thoroughly commercialized, meaning speakers were routinely paid, often handsomely, and this helped encourage women's influx into this new type of activism. The skyrocketing popularity of the lyceum as public entertainment meant there were ample job opportunities for lecturing women in the postwar years.[31]

These new realities drove large numbers of women's rights activists into lecturing, where they mounted a series of independent, one-woman movements. Most of these women's rights lecturers did not work for a suffrage organization, although they may have belonged to one. This was because organizations were cash strapped and had little money to pay women for their services. Yet activists needed to earn a living, so they pursued opportunity on the open market. Their choice to venture into the lyceum lent women's activism a great deal of independence, since they did not need to coordinate their messages with any central clearinghouse. Rather, they proffered their own analyses of what the hour required.[32]

The positive reception suffrage lecturers received also underscored a sea change in public opinion after the war. "In the course of the next ten or twelve years," one suffragist recalled, "the whole country was seething with interest in the questions that relate to women."[33] People from all walks of life—opponents, supporters, neutral observers, and curious onlookers—flocked to suffrage lectures. Suffragists sometimes spent as much as 100 to 200 nights a year lecturing, crisscrossing the nation by stagecoach and train. As these women canvassed the country, the *Woman's Journal* began running a regular feature, "Notes from the Lecture Field," to capture the feverish activity. Indeed, the ground was positively cluttered with itinerant suffrage speakers, who sometimes drew audiences of several thousand. Some of their names are known today, but most are not.[34]

With all this agitation, the press and the general public sometimes had a very different sense than movement veterans of who the leaders were at any given time. Women shot to prominence quickly. For example, celebrated lecturer Anna Dickinson became perhaps the most famous woman in America in the 1870s. She ardently supported suffrage, and for a time the National Association curried her favor, but she refused affiliation with any suffrage organization, preferring independence. There were regionally famous suffrage lecturers too, such as Michigan suffragist (Mary) Adelle Hazlett, whom the New York press dubbed the "Michigan Anna Dickinson." Hazlett, for one, abhorred eastern suffragists' sense that they ran—or at least, ought to run—the campaign.[35]

Anthony perceived mixed blessings in the new popularity of lecturing women and the now routine coverage they garnered in the mainstream press. More women speaking to more audiences in more places, along with the routine press coverage that such events generated, meant that their message, or messages, were reaching more Americans, perhaps, than any other form of movement work. Such popularity and presence suggested that the achievement of women's rights was closer than ever before, even as a new generation seized the torch rather than awaiting its passing. "How rapidly now the ball rolls on," she mused, ". . . but how different the times." Antebellum women who had dared to speak publicly endured "ridicule & scorn," she recalled, paving the way for the "profit and emolument" now accruing to "the newly awakened . . . [who] push their way into prominence . . . & . . . take the front seat of the public movement." The best Anthony could make of the "pitiable" ingratitude of so many new recruits was that their sheer numbers demonstrated "the nearness . . . of our demand."[36]

It was not only "the newly awakened" who pushed in this direction. Even Stanton preferred solo engagements during these years. In truth, she hated conventions (where she was often attacked for her uncompromising ideas and bold personality), and she only attended the National Association's annual meetings under extreme pressure from Anthony.[37] Not only did Stanton find conventions too rehearsed and repetitive, the format was beginning to strike her as old-fashioned. On the lecture circuit, Stanton could earn a living and develop her philosophical ideas and political arguments without hindrance. "So long as people will pay me $75 & 100 every night, to speak on my own," Stanton quipped, "there is no need of my talking in Convention."[38] At one point, she even offered to donate $100 to convention organizers if they would leave her alone "to pursue my individual work."[39]

The "individual work" of women who invaded the lyceum following the Civil War fundamentally changed how the movement operated. It exerted a decentralizing effect, pulling women away from organizational work and away from a coordinated message. Nevertheless, the multiplying voices of both the famous and the unknown helped to convince average Americans that woman suffrage was not necessarily a dangerous idea. Everywhere, older activists commented on the vast sea change in public opinion since the antebellum era.[40] And the opportunities women found on the lyceum fueled the grassroots expansion that remade postwar suffrage into a diverse and uncontrollable social movement.[41]

❖ The Challenges of Coordination

Decentralized and independent activism even reshaped more conventional suffrage work in the ways that state and local suffrage societies positioned, and even imagined, themselves. As Stanton herself acknowledged, national organizing was in many ways a response to the new vitality of grassroots activism—an effort to make a national movement cohere from the uncoordinated but seemingly ubiquitous local actions.[42] Whereas the American Association's public mission was to redouble that state activism, the National Association hoped to redirect it toward national objectives. Both goals remained sometimes elusive, however, as various state and local organizations determinedly tried to remain independent.

Some state and local societies did formally affiliate with national organizations, but equally notable was the refusal of others to do so. In 1869, the well-established Missouri Woman Suffrage Association declined to affiliate with either the National or the American Associations.[43] Iowa, which formed its first state association in June of 1870—with area representatives present from both the American and the Union Associations, presumably there to persuade the new association to affiliate—voted to embrace independent action, affiliating with neither.[44] In that same year, California women held their first state convention and voted, after a heated debate, to remain independent of eastern associations for at least one year.[45] Sometimes state associations reconsidered their auxiliary status, as the Indiana Woman Suffrage Association did in 1871, taking up a motion at its annual convention to withdraw from the American Association and remain independent.[46]

Although a national society might claim a state organization or person as an affiliate, this did not mean that the state suffragists understood themselves to be auxiliary. As late as 1878, Stone wrote Iowa suffragist Martha Callanan regarding disgruntlement in that state about the American Association's claim upon the allegiance of the Iowa Woman Suffrage Society. Stone's letter outlined the rather loose policy by which the American Association determined auxiliary membership. "We assumed," Stone explained, "that those states which were represented at its [the American Association's] formation were auxiliary."[47] A number of suffragists in the corn state disagreed. Wisconsin suffragist Lillie Peckham was furious when her name was used, without her authorization, on the public call for the American Association's inaugural convention. When she agreed to attend the American Association's founding convention as a Wisconsin delegate, she did so simply to see what the event was about. She was quite clear that her attendance did not constitute a formal endorsement of this society over any other.[48] Fanny E. Russell of Maple Plain, Minnesota, publicly protested the National Association's 1872 listing of her name as a vice president from that state, since she was, by choice, not a member of that association. "I was a little astonished," Russell explained, ". . . and a little curious to know how many of the names upon the same list of officers were also used without permission." "Let us each work in our own way," she continued, underscoring the independence of action, "and not force any one to train in a company one does not voluntarily join, by using names without permission."[49] Where state affiliations were concerned, confusion reigned.

In some cases, state-level suffragists made alternative attempts to coordinate action across state lines, bypassing national association efforts to do so. In June of 1869, activists at an Indiana suffrage meeting backed the creation of a new regional association, the Western Woman Suffrage Association.[50] Women and men throughout the Midwest also supported the idea. In the fall of 1869, the same year the National and American Associations were created, midwestern women held a large convention in Chicago to launch the Western Woman Suffrage Association.[51] Testifying to the frequency and preexisting variety of organizing on the ground, that association's call invited all organizations, "whether state, county, or town, whether American or of any other nationality," to attend.[52]

A year later, in November 1870, a different regional organization, the Northwestern Woman Suffrage Association, held a mass convention in Detroit.[53] It was chaired by the noted Michigan lecturer Adelle Hazlett, who registered her distaste for eastern divisions and oversight by insisting upon midwestern women's independence.[54] Women in Illinois agreed. When the American and National Associations failed to unify in 1870, the Illinois Woman Suffrage Association registered its dissatisfaction by withdrawing from the American Association and voting overwhelmingly to affiliate instead with the Northwestern Woman Suffrage Association.[55]

An independent, regional association was soon formed in the far West as well. In May of 1871, activists in San Francisco hosted the first annual Pacific Slope Convention, an organization that lasted for several years. Those attending the four-day convention included persons from California, Oregon, Nevada, and Idaho.[56] Although these organizations are virtually forgotten today, they were a vital part of postwar activism. When asked about suffrage organizing in 1871, Stanton explained that there were four national woman suffrage organizations: the Pacific, the Northwest, the National, and the American.[57]

State organizing was no more harmonious than national organizing, however, further underscoring the atomized and sometimes conflicting nature of suffrage activism in these years. California, for example, was wracked by internal division, with suffragists clashing over matters large and small.[58] Divisions characterized organizing in Pennsylvania, Ohio, and New York as well.[59] And divisions on the national scene sometimes spilled over into organizing on the state level. The thriving state organization in Missouri, for example, founded in 1867, suffered near collapse when American Association allies attempted to drive National Association sympathizers Virginia Minor and Phoebe Couzins from office.[60]

A group of white suffragists in Illinois rejected what they derisively called the movement's "self-appointed" leadership. Area suffragists became so divided during the planning stages for an Illinois State Suffrage Association in early 1869 that they split into two rival factions, which held simultaneous conventions that February. Sarah Mills headed a group calling itself the "People's Convention," which derided Stanton, Anthony, and Stone as "self-appointed leaders." Mills accused these women and Chicago resident Mary Livermore, who rose to prominence during the war and headed the rival state convention, of trying to bar controversial views and wider perspectives. She viewed their leadership claims not as legitimately won through popular acclaim but as something they were busily trying to impose upon women. Reflecting the grassroots energy that animated the vastly expanded movement of the early 1870s, she countered that leaders ought to be chosen from "the People," who could better define the demands of the hour.[61] Even the nationally prominent Antoinette Brown Blackwell, Stone's sister-in-law and the first woman ordained as a minister in the United States, rejected the idea that victory required strong leaders. The new grassroots army, she countered, was enough to win the day. "There are thousands of 'women of the hour,'" she told Stanton, "we dont [sic] need one preeminent over all the others."[62]

Anthony positively disagreed. The incredible postwar ferment and the pervasive sense that victory was nearly at hand made it even more incumbent upon National Association veterans to assume responsibility for the course of women's rights, she believed. In her view, she and Stanton best understood how to coordinate that action and how to deliver the necessary, precise final blows to women's disenfranchisement. "Washington is *the point* of attack, — & if *we are not there to make it*," she explained, "some *others—less competent—surely* will be—It will not do to leave that *fortress unmanned.*"[63]

❖ Victoria Woodhull and the New Departure

The January 1871 Union Association convention underscored just how quickly and how spectacularly new recruits rose to prominence during these early years. The events that followed confirmed Anthony's fears that chaos within the movement left it open to misdirection, and it prompted her to seek tighter control. The 1871 convention proved notable for two things: the entrance into the campaign of a controversial new figure, the free-love advocate Victoria Woodhull; and the Union Association's adoption of a new suffrage strategy born at the grassroots, the so-called New Departure.

On 11 January 1871, the Union Association delayed its convention's opening session for a historic occasion—Woodhull's address to the House Judiciary Committee advocating women's enfranchisement. Congressional committees did not usually invite women to address them, so the event itself, apart from the subject, was thrilling and not to be missed. Equally electrifying was the person invited. Victoria Claflin Woodhull was born in Homer, Ohio, in 1838. Her father, a con man, had marketed his young daughter as a gifted spirit medium, selling her powers—powers that many nineteenth-century Americans believed certain individuals possessed—to put the living in communication with the dead.[64] At age fourteen, she married Canning Woodhull, an Ohio doctor, who descended into alcoholism and infidelity, leaving Victoria responsible for supporting the family, including their two small children. In 1865, well before it was socially acceptable, the pair divorced. Yet they continued to live together, as Victoria cared for her incapacitated ex-husband. Woodhull then remarried and lived under the same roof with her new husband as well as her ex-husband, a doubly scandalous arrangement. Woodhull, already an ardent spiritualist and a traveling spirit medium (who claimed to be animated by the spirit of the ancient Athenian statesman Demosthenes), also began to embrace the ideas of free love. Considered degenerate and even heretical by most Americans, free lovers encouraged the expression of women's sexuality, at a time when women were considered to have no sexual feelings whatsoever, only a maternal instinct arising from their duty to procreate.[65]

Woodhull and her sister, Tennessee Claflin, first catapulted to national notoriety when, in 1870—just one year before her address to Congress—the pair had persuaded Cornelius Vanderbilt, the obscenely wealthy railroad magnate, to set them up with a Wall Street brokerage firm. Vanderbilt had been grateful to Woodhull for allowing him to communicate with his dead wife, and he rewarded her handsomely. Woodhull and Claflin's arrival on Wall Street created a sensation and delivered a blow for women's rights, with their shocking appearance in this staunchly all-male bastion. Soon, the sisters also began publishing a new reform newspaper, *Woodhull & Claflin's Weekly*. They used it to advocate a broad reform agenda, including free love, women's rights (including women's suffrage), spiritualism, radical labor politics, and communism. Revealing Woodhull's deep immersion in the world of radical politics, her newspaper was the first to publish an English translation of Karl Marx's 1848 *Communist Manifesto. Woodhull & Claflin's Weekly* sought complete social transformation. Tennessee Claflin, meanwhile, shocked the public by her choice to wear men's clothing and smoke cigars. That someone as controversial as Woodhull would be chosen as the first woman to address Congress on the question of women's voting was somewhat surprising, given she had no longstanding women's rights credentials. She, like so many after the war, was new to the women's suffrage scene, and she contributed to its redefinition.[66]

On the morning of 11 January 1871, Woodhull schooled the House Judiciary Committee on points of constitutional law. Under the logic of the New

Victoria Woodhull
(Portrait by Matthew Brady,
c. 1870, Collection of the
New-York Historical Society)

Departure, she argued, women already possessed the right to vote. She based her argument on a dazzling new legal interpretation of the Fourteenth and Fifteenth Amendments. Whereas women had previously protested their exclusion from those amendments, Woodhull turned this around. She insisted that the rights and protections contained within those amendments applied to women. Although the second clause of the Fourteenth Amendment stipulated that federal citizenship applied only to the "male" populace, Woodhull refocused attention on the first clause, where federal citizenship was conferred upon all "persons"—which she insisted must include women. She explained that the Fourteenth Amendment, in conferring federal citizenship (which had previously been conferred by the states), made the federal government responsible for protecting "the privileges" that came along with national citizenship. The Fourteenth Amendment had not spelled out what those "privileges" were, however. So Woodhull did. Because the only legitimate basis for a democratic government could be the will of the people, she continued, the most basic of these privileges must be the right to vote. Woodhull then turned to the Fifteenth Amendment. It banned disenfranchisement on the basis of "race, color, or previous condition of servitude." A "race," she asserted, "comprises all the people, male and female." The federal government, then, had an incumbent right to protect women against voting discrimination. Women, she argued, needed only to march to the polls and begin casting their votes.[67]

Reflecting the shape of the movement in the late 1860s and the early 1870s, the New Departure had been born at the local level, with activists on the ground. Woodhull merely ushered it onto a national stage. As early as 1868, women had begun a direct action campaign in Vineland, New Jersey, when nearly 200 women showed up to the polls on Election Day to cast their ballots. In 1869, Mary Olney Brown, on "the other side of the continent" in Washington Territory, took advantage of a loophole in territorial law, which enfranchised "all white American citizens above the age of twenty-one," and marched to the polls to cast her vote. These efforts and scores of others became part of a larger constitutional argument when, in October 1869, Virginia and Francis Minor of Missouri first articulated the New Departure strategy. The idea quickly spread through grassroots networks, and by 1870, the year before Woodhull addressed the House Judiciary Committee, women—both black and white—were marching to the polls in significant numbers. Congress's May 1870 passage of the Enforcement Act, designed to strengthen the Fifteenth Amendment by providing citizens recourse to the federal courts if local election officials refused their ballots, encouraged and accelerated women's direct action voting. Already by 1871, New Departure cases were winding their way through the federal courts.[68]

The main difference between Woodhull and the Minors was the branch of government they assailed. The Minors encouraged women to vote, to risk arrest, and to test their claims in court. They hoped the judicial branch would affirm their reading of the Reconstruction Amendments and thereby obviate any need to press women's claim at the legislative level (state or federal). Woodhull, by contrast, emphasized federal legislative action. She called upon Congress to pass a declaratory act affirming this broad reading of the Reconstruction Amendments and thereby granting women's voting rights.[69]

Anthony and Isabella Beecher Hooker were so thrilled that they invited Woodhull to deliver her remarks once again, that afternoon, at the Union Association's convention, where she spoke to an enthusiastic packed hall. The Union Association threw its energies behind Woodhull and made the New Departure the centerpiece of its January 1871 convention, abandoning its work for a federal amendment. It was a creative and promising argument, and the Union Association adopted it wholesale. Urging women everywhere to drop work for a Sixteenth Amendment in favor of the New Departure, Anthony advised activists to give up that "old stage-coach method" and instead "use the new method—the telegraph system—and do the work quick." Anthony's elation was palpable.[70]

The National Association urged women everywhere to vote in the upcoming 1872 presidential election.[71] Believing the final phase of their long struggle was now at hand, Anthony cheered: "I have new life, new hope that our battle is to be short, sharp, and decisive under this 14th & 15th Amendment clause—it is unanswerable."[72] She, Hooker, Stanton, and others enthusiastically welcomed Woodhull into the organization, where Woodhull became an overnight star, identified by the press as "the leader of the party."[73] As Woodhull stepped into the national suffrage spotlight, Union Association members confidently predicted that woman suffrage was practically won.

The Union Association, which set up a congressional lobby committee at its meeting, began petitioning Congress for a declaratory act, and Hooker remained in Washington, D.C., throughout the first part of 1871 to pressure Congress for its passage. In an unprecedented move, Congress officially acknowledged these female lobbyists by setting aside two congressional rooms specifically for their use—more evidence that victory was surely at hand.[74] Yet as the momentum within the Union Woman Suffrage Association swung behind Woodhull and the New Departure, Anthony also began to feel eclipsed and rudderless: "I tell you I feel utterly disheartened—not that our cause is going to die or be defeated, but as to my place and work."[75]

Stone and her close colleagues in the American Association were neither elated nor amused. Always more socially conservative, they feared that Woodhull's controversial free-love views would cost the movement public support and thereby delay victory. They had a larger legal quibble as well. Like many Americans, they disagreed that the Fifteenth Amendment had transferred the power to appoint voters to the federal government. They, like others, insisted that this power continued to reside with the states. An editor of the *Woman's Journal*, Thomas Wentworth Higginson, further argued in its pages that voting rights were not synonymous with citizenship, and therefore were not among the privileges of the Constitution.[76]

Here, the American and National Associations entered into larger national debates over a point of constitutional law that remained uncertain. Although it is hard to imagine today that voting is not among the most basic rights of citizenship, this was by no means agreed upon in the nineteenth century. Nor was there yet agreement, as there is today, that federal authority had the right to regulate suffrage. Emancipation had forced a national debate on just these questions, and the arguments of the New Departure advocates held implications for issues well beyond the rights of women.

They went to how broadly the nation would interpret the Reconstruction Amendments and thus how broadly they would interpret the rights of African Americans.

✤ The People's Party

Stanton's admiration for Woodhull differed from Anthony's. If Anthony was impressed by Woodhull's focused method of attack, Stanton was impressed by Woodhull's breadth of vision. Some northerners, particularly those in abolitionist circles, perceived that the Civil War had fundamentally remade the world. And they believed that from the pieces of that fractured old world they could put together a new and better society. They believed they could finally perfect American democracy and usher in a new age of enlightenment. The war, it seemed, had made this possible, and reformers believed they needed to act quickly. That belief produced a broad range of reform impulses, reflecting people's competing ideas about what that new world ought to be and what it required. Abolitionists and freedpeople, on the one hand, each put forth a wide range of plans aimed at creating a new age of racial equality. Immigrant and native-born wage laborers, who felt exploited by the rapid industrialization that overtook the North during the war, put forth a wide range of plans to remake the nation's political economy in order to inaugurate a new era of class equality.[77] For Stanton, women's emancipation needed to be at the heart of any national rebuilding, and in her mind, this needed to join other comprehensive changes. She advocated revision to things as dry as tariff reform and monetary policy. She took positions on labor strikes and much more. Stanton was an expansive, comprehensive thinker who dreamt of a radically new and better world. She was always oblivious to the ways her elitism bounded that vision, however. She loved the rocky seas of political protest and the world of ideas, and she was particularly attracted to Woodhull's advocacy of a new national political party—the "People's Party."[78]

Within the year, Woodhull had successfully parlayed her overnight fame into leadership of a broad new reform coalition. She persuaded Stanton and Hooker to join her in devoting the Union Association's 1872 spring convention to the creation of this new political venture. In short, they proposed a new national political party made up of labor radicals, temperance reformers, peace crusaders, woman suffragists, and assorted others. Their goal was to unseat the Republican Party, which they accused of having abandoned any commitment to meaningful equality. The Union Association's invitation to its May 1872 meeting announced a "People's Convention," and it invited everyone to come in order to "inaugurate a political revolution."[79] When Anthony found her name on the call, along with those of Stanton and Hooker, she was furious. She thought the idea ridiculous. A women's political party would be a party without electors, she charged, making it completely nonsensical. So she privately opposed the plan.[80]

When the People's Convention's opened, confusion erupted. Although organizers hoped to "inaugurate a political revolution," the affair underlined the many challenges of building reform coalitions, particularly across so many issues on which little agreement existed. Likely cognizant of the problem, organizers tried to exert some control over the affair. In a fairly unprecedented move, they decided to charge twenty-five cents admission to the morning and afternoon sessions, "in order to secure quiet and order."[81] (Admission was generally charged only for evening sessions, when prominent speakers appeared.) Protests began outside the hall as interested parties, some of whom had traveled long distances, arrived and expected to enter the hall unimpeded. Upon discovering they would be charged admission, large numbers left in angry disgust. Inside, Stanton read the platform for a new political party—a platform drafted entirely by women. It included everything from woman suffrage to financial reform. More chaos ensued when organizers opened the platform and resolutions to discussion. The audience demanded to know on whose authority these subjects had been introduced, and Hooker rapped her foot in an attempt to call order.[82]

Anthony had had enough. That evening, she attempted to contain Woodhull, Stanton, and Hooker. Although Anthony had warmly welcomed Woodhull into the Union Association, she now disagreed with the direction in which Woodhull and Stanton were heading. And she sought to contain them. Woodhull had earlier issued a second call, in addition to that for the Union Association's "People's Convention," urging a more general reform meeting that was slated to open the following day.[83] Woodhull closed her Union Association remarks by inviting everyone to adjourn and reconvene the following day in Apollo Hall with a host of other reformers to finalize creation of this new political party. Anthony swiftly interjected. She insisted the woman suffrage convention would continue for its planned second day and would not dissolve itself into another's agenda.[84] Mayhem broke out, as a man from the floor called for a vote on whether to join with reformers in Apollo Hall. Anthony swiftly declared the evening session concluded. But a spontaneous chorus arose strongly in favor of Woodhull's proposal. Finding herself in a distinct minority, Anthony ignored the shouts, once again declared the meeting adjourned, pushed those on the stage to make a hasty exit, and attempted to get in the last word, shouting over the clamor that the woman suffrage convention would continue at eleven o'clock the following morning.[85]

❖ Anthony's New Compass

Anthony took swift control of the Union Association the following morning, and she would never again release it. From this point forward, she and Stanton began to part ways. They remained close allies, each dependent on the other, but their temperamental differences became more and more evident in the divergent, if still tightly joined, work they pursued. During the early years of Reconstruction, Anthony had been willing to join Stanton on her free-ranging exploration of radical ideas, but she was increasingly unwilling to indulge her friend. Anthony herself was not philosophically inclined in the same way that Stanton was. She had her own philosophical ideas about what the vote meant (notably, economic independence),[86] but she was always an organizer at heart. She began to view Stanton's free-wheeling tendencies throughout the early years of Reconstruction as potentially damaging to the suffrage cause. She became less and less willing to join Stanton on the rocky, open sea of ideas, where Stanton blended woman suffrage with other agendas. She found within herself a new center, separate from (if never divorced from) her friend. She became increasingly convinced that winning the vote required a strong, suffrage-only organizational stand, moving her closer to the position of the American Association. It was not that she became narrow minded so much as she insisted upon greater focus. Woodhull's efforts to capture suffrage organizing and merge it with a larger reform agenda would soon turn disastrous, and the episode would teach Anthony both to insist upon the priority of the vote and to keep the vote separate from other political entanglements. This became her new compass over 1872 and into 1873, and she would stand firm on that ground for the rest of her career.

When the National Association's meeting convened for a second day, Anthony greeted only a small audience, most of the previous day's audience having joined Woodhull in Apollo Hall.[87] There, attendees formed the short-lived Equal Rights Party, and they nominated Victoria Woodhull as their 1872 candidate for president of the United States. She was the first woman in history to run for the office. Woodhull, who loved controversy, accepted Frederick Douglass as her running mate, though he himself did not endorse this ticket.[88] Back in Steinway Hall, Anthony worked overtime to salvage the struggling organization, which she perceived as nearly destroyed. "There never was such a *foolish muddle*," she confided to her diary, "all come of Mrs. S. [Stanton] consulting *with* & conceding *to* Woodhull—& calling *Peoples* [*sic*] Con—instead of W.S. [woman suffrage] Con[vention]—."[89] "I *never* was so *hurt with folly of Stanton*," Anthony wrote, "all came near being lost."[90]

Taking control of what was left of the tattered organization, Anthony strove to contain the damage. She declared that her organization endorsed no woman for the U.S. presidency. Rather, it pledged to work for whatever viable party supported women's voting rights, and the Equal Rights Party was not viable, in her view.[91] This put her at odds with Stanton and Hooker, who supported Woodhull's candidacy.[92] In the coming months Anthony would work hard to redirect the woman suffrage organization she held so dear. That organization, the National Woman Suffrage Association—which had, by this point, lived several lives—was officially reconstituted at that second day of the Union Association's May 1872 meeting. And Anthony was for the first time elected its president. The Union Association was now dead. Although Anthony believed she had rescued the National Association "by a hair breadth escape,"[93] she fretted about how to rebuild it. "Our movement as such is so demoralized by the letting go of the helm of ship to Wood-hull."[94] "I am thrown half off my own feet—really not knowing whether it is *I* who am gone *stark mad* or some other people."[95]

The sex scandal Woodhull unleashed months later seriously hampered Anthony's efforts to breathe new life into the National Association. In October, Woodhull accused the nation's most prominent minister, Henry Ward Beecher, of an affair with his parishioner and best friend's wife, Elizabeth Tilton. Woodhull had grown tired of the near-continual attacks upon her reputation by the ostensibly upstanding men of the nation for her free-love views and her purported immorality. In retaliation, she decided to expose their hypocrisy and strike another blow for women's rights by attacking the sexual double standard—which condemned women for sexual expression but tolerated it in men. As usual, Woodhull acted with flair. Days before the 1872 presidential election, on the front page of her newspaper, she branded Beecher—the American Association's first president, Isabella Beecher Hooker's brother, and one of the nation's most respected men—an adulterer.[96] The issue sold out within hours and caused gridlock in downtown Manhattan. To compound matters, Woodhull named Stanton as her source. Leading figures in the movement had known about the affair for some time, but no one dared publicize it. It was not the type of thing respectable women talked about in public. Woodhull would pay a heavy price for airing it. Officials soon jailed her on charges of obscenity. Because of Woodhull's close alignment with the suffrage movement, the public and the press began to brand all suffragists as immoral free lovers, and a heap of bad publicity rained down upon the movement.[97]

Woodhull's accusations set off the most famous sex trial of the nineteenth century—a trial that did significant damage to the movement's public image, further convinced Stone of her rivals' recklessness, and left Anthony scrambling to do yet more damage control. When Beecher's criminal trial for adultery concluded in July 1875, the guilty Beecher was acquitted. In a stark illustration of the sexual double standard, Elizabeth Tilton—wife of Theodore Tilton, who had helped create the Union Woman Suffrage Association—was excommunicated.[98] Woodhull, meanwhile, remained defiant. She was let out on bail, once again arrested for obscenity, rejailed, and once again released.[99] Branded by a famous cartoonist as "Mrs. Satan," she proved to opponents that woman suffrage meant sin and perversion.

The Woodhull affair drove a deeper wedge between the New England and New York branches of the movement, a division that showed initial signs of rapprochement during the campaign season of 1872.[100] After the Woodhull alliance, Stone never trusted Stanton and Anthony again. Stone shared the view pervasive in the early 1870s that suffrage was nearly won. She believed public opinion had turned in suffragists' favor, and the campaign season of 1872 suggested that politicians might now follow suit. Stone believed the Republican Party's choice to include a plank on women's rights in their 1872 national party platform was a promising omen. For the first time in political history, a major national political party affirmed that it remained "mindful of its obligations to the loyal women of America" and treated their demands "with respectful consideration."[101] Suffragists, in Stone's mind, only had to keep up the pressure and not give politicians (or the public) any reason to reverse course. Stone believed that in aligning with Woodhull, Stanton and Anthony had done just that: they had turned back progress. They had turned the tide rolling inexorably toward universal suffrage back upon itself. Whether they actually did this is unclear, but for Stone the damage was unmistakable. She now viewed the pair as untrustworthy loose cannons who caused more harm than good.[102]

Stanton and Anthony each handled the scandal differently, revealing differences in their temperaments and priorities. Stanton refused to sanction the sexual double standard as it was being applied to Woodhull and Elizabeth Tilton. It galled her that the press demonized Woodhull and Tilton as

Illustration of the Henry Ward Beecher & Elizabeth Tilton Sex Scandal, with Victoria Woodhull swimming, top left (Courtesy of the Prints & Photographs Division, Library of Congress, LC-USZ62-121959)

immoral, while remaining reverent toward the guilty Beecher. Never shy of controversy, Stanton defended the two women by publicly corroborating Woodhull's charges and revealing herself as the source of Woodhull's information.[103] The degree to which Anthony was moving toward a more focused strategy, centered on the vote, was evident in her reaction. She refused to get embroiled in a debate on morality and the sexual double standard. Unlike Stanton, Anthony attempted to dissociate herself and the National Association from the scandal by declining public comment.[104]

As the accusations of Beecher's infidelity became public, Anthony went to the polls to cast her vote in the November 1872 election, and this act helped her chart a course through the public-relations disasters that followed Woodhull's revelations. Anthony, who had sometimes wondered about her place in the work during the late 1860s and early 1870s, was reinvigorated by her decision to cast a ballot. She voted for the Republican incumbent, General Ulysses S. Grant. "Well I have been & gone & done it!!—positively

Cartoon of Victoria Woodhull as Mrs. Satan. Caption reads: "Get thee behind me, (Mrs.) Satan! Wife (with heavy burden): I'd rather travel the hardest paths of matrimony than follow your footsteps." Full page cartoon by Thomas Nast in Harper's Weekly, *17 February 1872. (Courtesy of the Prints & Photographs Division, Library of Congress, LC-USZ62-74994)*

voted the Republican ticket," she wrote Stanton.[105] Anthony did not share the American Association's commitment to the Republican Party, but she believed that if the Republicans won, they would be forced to affirm the logic of the New Departure.[106] She hoped the Republicans' plank urging "respectful consideration" to "the loyal women of America," along with what Anthony hoped would be a massive voter turnout among women, would compel it. Although she turned her back on Woodhull, Anthony remained confident that the New Departure put suffrage within reach.[107]

A few weeks later, a U.S. marshal knocked on Anthony's door and arrested her for voting illegally.[108] She served no jail time. Yet her arrest, which one historian speculates came from the highest levels of the federal government, signaled the Republicans' unwillingness to sanction the New Departure logic.[109] In all, dozens of women, black and white, attempted to vote in the 1872 election, and some of their cases began to wind their way through the courts.[110] It was not the massive showing Anthony and other New Departure advocates had hoped for. Not even Stanton voted. She had considerably less faith than Anthony that the Republican plank regarding women, which Stanton derisively called a "splinter," promised anything.[111] But a somewhat rudderless and besieged Anthony was rejuvenated, and she had a mission. Her pending trial gave Anthony a focal point during the rough year of 1873, when Beecher's ongoing trial spiced up the news.

Anthony hoped her trial might serve as a test case.[112] If she could get a favorable ruling at her June trial, then suffrage might be won. So she began lecturing widely over the early months of 1873, delivering her "Is It a Crime for a U.S. Citizen to Vote?" most nights of the week.[113] She hoped to defend principle as well as to sway potential jurors. Matilda Joslyn Gage did the same. Gage was a prominent New York suffragist, with roots in antebellum reform, who from its inception, helped lead the National Association. She nightly delivered her "The United States on Trial, not Susan B. Anthony."[114]

The *Woman's Journal*, by contrast, ran a piece expressing their disappointment in voting women, calling theirs an unhelpful "belligerent attitude," forcing the issue instead of waiting for public opinion to grant it.[115] This further retarded the cause, the editors argued. The power to determine who could vote belonged to the individual states, they continued, and to suggest otherwise was a constitutional violation that threatened "despotism."[116] The National Association's strategy, in other words, did more than retard the woman suffrage cause, they warned. It threatened to disrupt democracy itself by advocating a dangerous balance between the powers of state governments and of the federal government. In opposing the National Association, the editors of the *Woman's Journal* believed they were busily safeguarding the very foundations of American democracy.

❖ Back to Seneca Falls

For Anthony, who believed that safeguarding democracy required safeguarding a national strategy for women's full suffrage, the year 1873 dawned with both pessimism and determination. In a New Year's Day letter to Wright, she worried that so many veteran activists "are *relaxing from* thought & work—feeling that the *move*ment will go forward with its own momentum." Anthony allowed that this was possible, "but I do not believe it—hence I cannot relax our effort."[117] The National Association was in a bit of a holding pattern that winter, as the New Departure cases slowly wound their way through the courts. At the same time, Anthony was eager to counter the bad publicity generated around the Beecher-Tilton scandal, which raged throughout 1873. Unwilling and temperamentally unable to "relax our efforts," Anthony channeled these various worries into affirmatively creating some momentum to ensure that "the *move*ment will go forward." Commemoration was still very much in the air nationally, as postwar fervor subsided and evolved, and as Americans looked toward the approaching national centennial. Women were visible and active commemorators in these contexts, but a celebration of the cause of women's rights, not just women, in public memory promised to impose some coherence on the sprawling and chaotic new suffrage movement. Anthony and others would make the upcoming meeting of the National Association, to be held in May in New York City, the occasion for such an event.

It may have been no more than coincidence or happenstance that the Seneca Falls meeting was now exactly twenty-five years ago and ripe for a silver anniversary when Anthony cast about for some reason to celebrate. In other words, what was happening in 1873 contributed as much to the myth of Seneca Falls as what had happened in 1848. Paulina Wright Davis's 1870 anniversary call had stated unequivocally, "The movement in England, as in America, may be dated from the first National Convention, held at Worcester, Mass., October, 1850."[118] And Stanton had stood upon the stage of that event and enthusiastically agreed. Now, for a variety of reasons, 1848 was the right time, and not just because it happened two years earlier than the Worcester meeting. Set against the background of turmoil and scandal of the early 1870s, the anniversary of Seneca Falls would be as useful as it was convenient. Although Anthony held the 1873 anniversary meeting in New York City, figuratively the moment had arrived to go back to Seneca Falls.

As commemorative events go and by the standards of post–Civil War pageantry, the anniversary session was fairly meager in ceremonial display—perhaps underscoring just how tentative and tenuous this new point of origin was. Not yet a sacred myth, Seneca Falls was not yet even a *story*. Its most sacred text—the original copy of the Declaration of Sentiments—was not on display, because back in 1848 it had not been deemed important enough to preserve. And so, aside from the "wreath of laurels, interwoven with a silver thread," no other trappings or relics graced the stage, save for three of the original organizers: Mott, her sister Martha Coffin Wright, and Stanton.[119] Reluctantly attending to please Anthony, Stanton had for months been dreading the "crucifixion" of the inevitable attacks she faced at conventions. "I usually preserve the exterior of a saint," she had confided to Wright in March, and "there is no use of everybody knowing how like a fallen angel I often feel."[120] Perhaps for these reasons, Stanton did not make good on the convention call's promise that she and Mott would share reminiscences of 1848.[121] Neither did Mott (who did not try to appear a saint but was universally regarded as such). In fact, Mott failed to credit Seneca Falls as the birthplace of the movement, instead telling a more collective origins story and giving "considerable credit for it to the Quakers."[122] Having stayed relatively neutral when the movement split in 1869, Mott lent a nonpartisan dignity to this deeply partisan celebration.[123]

Without any need to resort to outright exclusion, the commemoration event acted as a historical sieve: keeping offstage both newcomers and longtime leaders such as Lucy Stone, who had not been present at the 1848 meeting. The same logic might as well have excluded another 1848 absentee—Anthony—but Stanton's presence onstage made it plausible for her longtime collaborator to be there, too. Unable to reminisce about an event she had not attended, there was literally nothing for Anthony to do to commemorate it—except to preside. Taking the role of onstage historian, she narrated events she had not witnessed and imbued them with retrospective significance. She opened by announcing that they had gathered to celebrate "the twenty-fifth anniversary of the movement." She then read from the printed report of the Seneca Falls convention, since most in attendance would not have been familiar with what had happened or what had been discussed there.[124]

Only a few years earlier, getting one's hands on a printing of the 1848 report would have been nearly impossible. The offices of Frederick Douglass's newspaper, the *North Star*, had printed a small run of the report in the form of a pamphlet that included the Declaration of Sentiments—the original of which may simply have ended up on the print shop floor after the compositor had set it in type.[125] By 1868, Theodore Tilton noted that copies of this report "are now rare, and will one day be hunted for by antiquarians."[126] (Today, fewer than twenty-five copies survive.)[127] In 1870, however, in the wake of the split, Stanton had worked with Amy Post to have the proceedings reprinted, many without any visible clue (intentionally or accidentally) that they were not originals from 1848.[128] (Post, an abolitionist and Quaker, had signed the original Declaration of Sentiments.) These once "rare" proceedings had begun to circulate more widely as a result, establishing a documentary basis for what would become the movement's origins story. Isabella Beecher Hooker, who was kept away from the 1873 convention, made this point in a letter that was read aloud to those assembled. "First, let me beg you my friends, one and all," she began, "to read the report of the first convention at Seneca Falls twenty-five years ago . . . that you may join me in heartfelt admiration." Hooker enthused that she had just finished reading the report herself "for the third time," and that "had I the means, the printed reports to this convention should be placed in the hands of every woman in the United States."[129] It was surely a reprint that Hooker had in her hands. As Mott had done in 1866, Hooker exhorted young women activists to learn their history—now available in convenient and plentiful form. Together with Stanton's decision to reprint the report, Hooker's urging that women get their hands on this movement talisman began the long process of turning the Seneca Falls report—and more specifically, the Declaration of Sentiments therein—into a sacred text.[130]

As the 1873 commemoration taught, to have been at Seneca Falls in 1848, or to choose to join the struggle that purportedly began there, was to be on the right side of history. Anthony said as much from the stage, when she predicted triumphantly—if also hopefully—that this "little meeting and its doings would one day be as famous as the Declaration of Independence."[131] In what amounted to its first public telling, this nascent myth emphasized that the historic road from Seneca Falls led directly and exclusively to Stanton, Anthony, and the National Association. And while it was slightly inconvenient that only one of them had actually attended the local gathering at Seneca Falls in 1848, *neither* of them had attended the first national women's rights meeting at Worcester in 1850. That alternative point of origin, which they had previously embraced, drew the wrong lessons about which side of the divided movement, which side of history, suffragists should choose in 1873. That story pointed to Stone and her allies who had been moving influences at Worcester in 1850. By contrast, a Seneca Falls origin excluded them. It was exclusive, rather than inclusive. And Stanton and Anthony preferred it for just this reason. It limited the movement's legitimate leaders to a very small contingent. Stone and all those activists who had taken a robust part in the antebellum movement over the 1850s, who toiled to build and sustain it, were erased—simply because they had not been present at the ostensible creation in Seneca Falls. In this way, the 1873 commemoration was less about preserving history than it was about creating a collective memory that drew a clear line of succession.[132]

That line of succession was made explicit in a resolution emerging from the anniversary: "Resolved, That Lucretia Mott and Elizabeth Cady Stanton will evermore be held in grateful remembrance as the pioneers in this grandest reform of the age; that as the wrongs they attacked were broader and deeper than any other, so as time passes they will be revered as foremost among the benefactors of the race, and that we also hold sacred the memory of their co-labors in the convention of 1848."[133] Worded in the future tense, this resolution looked ahead, not backward. Mott, who was eighty, was visibly frail and wondered aloud whether the commemoration might be her last public appearance. It wasn't, but the point weighed heavily. Thus, the torch was all but passed in 1873 to Stanton "evermore," not only as Mott's "foremost" successor but as the woman who, as the story went, had almost singlehandedly inaugurated the women's rights movement in the United States. The resolution notably made no mention of other organizers such as Martha Coffin Wright, who sat beside Mott and Stanton on the stage of that first anniversary celebration.[134] Ironically, Wright, who had been present at the creation, was unnecessary to the logic of this story, while Susan B. Anthony was emerging at its center, although she had not attended. A variety of objectives and strategies had been discussed in 1848, but only one served the needs of 1873: national suffrage. In this sense, Anthony's decision to vote in 1872 made her the torch carrier for that narrowed memory of Seneca Falls. Her two-hour evening keynote at the 1873 commemoration bolstered this impression. She dedicated it to her arrest for voting. Although Anthony mentioned and praised other women who had voted, she emphasized her own effort and experience.[135] If Mott was the godmother of Seneca Falls, and Stanton was its architect (and Mott's successor as patron saint), then Anthony embodied the single-minded pursuit of its greatest promise—namely, that someday all women would vote.[136]

Thus, Anthony emerged from the twenty-fifth anniversary convention as the narrator and historian of a nascent myth, as important as any of the women who were actually at Seneca Falls and co-equal with the greatest among them. She not only embodied the solitary mythic goal selected from many, she was a major advocate of a national strategy for victory and arguably the major opponent of what she perceived to be the threat of decentralization. Anthony was happy for women to work locally, and she encouraged their independence—to a degree. Yet she believed that the postwar movement was too atomized to win the future and too shortsighted in losing its past. Mary Livermore, for example, was a wartime leader of the Northwestern Sanitary Commission who became a suffragist, a leading figure of the American Association, and a popular speaker after the Civil War. But when Livermore lectured on the history of the movement, she dated it to 1869, when she and others radicalized by the war had become active. Privately, Anthony criticized Livermore for ignoring or being ignorant of the movement before Fort Sumter, for thinking, like so many of the new suffragists, that the cause began with their own entrance into it.[137] Anthony worried that self-regard was as much a cause of atomization as strategic disagreements. Yet she and Stanton were human enough not to see clearly that they, too, were touting as collective memory a version of history that began the movement with Stanton's personal entry into it. Nevertheless, beginning with the 1873 anniversary convention they amended Mott's 1866 admonition for women to learn their history. If women were to understand where the movement had been and where it must go, the version of history they learned mattered.

Anthony and Stanton shared a deep faith in their mission and a righteous belief that a story of women's rights was historically significant, in a larger political climate that did not treat the history of women's rights as worth recording or celebrating. They each understood, on some level, that recording and celebrating that history could serve as an important movement resource. And each believed that the new generation of recruits was taking hold of an important legacy, and that these recruits needed to understand the gravity of their mission—something best underscored by appealing to history. On these points, Stanton and Anthony aligned. But the inflection each would give to this ongoing project over the years to come differed. That inflection would reflect the larger political sensibilities of each woman: Anthony, the peerless organizer, and Stanton, the consummate philosopher.

❖ The National Association Adrift

In June of 1873, one month after the first commemorative convention for Seneca Falls, Anthony lost her voting trial. Judge Hunt found Anthony guilty and fined her $100 plus the costs of prosecution. She defiantly refused to pay. More important, she was denied the possibility of appeal. This meant she could not continue to pursue her case and secure a favorable judgment from a higher court. The judge clearly meant to put an end to the New Departure. He would not sanction its logic. Neither would he allow any other judge to sanction it.[138]

Meanwhile, other women managed to appeal their decisions, until Virginia Minor, an originator of the New Departure strategy, found herself before the U.S. Supreme Court. Women had been losing their cases in lower courts, so optimism was tempered. In March of 1875, the court ruled unanimously in *Minor v. Happersett*. The justices decided that the Reconstruction Amendments had not given the federal government the right to regulate voting. In a vindication of the American Association's position, they ruled that the power to determine voter qualifications remained with the individual states, where it had historically resided. The court also ruled that voting was not, in fact, a right of citizenship. It was, rather, a privilege, to which not all citizens were entitled. The New Departure as a quick path to victory was decisively dead.[139]

The decision was about more than women's rights. It was about how loosely the court was willing to read the Reconstruction Amendments. Those amendments had not only granted new rights, but they had put the federal government in charge of defining and defending those rights. The arguments women pushed, then, had implications for the rights of African Americans. Was the federal government going to interpret the rights outlined in those amendments broadly or narrowly? Already by Anthony's trial in 1873, just three years after the ratification of the last of those amendments, northern white will to protect African Americans was waning. Whites' tepid commitment to black rights had eroded further still by 1875, and this meant whites were less and less willing to sanction the logic of the New Departure. Not because they necessarily opposed women's voting, although they may have, but because they were not willing to sanction a broad expansion in black rights. With the *Minor* decision, the Supreme Court dealt a severe blow to women's rights, but the subtext lurking behind the decision was a denial of black civil rights.[140]

After 1873, when it became increasingly clear that women would not win their New Departure cases, the National Association was left with no viable strategy. Anthony had used the May 1873 anniversary convention to urge women to unite under the National Association's banner, but for several years after Anthony's June defeat, her organization had no concrete plan to offer. The National Association had given up pursuit of a Sixteenth Amendment back in 1871, when Woodhull first addressed Congress, and it now appeared they could not return to it. The *Minor* decision appeared to put an end not just to the New Departure, but also to the likelihood of winning a federal amendment. The court had ruled that Congress could not appoint voters. Voters could only be appointed by individual states, as the American Association had long argued. So Anthony, who hated what she perceived to be inefficient state-by-state work, was forced back into the expanding, vibrant, uncontrollable world of local activism, where women sometimes pushed right past her.

3. *Women's Rights from the Bottom Up*
✤ 1873–1880

Women's suffrage now had to be won on a state-by-state basis, just as the American Association's leadership had been saying all along. The cause of women's rights confronted the same postwar challenge as African American civil rights: a war that began over the question of freedom or slavery in the territories ended without settling the question of federal versus state power. All states would now be nominally "free states," but *how free*? The scope of the franchise and the meaning of freedom itself remained open questions well after the ratification of the Fifteenth Amendment, and states played a pivotal role in that debate. They debated expanding (and restricting) the franchise in the flurry of state constitutional conventions following the Civil War as well as the broader wave of legislative revisionism that altered state governance in other ways. That complex world of state politics defined and redefined citizen's rights. And here, after 1873, state-by-state proponents controlled women's suffrage politics, and they had every reason to hope for success. That women had already won full voting rights in the territories of Wyoming and Utah was cause for optimism. But votes on women's suffrage were coming up regularly in state legislatures, and the signs were often promising. Moreover, state-by-state proponents pioneered a range of different strategies, some of which began to bear fruit. Yet when Stanton and Anthony tried to enter those state campaigns after the collapse of a federal strategy, they were alternately welcomed and unceremoniously rebuffed, exposing tense undercurrents in the suffrage movement.[1]

Meanwhile, still others argued that voting was not the best way to emancipate women at all. Women's rights activism expanded rapidly after the Civil War, and the women's suffrage movement soon found itself engulfed by other movements that offered competing definitions of women's rights. These contending women's rights voices successfully competed with the suffrage movement for the allegiance and energies of new recruits. They ranged from the free-love movement's farsighted notions that a woman's control over her body had to be the foundation of women's rights to working-class women's demands for economic parity. The biggest challenge to the suffrage movement, however, came from the Woman's Christian Temperance Union, organized in 1874 not only to combat liquor sales and consumption but also to protect women from men's excesses and abuse. In just a few years, it became the largest women's organization of the nineteenth century, by far. Its membership dwarfed suffrage organizing, and the temperance movement recruited both veteran and newly activist women onto a "separate path," taking them away from suffrage work. The WCTU eventually undertook its own suffrage campaigns, aggravating its already tense and fraught relationship with the diverse goals and leaders of organized suffrage movements.[2]

Stanton and particularly Anthony searched for a way forward after the defeats of the New Departure. They searched for some way to lead the diverse and expanding movements of American women back to a common goal, what they believed to be the only sensible agenda: full suffrage achieved nationally. Having responded to the challenges of the early 1870s, in part by experimenting with the tools of collective memory, Stanton and Anthony tentatively sketched out the story of Seneca Falls as a usable past. Over the remainder of the decade, they would return to this fledgling story again and again. As time wore on, they learned to tell it more effectively and more usefully. Decades before, at an 1854 women's rights convention in Philadelphia, Anthony had heard Lucy Stone make what seemed at the time to be an absurdly frivolous suggestion. Women's "rights, should be illustrated in fiction. Prizes should be offered for the best stories," said Stone, who "pointed to 'Uncle Tom's Cabin' to show what fiction could accomplish." Stanton was even named to the prize committee, but "nothing was ever done to carry out the proposition."[3]

By the 1870s, Stanton and Anthony were coming to see that persuasive speeches, articles, petitions, letters, and calls to meeting were one thing, but the hardly simple art of storytelling was another form of activism entirely. The expanding, localized, and sometimes competing world of women's rights activism inspired them to learn and hone this art over the coming years, as they struggled to redefine a federal strategy born of their frustration with state work, to persuade women that suffrage was the pinnacle of a rights agenda, and finally, to disrupt national storytelling, embodied in the nation's 1876 centennial celebration. This would become one of the most important lessons Stanton and Anthony took away from the remainder of the 1870s. But their story about where women's rights had begun—and the constellation of meanings it contained—did not go unchallenged.

❖ States' Rights for Women

Throughout the 1870s, pursuit of state voting rights was a rich and vibrant world. That vibrancy grew after the *Minor* decision, when suffragists who had been working for a federal strategy switched to state and local strategies.[4] In short, state work involved getting individual state governments to strip the word "male" from the eligible voters clauses of state constitutions. Those clauses had historically limited voting to persons who met certain qualifications, such as race, age, and property holding.[5] Most clauses also defined voters as "male." (New Jersey had historically allowed women to vote, until it inserted "male" into its voters clause in 1807.)[6] After the Civil War, as they had before the war, women strove to get the offending word removed from state constitutions and thereby win the right to vote. As they had in Wyoming and Utah, suffragists hoped that women would begin to get voting rights in other states and territories, setting in motion a force that could quickly carry the question throughout the country.

The postwar wave of constitutional revisionism—in which countless states revised and redrafted their constitutions—opened up a promising arena for attack. After the Civil War, Congress required that southern states revise their constitutions in order to be readmitted to the Union, with the stipulation that those states affirm black civil rights. But this wave of constitutional revisionism was not confined to the South. Northern and western states revised their constitutions again and again, sometimes in quick succession.[7] Suffragists had every reason to hope that this radical remaking of rights at the state level would produce changes in the status of women. Indeed, woman suffrage was a subject of frequent discussion. Constitutional conventions of all male delegates, black and white, considered women's enfranchisement in New York (1867), Arkansas (1867), Illinois (1869–70), Vermont (1870–71), Nebraska (1871, 1875), Pennsylvania (1872–73), New Jersey (1873–74), Ohio (1873–74), Missouri (1875), Texas (1875), Colorado (1876–77), California (1878–79), Washington Territory (1878), and Louisiana (1879).[8]

In some states, women pushed the issue onto convention agendas, whereas in others the broader climate of rights remaking moved convention delegates to take up the question on their own initiative.[9] The Nebraska House of Representatives, for example, sent a memorial (a nonbinding resolution) to that state's constitutional convention urging delegates to support woman suffrage because an invidious distinction between the sexes was "unbecoming to the people of this State in the year 1871 of the world's progress."[10] A delegate to the Ohio constitutional convention similarly stated that "the question of woman suffrage is, in my opinion, one of the most important . . . political problems of this century."[11] Illinois convention delegates voted to remove the word "male" and agreed to submit the question to that state's eligible voters in a referendum. They then narrowly reversed their decision a month later.[12] Similarly, Michigan constitutional delegates approved woman suffrage at its 1867 constitutional convention but then reversed themselves on a second vote.[13] By 1874, when they convened yet again, they kept women's voting in their proposed revision.

Michigan's convention delegates (all male) appear to have taken up the question without any organized pressure from women's groups, who then had to hastily organize a campaign to support the referendum. The constitutional convention put forth the clause about women's voting as a separate question. Eligible voters (men) were to cast ballots on the new constitution as a whole, and then to cast a separate ballot for women's voting. As they had in Kansas in 1867, out-of-state suffragists descended upon Michigan, where they mixed with local suffragists. This added another layer of chaos to the 1874 Michigan campaign, as the diversity of personalities and strategies stirred tensions among national leaders, independent state suffragists, and local-level suffragists.

Stanton and Anthony, moreover, found themselves outflanked when the American Association held its 1874 annual convention in Michigan, bringing in large numbers of its partisans and luminaries, some of whom then stayed to campaign for the measure. Margaret Campbell, an American Association loyalist, confided to Lucy Stone that she was "afraid Susan will go."[14] Go she did. After Stanton and Anthony had each campaigned in Michigan for roughly a month, Stone replied to Campbell, "I was sorry, when I found that Mrs. S. was to be in Mich. for she is utterly indiscreet."[15] Some local suffragists, like the well-known (Mary) Adelle Hazlett—head of the Northwestern Woman Suffrage Association and a notable opponent of what she perceived to be eastern paternalism and internecine strife—struggled to keep local control over the campaign.[16] And a group of local suffragists declined Margaret Campbell's services, offered by the New England Woman Suffrage Association, mistaking her for a woman of the same name who was a supporter of Victoria Woodhull.[17] Other local women invited national support. How well they all cohered on the ground was an ongoing struggle. Personalities clashed. Priorities differed. And confusion and conflict arose about who ought to be in charge.

Quite aside from being unwelcome by some, Anthony went to Michigan somewhat reluctantly. Forced back into state-by-state work after New Departure defeats, Anthony nevertheless continued to believe that state strategies were a fatal drain on movement energies. She doubted whether incremental gains would ever amount to nationwide women's suffrage, and she worried about dividing scarce labor, with women fighting many fires in the states and territories, rather than fighting one big fire in the nation's capital. "Do you see any way we can *even hope* to make Congress look at us?" Anthony queried a friend as the New Departure faced defeat.[18] "I do not believe in getting suffrage by *state action*," she lamented, "but it is the only way the politicians will allow us to *agitate* the question—So I accept it of necessity—not choice."[19]

Anthony's presence in Michigan also provided ammunition to the enemies of suffrage. One local newspaper editor criticized Michigan's homegrown suffragists for not ordering Anthony out of the state and cited this failure as evidence that they harbored a covert agenda for greater sexual freedom.[20] Aftershocks of the Woodhull scandal continued to plague Anthony's reputation, despite her attempts to distance herself, and they plagued the movement more broadly by tarring suffragism with the brush of immorality and eastern cosmopolitanism. This deepened already-strong prejudices among some against suffragist carpetbaggers from the East who condescended to save the provinces from inexperience. When Anthony attempted to speak in Hazlett's hometown of Hillsdale, Michigan, the local Woman Suffrage Association refused to help with arrangements, bluntly fearful that Anthony would "do more harm than good." For better or worse, Anthony drew large audiences—even in Hillsdale—but in the flagship suffrage newspaper, her voice did not carry beyond the lecture hall and into print.[21] The *Woman's Journal* amply covered the 1874 Michigan campaign but barely mentioned Anthony's involvement.[22]

Stanton, likewise, came in for rough treatment by Michigan's major newspapers, even though most of them favored women's suffrage. Her sweeping and often-controversial pronouncements—her continued criticism of the Republican Party, for example, and her unapologetic confirmation to reporters that she was the source for Woodhull's knowledge about Beecher's infidelity—did not sit well with many.[23] Stanton and Anthony both blamed Hazlett, who disapproved of eastern interference, for the bad press coverage.[24] Soon national newspapers picked up on the tension, reporting that Stanton's presence in Michigan had "dealt her own cause a severe blow."[25] The claim underscored the ways in which Stanton was undermined by her own fierce refusal to sanction the sexual double standard, along with her uncompromising stands. Her willingness to pursue ideas to their logical end made her a dazzling thinker, but not always the most effective strategist.

Another overriding tension in the campaign was the relationship between woman suffrage and temperance, the rapidly accelerating campaign to abolish liquor. Michigan was a hotbed of temperance activism, and many women supported both causes. If the Woodhull scandal had linked suffrage with free love, Michigan women's temperance fervor infused suffragism with sober morals. Although many eastern and national-level suffragists did not share local concerns about demon rum, two rationales for women's suffrage might well have seemed better than one, save for the fact (which Stanton and Anthony certainly recognized and feared) that temperance suffragists awakened a powerful new opponent: the liquor lobby.

On Election Day, woman suffrage lost by a large margin: 135,000 to 40,000.[26] Suffragists tossed around blame, not infrequently pointing fingers at one another. Some blamed liquor interests. Others blamed immigrants, a common scapegoat. And some blamed local suffragists for being poorly organized.[27] The *Woman's Journal* blamed Stanton and Anthony, claiming the Beecher-Tilton scandal had cost the campaign thousands of votes.[28] Anthony, in turn, blamed "every whiskey maker, . . . drinker, . . . [&] gambler . . . every ignorant besotted man . . . & then the other extreme —every narrow selfish religious bigot."[29] She also blamed herself for not having taken inexperienced state and local workers more firmly in hand.[30] As the chair of the National Association's executive committee, she wrote, "I . . . failed to go to their *state* W. S. Ex. Com. [Woman Suffrage Executive Committee] and show them how to do the work."[31] Opposition to women's suffrage, per se, was no longer the only challenge. Coming up with plans to cohere the varied campaign into an effective front of attack was, to Anthony's mind, equally perplexing.

Besides continuing to try to influence state constitutional conventions, state-by-state strategists also attacked a second front: state legislatures. Most state legislatures were empowered to pass amendments under existing state constitutions, although a subsequent voter referendum was usually required. Meaning if state legislators voted in favor of a constitutional amendment granting woman suffrage, that amendment then had to go to a statewide referendum of eligible voters. This was a cumbersome path to be sure, since many states required that any constitutional amendment first pass two successive legislatures. In some states, the legislature only met every two years, requiring suffragists to undertake multiple, drawn-out campaigns. Needing to win *three* favorable votes, spaced at significant intervals, two legislative and one statewide, was a significant hurdle. And activists had to monitor and influence *five* votes when both chambers of the legislatures were considered. Anthony's distaste for state work was certainly understandable. But the *Minor* decision seemed to confirm it as the only route available. Fortunately, public support for woman suffrage surged in the 1870s, and state legislators gave suffragists reasons for optimism.

A dizzying array of state legislatures considered woman suffrage measures in these years. The Minnesota legislature held a hearing on a woman suffrage amendment in 1867.[32] The Massachusetts Senate Committee on Woman Suffrage voted nine to one for a state constitutional amendment striking the word "male" from its list of voter qualifications in 1869.[33] That same year, the Nevada Senate narrowly defeated a woman suffrage amendment, which failed by only one vote. On a second vote, they approved the measure, only to see it fail in the Nevada House by two votes.[34] Rhode Island held hearings on the expediency of an amendment in that same year, while the Vermont Council of Censors appointed a body to enquire into a constitutional amendment to enfranchise women, an action the committee later endorsed in a lengthy report.[35] In 1870, both houses of the state legislature in Michigan had approved an act to amend the state constitution in order to allow woman suffrage. It was struck down, however, by gubernatorial veto.[36] Also in 1870, a bill for women's full suffrage was introduced into the New Mexico territorial legislature.[37] And women's full suffrage failed in 1872 in the territory of North Dakota by a single vote.[38] That same year, the South Carolina legislature, heavily African American, debated a woman suffrage amendment to that state's constitution.[39] The Indiana legislature voted on woman suffrage in 1877.[40] The Massachusetts legislature voted on women's equal suffrage almost every year between 1868 and 1882.[41] Those votes were often close, with a majority of one house deciding in favor of the reform.[42] And Oregon legislators twice voted on full suffrage bills in the 1870s.[43] This brief inventory is necessarily selective. Yet even this partial glimpse reveals how regularly and how seriously state politicians addressed the question.

Iowa became the next hope for suffragists after Michigan. As early as 1861, the Iowa legislature instructed its committee on constitutional amendments to enquire into the expediency of striking the word "male" from that state's founding document.[44] That legislature had then put woman suffrage to a vote in every session since 1868.[45] By 1874, the measure passed overwhelm-ingly and was scheduled for referendum in 1876. This buoyed suffragists' spirits in the wake of the Michigan defeat.

Anthony had no intention of risking a loss in Iowa in 1876 by making the same mistake she felt she had made in Michigan, deferring too much to statewide activists. "So now," she wrote a colleague in January 1875, "I propose that the *National Society shall mother Iowa* & help her on to her two feet."[46] Iowa women did not always feel they needed out-of-state mothering, however. From 1872 to 1874, while the legislature considered women's vot-ing rights, a contingent of Iowa suffragists had asked Stanton and Anthony to stay out of the state for fear that their ties to Woodhull would cost votes.[47] Despite Anthony's assistance (or because of it, in some eyes), state-level suffragists lost another chance for a referendum in 1876, when the Iowa leg-islature failed to pass the provision for a second time.[48] Still, state work con-tinued apace, where state-by-state proponents argued among themselves over strategy and what their immediate goal ought to be.

✢ Of Tax Revolts and Tea Cups Half Full

The range of strategies state-by-state suffragists used and the myriad differ-ent goals they pursued—from full to partial suffrage measures—meant state work defied easy characterization. Tax revolts, refusing to pay until enfran-chised on the grounds of "no taxation without representation," was one popular approach. Although the method dated to the 1850s, the centennial of the Boston Tea Party in 1873 gave women's tax revolts new life.[49] With the collective memory of the American Revolution newly relevant and thus ripe for reinterpretation, suffragists made a powerful claim for both women and men. Despite the impact of the Civil War and Reconstruction, univer-sal male suffrage had still not been won in all states. Some still tied voting rights to taxation or property ownership, even for white men.[50] In many ways, women's tax revolts built upon a more convincing argument than the New Departure, which had promoted a clever but controversial reinter-pretation of the law.[51] Tax-protesting women appealed to an already well-established principle: the obligation of paying a tax demanded the demo-cratic right to vote against it.[52] The *Albany Times* noted the strategic change: "Having failed after many years to secure representation, they [suffragists] now demand exemption from taxation."[53] A contributor to the *Woman's Journal*, meanwhile, commented in 1871 that "hostility to excessive taxation seems to be the main plank in the present political platform."[54] As a platform that had to be deployed individually, whether by women acting independently or by organized protests of women acting in concert, tax protests became widely popular among all kinds of suffragists in the 1870s.[55]

The 1873 centennial prompted larger-scale tax protests. The demonstrations were called Women's Tea Parties, and Lucy Stone and Julia Ward Howe organized and spoke at an especially large one in Boston a day before the official anniversary that December. In New York, a state suffrage society used their Tea Party to kick off an 1874 campaign demanding New York women be exempted from taxation until enfranchised by that state's legislature.[56] Suffragists launched a similar campaign in Connecticut. Through the pages of the *Woman's Journal*, Lucy Stone, who had refused to pay her taxes as early as the 1850s, called upon women everywhere to protest taxation without representation.[57]

A pair of elderly sisters, Abby and Julia Smith, mounted the highest profile individual tax revolt, also in 1873. Unmarried and living together in Glastonbury, Connecticut, the Smith sisters claimed to pay the highest property taxes in town. Upon returning from the American Association's annual convention in Boston that October, they found their tax assessment had gone up further still. They refused to pay, and Glastonbury officials began seizing and selling off their property. The sisters themselves began lecturing about their ordeal to public audiences in order to generate sympathy and recruits. Audiences roared when the two elderly women recounted how the taxman had confiscated all their livestock but two cows: Taxey and Votey.[58]

William Ingersoll Bowditch, a former abolitionist and an officer of the Massachusetts Woman Suffrage Association, angrily pointed out that the women of Lexington and Concord, along with neighboring Acton, paid enough taxes between them—more than $7,000—to have paid for the pricey statue of a minuteman about to be erected in Concord. Bowditch sardonically suggested that the town instead erect a centennial statue with a revolutionary hero challenging his unfair taxation alongside Glastonbury officials unjustly selling Abby Smith's cows.[59]

In the other high profile case of the mid-1870s, Stephen Foster, Abby Kelley Foster, Sarah Wall, and Marietta Flagg—all of Worcester, Massachusetts—refused payment of taxes in 1874. That same year, the Fosters convened an Anti-Tax Convention in Worcester.[60] They were not alone. In New York and California, women also formed anti-tax-paying leagues.[61] A group calling itself the Woman's Anti-Tax Paying League of San Francisco circulated a tax protest statement to the tax collector's office of Alameda County and to the press, including the *Woman's Journal*.[62] And by the mid-1870s, women had formed the Monroe County New York Tax Payer's Association, based in Rochester.[63] The newspaper editor turned law school student Mary Ann Shadd Cary arrived at City Hall in Washington, D.C., in the spring of 1871 and argued before the seven-member board that as a citizen, a district resident, a taxpayer, an African American, and a woman, she possessed a legitimate claim to the ballot.[64] In Massachusetts and elsewhere in New England, women demanded relief from taxation until enfranchised.[65] So did Martha Schofield, a white woman in South Carolina.[66] Conversely, some women began arguing for the extension of voting to tax-paying women only.[67]

Once again, as it had with the New Departure, the National Association tried to translate this local strategy onto the federal stage.[68] At their annual 1874 and 1875 conventions, when the National Association cast about for some way to attract congressional notice, members looked upon these many actions.[69] They adopted and submitted a memorial petition to "exempt women from taxation for *National* purposes, so long as they are unrepresented in National Councils."[70] National Association loyalist Jane H. Spofford held a reception honoring Julia Smith, to give "people an opportunity to meet this heroic woman."[71] Stanton even composed a speech on the subject.[72] In Washington, D.C., Isabella Beecher Hooker, the National Association's representative in the capital city, began lobbying Congress to exempt women from taxation until they were enfranchised nationwide.[73] That effort was short lived. But it epitomized the ways in which Anthony struggled throughout these years to superimpose a federal, unifying plan onto the outpouring of state suffrage work.

Partial suffrage also became an important strategy. Partial suffrage measures gained momentum during these years, as some began arguing that limited voting rights were a worthwhile goal. The expense and onus of working for so-called full suffrage at the state level made it increasingly unattractive, even to the American Association. By 1871, they began to advocate presidential suffrage, where women could vote for the U.S. president, but no other office. Henry Blackwell was particularly fond of this approach. Blackwell and others argued this did not require a state constitutional amendment, thus lifting the onerous demands of accomplishing one. Instead, state legislatures could directly enfranchise women for these types of elections—meaning *one* favorable vote, not five. In this way, the American Association hoped to persuade the Republican Party that women's votes were necessary for its survival. They hoped, in turn, that Republicans would court women's votes by supporting more extensive voting rights, eventually moving toward full suffrage. Presidential suffrage was to be an "entering wedge" in the fight, not an end in itself. The Massachusetts Woman Suffrage Association followed this path and pressed its state legislature for partial suffrage rights beginning in 1872.[74]

At the local level suffragists were advocating another partial measure: municipal suffrage. The special status of the city of Washington, D.C., had prompted this approach immediately after the Civil War.[75] In 1867, African American and white women and men of the District of Columbia organized the Universal Franchise Association to secure local voting rights for women. In other words, they sought voting rights in city affairs. Electing as their president a U.S. senator from Kansas, they sought passage of a suffrage bill like the one just passed to enfranchise black men in the capital.[76] By the end of the 1870s, the New England Woman Suffrage Association, the American Association, and the Massachusetts Woman Suffrage Association began promoting municipal suffrage, and they brought municipal suffrage bills to votes in the Massachusetts legislature.[77] Whether pursued by African American or white women, for overt or covert reasons, the municipal suffrage movement (which was sometimes linked with tax protests) was a kind of bottom-up approach to voting rights.

Another group of women did even more to push the idea of municipal suffrage: temperance women. The newly formed Woman's Christian Temperance Union (WCTU) held fast to notions of women's supposedly superior morality. They used housekeeping ideas, suggesting that women could improve city and municipal health by application of their home caretaking skills. And they liked the idea of municipal suffrage giving them a voice in local liquor laws. Municipal suffrage was, for some temperance women, a sufficient extension of rights. Over the 1880s, these campaigns bore fruit, and women began voting in certain types of local elections. But the alliances sometimes formed in these municipal suffrage campaigns between temperance and suffrage women also brought powerful enemies in the liquor lobby, meaning that municipal campaigns were not always an easier row to hoe.[78]

A final partial suffrage strategy was born entirely at the grassroots: school suffrage. More successful and common than presidential or municipal enfranchisement efforts, school suffrage campaigns owed little or nothing to either the National or American Associations. Many were not the product of any kind of suffrage organizing per se, but rather grew out of other dynamics that were peculiar to a given town, county, or state. Moreover, school suffrage both predated the woman suffrage movement and itself quickly acquired the status of an actual movement, notwithstanding its diversity and particularity. Kentucky allowed school suffrage for widows and unmarried women who owned property as early as 1838. Michigan followed suit for taxpaying women in 1855, as did Kansas in 1861. Colorado approved school suffrage in 1876. Minnesota and Mississippi (rarely mentioned in the same sentence) both granted school suffrage in 1878. Massachusetts approved it the following year. Twelve more states followed in the 1880s. Temperance women often joined or launched these campaigns, hoping to require temperance education in public schools. Local school suffrage laws varied widely, of course, and imposed myriad eligibility requirements and restrictions. But as an uncoordinated and inherently decentralized movement, its success was unmistakable.[79]

In fact, its success placed national leaders and associations in the uncomfortable reactive position of being led from below. The school suffrage movement succeeded where neither the National nor the American Association had been able to, in exploding the canard that few women actually wanted to vote. What worried national leaders, however, was the prospect of enfranchised women not actually registering or turning out to vote in school elections. The American Association found that getting out the school vote required significant resources. The time invested yielded only a small result, since few women (when compared to half of the adult population) were actually enfranchised by these laws. Anthony found school suffrage, along with presidential suffrage, a complete waste of time.[80] Harriet Robinson, a prominent suffragist in Massachusetts allied with the National Association, later called the 1879 Massachusetts measure a "sham," an effort that only tried suffragists' nerves. Blackwell and Stone, on the other hand, although not strong proponents of such laws, thought they might have a salutatory effect. They tried to remain positive, calling the 1879 Massachusetts law a start "in the right direction" and "the thin end of a wedge." Women enfranchised by school suffrage law in Massachusetts did, moreover, begin to support larger woman suffrage aims. But Stone herself chose not to vote. Registration required using her husband's last name, her legal name, a concession she refused. Despite this, partial suffrage measures continued to be an important strategy of state-level activists and of the American Association, avoiding the challenges of amending state constitutions through cumbersome conventions, legislation, and referendums, while creating an entering wedge for winning full suffrage.[81]

❖ What Are Women's Rights?

At the same time that women who identified primarily as suffragists fought their battles on many fronts and in many ways, other women began to vie for the soul of a rapidly expanding women's movement. By the mid-1870s, just what constituted women's rights became a topic of heated debate, with no agreement that suffrage stood or should stand at the pinnacle of a women's rights agenda. Women's rights were many things in this era, as multiple, overlapping movements rapidly assumed proportions that would have been unimaginable in the antebellum decades. This meant older suffragists had another battle on their hands: trying to convince other women that suffrage was the best path to liberation.

The WCTU was by far the most successful post–Civil War women's rights organization. Temperance women understood suppressing demon rum as a women's rights issue, albeit one based in religion and a culture of domesticity rather than in liberal individualism and electoral politics. In 1873, while the National Association was busy commemorating the twenty-fifth anniversary of Seneca Falls, midwestern women were moving in a different direction. In Hillsboro, Ohio, a temperance advocate and professional lecturer named Dr. Diocletian Lewis exhorted his audience to defend women, family, and the home from the degradation and violence of drunken men. Lewis had delivered this lecture many times, in many places, and groups of women had, for decades, taken local action against liquor. But neither had sparked what began that day in Hillsboro. Something moved these women to march en masse to their town's saloons, hotels, and drug stores and demand that the owners sign pledges to stop selling alcohol. Where owners refused, women invaded their establishments, knelt on their rough-hewn floors in prayer, and sang hymns—often for hours, sometimes for days. Within a few weeks, businesses dispensing alcohol in Hillsboro dwindled from thirteen to four.[82] The fervor quickly spread to other towns as well, sometimes following Lewis's appearances, sometimes not. Liquor sellers in other midwestern and northeastern states soon found themselves besieged by bands of militant praying women. The spontaneous momentum behind the Woman's Crusades propelled the 1874 creation of the WCTU, which rapidly grew into the largest women's organization of the nineteenth century (and remains in existence today).[83]

The women who joined the WCTU were deeply religious, and many would not have joined the women's suffrage movement. They perceived politics and political protest as unladylike. Political involvement defied women's proper domestic sphere as well as their accustomed and proper mode of exerting passive influence within the home. The WCTU preached "gospel temperance" and moral suasion, meaning reform through prayer and moral appeals, considered permissible actions for women. The ascendancy and popularity of such thinking was anathema to Stanton, who in a public lecture compared the "Woman's Whiskey War" to "mob law" and worried about resurgent religious conservatism.[84] Anthony dismissed the crusades as "only a spasm."[85] But temperance was no mere spasm.

Temperance drew massive numbers of women into public action, where they began to gain an education in formal politics. As they tried to rid the nation of demon rum, temperance women began to emphasize the need for legislative reform (in addition to moral suasion), and they launched massive petition drives (considered permissible for women) to demand, among other things, laws banning the sale of alcohol. They justified such political actions by appealing to their God-given duty to protect the home. Temperance laws would prevent drunken men from spending a family's income on liquor and leaving women and children destitute. They hoped such laws would also prevent men's abuses against women in the form of battery, rape, and more—which they reductively contributed to alcohol consumption. Theirs was a women's rights analysis, but one founded on very different principles than the mainstream suffrage movement. In any case, during the last decades of the nineteenth century, it is undeniable that the cause of temperance—not suffrage—awoke massive numbers of women to a desire for political participation.[86]

The 1874 creation of the WCTU created complications for the mainstream suffrage movement, which began to lose recruits and cede momentum to temperance work. The temperance campaign proved electric, and some suffragists jumped ship in order to devote more time to temperance work. Emily Pitts Stevens was a California suffragist, and she published an important suffrage newspaper, the *Pioneer*, which she began in 1869, the first woman suffrage paper in the West.[87] By 1873, she sold her newspaper to become a temperance lecturer and, eventually, a national organizer for the WCTU.[88] Others began to split their time between the two causes. Mary A. Livermore, the renowned orator and an officer of the American Woman Suffrage Association, for example, became prominent in both causes, lecturing for both. Within a few years, the two causes were so intermingled that Livermore declared in September 1876 that "the prohibition and woman suffrage movement[s] were joined together, like Chang and Eng, the Siamese twins, so that you cannot tell which is Chang and which is Eng."[89] The temperance movement was vast and complex, with many on-the-ground women readily supporting voting, although it was not yet a stated goal of the WCTU. Meanwhile, many if not most on-the-ground suffragists supported temperance, blending together seemingly divergent ideologies—producing yet more variation in the suffrage movement. The fact that many, if not most, local-level suffragists supported temperance greatly worried some national suffrage leaders who believed that advancing suffrage required more focused allegiance.

The relationship between temperance and suffrage organizing at the national level remained uneasy, even after the WCTU formally endorsed women's suffrage in early 1800s. In that year, the redoubtable Frances Willard, an Illinois college president and dean of women, began a two-decade stint as president of the WCTU (which she had helped to found). God had asked her to pursue women's suffrage, she explained, in the name of saving the home. Willard's appeal to God's will helped persuade the movement's base that the vote—associated with the public (as opposed to domestic) sphere and therefore considered appropriate only for men—was a permissible goal. Willard's "Home Protection" platform grafted suffrage onto the organization's mission and explicitly called it "a movement . . . to secure for all women above the age of twenty-one years the ballot as one means for the protection of their homes from the devastation caused by the legalized traffic in strong drink." More than any other woman who crossed or straddled the line between suffrage and temperance activism, Willard's ascendancy offered to "the average woman" not merely a choice among local, state, or national strategies but more fundamentally a choice of ideological bases and movements for women's rights.[90]

At the opposite end of the spectrum from the conservative WCTU were the sex radicals, who formulated a different critique of women's subordination. Although Anthony cast Woodhull out of the National Association, Woodhull did not go away. To escape vilification in the East, Woodhull went west. She emerged as a focal point of the free-love movement throughout the mid-1870s, and she did more than perhaps any other person to bring free-love ideas before the general public. After fleeing the East, she spoke night after night throughout the Midwest and the West, where she became a celebrity on the lecture platform. Rural women became radicalized by hearing her speak. Those who were too nervous to attend her public lectures consumed free-love ideas in the privacy of their own homes, through the pages of *Woodhull & Claflin's Weekly*, which Woodhull continued to print. All these women then used the pages of the *Weekly* to form grassroots networks that developed into a grassroots women's rights movement. Its pages, in turn, helped groom other female sex radical voices, such as Laura Cuppy Smith and Lois Waisbrooker. These women helped sustain the movement after Woodhull ceased publication of the *Weekly* in 1876 and permanently left the country for England in 1877. Woodhull never again played a prominent role in the U.S. women's rights movement. Yet she left a powerful legacy. (In England, Woodhull married a wealthy banker and lived the rest of her life as a respectable lady in material comfort.)[91]

Free love grew into a significant movement in these years. Although it was vilified in the press as nothing more than immorality and licentiousness, it was actually a radical critique of women's unequal position in society. Philosophies varied, but one consistent theme emerged. All sex radicals argued that meaningful freedom required women's control over their own bodies. For them, the heart of women's inequality lay in private relationships, not in politics. The seat of that inequality was marriage. Because women had no economic options, they were forced into marriage for access to male economic support. In turn, the state gave a husband complete ownership of his wife's body—including expectations that she submit to his sexual requests (there was as yet no concept of marital rape). Marriage, they argued, was a coercive institution tantamount to state-sanctioned prostitution. Only when women had access to economic independence could they freely enter into marriage. And only when women had access to information about their bodies and contraceptive control could they freely choose motherhood.[92]

If calling marriage prostitution was not inflammatory enough, sex radicals went further. Women in the nineteenth century were thought to have no sexual desire, only a maternal instinct.[93] Sex radicals countered that women experienced sexual passion and had a right to cultivate their sexuality, which included both the right to say "yes" as well as "no." Sex radicals also attacked the sexual double standard, in which women's sexual expression was socially condemned while men's was encouraged and excused. Finally, they supported the labor movement and plans for radical economic reform, which they saw as necessary for women's economic independence. Like most reformers in their day, free lovers had overlapping reform allegiances, and many supported suffrage, even if they did not think it was the primary seat of women's oppression. After Woodhull's brief, if memorable, association with the National Association, however, mainstream suffragists were not eager to welcome sex radicals into their ranks. They feared free lovers might further discredit the cause. Free lovers, meanwhile, thought the mainstream suffrage movement failed to tackle the real problems underlying women's subordination. As with the WCTU, the relationships between the two organized movements was uneasy, even as women on the ground blended support for both causes.

Sex radicals formed their own independent women's rights organizations, and these contributed to the movement's growth over the mid- to late 1870s. When the distributor of *Woodhull & Claflin's Weekly* refused to send it out due to its ostensibly obscene content, readers banned together and formed clubs to ensure the paper's continued distribution nationwide.[94] In 1873, women and men helped form the New England Free Love League. And in 1874, they formed the Western Women's Emancipation Society.[95] From the stage of the Western Women's Emancipation Society's meeting in Ravenna, Ohio, delegates made their priority clear: "Woman's first great, and all embracing right, without which all talk of other rights is but mockery and nonsense, is the Right to Herself."[96] The example of these organizations led to the creation of others.[97] The sex radical press grew as well, with newspapers like the *Word*. These papers helped to cultivate and distribute movement philosophy.[98]

Free lovers sparked a powerful backlash in the form of purity and anti-obscenity campaigns. These campaigns purported to protect vulnerable women from predatory men and sexual danger, but they were in many ways men's continued effort to control women's bodies. Anthony Comstock, a dry goods clerk with service in the Union Army, spearheaded the movement and successfully lobbied for the 1873 passage of a federal obscenity law. The so-called Comstock Law forbade the circulation of "obscene" material through the mail.[99] Comstock also successfully worked to classify information about abortion and contraception as obscene. Following Comstock's lead, states began to criminalize the practice of abortion and contraception, both of which had been legal. Comstock especially relished assaults upon editors of the sex-radical press, whose newspapers circulated through the federal mail, making them vulnerable to prosecution. Their frank discussions of women's bodily freedom, which included information on limiting pregnancy, made them vulnerable to prosecution under the Comstock Law. Woodhull, who made sport of offending Comstock, was arrested and jailed multiple times, as were others.[100]

Working-class women simultaneously launched their own women's rights movements and offered their own analyses of women's oppression. They agreed with the free lovers that women's economic subordination lay at the heart of the problem. But they did not share free lovers' emphasis on critiquing marriage and sexuality. The women's labor movement was, in important ways, an offshoot of the male labor movement, from which women were routinely excluded simply because they were women. Sexism in the labor movement was rife. Barred from most branches of the male labor movement, women had to organize on their own.

Working-class women, like men, responded to the changed conditions of their lives after the Civil War in a process historians have called "Northern Reconstruction." Wage work was not new, but the expansion in that work was. The United States emerged from the Civil War as the world's second-leading industrial power, and it would soon surpass Great Britain as the world's leading industrial power.[101] That meteoric growth in the manufacturing sector had largely been a northern phenomenon, and massive waves of European immigrants along with rural migrants moved into industrializing northern cities to find wage work. With the growth in manufacturing came a new wave of labor unrest. Industrial workers were caught in an often-inescapable web of dire poverty, and they routinely equated their lives with those of former slaves, referring to their condition as "wage slavery." For the most part, no laws governed the conditions of work. There existed little protective legislation of any sort and no minimum wage. Hours were exceedingly long, pay was scant, working conditions were dangerous, and exploitation (including sexual exploitation for women) was common. Working women generally made even less money than working men, being paid less for the same work or being sex segregated into lower-paying occupations. Impoverished wage workers, men and women, demanded that Reconstruction—the remaking and redefinition of rights—be extended to them as well.[102]

After the Civil War, industrial wage workers launched a varied movement, which frequently called upon government to take a more active role in addressing the needs of working people. They demanded, for example, laws limiting the length of the work day, laws for child-labor protections, laws to encourage a redistribution of wealth, and more. In short, the labor movement wanted the government to intervene in order to address the problems of working people, much as it had intervened to address the problems of freed people. Workers launched protests, appeals, and general strikes, some of which shut down American cities. And they successfully inserted themselves into national political debates, moving the so-called labor question to the forefront of Reconstruction-era politics. But sex discrimination, combined with fears that lower-paid women would take men's jobs, undergirded women's exclusion from men's labor organizations.[103]

Working women, and the labor movement more generally, were split over the utility of the ballot. Some believed that the ballot could be used to enact their demands. They believed they could vote themselves a shorter work day, for instance. An equally large contingent of the labor movement argued that the vote had limited utility. For those working men who had the ballot, they pointed out, it had made little impact upon the conditions of their lives. Voting, some labor activists suggested, was merely illusory power. Better, they urged, to organize in massive numbers and confront industrial capitalists head on, in strikes, slow downs, and direct-action campaigns. Although many working women supported women's voting rights, they often prioritized other demands, remaining circumspect about the vote's potential to meaningfully affect their lives.[104]

At the same time, working women sometimes turned to the organized suffrage movement for support, but this too was an uneasy alliance. Because of the organized male labor movement's hostility, working-class women needed allies in their efforts to organize. Conversely, suffragists wanted to draw attention to working women's plight, at least as they understood it, because they saw in them a stark example of the need for sexual equality.

The two groups hardly made ideal partners, however, with mainstream suffragists attempting to persuade wage-earning women of their preeminent need for the ballot, and wage-earning women insisting upon their own, independent ability to offer solutions to the problems confronting their lives. The New England Women's Club, for example, composed of numerous suffragists, investigated the conditions of Boston sewing women and published a landmark report with dire findings.[105] The short-lived Boston Working Women's League, an independent organization composed of working-class women, appreciated the concern, but firmly rejected the suffragists' efforts to impose solutions.[106] So too did the Working Women's Association (WWA) in New York City, organized through the offices of the *Revolution*, Stanton and Anthony's short-lived newspaper (which they had been forced to sell in 1870).[107] Composed primarily of female typesetters, the WWA "rejected Stanton's suggestion that they name their organization the Working Women's Suffrage Association."[108] They also rejected Stanton and Anthony's suggestion that enfranchisement be the association's top priority.[109] Still, the typesetters desired an alliance, both because of the antagonism they received from male workers in the National Typographical Union and also because of their shared commitment to sexual equality.[110] Leading suffragists frequently imagined a universal woman (a married, white woman of the middling classes), and therefore a universal conception of women's rights—one centered on the vote. But working women such as Jeannie Collins of

Massachusetts challenged them head on, understanding that women did not constitute a single, unified group but were, in fact, divided by class. There could be no single conception of women's rights, working women like Collins argued, because "there are not certain wrongs that apply to the whole sex."[111]

In October 1873, northeastern club women launched yet another women's rights organization, the Association for the Advancement of Woman (AAW), at what they called the Woman's Congress. Club women put their emphasis on yet another set of issues, many of which reflected their own social positions. Club women's political leanings ranged from progressive to conservative. Some had deep roots in reform networks, some were career women, and some were upstanding society women. The two most influential clubs, both founded in 1868, were Sorosis, based in New York City, and the New England Women's Club, based in Boston. These and other clubs met every few weeks to educate members on various topics such as the "Pulpit as a sphere for women," and, "Does society properly recognize and respect business women?"[112] They worked on broad-ranging issues, including "homes for unwed mothers; pensions for widows and dependents; protection for industrial workers; child-labor laws; [and] maternal and infant-care clinics."[113] The club movement grew rapidly in the half century after the Civil War, with clubs forming in cities across the nation. Yet membership was generally restricted, often by invitation only. What united clubwomen, many of whom also had overlapping membership in suffrage organizations, was their desire to press for women's emancipation through education, physical activity (considered too delicate for girls), uplift, and self-improvement.[114]

The AAW and the 1873 Woman's Congress grew partly out of club women's dissatisfaction with certain dimensions of the suffrage movement, including Stanton and Anthony's alliance with the controversial Woodhull.[115] As one newspaper put it: "Justly, or unjustly, the taint of the abominable free-love doctrine enunciated so unblushingly by certain female agitators has become attached, in the public mind, to some degree at least, to the whole 'woman movement.'"[116] Charlotte Beebe Wilbour and other AAW organizers tried to uncouple the sometimes-negative publicity surrounding suffrage (in the wake of the Beecher-Tilton scandal) from women's progress. Wilbour, herself a suffragist, felt there needed to be a less controversial organization to emphasize and promote other aspects of women's advancement. Roughly 150 leading women, including Lucy Stone, signed the call to the October 1873 Woman's Congress.[117] Anthony's name, however, did not appear; irritated, she complained privately over the omission.[118] Neither did

Anthony attend the congress, being evidently unwelcome. Yet her absence at something such as this—a Woman's Congress—was conspicuous, so to minimize any appearance of division and disagreement, one suffrage newspaper diplomatically attributed her absence to her sister's illness. In fact, it seems, organizers had excluded her.[119]

Although the 1873 Woman's Congress had a sprawling agenda, it stopped short of endorsing woman suffrage, likely because of the fact that some now associated the demand with sexual scandal.[120] Wilbour, who presided, squarely challenged leading suffragists. A woman should "no longer be satisfied," she stated, "to follow the lead of others but should herself inaugurate more great movements in the best interests of women."[121] Club women intended the 1873 congress to be an umbrella organization, encouraging the formation of local clubs and coordinating their action.[122] The congress itself was to remain an elite body of several hundred, and organizers carefully orchestrated the 1873 meeting, controlling who spoke and preventing any one subject from dominating. Thirty-five papers were presented over several days, on everything from motherhood to women's colleges.[123] One speaker briefly broached the subject of woman suffrage, but it was never thoroughly discussed.[124] Yet the 1873 congress also elected two prominent suffragists, Mary Livermore and Julia Ward Howe, both of the American Association, the AAW's president and vice president.[125] After its founding in 1873, the AAW became a fairly long-lived organization, holding annual Woman's Congresses in cities around the country. The AAW, too, vied for a claim over the tone and definition of a women's rights agenda.[126]

Black women forged their own definitions of rights. The "era's sea changes opened the door to broad rethinkings of the meanings of manhood and womanhood for black Americans," one historian argues. Formerly enslaved people, men and women, as well as northern blacks, male and female, all joined the vibrant and cacophonous discussion about the standing of women in public life. Because no universal black woman existed, just as no universal white woman existed, black women's definitions also varied. One thing united them: an emphasis on race concerns as an integral part of any women's rights agenda. These debates about women's standing sometimes took place within a black community and sometimes took place amid larger national discussions. Freedwomen often emphasized access to employment—away from the gaze of white eyes—reunion of their families, and physical safety from the threat of rape and lynching that hung like a pall over their lives. They fought for desegregation and for expansion of job opportunities (most black women were relegated to domestic service, even after the Civil War). Other black women, often more elite northern women, fought for women's rights by arguing for black women's basic humanity, offering themselves as exemplars of respectable womanhood. Whereas white women were presumed to be respectable, black women were not. And elite northern black women's public conduct as respectable women, emulating the very norms other white women's rights activists challenged, was itself often a claim to rights. Mocked and degraded in minstrelsy, popular cartoons, and other forms of popular culture, black women argued by their conduct that they belonged to the class of humanity known as "woman."[127]

Because the white women's rights movements often overlooked the concerns of black women—sometimes overlooking black women's basic existence—they often had to organize on their own. The failure of white women's organizing to address their concerns, and black women's simultaneous insistence that they control their own lives, meant black women often preferred to organize on their own. They were present in the ranks of the WCTU, the organized suffrage movement, the labor movement, and eventually the club movement, but even there, they frequently used those organizations for their own ends. The sexism black women also encountered from within civil rights movement, from black brothers-in-arms, made voicing their concerns even more difficult at times. But they did voice them. Rarely, though, did they turn against black men. The black church emerged after the Civil War as a central organizing site for black women fighting to improve the conditions of their lives. There, one historian notes, "many new organizations were conceived, led, and operated entirely by women," supporting work within their communities and casting themselves as public actors. Women became teachers to uplift the race; laundresses staged strikes to protest exploitation; and lecturers publicized race concerns. Throughout all this activism, black women developed their own unique analyses. They insisted upon what scholars call an "intersectional analysis," one that simultaneously took up race and gender, seeing the two as inextricably linked.[128]

The sprawling, expansive women's movement grew over the 1870s into a multifaceted, broad-ranging campaign. And it offered trenchant, if competing, critiques about women's unequal position in society. Support for woman suffrage was in some ways a common denominator, but many disagreed over making it a primary emphasis. Those that supported woman suffrage, moreover, disagreed about what voting rights even meant. Throughout the 1870s, women grappled with important questions about the nature and foundations of sexual discrimination. And in this vital debate, white suffragists did not occupy center stage. These different and simultaneous impulses represented a maturing women's movement. And given women's many different subject positions, it expanded in many different directions. There could be no single conception of woman's rights, because, in the words of working woman Jeannie Collins, "there are not certain wrongs that apply to the whole sex."[129] All this challenged leading suffragists, who urgently wanted women to rally around the vote.

❖ An Amendment and a Declaration

As the women's movement expanded dramatically over the 1870s, the National Association had to deal not only with public opposition to enfranchisement and with its leaders' own reluctance to be back in the world of state work, but also with other visions of women's rights. As those movements became more powerful, Stanton's and Anthony's concern mounted. Their growing awareness about this challenge was reflected in the National Association's pronouncements. Their annual convention in January 1874, for example, gently condemned the outpouring of women's rights activism for being misdirected. From the convention floor, officers read a resolution advising that women's "proper self-respect and . . . best interests" lay in the "enfranchisement of their own sex"; this being "of far more importance than all" the other activities that "now absorb . . . a large majority of . . . women."[130] Although the leaders of the National Association believed a federal political solution could best free women, they were constrained by the *Minor* decision. All that changed in 1876, when they tried once again to weave these many strands into a single, coherent movement.

That November the National Association issued an appeal and a petition for what it hoped would become the Sixteenth Amendment to the Constitution of the United States, announcing the organization's refusal to concede a federal strategy. The courts had seemed to close this door definitively, but as Anthony explained—employing new logic—her 1873 trial loss actually proved the *legality* of a federal strategy. If federal authorities could punish her for voting in the state of New York, then it stood to reason they could also *protect* her right to do so.[131] In other words, if the federal government had the right to intervene negatively in state matters, then it could also intervene *positively*. (Such thinking drew upon general postwar debates over new conceptions of positive versus negative liberty.) The National Association simultaneously insisted that the Reconstruction Amendments had created federal authority to regulate voting, directly challenging the Supreme Court.[132] They pointed to the ability of the federal government to interfere with voting in the territories as proof positive.[133] The wording of their new appeal for a Sixteenth Amendment was revealing: "If Women who are laboring for peace, temperance, social purity and the rights of labor, would take the speediest way to accomplish what they propose, let them demand the ballot in their own hands. . . . Thus only can they improve the conditions of the outside world and purify the home."[134] Stanton's and Anthony's renewed bid for a Sixteenth Amendment was not simply a bid for voting rights, but also a renewed bid for the heart and soul of the woman's movement.[135]

Stanton and Anthony unveiled their plan for a Sixteenth Amendment at a difficult political moment. Suffragists' optimism, born of the radical ferment of the early Reconstruction years, was now dissipating, as women watched politicians lose their will to remake individual rights. The Republican Party, once the radical party of emancipation, was becoming the party of big business. Radical Republicans, who had supported abolition and an expansive civil rights agenda, had either died or been purged from the party. And in November of 1876, the same month the National Association launched its new federal strategy, a contested presidential election brought a formal end to Reconstruction. Southern electors agreed to throw the presidency to the Republicans in exchange for the removal of federal troops from the former Confederacy. When that came to pass in 1877, African Americans in particular and the cause of voting rights in general suffered the consequences. Southern white supremacists had always maintained that policing African Americans—which was tantamount to terrorizing them—was a matter of states' rights. Many white northerners, weary of Reconstruction-era battles (and always tepid in their support of freedmen), increasingly capitulated to this view. As the Supreme Court had signaled in deciding *Minor*, the nation remained unwilling to accept the Reconstruction Amendments as expansions of federal power.[136]

Although these realities made this an inauspicious moment to demand a federal constitutional amendment to confer voting rights, the nation's hundredth birthday in 1876 represented a unique opening for women. Americans were so eager for the centennial that they had started celebrating in the countdown to midnight on 31 December 1875. Stanton and Anthony realized that the entire coming year would be "a never-to-be-forgotten hour"—perhaps even, finally, the woman's hour that had been denied them in 1866, ten long years ago. In January, National Association president Matilda Joslyn Gage, a veteran suffragist, announced plans "to prepare a woman's declaration, and to celebrate the coming Fourth of July with our own chosen orators and in our own way."[137] The Centennial International Exposition outside

Philadelphia looked both backward and forward, emphasizing an ongoing story of progress. The centennial committee's reneging on promised space for a women's exposition revealed some of the limits of that ongoing story. The Women's Centennial Executive Committee, a mainstream organization who celebrated women's sphere, miraculously raised $30,000 to erect a Woman's Pavilion within the fairgrounds, ensuring women's inclusion. The exhibits, however, celebrated domesticity and touted the dignity of American woman as an aspect of national greatness.[138] Lucy Stone sent the Women's Committee a ready-made display of "The Protests of Women Against Taxation without Representation." Fearing controversy, organizers put the case in an inconspicuous location, out of view.[139]

The National Association refused cooperation with the entire event. Its members designed uncensored exhibits on women's rights in rented rooms near the fairgrounds, rooms that doubled as the organization's summer headquarters and woman suffrage recruiting station. (Anthony had to be the official leaseholder, since, in this year of democratic triumph, married women still could not sign contracts under Pennsylvania law.)[140] In its small, makeshift quarters, the association used its exhibits to demonstrate "that the women of 1876 know and feel their political degradation no less than did the men of 1776."[141] Women in places such as Milwaukee and Chicago also issued centennial protests.[142] The experiences of the centennial year seemed to teach Stanton and Anthony the power of disrupting historical narratives.

In an audacious move, they went so far as to disrupt the ceremonies around the Declaration of Independence itself. "On July Fourth, while the men of this nation . . . are rejoicing that 'All men are free and equal' . . . , a declaration of rights will be issued from these [Philadelphia National Association] headquarters," Anthony and Gage declared that May, along with "a protest against calling this centennial a celebration of the independence of the people, while one-half are still political slaves."[143] They announced a program to be held on the Fourth of July at Philadelphia's First Unitarian Church, where they would read their protest. Anthony hoped for something more dramatic, so she applied for platform seats at the centennial's Grand Ceremonies, designed around Independence Day. Her application was refused.[144]

On 3 July, the day before the Grand Ceremonies—when Stone, Howe, and the American Association presented a dignified program in Horticultural Hall on the fairgrounds about women voting under New Jersey's state constitution of 1776—Stanton made a final attempt for recognition at the official proceedings, requesting a momentary, nonspeaking slot on the centennial program. "We do not ask to read our declaration," she explained, "only to present it to the president of the United States, that it may become an historical part of the proceedings." They were again refused. The women spent the morning of the Fourth debating what to do next, deciding that Mott and Stanton would go to the First Unitarian Church as planned. Meanwhile, Anthony had quietly procured a press pass for the ceremonies (through her brother's newspaper), and she scrounged four additional tickets. She and four others planned to disrupt the official proceedings, refusing to take no for an answer. They were determined "to take the risk of a public insult in order to present the women's declaration and thus make it an historic document."[145]

The centennial's culminating Grand Ceremonies were held in Independence Square behind its namesake hall, before a crowd that quickly filled up every inch of pavement, the stoutest limbs of the oldest trees, and bleachers seating 4,000. On the platform were Emperor Dom Pedro II of Brazil and other foreign dignitaries, Civil War generals William T. Sherman and Philip Sheridan, and many state governors. Acting Vice President Thomas W. Ferry represented President Grant. After a fair amount of fanfare, the mayor of Philadelphia gingerly brought forward the original 1776 Declaration of Independence, framed and under glass (brought in from Washington, D.C., for display). "It was placed upon the speaker's stand facing the vast multitude in the square," reported one newspaper, "and for five minutes the vicinity fairly rang with cheers." The event of the day was to be a reading of the fabled document by Richard Henry Lee, grandson of an original signer. The famous "created equal" passage was interrupted by cheers, but thereafter the crowd grew bored, and "a buzz of conversation swept across the platform and the square." Anthony's little band prepared to move. As Phoebe Couzins, one of the group, told it: "We were about to commit an overt act."[146]

When the reading concluded and the dignitaries began to stand for yet another hymn, Anthony and her entourage pushed their way up the center aisle to the lectern, where she said a few "fitting words" before handing a three-foot scroll tied with patriotic ribbons to the acting vice president.[147] "He was seen to bow and look bewildered," one newspaper recounted.[148] Matilda Joslyn Gage and the others distributed printed copies of their protest declaration, while "on every side eager hands were stretched; men stood on seats and asked for them." Then they were gone as quickly as they had come, leaving the presiding officer shouting "Order! Order!" as they scurried out of the park and around to the front of Independence Hall.[149]

There, drawing a crowd and applause, "Miss Anthony read the Declaration of Rights for Women by the National Woman Suffrage Association, July 4, 1876."[150] Here and there it echoed the original Declaration of Independence, as in its reference to "a series of assumptions and usurpations of power over woman." More than half of it was devoted to "Articles of Impeachment Against Our Rulers." A number of newspapers later printed the entire declaration verbatim.[151] Upon finishing their surprise reading, Anthony's group joined the other leaders and a large audience for the preannounced reading at the First Unitarian Church. Five hours of speeches (including Anthony's on taxation without representation) followed, interspersed "with appropriate and felicitous songs." A few weeks later, an attendee who lived in nearby Bristol, Pennsylvania, explained that the disruption at Independence Square aimed to ensure that the women's declaration "shall go on file with the general archives of the day, so that the women of 1976 may see their predecessors of 1876 did not allow this centennial year of independence to pass without protest." The anonymous commentator recalled that the final speaker at the church—an Englishman who eagerly quit the Independence Square festivities to attend the suffrage meeting—had stated "that he considered *their* meeting *the* meeting of the day, and the event of the day which would be handed down in history." The column concluded, however, that "to make his words good, the women will have to furnish a historian, for . . . the newspapers make very little mention of the meeting."[152]

Stanton, Anthony, and Gage had been thinking similar thoughts for some months: women needed to furnish their own historian if women in general, and the movement in particular, were to find a place in both future accounts and in the collective memory of their day. It would not do to grovel to generals and vice presidents for the momentary chance to "become an historical part of the proceedings" or to resort to carrying out public stunts, however thrilling, in hopes that their important work "shall go on file with the general archives." The three women were beginning to understand that they needed "to commit an overt act" not as protesters but *as historians*, writing up their *own* historic proceedings and making a place for their *own* archives. Ideally, such chores might help promote the cause and also help pay the rent. As a start, during the centennial they solicited $5 donations with the promise to thank contributors by sending them, as a premium, "a history of the woman's rights movement, which they expected to be a pamphlet of several hundred pages." Fifty-two women responded, and with the $260 proceeds, they secured their Philadelphia headquarters for the summer.

Subscribers were told to expect the history book before the centennial year was out.[153] The women would not meet that deadline, but history remained very much on their minds.[154]

Fall 1876 was presidential election season, and Stanton, Anthony, and the National Association campaigned hard for the Sixteenth Amendment—lecturing, lobbying, and petitioning. Three days after the election in November, as the Tilden-Hayes dispute over which candidate had won the 1876 presidential race preoccupied everyone in the country, they issued their appeal for a federal amendment—more inauspicious timing. Still, they made headway. "Having celebrated our Centennial birthday with a National jubilee, let us now dedicate the dawn of the Second Century to securing justice to Woman," they urged.[155] It was a full-court press. "Mrs Stanton is on the 'War Path' . . . in Ohio," Anthony cheered in March of 1877; "I have spoken six nights out of every seven for the past *seven weeks* & have about as many more before me—so am up to my ears in packing & unpacking getting to & from trains—& to & from lecture halls."[156]

The American Association did not welcome this revived federal initiative (or the National Association's political theater during the centennial). When the National Association sent its November 1876 appeal and petition to the *Woman's Journal*, along with money for printing, Stone refused it.[157] She eventually relented and sent the federal petition to *Woman's Journal* subscribers. She undercut the action, however, by also including petitions for state legislative action. The mailing further explained: the American Association "recognizes the far greater importance of petitioning the State Legislatures," since "suffrage is a subject referred by the Constitution to the voters of each state."[158] When Anthony asked William Lloyd Garrison, American Association member and *Woman's Journal* contributor, for a letter endorsing the new campaign, he declined, calling the notion "quite premature" and likely to bring the woman suffrage cause "into needless contempt." Better, he argued, to spend more time bringing around public opinion first.[159]

The Sixteenth Amendment drive nevertheless gathered steam and generated significant enthusiasm. Having gathered tens of thousands of names in a few short months, the National Association prepared to present them to Congress at the beginning of 1877, in conjunction with its annual January convention in Washington, D.C. News about agitation for a federal amendment in the states came in from all quarters. In the complicated way that the many rights causes often blended together on the ground, Elizabeth Boynton Harbert, a Chicago suffragist and National Association ally, reported on the temperance work being done in Chicago in conjunction with advocacy of a Sixteenth Amendment (even though the WCTU had yet to endorse women's voting).[160] Not everyone attending the convention supported the idea, however. Anthony was reportedly "roused . . . to the boiling point" when one man suggested they instead concentrate forces in Colorado, where that same month the new state government had agreed to submit woman suffrage to a statewide referendum (scheduled for October). This, he argued, would be "a shorter way to success" than a federal amendment. An irritated Anthony fired back that this was the work of the American Association.[161] Sarah A. Spencer, who received, sorted, counted, and rolled up the petitions, worked with Anthony to copy thousands of names so that a duplicate set could be submitted to the House as well as the Senate. Spencer received petitions from twenty-three states, and she presented them by pointedly offering individual congressmen a petition from their home state. Within the space of one day, Spencer submitted 40,000 names.[162]

Mixed success came of the multiple efforts of 1877 and 1878. Eastern and midwestern suffragists descended upon Colorado that fall, where they mixed with western and local suffragists also campaigning for the state amendment. The American Association cancelled its annual conventions in order to concentrate on Colorado, holding hope high. When the votes were counted that October, the measure lost by a margin of two to one.[163] But at least one more state had pushed the question to a vote. The defeat, however, left the American Association even more committed to partial suffrage as a more winnable, if gradual, path to full suffrage. A few months later, the National Association's federal campaign bore fruit when Sen. Aaron Sargent (R-Calif.) introduced the Sixteenth Amendment to the U.S. Senate. He did so on 10 January 1878. Senate Resolution 12 read: "the right of citizens of the United States to vote shall not be denied or abridged by the United States or by any state on account of sex." The amendment, written by Stanton, was modeled after the Fifteenth Amendment, and like that measure, its final section gave Congress the right of enforcement. The amendment was read twice and then referred to the Committee on Privileges and Elections. Women delivered remarks before that Senate committee for two days. The crowds were so large that the committee had to move to a bigger room.[164]

In a complicated legal argument, Stanton conceded that states retained the right to regulate suffrage, but they could not, she insisted, *deprive* citizens of the franchise. Ever since the Reconstruction Amendments, she argued, the balance of national power had shifted, and the national government had an obligation to protect national citizenship rights, including those of women.

"*Flocking for Freedom.*" *Cartoon of a petition drive for a federal amendment, featuring caricatures of leading women suffragists taking their petitions to Congress and errone-ously including Lucy Stone, far left. Cartoon by Joseph Keppler, in* Puck, *23 January 1878. (Courtesy of the Prints & Photographs Division, Library of Congress, LC-USZ62-73990)*

The committee chairman's "studied inattention and contempt" exasperated Stanton to such a degree that she barely "restrained the impulse . . . to hurl my manuscript at his head." The Senate took no vote, but the measure had (for the second time) been introduced to Congress.[165]

❖ To Furnish Her Own History

After the revived federal amendment met with defeat in early 1878, Stanton and Anthony reacted much as they had after the crises of 1873. Trying to maintain morale and enthusiasm during a year that also coincided with the thirtieth anniversary of Seneca Falls, and faced with ongoing challenges from other groups of activists, they organized yet another commemora-tion.[166] Planning for the thirtieth anniversary celebration was considerably more elaborate than in 1873, when they had incorporated a few commemo-rative utterances into a regular National Association annual May conven-tion, held in New York City. They now proposed a free-standing celebration to take place in July, the month of the original convention. They billed the latest commemoration as a "mass reunion" (although only about 300 had been present originally) and invited all suffragists—indeed, all women's rights activists—to unite under the banner of Seneca Falls. The anniversary call deemed Seneca Falls "the first convention ever held in this country and so far as known, in the world."[167] The reunion banner would not, however, actually hang in Seneca Falls, New York. It had been a sleepy village in 1848, and three decades later, it was still no metropolis. Fifty miles west of Seneca Falls, the thriving city of Rochester would be close enough and more convenient (Anthony lived there), not to mention more suitable as a transportation hub.[168] It was also fitting. The original meeting in Seneca Falls had adjourned to reconvene two weeks later in Rochester's Unitarian Church. The thirtieth anniversary commemoration would be held in the very same church, they announced, marking it as sacred ground.[169]

The National Association's invitation to what became known as the "Third Decade Celebration," which asked suffragists of all stripes to accept the 1848 gathering at Seneca Falls as "the first women's rights convention ever held" in America or the world, was a provocation that did not go unnoticed—or unchallenged. In June 1878, six weeks before the much-ballyhooed event, a debate erupted over which of the early conventions could be called the first. The editorial staff at the *Woman's Journal* issued a direct challenge to the National Association's anointing of Seneca Falls. "The Thirtieth Anniversary of the *Second* Woman's Rights Convention the world ever knew will be celebrated . . . in Rochester," they noted tersely. "The *first* one," they countered, "was held in Akron, Ohio, the year before, by Mrs. Frances D. Gage and other Western women."[170] Several other women's newspapers—including the *Englishwoman's Review* (Great Britain), and the *Woman's Exponent* (Utah)—picked up and reprinted this correction, spreading the notion that credit belonged to Akron.[171]

"Mrs. Frances D. Gage" herself soon wrote the *Woman's Journal* to correct its correction. The meeting she had helped organize in Akron had been in 1851 and had not preceded Seneca Falls. Setting the *Journal* straight, Frances Dana Gage affirmed the primacy of Seneca Falls, which she credited to Amelia Bloomer and Stanton, although she claimed not to know whether Seneca Falls was the first "in the world" (as the anniversary call had claimed). In correcting the record, however, Gage inadvertently inserted an error of her own, mistakenly including Bloomer as one of the 1848 meeting's organizers.[172] Yet another women's rights newspaper, the *National Citizen and Ballot Box*, subsequently published a column to dispel all these circulating errors.[173] This column also took pains to correct a common and growing misimpression (which has nevertheless endured) that Anthony had been at Seneca Falls in 1848.[174] Although Anthony never made such a claim, her ubiquity and centrality in commemorating Seneca Falls and her enduring friendship with Stanton made the conclusion an easy jump.

On 19 July 1878, as crowds assembled in Rochester for the thirtieth anniversary, temperatures ran into the nineties. Inside the Unitarian Church, where pews filled to capacity, temperatures ran even higher. Contrasting with the short anniversary program of 1873, organizers now devoted the entire day to celebration. Urgings to keep cool punctuated the numerous speeches from young and old. Amy Post, who had helped to arrange the original August 1848 meeting in Rochester, set the tone. Following the inflated rhetoric of the event's invitation, she called the Seneca Falls meeting "the first Woman's Rights Convention known in history." Though the 1848 Declaration of Sentiments had contained numerous demands for women's rights, Post quoted only the resolution for the franchise. The focus on suffrage thus established, Post worked to connect Anthony to Seneca Falls, eliding more than two decades of history by jumping directly to Anthony's 1872 voting attempt, something that was becoming a familiar pattern in the telling of Seneca Falls. Post then acknowledged what had to be on the mind of many: "Perhaps some of you think that there is small hope of success since we have already been at work thirty years."[175]

Post's remarks and the event itself signaled the shift in mood by 1878. That shift gave this anniversary celebration a different inflection than previous commemorations. The heady optimism of Radical Reconstruction, when a broad redefinition of rights seemed possible, had cooled. Reconstruction was officially over, and the goal of women's full suffrage had suffered continual setbacks. Yet as speaker after speaker took the stage, they recounted the extensive gains in women's rights over those thirty years, such as women's admission into the nation's universities and esteemed professions. The long view showed reason for optimism and for continued work, speakers suggested. In fact, the long view made it incumbent upon young women to take up the suffrage cause. Because you have had all the advantages we lacked, and because "you hold to-day the vantage ground we won by argument," the older women told the younger, you must "show now your gratitude . . . by making the utmost of yourselves."[176] Where the influx of new women into the cause following the Civil War had disoriented some veterans, the failure of suffrage to be won now made those same veterans acutely aware of the need for young recruits to sustain the movement well into the foreseeable future. The anniversary celebration simultaneously strove to discipline the younger women, saying: follow our more experienced lead.

Various pioneers were on hand, but leading figures in the American Association absented themselves from this so-called mass reunion. Sojourner Truth was one of the few prominent black women to attend National Association events. In her anniversary remarks, she urged women to take their rights rather than plead for them, a position that aligned with the National Association's philosophy.[177] Truth had been a slave in New York, freed in the 1820s, who then preached the gospel as an itinerant minister. She was also an active abolitionist who met with Lincoln during the Civil War, and she was well known among reformers. She dictated an autobiography, which she sold along with her photograph to support herself, and she closed the morning session by taking the opportunity to sell her photograph as a souvenir.[178] Frederick Douglass, who was also on hand, urged participants to buy the photographs.[179] Douglass's support for woman suffrage had remained steadfast throughout his long career.[180] And he took the stage with Stanton and Anthony at this and other events, despite the harsh words the three had exchanged in the 1860s. In many ways, their primary fights were not with each other but with the larger power structures that denied women and African Americans rights. The three remained friends, if not close friends, throughout their long careers. Still, Anthony privately encouraged suffragists to remember the insult of the "negro's hour."[181] Meanwhile, some of those assembled openly criticized Douglass for urging women in his anniversary remarks to be "self-sacrificing," with Stanton quipping that women had done that for long enough.[182] Yet Stanton effusively praised him as the one voice at Seneca Falls who had been willing to support her demand for voting rights. Douglass was now an elder statesman and a national institution; his very presence helped enhance the power of the story and the legitimacy of the event.[183]

This was the last major suffrage convention Lucretia Mott attended. She was in her mid-eighties. Her family had insisted she remain home, but at least as one newspaper reported it, she was determined to be present. She offered general reminiscences from her own life, punctuated by urgings to improve women's physical, "civil, religious, educational, and industrial" standing, and thereby improve the health of the nation.[184] She also spoke of the need to separate "true Christianity" from oppressive theological doctrine.[185] But, notably, once again, Mott did not focus on Seneca Falls as a singular watershed. The temperature inside the church was oppressive, and friends urged Mott to leave for fear she would suffer heat exhaustion. As she departed the stage, the audience stood as a sign of respect. They shook her hands as she made her way down the church's long aisle, with Douglass calling after her and bidding her a "goodbye" on behalf of those assembled.[186]

Stanton and Anthony may well have hoped that the 1878 anniversary celebration would heal or at least thaw the movement's divisions. "In union," Anthony explained to Lucy Stone in the wake of that anniversary, "there is strength."[187] But she could not get Stone or other women's rights activists to agree with her on points of strategy, organization, or theory. Organizers solicited letters of greeting and support from those unable to attend, received many, read some at the event, and published many more in the *National Citizen and Ballot Box*, the National Association's new newspaper (its first since the *Revolution* had been sold in 1870), owned and edited by Matilda Joslyn Gage. Such letters were opportunities for women to begin telling the Seneca Falls story as *their story*, acknowledging and commemorating it whether or not they were actually there. Testimony that Seneca Falls was the movement's shared origin no longer came primarily from Stanton and Anthony. In Maquoketa, Iowa, women even held their own thirtieth anniversary celebration—with roughly sixty women showing up for a lawn picnic, complete with flags, flowers, and banners—surely one of the first times women outside New York had actively participated in the collective memory of Seneca Falls.[188]

The question of origins was still far from settled inside the suffrage movement, however. In 1880, the Massachusetts Woman Suffrage Association held a different thirtieth anniversary celebration. They commemorated the 1850 Worcester convention as the movement's beginning. And they held the anniversary in Worcester. Stone opened by quoting scripture: "Put off thy shoes from thy feet, for the place where thou standest is holy ground." Where they now stood, she continued, "the first public protest" had arisen against those laws that bound women in servitude. Thomas Wentworth Higginson, a prominent abolitionist and a *Woman's Journal* editor, began his remarks by calling Worcester the "first Woman Suffrage meeting." This commemoration differed, however, from those staged by Stanton and Anthony, and not just in celebrating a different origin. This was very much a local affair, organized by the state society and drawing mostly Massachusetts residents. Harriet Hanson Robinson (a rare National Association partisan in Massachusetts and a rival of Stone) read a sort of historical minority report into the record, commenting amid the proceedings that "the first Woman's Rights convention was held at Seneca Falls, N.Y. in 1848." Stone's ensuing column about the Worcester celebration noted pointedly that Robinson's version of history contained "points she will have to correct."[189]

Stanton and Anthony's version of history—the volume they had promised to write for contributors at the 1876 centennial—hoped to correct many points, too, but their Sixteenth Amendment campaign deferred the hope and the promise alike. In February 1877, Anthony had penned a short piece for an Ohio women's rights newspaper, acknowledging the delay. "The proposed history of the woman suffrage movement is progressing slowly," she conceded. "The work grows in the hands of its editors—much time and labor have been expended in getting material together."[190] Stanton and Anthony did, however, manage to get a short historical account into print to coincide with the thirtieth anniversary in 1878.

Two years earlier, Anthony had accepted an assignment to edit the women's rights entries for *Johnson's New Universal Cyclopaedia,* a four-volume reference edited by some of the most distinguished men of the day.[191] Anthony was asked to select women to profile and to compose the entry on "Woman's Rights."[192] Never being much of a writer, she asked Stanton to help her compose the main entry.[193] It was the first time Anthony had written history for publication, and she knew full well that every inclusion, exclusion, and interpretation would be read politically by those most in the know. Trying to stave off dispute, Anthony implored a friend: "Please don't mention the fact of my editorship to any of the *Boston ring*" (meaning Stone and the American Association).[194]

The 1870s had imposed hard lessons on Anthony and Stanton, as rival organizations and alternate motivations rapidly produced many movements with many definitions of women's rights. That stopped here. Now a widely distributed and respected reference volume had asked Anthony "to give the defenition [*sic*] to *woman suffrage.*" She did so, pointedly, in the entry's first sentence: "Woman's Rights, a term used in the U.S. to designate the movement for woman's equal social, civil, political, industrial, religious, and educational rights with man."[195] Without apology to Mary Wollstonecraft (whom she later mentioned in passing), the entry immediately clarified that in the United States, "woman's rights" meant first and foremost the "social, civil, [and] political" rights necessary to gain other kinds of equal rights with men. In other words, "woman's rights" meant exactly what Anthony had been insisting: woman suffrage, above all else.

The second sentence dispelled any doubts about where it all began: "The first convention was called July 19, 1848, at Seneca Falls, N.Y., by Lucretia Mott, Elizabeth Cady Stanton, Martha C. Wright, and Mary Ann McClintock" (Jane Hunt being mysteriously absent from the list). A long first paragraph of details about the meeting followed, including the passage of resolutions demanding educational and professional rights for married and unmarried women alike. The meeting had not been without discord, however. "The resolution asserting 'the duty of the women of this country to secure to themselves their sacred right to the elective franchise' was the only one that met with opposition. . . . Mrs. Stanton and Frederick Douglass, seeing that the right to make laws was the power by which all others could be secured, advocated and carried the resolution." Explaining that "a declaration of rights was adopted, setting forth similar grievances under a masculine dynasty to those the colonies endured under King George," the entry noted that although it "was signed by over 100 persons: many withdrew their names when the storm of ridicule began to break." Nevertheless, "the brave protests sent out from this meeting touched a responsive chord in the hearts of women all over the country. Conventions were held soon after in Ohio, Indiana, and Pennsylvania, and one in Rochester, N.Y., within two weeks." All this before the end of the first paragraph. Here was a rough draft of the myth of Seneca Falls—the first account, not exactly written for the history books, but certainly written *as history*.[196]

The *Cyclopaedia* entry accomplished more than literally putting Seneca Falls first: it made clear why it mattered so much that Seneca Falls be recorded and accepted as the origin of the struggle. The very definition of "Women's Rights, a term used in the U.S. to designate the movement" was at stake. Those rights, and that movement, were, since the Civil War, keyed, in Anthony's mind, to suffrage—"the right . . . by which all others could be secured." But not everyone understood or affirmed this, even at Seneca Falls. The "progress of civilization" itself, the entry read, had "prepare[d] the way for the woman's rights movement in 1848."[197] That year mattered because the unfinished work of the American Revolution had been revived, and in due time, carried on through the Civil War and Reconstruction. From the vantage of 1876, when the entry was composed, it mattered that well-meaning but timid people had to be persuaded by brilliant and farsighted political thinkers such as "Mrs. Stanton and Frederick Douglass" to pass the suffrage resolution at Seneca Falls. Anthony herself made no appearance in the *Cyclopaedia*'s historical narrative until the fourth paragraph, stuck in the middle of a long list of delegates and organizers of conventions that had followed in 1850 and 1851. Her name recurred at least once in all but two of the remaining nine paragraphs, however—twelve times in all, not counting her byline, in a text of less than four pages. That mattered, too, in an entry that otherwise took great pains to acknowledge dozens upon dozens of important activists, including Stanton's and Anthony's bitterest rivals. The narrative stated frankly that after the Civil War, "there was a division in our ranks" (and here, the encyclopedic tone slipped momentarily into a more personal voice), "growing out of personal hostilities—a difference as to our affiliations, as to the discussion of social questions, and as to the true interpretation of the Constitution, the limits of State rights and Federal power." Writing just fifteen years after Fort Sumter, Anthony continued, "The seceders, led by Lucy Stone, centred [*sic*] in Boston." So, there it was, the specter of secession, which had betrayed the sacred principles of the Declaration of 1848 as much as that of 1776.[198]

The definition of women's rights, the primacy of suffrage, the federal strategy: all of this rested upon fixing the movement's origin at Seneca Falls. Even "division in our ranks" mattered, in this sense, because internal division meant that there was a right side and a wrong side ("the seceders"). This is why Seneca Falls had to come first: because right and wrong had been there in 1848, too, and right had won the day. Although it surely mattered that a hundred conventioneers had put their names to the Declaration of Sentiments, it mattered even more to record for history—although it was not true—that "many withdrew their names when the storm of ridicule began to break." It mattered to exaggerate the storm and the ridicule (press coverage in 1848 was generally favorable or neutral), because three decades later the goal was still far from won. It mattered, in short, that the story of Seneca Falls was *becoming a myth at the same time that it was becoming history*. The myth of Seneca Falls was the myth of America, but an America that only the likes of Douglass, Stanton, and Anthony saw clearly at the centennial mark: an unfinished America where "brave protests" could "strike a responsive chord" and change the way things are.[199]

If so much political work could be accomplished in a brief historical sketch for a multivolume encyclopedia, how much more could be done in a multivolume work of women's history by women historians? The last sentence of the entry (before the *Cyclopaedia* moved on from "Woman's Rights" to the next alphabetical entry, "Womb," written by the good doctors E. Darwin Hudson Jr. and Willard Parker) read simply: "For further information, see *History of Woman Suffrage Movement*, edited by Elizabeth Cady Stanton, Matilda Joslyn Gage, and Susan B. Anthony."[200] Looking toward the long-term usefulness and relevance of the entry, they included a savvy plug for the definitive work, which did not yet exist. Like the nascent myth of Seneca Falls and like the ongoing movement itself, the full *History of Woman Suffrage* was still a promise not yet kept.

4. Inventing Women's History
✥ 1880–1886

After more than a decade of constant travel, Stanton retired from the lecture circuit in 1880. Now sixty-five years old, she found the exhausting travel less appealing. Sleeping night after night in new places, in sometimes crude accommodations, rushing to make engagements scheduled over short times across far distances, and anxiously waiting for delayed trains had lost its allure. Stanton had spent the better part of the postwar decade and a half on the road. With her children now finished with their expensive college educations, she no longer needed steady nightly door receipts.[1] She continued to lecture, but not nearly as often. Her lyceum retirement freed up enormous amounts of time, and she sought another place to apply her voracious intellect. Soon, Stanton persuaded Anthony, age sixty, to also leave the lecture circuit temporarily, so that they could finally devote intensive time and energy to their long-promised and -deferred *History of Woman Suffrage*.[2] They vowed to complete it that winter, once and for all. By October 1880, Anthony had relocated to Stanton's home in Tenafly, New Jersey.[3] Soon they were joined by their younger colleague, fifty-four-year-old Matilda Joslyn Gage, an officer of the National Association who had been its president during the centennial. For the last three years, she had been the editor and owner of the monthly *National Citizen Ballot Box*, a new National Association organ, which had serialized some early chapters of what the three women were now determined to complete as a major book.[4]

Although they certainly had posterity in mind, their mission was far more immediate and political: to give younger women a source for learning about—and understanding—the movement's legacies, objectives, and strategies. It had become clear during the past decade that woman suffrage was not going to be won anytime soon—the work begun by their generation would have to be completed by the next generation. Large number of young woman had taken up the call, but Stanton, Anthony, and Gage still despaired over the campaign's future, especially as other rights agendas and even other approaches to suffrage divided the movement, diluted its strength, and, in their view, misdirected its energies. The three were keenly aware of getting older themselves, and their mentors and collaborators had already begun to die off. That reality weighed heavily, especially when they lost Lucretia Mott that November, just as they resumed work on the *History*. "We . . . have been moved by the consideration that many of our co-workers have already fallen asleep," they wrote in the preface to volume 1, "and that in a few years all who could tell the story will have passed away."[5] The *History*'s authors hoped that if they could give younger activists a collective memory of where the movement had been, they would learn the right lessons about where it needed to go. The *History* would be both a gift and a lesson. It would be a legacy and a directive—which the authors fervently hoped would redirect the movement and keep it on course after they, too, "fell asleep."

The project also reiterated and expanded the hard but crucial lesson Stanton and Anthony themselves had learned over the past decade: history mattered. It had simply not been enough for women to make their political voices heard. They also had to make women's rights self-evident in the postwar politics of collective memory by speaking *with* history as well as for it. It was no accident that their long-held but vague desire to write the movement's history coalesced during the centennial. Between the war itself and the nation's hundredth birthday, collective memory had become both a boom industry and a political proxy. Particular ways of remembering the war had, in less than two decades, been used first to enfranchise and then to disenfranchise black men. Woman suffragists, however, had failed to make their cause an integral part of the war's legacy.

By the time Stanton, Anthony, and Gage were in a position to commit themselves to completing the *History*, publishing had taken its place alongside monument building and public celebrations as a pivotal arena where Americans reshaped the past for present political purposes.[6] In 1877, as Reconstruction ended, the War Department finally established an official publications office to revive a stalled documentary history of the late conflict. The first volume of *The War of the Rebellion: A Compilation of the Official Records of the Union and Confederate Armies* appeared in 1881 (the same year as volume 1 of *The History of Woman Suffrage*); 127 further volumes followed by 1901, produced by a staff of more than one hundred.[7] Meanwhile, commercial and popular publishers issued so many war-related magazine articles, memoirs, novels, biographies, and histories that the tide "pouring forth from the presses," one scholar observes, "seemed unstoppable."[8]

Nearly all of it was military in nature, and nearly all was written by, for, and about men.

The coauthors of the *History of Woman Suffrage* hoped that their work might take its place among the military memoirs and countless other volumes devoted to the war.[9] This aspect of their motivation and the volumes that resulted is easy to overlook: *The History of Woman Suffrage* was, in an important sense, a book about the Civil War and Reconstruction. It was a piece—an important and overlooked piece—of the Civil War publishing boom. From the introduction's unmistakably provocative first sentence, "The prolonged slavery of woman is the darkest page in human history," to a late chapter's embrace of a particular memory of "'the war of the rebellion,'
. . . the final struggle between freedom and slavery," the authors framed the story of their movement within antebellum, wartime, and Reconstruction politics.[10] Simply put, the *History* made their case for woman suffrage by presenting it as inextricable from "the great lesson of the war, National protection for United States citizens, applied to women as well as to the African race."[11] The whole of volume 1 unfolded in uneasy tension with this lesson, as the coauthors worked to forge a new Civil War memory paradigm, one to join and challenge those already in circulation, just as the balance between those circulating memories and their attendant politics was beginning to shift and change.[12]

❖ Friction in the Archives

At Independence Hall in 1876, when Anthony and Gage gave the acting vice president their scroll to get it "on file with the general archives of the day," their triumph was symbolic—and *only* symbolic. The official history and proceedings of the centennial had not reprinted any part of the Woman's Declaration of Rights, nor even noted the women's presence, much less their "overt act" of protest. Later that year, launching the Sixteenth Amendment drive, they complained that their unheeded "petitions . . . by the tens of thousands, are piled up in the national archives." In truth, there simply was neither anything like a "general archives of the day" nor a U.S. "national archives" in 1876, and there would not be for nearly sixty years. After the British burned Washington, D.C., in 1814, government records that had not been lost had been published in the thirty-eight volume *American State Papers* series, but not until 1894 did Congress employ a historian (actually, a former Tennessee congressman) to compile, edit, and publish *The Messages and Papers of the Presidents* in ten volumes.[13] Well into the twentieth century, original government documents were still preserved (or not) haphazardly, scattered among the departments that created them, while the papers of politicians, poets, and jurists knocked around in family hands until perhaps some portion went to distinguished universities or ended up in various antiquarian libraries and societies. Women were in these collections, of course, just as there were a few history books about them, because women were part of the national fabric; but their presence was more incidental—a byproduct rather than an organizing principle.[14] The concept that the deeds and documents of women merited preservation along with those of statesmen was itself as radical a concept as any of Stanton's, Anthony's, or Gage's political ideas. The *History* authors' growing awareness that remembering also required a paper trail—in essence, an archive—shaped the unique way in which they wrote their *History*. It would become the story and the archive all in one.[15]

Theirs was a stunning act of historical imagination at a time when there was barely any such thing as a public archive in the sense that modern scholars take for granted: documents collected, organized, and preserved systematically, both for their own sake and to furnish historians with a record as complete, authoritative, and accessible as possible. Yet, this is exactly what Stanton, Anthony, and Gage conceived of and set out to build from scratch—with a staff of only three: themselves. As modern scholars do, they put research before writing and set out assiduously to collect what today would be called primary sources, of many kinds: letters, newspaper reports, speech transcripts, pamphlets, legislative reports, legal treatises, and more. By 1880, they had been soliciting material for four years and had published a few early draft chapters in Gage's newspaper to generate reader corrections and suggestions (in a rudimentary form of peer review). Published excerpts and announcements invited "one and all . . . [to] send your facts and help us prepare a grand and true history, one of which all women and the nation will be proud."[16] They also wrote countless letters asking colleagues to write up recollections about their lives or incidents in the campaign and to send along any scattered fragments and old documents in their possession. Besides historical and archival vision, there was genuine humility not only in the recognition that they could not possibly remember all that they and women they knew had done, across nearly fifty years and an ocean besides, but also in the admission that many women they did not know had done many important things they knew nothing about.[17]

The solicitation to "send your facts" soon buried the three under an avalanche of letters and enclosures. They set about the seemingly never-ending task of sorting, dating, and trying to put the papers into some meaningful order. "We stood appalled before the mass of material," Stanton remembered, "growing higher and higher with every mail, and the thought of all the reading involved made us feel as if our life-work lay before us. Six weeks of steady labor all day, and often until midnight, made no visible decrease in the pile."[18] To compound matters, the reminiscences arriving in the mail were much longer than they could use. "Sketches of persons must be *very brief*," Stanton pleaded with contributors. "We are already swamped with material. My head turns to look at it. Everybody amplifies."[19]

But not everybody cooperated, of course. Some preferred to squelch. Lucy Stone opposed the project from the start, fearing that it would be a polemic, heavily skewed toward Stanton, Anthony, and the National Association. Stone refused to supply even basic information. "I cannot furnish a biographical sketch, and trust you will not try to make one," she replied. She closed her letter: "Yours with ceaseless regret that any 'wing' of suffragists should attempt to write the history of the other."[20] The *History*'s architects were undeterred, believing that the goal of suffrage was too important "to linger over individual differences."[21]

With the research phase well under way, the three quickly set up a rough division of labor to tackle the enormous scope of the work. "What planning, now, for volumes, chapters, footnotes, margins, appendices, paper, and type; of engravings, title, preface, and introduction!" Stanton remarked. "I had never thought that the publication of a book required the consideration of such endless details."[22] The three agreed that Stanton and Gage would do most of the actual writing; Stanton would edit everyone's prose; and Anthony (who was nearly as gifted and driven to organize paper as she was people) would manage production details and the vast correspondence the project generated.[23] The sheer mass of material very quickly led the women to divide the projected book in half. Instead of a single volume, they now proposed two. Volume 1 would tell the antebellum story, and volume 2 would pick up the narrative from the Civil War and bring it forward. The three worked together to outline the *History*'s general vision, chapter structure, and content. Stanton and Gage divided up the chapters and each drafted different ones. With the general shape and the division of labor decided, Gage worked mostly from her own home in Fayetteville, New York.[24] Because of the loss or possible destruction of her editorial correspondence with Stanton and Anthony (who were usually together in Tenafly, the center of production), it is difficult to say how much Gage ultimately shaped the final narrative, but she certainly had less control.[25] In both locations, the women taught themselves how to write history for publication, discovering a frustratingly improvisational yet deeply satisfying process that every modern historian knows well. Gage surveyed the wreckage in her front parlor: "In my bay window, stands a table from my library and a stand and two chairs, all covered with books and papers. I say nothing of books, papers & boxes . . . on the floor. It is confusion, but out of it grows a history chapter."[26]

The *History*'s chapters were innovative in design as well as content. Nearly every page contained excerpts (of varying lengths) from diverse kinds of original source material. In a chapter on, say, an antebellum women's rights convention, they included not only actual proceedings and (where available) organizers' correspondence; they also interwove substantial excerpts from contemporary newspaper accounts, speeches by supportive and critical politicians, legislative hearings, reports, bills, political party platforms, judicial decisions, and more. Sometimes they reprinted original material in its entirety, filling several pages. Offsetting these documents in a smaller typeface, they silently cued the reader to perceive and value the privilege of examining original sources for themselves. This extensive reprinting of documents accounted for the volumes' massive size, consuming nearly 1,000 pages each. More than 125 years after their publication, they remain an indispensable source, having stood for much of that time as the richest repository of published, accessible documentary evidence of nineteenth-century suffrage movements.[27]

The three women learned an enormous amount about writing history during that long, productive first winter. They grappled with the complex tensions between constructed narratives and notions of objectivity. "*In our history*—we want to get actual *facts about persons* & dates & names in their proper order—*not* the individual's [personal] *feelings*," Anthony confided to a friend, "and we *try*—but oh how difficult—almost impossible—to accomplish."[28] As chapters were finished, Anthony took them for typesetting at the printer's, where second thoughts or production issues sometimes resulted in last-minute changes made on the spot.[29] But come spring 1881, after months of painstaking research, organization, outlining, writing, revision, and editing, Anthony triumphantly declared that they were "in the last agonies of going to press with the history."[30] In May, their publisher delivered a finished copy of volume 1, covering the antebellum years and making many documents widely accessible for the first time. "It was an octavo, containing

Matilda Joslyn Gage (The Schlesinger Library, Radcliffe Institute, Harvard University)

871 pages, with good paper, good print, handsome engravings, and nicely bound," Stanton beamed. "I welcomed it with the same feeling of love and tenderness as I did my firstborn."[31]

Although the title page billed Stanton, Anthony, and Gage as the *History*'s editors, they were not merely editors but authors who created a narrative of American women's history where none had existed before. Emphasizing their editorship (over their authorship) and including a documentary foundation within the text, however, projected an objective, professional tone undoubtedly intended to enhance the volume's authority. This was surely not coincidental. Not only did women's history not yet exist as a recognized worthwhile field, the discipline of history, as a professional discipline with objective standards, was in the midst of being born. In 1880, the year they began writing, Herbert Baxter Adams founded the history seminar at Johns Hopkins University, from which J. Franklin Jameson would earn the first doctorate in 1882, the same year the women published volume 2. In 1884 Adams, Jameson, and other men would found the American Historical Association, an all-male bastion, like the new profession itself.[32] But Stanton, Anthony, and Gage insisted they were every bit these men's peers. And, indeed, they were.

Yet the *History*'s authors were activists, not academics, and as the first sentence of their preface clearly stated, they had intertwined goals. "In preparing this work, our object has been to put into permanent shape the few scattered reports of the Woman Suffrage Movement still to be found," they began, "and to make it an arsenal of facts for those who are beginning to inquire into the demands and arguments of the leaders of this reform."[33] The authors thus carried their book back into the fray. When Stanton addressed the Senate Committee on Woman Suffrage in 1882, she pointedly began by presenting a copy of volume 1 to every senator in attendance (which charmed even the southern Democrats, known for their fierce opposition to her cause).[34] Until that day, few if any civilians had ever walked into a congressional hearing armed with such an impressive "arsenal of facts."[35]

The way they compiled and deployed history revealed that Stanton, Anthony, and Gage understood history writing to be a critical form of social activism. They thought deeply about the relationship between these undertakings (in ways that professional historians would not begin to honestly confront until much later).[36] Rejecting the idea that, as they put it, "the actors themselves cannot write an impartial history," they remarked: "to be historians of a reform in which we have been among the chief actors, has its points of embarrassment as well as advantage. Those who fight the battle can best give what all readers like to know—the impelling motives to action; the struggle in the face of opposition . . . ; and the despair in success too long deferred."[37] Stanton, Anthony, and Gage began their labors convinced that "there is an interest in history written from a subjective point of view, that may compensate the reader in this case for any seeming egotism or partiality he may discover."[38] Although one might ponder whether they referred to "the reader" as "he" by mere literary convention or to emphasize that men, too, could learn a lot from their book, the more fundamental point here is that Stanton, Anthony, and Gage intuitively and remarkably reached toward the modern (and even postmodern) dilemmas of writing professional history. Yet some readers were disappointed and even angered by the "subjective point of view" in the work.[39]

Contemporary reviews of volume 1 were favorable to mixed. "We have long needed an authentic and exhaustive account of the movement for the enfranchisement of woman," wrote the *New York Sun* approvingly. The *Home Journal* chimed in with enthusiasm: "reminiscences, correspondence, speeches, essays, newspaper articles, reports of meetings, everything that bears on the topic has been made to do service." E. L. Godkin's liberal periodical the *Nation* was less charitable, dubbing the *History* an "unedited work of many hands, [and] a disorderly repository of facts."[40] Lucy Stone reviewed it critically for the *Woman's Journal* in August 1881. "We were asked to contribute to this work, but we have neither time nor inclination to write personal sketches of ourselves," she sneered, ". . . while the work remains unfinished." Although she expressed concerns about fairness and misrepresentation, given the movement's organizational and strategic divisions, Stone's most telling criticism was that such a historical enterprise was simply "premature." Stanton, Anthony, and Gage had anticipated this very criticism (very likely with Stone in mind) on the volume's first page, quoting nameless naysayers who had discouraged the project: "It is too early to write the history of this movement; wait until our object is attained." [41] To the three coauthors, who firmly believed that writing history could shape the future, this was all the more reason not to wait.

Stone's failure to grasp this revealed a more traditional conception of the relationship between the past, present, and future—a conception that ultimately worked to her disadvantage. In the arena of history and collective memory, Stone's rivals consistently outmaneuvered her. While she balked, they created the movement's first—and most enduring—master narrative. Yet Stanton and Anthony could not have set out to accomplish, or even imagined, all that they ultimately did accomplish with the *History*. Now, having first taught themselves how to write history, they turned to learning how to use it. [42]

❖ Volume 1 (1776–1861): The Origins of an Origins Myth

Despite E. L. Godkin's dismissive review calling volume 1 "an unedited . . . disorderly repository of facts," the *History*'s editor-authors actually constructed very orderly story lines. But the story they crafted from those facts was itself, like the archival repository they compiled, a new invention. As lived, history has no beginning, middle, or end, but as written, history's beginning is always a choice made by the historian. Where to start? How far back to go? In trying to make sense of antebellum women's history, Stanton, Anthony, and Gage had no choice but to select some origin point. They chose to present that point as the 1848 convention in Seneca Falls. Rendered much more fully than ever before, that story now took on grander proportions, becoming the key to understanding the entire movement.

But if Seneca Falls was the beginning, what to do with relevant events and influences that came before the beginning? Stanton, Anthony, and Gage collected three chapters' worth of material that they had to get through before they could get to Seneca Falls in chapter 4. They characterized this early history as prehistory, giving chapter 1 the punning title, "Preceding Causes." Here they discussed both earlier movements, such as the antislavery cause in which many suffragists learned how to be activists, and early influences—people and events that caused the distinct movement that began at Seneca Falls in 1848. Chapter 1 roamed through the intellectual and philosophical underpinnings of woman suffrage, featuring a host of figures from early European authors to the great women of the American Revolution, such as Mercy Otis Warren and Abigail Adams, identified as "the first American woman who threatened rebellion unless the rights of her sex were secured." In March of 1776, Abigail urged her husband, John, a member of the Continental Congress, to "remember the ladies" when drafting the laws of the new nation. "If particular care and attention are not paid to the ladies," the *History*'s authors quote Adams as saying, "we are determined to foment a rebellion, and will not hold ourselves bound to obey any laws in which we have no voice or representation." Chapter 1 detailed other domestic influences, including "Frances Wright . . . the first woman who gave lectures on political subjects in America" and the sisters Sarah and Angelina Grimké, who "from the beginning took an active part in the Anti-Slavery struggle." All this encouraged Americans to recognize just how *long* women had been demanding rights for themselves and others. Nevertheless, the *History* treats these antecedent women as either individually heroic or working for something other than women's rights.[43]

Stanton herself wrote up the first substantive, document-based account of a "preceding cause," devoting the entirety of chapter 3 to "The World's Anti-Slavery Convention, London, June 12, 1840," an event that had changed her own life, setting her on the path to becoming a reformer. "The first public demand for political equality by a body of women in convention," she wrote, "was a link in the chain of woman's development, binding the future with the past." Nevertheless, she prefaced the London story by insisting that "the woman suffrage movement" was "the legitimate outgrowth of *American ideas*—a component of the history of our republic," adding that "above all other causes of the 'Woman Suffrage Movement,' was the Anti-Slavery struggle *in this country*." Stanton described being radicalized by anger when Englishmen refused to seat American women delegates including veteran reformer Lucretia Mott, whom the decades-younger Stanton had just met. "As Lucretia Mott and Elizabeth Cady Stanton wended their way arm in arm down Great Queen Street that night," she recalled (even if Mott did not), "they agreed to hold a woman's rights convention on their return to America."[44]

Two elements of Stanton's narrative made this an important prologue to Seneca Falls. For one, the experience had radicalized Stanton. And in many ways, this story, which Stanton now mapped onto the movement, was—more accurately—her own personal story. Secondly, for Stanton, who was never an ardent abolitionist, the story recast abolitionism. The antislavery movement's most notable trait was its outrageous hostility to women's rights. Whereas Stone and others depicted women's rights arising from *within* abolition, for Stanton, it arose from without. It arose from a necessary break with abolition. "The movement for woman's suffrage, both in England and America," she concluded, "may be dated from this World's Anti-Slavery Convention." Stanton's choice to emphasize and craft origins in this way surely resulted from her continued animus over the Fifteenth Amendment. Stanton made this 1840 story "a link in the chain" of the woman suffrage movement's independence and divergence from the abolitionists, who had in 1840 excluded women as participants in an important meeting, and who had in 1870 excluded them from the American Constitution.[45]

The early chapters thus acknowledged "preceding causes" but kept them apart from the true beginning of the story: how an independent and fully developed movement was born at Seneca Falls in 1848. It was there that myriad antecedents "culminated at last in a woman's rights convention."[46] The Seneca Falls story elaborated in volume 1 borrows many phrases from the account that opened the 1878 encyclopedia entry on "Woman's Rights" that Stanton had helped draft for publication under Anthony's byline.[47] That text clearly functioned as a preliminary draft for telling the story in their own book, where they could now allot all the space they wished. The version in volume 1 actually begins with a document, "a startling announcement" that appeared in the *Seneca County Courier* on Saturday, 14 July 1848. Mott, Stanton, Martha C. Wright, and Mary Ann McClintock—"four ladies, sitting around the tea-table" of a fifth, Jane Hunt—penned this original call to meeting. Its publication in a weekly rural newspaper, only five days ahead of time, suggests the local and improvisational nature of this founding moment. This is the story of how a small "circle" (a word that appears throughout the volume, as in "our circle") sparked an entire movement.[48]

"On Sunday morning," the day after the newspaper announcement appeared, with only three days to go before convening on Wednesday, the organizers "met in Mrs. McClintock's parlor to write their declaration, resolutions, and to consider subjects for speeches." The implication of naiveté is surely intentional and reinforces the utter newness of what they were doing. Mott was a seasoned reformer and speaker (and the others were antislavery

Quakers), but the narrative emphasizes that they had "no experience in the *modus operandi* of getting up conventions, nor in [composing] that kind of literature" and "were quite innocent of the herculean labors they proposed." The meeting's (and the chapter's) key "historic documents" Stanton reported, evolved from the women's dissatisfaction with "various masculine productions" they discussed while seeking possible models for a manifesto. "The reports of Peace, Temperance, and Anti-Slavery conventions were examined, but all alike seemed too tame and pacific for the inauguration of a rebellion such as the world had never before seen." These women were "quite innocent," and yet also quite radical.[49]

Finally, "one of the circle took up the Declaration of 1776" and read it aloud with gusto. "It was at once decided to adopt that historic document" as the basis for their protest by revising its famous list of grievances against the King as a list of grievances against "all men." Now, sitting around McClintock's "antique mahogany center-table," Stanton and the rest wrote out their own "historic document"—the soon to be famous Declaration of Sentiments.[50]

On 19 July, the "eventful day dawned at last," Stanton continued, and crowds assembled outside Wesleyan church, waiting to be let in. But "lo! the door was locked," and Stanton's son had to be "lifted through an open window to unbar the door" from inside. After speeches, Stanton read the Declaration of Sentiments, which the chapter then reprints in its entirety. "When, in the course of human events, it becomes necessary for one portion of the family of man to assume . . . a position different from that which they have hitherto occupied, but one to which the laws of nature and of nature's God entitle them," it began, ". . . [then] they should declare the causes that impel them to such a course. We hold these truths to be self evident: that all men *and women* are created equal." Thus the organizers transformed a sacred document of the American status quo into a clarion call for women's rights. The authors of the Declaration of Sentiments had even taken pains to think up exactly eighteen grievances, the same number put forth in 1776. There followed a corresponding series of demands, which the *History* also reprinted, and which included property rights, access to the professions, higher education, and an end to the sexual double standard.[51]

Reprinting the entire 1848 declaration not only preserved it for history and made it even more widely accessible, the scope of its demands demonstrated the completeness of the movement born at Seneca Falls. An interpretive passage that followed the text of the document emphasized, "Thus it will be seen that the Declaration and resolutions in the very first Convention, demanded all the most radical friends of the movement have since claimed." Paradoxically, the gathering of organizational innocents had nevertheless given birth to a full-grown women's movement, already *complete* in its ideological development. All that followed, the remaining hundreds upon hundreds of pages, was, by implication, derivative. In another passage (taken almost verbatim from the "Woman's Rights" encyclopedia article), they asserted that "the brave protests sent out from this Convention touched a responsive chord in the hearts of women all over the country" and that "conventions were held soon after in Ohio, Massachusetts, Indiana, Pennsylvania, and at different points in New York."[52] It was Seneca Falls that cohered a movement.

The author-editors reiterated the ripple effect of Seneca Falls in the state chapters that alternated with individual women's personal stories throughout the rest of the volume. The recollections of Emily Collins, a relatively obscure suffragist, followed this Seneca Falls–focused chapter on New York. Collins described her conversion, born of the convention in Seneca Falls. Since childhood, she "pined for that freedom . . . denied to all womankind. . . . But not until that meeting at Seneca Falls in 1848 . . . gave this feeling of unrest form and voice, did I take action." The Pennsylvania chapter reprinted Lucretia Mott's remarks at an 1852 convention in Westchester, reminding delegates that their ideas sprang full born from "the first Convention held at Seneca Falls, in 1848, where a few women assembled, and not withstanding their ignorance of the parliamentary modes of conducting business, promulgated these principles, which took deep root." Where they could, then, the authors positioned subsequent history in relation to that 1848 foundational moment. The Ohio chapter included Gage's presidential address to the Cleveland National Woman's Rights Convention of 1853, which opened with "a review of what had been accomplished since the first Convention was held at Seneca Falls." As in the false claim first made in the 1878 encyclopedia entry and repeated here—that of the declaration's one hundred original signers, "many . . . withdrew their names as soon as the storm of ridicule began to break"—those who disbelieved only made the Seneca Falls story stronger. This, too, would become a recurring motif.[53]

The authors then sandwiched a chapter of Stanton's reminiscences between the chapters on New Jersey and yet another chapter on New York (the only state to receive double billing). Devoting the chapter to Anthony, Stanton gave the reader a full introduction to this famous woman, and notably she returned to Seneca Falls. "The reports of the Conventions held in Seneca Falls and Rochester, N.Y., in 1848," she began, "attracted the attention of one destined to take a most important part in the movement—Susan B. Anthony . . . the Napoleon of our struggle."[54] Later on the same page, an account of Stanton and Anthony's first meeting "in the month of May" (the year was somehow omitted in the first printing) gave the impression they had met in 1848, perhaps even at the Seneca Falls convention. (Later printings clarified, "it was in the month of May, 1851, that I first met Miss Anthony.")[55] In any case, "so entirely one are we," Stanton wrote, ". . . ever side by side on the same platform," that it hardly mattered whether Anthony had attended in 1848 or not. Indeed, "I soon convinced my new friend that the ballot was the key to the situation," Stanton recalled.[56] In sum, it was "reports . . . of Seneca Falls" that had brought Anthony to Stanton, and almost from the first moment the two were of one mind that suffrage was the primary goal. Here, Stanton clearly also spoke to the multitudes of women debating questions of strategy and emphasis in a broader women's rights movement. Then began the second New York chapter, featuring Stanton and Anthony's antebellum work there, which opened by reporting: "A full report of the woman's rights agitation in the State of New York would in a measure be the history of the movement."[57]

In other words, Stanton and Anthony *were* the movement. By the end of volume 1, which finished with an appendix that reprinted several more pages of reports, documents, and testimonials related to Seneca Falls, the mythic significance of that "eventful day" had been firmly established. Whether or not one accepted it as the movement's nativity, volume 1 makes the story of Seneca Falls a master narrative, the source of the movement's broad agenda yet narrow strategy, and the inspiration that brought to the cause its most brilliant strategist, Anthony, "the Napoleon of this movement." The myth of Seneca Falls was the very crux of that movement, with the comprehensive rights agenda outlined in 1848 culled down to one strategic goal—"the ballot was the key"—and distilled into the very title of the volume itself.[58]

❖ Mrs. Stanton's Blue Pencil

The chance to interpret the campaign was both a historic opportunity and a political minefield. When suffragists and reformers read volume 1, and as collaborations for volume 2 proceeded, disputes erupted. The preface to the *History's* inaugural volume downplayed any production tensions, suggesting that sisterly cooperation reigned supreme: "In collecting material for these volumes, most of those of whom we solicited facts have expressed themselves deeply interested in our undertaking, and have gladly contributed all they could."[59] They note minor dissention, but quickly dismiss it as having no effect on content. The reality was considerably more complicated. Disagreements extended well beyond Lucy Stone's vow of noncooperation and her critical review. Disagreements also characterized Stanton's and Anthony's relationships with their allies, where sometimes bitterly divisive disagreements arose over who had been asked to compose material, who had authorial control over that material, and the effect of Stanton's "blue pencil."

Stanton, a gifted stylist, edited contributions ruthlessly, and Anthony had to console outside authors, assuring them that they were "not alone in fearing Mrs. Stanton's reviewing of your chapter."[60] Indeed, the surgical strikes of Stanton's "blue pencil" transformed contributions and brought trouble. Early on, Anthony and Stanton had promised assorted contributors that their work would go in as submitted. This quickly proved untenable for a variety of reasons, including emphasis, style, agenda, tone—and, as always, length. Once into the project, Stanton and Anthony explicitly refused to publish pieces "exactly as . . . sent."[61] Contributors worried that Stanton's and Anthony's choices shaped meaning, unfairly discounted meritorious individuals, or excessively featured the undeserving. Disagreements also turned on how much internal history to reveal, some of which was deeply divisive.[62]

Laura de Force Gordon, a prominent California suffragist who was aligned with the National Association, raised her hackles when another area suffragist, Ellen Sargent—wife of Aaron Sargent, a pro-suffrage U.S. congressman who had introduced the federal amendment for woman suffrage to the Senate—was asked to write up California. Given that state-level suffragists were no less divided than those at the national level, Gordon likely believed that she and Sargent had different stories to tell. Gage shared her friend's surprise and dismay that Anthony had not asked Gordon to write the California chapter: "I myself was surprised [sic] when I went to Tenafly . . . to find that Mrs. Sargent had been asked to write the California chapter. Of course, I expected you to do it, but I was not even consulted. My coadjutors are very lawless, and sometimes very far from just, even in regard to myself."[63]

Harriet Hanson Robinson pulled her chapter on Massachusetts after a dispute with Stanton and Anthony over its content. Robinson was a rare New England ally, and Anthony commissioned her to write the Massachusetts chapter for volume 1. For reasons that are unclear but seemed to be about authorial control, Robinson grew frustrated and eventually pulled her contribution to the *History*'s first volume. She transformed her chapter into the basis of her own historical book. In 1881, the same year the *History*'s first volume appeared, Robinson published *Massachusetts in the Woman Suffrage Movement*. Robinson had been a Lowell mill girl, one of the early factory workers in the Massachusetts textile mills of the 1830s who struck for equal wages and encouraged women's self-development. Her emphasis, then, was different than that of the *History*'s author-editors and may have informed her decision to pull her chapter. Robinson treated Seneca Falls as one event among many, not as the inspiration for all subsequent organizing. Where the Lowell mill girls are an important early force for women's rights in Robinson's account, they are barely visible in the *History*.[64]

Another incensed contributor and reader was Amelia Bloomer, a temperance and women's rights newspaper editor perhaps even more famous as the namesake of the controversial "bloomers" costume. (Loose, flowing pantaloons that were less restrictive than the painfully tight corsets and long, heavy skirts of the era, bloomers were worn by antebellum dress reformers, including Stanton, for a time.)[65] A resident of Seneca Falls, she had introduced Stanton to Anthony in 1851. A few years before the Civil War, Bloomer had relocated from Seneca Falls to Iowa, where she remained an active reformer and suffragist. Stanton and Anthony had solicited both Bloomer's personal reminiscence of her years in New York and an additional chapter on Iowa (which had to be shelved when they divided the projected book into two volumes). As volume 1 continued to become more crowded, Stanton and Anthony decided not to include Bloomer's reminiscence either. They instead used the space for a sketch of Ernestine Rose, the mover behind New York's 1848 married women's property law (granting married women the right to own property, something historically denied them).[66] All that remained of Bloomer's submission was a long passage about temperance work, lifted from her recollection and dropped without attribution into the second New York chapter. Bloomer was furious. Stanton and Anthony offered repeated apologies, attributing the confusion to overwork and unknowingly making promises they could not keep.[67] Bloomer's anger mounted when, several weeks later, Anthony mailed back Bloomer's Iowa chapter requesting further revisions while adding that once the pages were resubmitted, Anthony could not promise "how or what we will do with them."[68] When Bloomer's Iowa chapter finally appeared five years later, in volume 3, she complained privately of "Mrs. Stanton making it read as she would like it to be and not as facts made it . . . I was disgusted and disheartened. . . . I feel that the thing ought to be rewritten. . . . It is all very discouraging, for they will leave in and take out whatever they please, and one don't [*sic*] know how it will come out."[69]

❖ Volume 2 (1861–1875):
Radical Women in Radical Reconstruction

Stanton, Anthony, and Gage cut short any celebration over the completion of volume 1 and laid plans to finish volume 2. They expected to return to work that summer of 1881, but Stanton became gravely ill, likely with malaria, and her bouts with fever delayed their plans.[70] Gage was thoroughly exhausted from simultaneously working on big books while editing a newspaper, and she was in personal financial trouble. She decided to sell the *National Citizen and Ballot Box* to make time for renewed work on the *History*. With the October 1881 issue of the newspaper, after three and a half years as editor, she bade her readership "Good Bye."[71] The National Association no longer had a newspaper, something that had long been an important goal for Anthony.

The three finally set to work again that fall, with a still-weak Stanton. "Buried in manuscripts" for yet another fall and winter, they faced the usual profusion of material.[72] To solve this ongoing dilemma, they decided—once again—to divide one projected volume into two.[73] The second volume would span from "the first gun on Sumter, April 12, 1861," through "the Negro's Hour" of postwar politics, to the Sixteenth Amendment campaign of the early 1870s. Beyond these battlefields, the chronology of this volume also meant that it would have to narrate the internal split in the women's suffrage movement. "And here will come the tug of the work," Anthony confided, "for from 1866 began the differences" that pitted former allies against one another.[74] Once again, the women sat buried in documents and drafts for month after month. They had taught themselves how to write history in struggling through volume 1. Now, however, the history itself had become more vexing and complicated, for the postwar nation and the postwar suffrage movement alike. "Oh! to see the end of it all!!" Anthony exclaimed in May 1882, when she, Stanton, and Gage completed a second volume of 952 pages.[75] In the context of war, race, and Reconstruction, the line of descent "from . . . the Convention at Seneca Falls in 1848, down to the present moment, . . . has been only the repetition of a traditional prejudice," they charged, against all who would be free. During this trying postwar hour, movement veterans and movement heirs failed to take to heart the lessons of Seneca Falls: freedom for all. These short-sighted activists subsequently jeopardized national security, as fights erupted about which was worse, "prejudice against race" or "prejudice against sex." "But from this opposition on all sides, *true* woman suffragists learned their power to stand alone, and to maintain the right against large and honorable majorities"; "few only," they added, "were equal to the emergency."[76]

Volume 2 was at once a significant contribution to the burgeoning culture of commemoration of "the war for freedom and for the restoration of the national unity," as the *History* put it, and a significant intervention into the continuing politics of "reconstruction . . . on the broad principle of equal rights for all."[77] Stanton, Anthony, and Gage organized volume 2 around what they deemed the salient feature of the era, national politics, and therefore around the only suffrage organization that fully understood that, the National Association. Chapters on both are interspersed throughout, being explicitly in dialogue with one another. As the nation united, the main chapters explain, old colleagues divided.[78]

This was a cruel irony, which Stanton, Anthony, and Gage felt keenly as activists, and which they demonstrated powerfully as historians in a stunning opening chapter titled "Woman's Patriotism in the War." Surveying the diversity of women's war work—from nursing to canning, sewing, fund raising, soldiering ("when she could do so without detection"), burying, dying, strategizing, politicking, and voicing "the solemn lessons of the war: liberty to all; national protection for every citizen under our flag; universal suffrage, and universal amnesty." Besides biographical sketches of "a few representative women" such as Anna Ella Carroll, Clara Barton, Dorothea Dix, Elizabeth Blackwell, Josephine Griffing, Anna Dickinson, and a remarkable array of women in male uniform, the authors devoted much space to the proceedings of the Woman's National Loyal League, formed by suffragists (including Stanton and Anthony) to press for transforming the war into one for emancipation and equality. The chapter argued unequivocally that women had helped to free the slave and to win the war. So "how was it possible that when peace was restored," they asked, in an incredibly moving passage, that women "received no . . . general recognition for their services, which . . . have been concealed from the people and ignored by the government."[79] No less than "the black man in the 'Union blue,'" they argued, women had earned the right to vote through wartime service; and yet, the former had been remembered and rewarded while the latter had been quickly forgotten or erased. By arguing that historical amnesia undergirded women's continued oppression, they also underscored their faith in the emancipatory power of writing history and shaping collective memory.

In essence, Stanton and Anthony explicitly challenge what later scholars have called an "emancipationist" or "abolitionist" memory of the war (and their attendant political demands for civil rights). Those overt efforts to remember that slavery and freedom were the war's root cause had cast a shadow over a more emancipatory, more inclusive, and meaningfully "true" story of the American past, argued the *History*'s authors. They forwarded their own more fundamental (in their view) "truths" about the nation's past—"truths" that were erased in all national memories, "emancipationist" and "reconciliationist" alike—in what they viewed as a broader, more egalitarian *suffragist memory*.[80]

Stanton, Anthony, and Gage developed a suffragist memory of the war and Reconstruction as a powerful indictment of the Republican Party and, to a somewhat lesser degree, their longtime abolitionist allies for ignoring or distorting the primary lesson of the war: national protection for national citizenship. That this lesson had been willfully overlooked at the expense of women was made glaringly clear by the insertion of "male" into the Fourteenth Amendment's definition of citizenship and the omission of "sex" from the Fifteenth Amendment's protection of voting rights. But, the *History*'s authors note, "Miss Anthony and Mrs. Stanton, ever on the watch-tower for legislation affecting women, were the first to see the full significance" of the Fourteenth Amendment's gendered wording "and at once sounded the alarm."[81] For disrupting the precarious consensus of Radical Reconstruction they were attacked and condemned by former friends and longtime foes, but they rejected any compromise "of our one grand, distinctive, national idea—UNIVERSAL SUFFRAGE." At an 1867 convention Stanton thundered, "We alone have struck the key-note of reconstruction. While man talks of 'equal, impartial, manhood suffrage,' we give the certain sound, 'universal suffrage.' While he talks of the rights of races, we exalt the higher, the holier idea proclaimed by the Fathers, and now twice baptized in blood, 'individual rights.' To woman it is given to save the Republic."[82]

Volume 2 brims with indignation, understandably—but sadly and painfully, it also brims with elitism and racism—both in the Reconstruction-era woman suffrage politics it depicts and in the framing and assumptions of the book itself. The chapter on women's wartime patriotism provided an early glimpse of this in its critique of the Radical Republican party, which by 1881 had been in power for twenty years and yet still "refused to secure [women] in the same civil and political rights enjoyed by the most ignorant foreigner or slave from the plantations of the South."[83] Stanton and

Anthony did not let go of their Reconstruction-era views. To the contrary, they defended them. Stanton had been right at Seneca Falls, and she was right now—or so the story went.[84]

Their account of the 1869 convention of the American Equal Rights Association (the last before the split) is devastating in its continued insistence upon Stanton's foresight in that moment. Once again in the *History*'s pages, Stanton openly engaged Frederick Douglass in debate about the pending Fifteenth Amendment and said flatly that she did not "believe in allowing ignorant negroes and foreigners to make laws for her to obey."[85] Stanton and Anthony's continued faith in educated suffrage, evidenced throughout the volume, revealed deep-seated prejudices expressed far too widely and far too often to be explained as mere demagoguery. They spared no ink in presenting them. In her evening keynote address to that same 1869 convention, Stanton recast the icons of Seneca Falls (standing in for what is depicted as a broader vision of freedom) into a breathtaking provocation. "Think of Patrick and Sambo and Hans and Yung Tung, who do not know the difference between a monarchy and a republic, who can not read the Declaration of Independence or Webster's spelling-book, making laws for Lucretia Mott," she said. Although Frederick Douglass called her out for race baiting, she repeatedly made, and the *History* continued to print, similar statements. The National Association's appeal to Congress, as it debated the enfranchisement of black men in the District of Columbia in 1869, is but one example: "You have added insult to injury by exalting another race above her head: slaves, ignorant, degraded, depraved, but yesterday crouching at your feet, outside the pale of political consideration, are to-day, by your edicts, made her lawgivers!"[86] Referring to the need for educated suffrage and praising their own stance against the Fifteenth Amendment, the pair, almost alone, rightfully understood "that with the incoming tide of ignorant voters from Southern plantations and from the nations of the Old World, government needed the intelligent votes and moral influence of woman to outweigh the ignorance and vice fast crowding round our polling booths."[87]

❖ A Suffragist Memory of the War

The frequency, even ubiquity, of such rhetoric in the making of suffragist memory frustrates scholars' efforts to understand post–Civil War memory culture as a two-way contest between emancipationist or abolitionist ways of remembering the era, on the one hand, and reconciliationist memories that erase black freedom in favor of appeals to racism as a basis for reuniting white Americans, on the other. Although a suffragist memory certainly undermined both abolitionist and emancipationist memories of the war in its degrading depictions of black men, Stanton and Anthony never tried to forget or erase emancipation or to deny it as the war's true goal and legitimate outcome. Nevertheless, they disagreed both with the masculinist bent of abolitionist memory culture and with its tendency toward self-congratulation, which erased the contributions of women. Although abolitionist men imagined themselves in the radical vanguard of human rights, they had grossly violated human rights, Stanton and Anthony charged, by compromising and granting suffrage to "ignorant" black men but not "educated" white women.

At the same time, a suffragist memory, as embodied in and undergirded by the myth of Seneca Falls, undeniably diminished emancipationist memory, which was under attack in the 1880s, amid the end of Reconstruction and the advent of Jim Crow. Volume 1's insistence that Seneca Falls had inaugurated "the most momentous reform that has yet been launched on the world"[88] and put forward "the most important demand of the century"[89] implicitly and explicitly (not to mention, intentionally) undercut the claim that African American suffrage was urgent. "While we have always demanded emancipation and enfranchisement for the African race," Stanton wrote in the *Revolution* in 1868, "we have no great enthusiasm for 'negro suffrage' as a party cry, because it is too narrow and partial for the hour." Suffragist memory rejected both "the Negro's hour" *and* "the woman's hour" in favor of "everybody's hour."[90] This memory simultaneously ignored and helped silence the many other rights demands that were embodied in an emancipationist memory forwarded by blacks themselves, including demands for land, education, and freedom from violence. If the race baiting of "Patrick and Sambo and Hans and Yung Tung" represented suffragist memory and the myth of Seneca Falls at its worst, the myth of Seneca Falls also seemed to contain ideas at their best—namely, universal suffrage.

Yet if these twin ideas seem at first contradictory, they were, in fact, two sides of the same coin. Stanton and Anthony defined universal suffrage *as* educated suffrage—a point that is easy to overlook. Both women and blacks should be enfranchised, in their view, but that abstract right should then be limited by practical means testing. This would ensure that disenfranchisement took place on what they viewed as "just" grounds, as opposed to the unjust grounds of abstract categories such as "race" or "sex." Flowing from what Stanton "termed her *isms*, her radical Anti-Slavery and Woman's

Rights, her demand for liberty and equality for women and negroes," suffrage memory was a radical woman's version of Radical Reconstruction.[91]

Nevertheless, suffrage memory in general and the myth of Seneca Falls in particular found little space for black women, who were almost invisible in the *History*. At their most combative, feeling pressed to defend or declare "the woman's hour," the work's authors envisioned the woman in question as white and privileged. Black women do appear in the *History*'s excerpted documents, because they were present and a part of the debates. But they are invisible in the *History*'s larger narrative arc. They are not an integral part of the story. Where black women do appear, rather than talk for themselves, they are more often talked *about*—as in Paulina Wright Davis's remarks (made at a National Association conference) that, if anything, black women should be enfranchised before black men. "The black women," she said, revealing evolutionary theories of race, "are more intelligent than the men, because they have learned something from their mistresses."[92]

And where the *History*'s authors permit black women to speak, the women tend to be folksy caricatures angry over sexism. Black women certainly did care about sexism, but that concern is distorted in Stanton and Anthony's telling. Black women developed some of the most important intersectional critiques of the nineteenth century, examining the ways in which multiple forms of oppression interlocked. Put differently, black women refused to separate the two causes. Yet Stanton and Anthony permit them only one or the other concern: gender or race. Stanton and Anthony, in turn, pick for them.

For example, the *History* included a rendition of Sojourner Truth's speech before an 1850s Ohio women's rights convention. The speech is recounted by a white woman, Frances Dana Gage, who recalls a supposedly thrilling moment when Truth stood and spoke, salvaging the cause of women's rights. When Stanton and Anthony wrote the *History*, Truth was fairly well known among a general audience in the North, thanks, in part, to biographical pieces about her by leading literary figures such as Harriet Beecher Stowe, author of *Uncle Tom's Cabin*. Truth was also a member of the postwar feminist-abolition coalition, and she attended some National Association meetings, one of the few black women to do so. Revealing the ways in which white women often exoticized Truth, Stanton and Anthony introduce the speech by informing readers that Truth "is still living . . . though now 110 years old."

The document Stanton and Anthony print is full of drama. As tumult grips the meeting, with cries of opposition to women's demands, "the leaders of the movement trembled on seeing a tall, gaunt, black woman in a gray dress and a white turban . . . march deliberately into the church, walk with the air of a queen up the aisle, and take her seat upon the pulpit steps." She then rises and speaks, quelling the tumult and dispelling the opposition. Truth's words are reported in dialect (which in all likelihood was not the way they were actually delivered), further exoticizing her and demeaning her intelligence. She dispels stereotypes, one after another, about women's supposed frail constitution, using herself as a countervailing illustration and underscoring each point by repeating the phrase, "And ain't I a woman?" "Amid roars of applause, she returned to her corner, leaving more than one of us with streaming eyes, and hearts beating with gratitude." In this story, as it is here told and reprinted, Truth chooses sex over race. Stanton and Anthony used her to argue that black women endorsed and deferred to a white women's rights agenda as representing the concerns of all women, including those of black women. As the story continues, Truth returns to her seat, sits quietly, and takes her direction from white women, who then run the meeting. She is a supporting cast member, not a main figure. And, of course, none of this comes from Truth herself.[93]

Stanton and Anthony, in turn, omit speeches by women such as Frances Ellen Watkins Harper, who explained at the 1866 AERA meeting that black rights and women's rights were "all bound up together." Stanton and Anthony used the published proceedings of the 1866 AERA meeting to compose their chapter on the AERA. They excerpt those proceedings at length, but Harper's speech, which appears within them, does not make the cut.[94] Stanton and Anthony reference her by name only, listing her as a member of the financial committee.[95] Harper never speaks. And of the roughly four dozen engraved portraits included in the *History*, none features an African American woman.[96] Overlooking the intersectionality of black women's experiences, Stanton and Anthony posit a universal woman who is encompassed by the concerns of white, educated women. There is little awareness in the volume of the ways in which womanhood is marked as white, however. To the contrary, Stanton and Anthony present themselves as—and surely believed themselves to be—the "*true*" representatives of meaningful inclusion. "Our Woman's Rights Convention has now taken the broad platform of 'Equal Rights,'" volume 2 explains.[97] Yet in their support for an educational test, Stanton and Anthony advocated the disenfranchisement of large numbers of black women, not to mention uneducated white and immigrant women. Stanton and Anthony wrote a history that helped bury black and working women's insights that no universal womanhood existed. That history insisted that educated, white, middle-class women could, and should, speak for all women.[98]

This whitening of Stanton and Anthony's history, of their rights agenda, and of the memory they forged had a distinct, if dubious, political advantage in the political climate of the 1880s. As increasingly large numbers of white Americans threw an abolitionist and an emancipation memory overboard, Stanton and Anthony's suffragist memory argued that women's rights need not be discarded with them. Americans knew that abolition and women's rights were tightly linked, with many prominent figures participating in both. By 1880, with women's voting rights still deferred and an abolitionist memory falling out of favor, Stanton and Anthony surely worried that women's rights might fall victim to these larger shifts in national memory culture and national politics. They tried to create a women's rights memory that could compete in the national arena, and whether they intended to or not, their *History* supported white supremacists' arguments about the tragedy of Reconstruction. That tragedy was not the 1880s collapse of black rights, as abolitionists and freedpeople argued, but rather the enfranchisement of supposedly ignorant and degraded black men in the first place. Stanton and Anthony knew of civil rights violations in the South, but in choosing to ignore them, they participated in the rehabilitation of white Confederates. Black men's voting is never threatened in this account. Their voting rights are granted and presumably freely exercised—doubling the insult to white women. In Stanton's and Anthony's view, the tragedy of Reconstruction was not retreat from African American civil rights, but rather the continued disenfranchisement of white women. And as more and more people began telling the story of Seneca Falls in the 1880s (which held together the *History*'s logic), they reinforced the racial politics encoded in that collective memory.

✦ The *History*'s Outliers

Not everyone bought this gathering suffragist memory, including some suffragists themselves. Lucy Stone and Henry Blackwell were the project's most obvious detractors. In 1881, the American Association published a short eight-page pamphlet outlining its history, presumably in response to the *History*'s first volume, published that same year. It contained no interpretative frame, however; and at eight pages, it was hardly a match for the magisterial *History*.[99] It was likely a preemptive strike as well, anticipating the publication of volume 2, and an effort to keep alive a different suffrage memory, one that was not antagonistic to black male enfranchisement.

In 1882, as the *History*'s authors were finishing volume 2, Stone authored a brief history, giving her version of postwar divisions. Blackwell also authored a competing account. "The causes of the division . . . has [*sic*] never been publicly stated," Blackwell explained. The American Association, he continued, had avoided any mention of them in order to preserve decorum and harmony. But those causes "are so wholly ignored in the Woman Suffrage History . . . that it is due to the truth of history that they should be put into permanent form. The seceders," Blackwell continued, aiming at Anthony and Stanton the damning language of secession introduced in the 1878 *Cyclopaedia*, "were the framers of the National W.S.A."[100]

Stone and Blackwell each emphasized the same message: the catastrophic damage they believed Stanton and Anthony had done to the cause of human rights. If Stanton and Anthony used Seneca Falls to defend themselves, as they put it in volume 2, as the only "true woman suffragists," Stone and Blackwell indicted them. Where Stanton and Anthony had defended their choice to align with George Francis Train and Victoria Woodhull in the pages of their *History*, and omitted any discussion of damage those alliances might have caused, Stone and Blackwell underscored a darker message. Those alliances—not abolitionists' choices or Stone and Blackwell's supposed shortsightedness—had cost women the vote. Stanton's and Anthony's ruinous alliances and their countless other offenses to the public morals, Stone and Blackwell charged, reversed the dramatic gains in public and Republican Party support after the Civil War, bringing ridicule and "discredit" to the cause. Stanton and Anthony seceded and broke ranks "because they found themselves unable to control" the AERA, the majority of its members opposing their disastrous stances. The American Association had been repairing the damage the pair had caused to woman suffrage's public image ever since. The superior wisdom of their own course, Stone and Blackwell countered, was reflected in the Supreme Court's rejection of federal power to appoint voters and in the fact that the National Association had since adopted the main strategies of the American Association by working in state canvasses.[101] Here, Stone and Blackwell depicted themselves as the vanguard of the movement, countering the *History*'s depiction of the National Association as the main (indeed, only) instigator.

Stone's and Blackwell's accounts were ineffective for a number of reasons. They remained unpublished, and they were too short, making them no match for the *History*. Stone and Blackwell were also hampered by their choice of topic: the reasons for postwar antagonisms. They failed to reach back into the prewar period and market the American Association as *the* rightful heir of an antebellum organizing tradition, and this made their accounts less persuasive. Rather than appearing authoritative, they seemed to be harping on the distant past. They could criticize Stanton and Anthony's ruinous postwar choices all they wanted, but as Blackwell's account acknowledged, by the 1880s there were many activists who had not been involved during the divisive postwar era. All they knew of the split were legends, if anything. With the publication of the *History*, Stanton and Anthony effectively monopolized a movement origins tale, one that anointed them, and they consequently appeared to be the movement's more legitimate strategists. Rooting their story in an origins tale that excluded their rivals made them seem by contrast the movement's authoritative center. They appeared to rise above the fray. Stanton and Anthony had effectively put Stone and Blackwell on the defensive, particularly in the eyes of younger activists. Stone's and Blackwell's defensiveness was evident in their dissenting accounts. Although they tried to paint the National Association as the deviation, they continually explained why they had separated. In doing so, they inadvertently corroborated Stanton and Anthony's depiction of the American Association as the "seceders," as the ones who broke away from the antebellum tradition. At the same time, Stone's failure to see memory as an important resource and skillful strategy limited her effectiveness. She learned only slowly, with the *History* as her teacher, that memory productions were "not a diversion from the real political work of fighting for" woman suffrage; they were "key sites of that struggle."[102]

By this point, Stone had a difficult battle on her hands. The American Association found almost no place in the *History*, not surprisingly. Stanton and Anthony increasingly controlled not just their own story, but the American Association's too. American Association figures were almost entirely missing from the second volume. They appeared from time to time, but Stanton and Anthony continually relegated them to supporting roles, if they allowed them to appear at all. During the second volume's main story, full of drama and betrayal, the American Association comes up only once. Discussing the 1869 creation of the American Association in a single paragraph early in volume 2, the authors wrote: "During the autumn of this year there was a secession from our ranks, and . . . preliminary steps were taken for another organization."[103] As with their 1878 *Cyclopaedia* entry, their use of secessionist language is damning. Readers can trust that the American Association broke ranks, and not the other way around, because these women and men were on the wrong side of Seneca Falls, meaning they were on the wrong side of Stanton and Anthony. A dry, final chapter on the American Association closes the second volume. Yet the chapter falls so far outside the main arc of the narrative that it reads as mere appendix, and there is no explanation of what the organization stood for.[104]

When the second volume was published, the *Woman's Journal* published two more reviews, one by fellow editor Thomas Wentworth Higginson and another by Stone. Higginson also alluded to what he depicted as the damage caused by Stanton and Anthony, but he diplomatically never named them, his points of disagreement, or the *History*. He opened gently, alluding to the *History* and adding how "he was struck anew with the difficulty of writing history . . . correctly," given that "the same occurrence looks so differently to different people." "What is still more important," he continued, building toward his critique, "is the immense amount of omission that takes place in any narrative." Maybe it was better, he urged, "to let by-gones rest" and avoid disclosures about "antagonisms" within the movement, guided by the age-old wisdom that "no doubt there was wrong on both sides." "But it may be," he went on, "that on the one side there is little wrong . . . and on the other little right." "The progress of every great moral movement" has included "a great many unworthy . . . incidents," he acknowledged. Yet "in rejoicing over the result, we must beware how we canonize all the performers as saints." This last line was clearly aimed at Stanton and Anthony. The fact that the movement did not die with your folly, he seemed to be saying, is not reason to celebrate you now.[105]

Stone reprinted Higginson's passage about false saints in her review several months later. "No one reading this book would get an accurate or adequate idea of the *real* history of the woman suffrage movement," she charged. The line came almost as a plea. "It will be read with interest by the increasing numbers who come into our ranks," she acknowledged, but readers who have "no intimate knowledge of the facts in the case" could easily be misled, "giving large credit to the book as one of uncommon interest." In other words, young people and new converts should not be led astray by what seemed to be a compelling story. Stone was beginning to understand that the *History* was perhaps not as big a diversion from the real work of the movement as she had first concluded.[106]

The children of William Lloyd Garrison also seemed to understand that the stakes over where one dated movement beginnings were significant. They were working on a biography of their father when the *History* was published, and they redirected their narrative to do battle with it. Although Garrison's children declared that the results of the 1840 London Anti-Slavery Convention "do not immediately concern this biography," they felt compelled to address it nevertheless, precisely because of how Stanton and Anthony had positioned it in their *History*. That event "is commonly treated," the Garrisons wrote, pointedly citing the *History*, "with some injustice to the Grimkés [sisters Sarah and Angelina], as the initial cause of the woman-suffrage movement." The Garrison biography depicted women's rights as supported by abolition (and certainly Garrison remained an ardent supporter over his lifetime), and it depicted women's rights originating earlier than Stanton would have it, coming out of a collaboration with, not a necessary and justified rejection of, the abolitionist movement. In this biography, Garrison and abolitionists in general went in for women's rights "to their utmost extent." The Garrison children understood that Stanton and Anthony's damning of abolition, subtly rooted in the Seneca Falls origins story, was helping to damage an abolitionist memory, which they hoped to salvage.[107]

Over the course of the project, Gage had also begun to feel excluded from Stanton and Anthony's vision for the *History*. It is easy to imagine that after a tight collaboration extending over thirty years, Stanton and Anthony had a difficult time incorporating a third person into that well-established dynamic. They likely invited Gage to join the project because she was known inside the movement as a historian, keeping rich files and filling her speeches with historical material.[108] Gage's complaints had begun small. Early on, she felt cut out of various editorial decisions. Today, she is eclipsed in accounts of the *History*'s production, partly because of the meager archival record.[109] But Gage's eclipse began in the collaboration itself. In the autumn of 1880, as Anthony decamped to Tenafly to restart work on volume 1, a reporter from the *New York Herald* visited to interview Stanton and Anthony about their plans for a women's rights history. The reporter, Gage griped, "called over before I went down [to Tenafly], and they [Stanton and Anthony] coolly appropriated the entire History to themselves,—never hinting towards me. Consequently only Mrs. Stanton & Miss Anthony were put in as its editors, & from the Herald it was copied and went to France in a paper—with myself left out. I feel such things and they wrong me."[110]

When Gage saw the second volume in print, tensions rose, this time over substantive matters of content. The authors had agreed Gage would compose (among other things) the chapter on "Trials for Voting," and they roughly agreed on its content.[111] Gage sat down to painstakingly reconstruct events, finding out who had voted where and with what outcome. Her chapter reflected the variety and abundance of women's voting efforts, including her own. The chapter that went to press, however, looked considerably different from the one Gage had authored. Anthony subjected it to Stanton's edits as well as her own. Their revised chapter omitted the stories of other voting women and added extensive material about Anthony, who became its focus.[112] This was now a reoccurring piece of the Seneca Falls story: Anthony's nearly solo 1872 voting effort as the embodiment of the 1848 convention's promise. Never consulted and never imagining such a radical overhaul, Gage was furious when she saw the chapter in print. Determined to correct the record, she tore apart her house looking for the original manuscript—material, she underscored, the three women had "*agreed upon.*" But she could not locate it, and her fury grew.[113]

The problems concealed within the "Trials and Decisions" chapter were not anomalous. On another occasion, Anthony again excised Gage's authorial and historical contributions. Gage had carefully prepared records of her battles with a Syracuse minister for inclusion in the appendix of the *History*'s second volume, but Anthony decided to cut them. Gage did not discover this until after pages had been sent to the printer, when changes were impossible. Furious, she complained privately to Lillie Devereux Blake, another prominent New York suffragist, who was having her own trouble with Anthony.[114] "Miss Anthony is and always was lawless," Gage fumed. "Even Mrs. Stanton did not know it until the History was out. I would tell you many things, but tell you too much, that you may see Susan B. does as she pleases, despite the protests of her co-workers or her own promises."[115] "It has always been the policy of Susan and Stanton to play into each others [*sic*] hands and to hold each other up at the expense of all other workers," she later railed. "I have seen it and I know it."[116]

❖ Volume 3 (1876–1885): Anthony's *History*

The third volume would cover work in the individual states. "If we could only get some one in each state to write what has been done in their several localities," Stanton groaned, "we could see our way out of this labyrinth."[117] She and Anthony asked various local women to write up the details of actions in their respective states, and they tried to determine what had been done where. This volume too, in many ways, falls outside the *History*'s main narrative arc. It begins with a few additional chapters on the National Association, then takes up the states. Those stories, while important, are largely derivative. Despite the ways in which the postwar campaign was decidedly local, Stanton and Anthony described a movement that was hierarchical and leader-driven, obscuring the ways in which women exerted their own independence and forged their own strategies. Stanton and Anthony, in essence, described a campaign as they (particularly Anthony) believed it should be, rather than how it was. In essence, they wrote into the historical record a program for the future.[118]

Stanton, Anthony, and Gage would not resume work on the *History*'s final volume until the middle of 1885, however, three years after the publication of volume 2.[119] Immediately upon completing the second volume, Stanton had sailed for Europe. She went to visit her son and daughter, both of whom lived abroad, and she remained overseas for a year and a half.[120] Anthony departed for Nebraska, which put woman suffrage to a statewide referendum in 1882. The amendment lost that fall, and a frustrated Anthony vowed never to work for a state initiative again.[121] After this disappointing defeat, Anthony, too, sailed for Europe, at the beginning of 1883, in what was her first overseas trip and likely her first extended vacation. Well-wishers and the press assembled to see her off. "I don't see why I can't have a little fun the same as anyone else," she joked with reporters.[122] Anthony planned a six-month tour of Rome, Paris, Geneva, and London. But before embarking, she made a point of telling reporters that she would return "to this country with Mrs. Stanton . . . to write the third volume of 'The History of Woman Suffrage.'"[123] The pair sailed back late that fall, aboard the *Servia*, but the ongoing demands of their activist and personal lives meant they did not resume work on the project for another two years.[124]

From this point forward, the *History* would become Anthony's—and Anthony's alone. She had earlier shared copyright with Stanton and Gage. The three had drawn up a legal partnership agreement, establishing joint ownership and a plan to split profits equally.[125] The agreement surely reflected their awareness of the commercial potential in Civil War publishing. It quickly became clear, however, that there would be no profits. And for volume 3, Anthony assumed sole copyright. The costs of production were enormous, and borne solely by Anthony, who eventually invested $20,000 (the modern equivalent of $500,000) into the *History*.[126] Over the years between volumes 2 and 3, Anthony had been unsure about a publisher. Deciding to bypass offers from Fowler & Wells, who had published volumes 1 and 2, Anthony pulled the third volume and self-published it, bringing added editorial control. She moved the entire enterprise to her home in Rochester, New York. There, she hired the printer Charles Mann to set type.[127]

Stanton, Anthony, and Gage finally returned to the project in the middle of 1885.[128] The women again withdrew from their usual flurry of activities and battened down the hatches.[129] Anthony even forwent a chance to vote in the 1885 fall elections as part of another large protest action by New York women, arguing that she could not leave work on the *History*. The authors' division of labor remained the same, but Anthony now spent a good deal of time consulting with Mann about production in Rochester, where changes were sometimes made on the spot.[130] They expected to finish the volume that fall, but despite near-constant labor, their work continued well into the following year, 1886. The intense, focused work went on for so long that Anthony found it hard to think of much else. She balked in response to a reception invitation, the type of affair she had attended thousands of times before, fretting about what to wear and how to make conversation. "I shan't know how to behave—I am all rusted out—know nothing . . . but *history* plodding!!"[131] By May 1886, they had finished the last bit of proof.[132] Anthony then took a vacation, reporting that she was "off duty . . . for a month—resting—while the Indexer & the Binder finish up Vol. III.!!"[133] She had hired a newspaperman to carefully index all three volumes.[134] This consumed yet more time, but Anthony remained committed to the need for a good index in order to make the volumes more useful to readers. Then came "atrocious" delays in typesetting.[135]

By the end of 1886—a full ten years after work on the project had begun—the last and final volume of the *History* was complete.[136] The volume's preface expressed the authors' intermingled sense of duty and triumph: "The three volumes now completed we leave as a precious heritage to coming generations. . . . This has been to us a work of love."[137] As if in dialogue with their detractors, they acknowledged the complexities of composition and the impossibility of writing anything complete. "After faithfully collecting material for several years, and making the best selections our judgment has dictated, we are painfully conscious of the many imperfections the critical reader will perceive."[138]

The third volume, like the others, was a remarkable piece of social history. In important ways, Stanton, Anthony, Gage, and the fleet of activists who worked with them, contributing reports, reminiscences, and state chapters, were the architects of social history, well before that field existed. They insisted that the deeds of women, not just military generals and statesmen, were critical pieces of national life. They argued that women, even obscure, ordinary women, could and did change the course of history. The state chapters chronicled the names of women who became the first doctors in their states, the first lawyers, and more. There was a compensatory bent to their project, which aimed to show women as persons of accomplishment. "Many who study the past with interest, and see the importance of seeming trifles in helping forward great events, often fail to understand some of the best pages of history made under their own eyes," they wrote; "Hence the woman suffrage movement has not yet been accepted as the legitimate outgrowth of American ideas—a component part of the history of our republic—but is falsely considered the willful outburst of a few unbalanced minds, whose ideas can never be realized under any form of government."[139] Stanton, Anthony, and Gage insisted that women—even unknown women—were component parts of the national fabric. They therefore deserved recognition, via the extension of the franchise, the emblem of national belonging.

Very quickly, the three-volume *History of Woman Suffrage* began to stand as the official record of the movement, and this had important consequences for the evolving shape of the campaign. There was nothing else to rival it. Stanton, Anthony, and Gage were not the only suffragists to write history, but they were the only ones to try to map a single narrative onto a sprawling, multifaceted campaign. The other volumes suffragists produced tended to be biographical compendiums, which contained short biographical profiles of great women arranged alphabetically.[140] Such volumes were useful, important works of social history in their own right. But they did not offer an overarching interpretation over fifty-plus years. Neither did they build a massive, readily accessible archive. The *History* alone held that distinction. It was a seminal achievement and a tremendous legacy. Nothing like it had ever been produced by a U.S. social movement. The mantle of authority the *History* quickly assumed augmented the arguments contained within it. Over the coming years, it would help to transform the movement, remaking it into Stanton's and Anthony's image. This did not happen by mere publication alone. The pair had to market this story to activists, which they believed was merely tantamount to bringing suffragists the truth.

Thanks to Anthony's efforts, this magisterial project greeted the world robustly. Without a readership, the volumes could have only limited value and influence, which Anthony clearly understood. She took swift charge of advertising and distribution. She arranged for the "some 1,500" who already owned sets to receive the final volume.[141] And she worked on expanding sales, both within and outside the woman suffrage movement. Originally sold for five dollars, the complete set now sold for between fifteen and twenty dollars (between $360 and $460 in current figures), and sales were somewhat restricted by its steep price.[142] Anthony surely donated more copies than she ever sold. She eventually gifted over a thousand copies to university and public libraries around the world.[143] Not all deemed the set worthy of their shelves, however. Harvard University returned Anthony's complementary copy.[144] Unfazed, Anthony energetically donated copies to congressmen, labor reformers, descendants of women's rights pioneers, women's rights advocates, and more.[145] This was not only a project for posterity; it was intended to be a usable past.

After the publication of volume 3, Anthony took even greater control over the *History* by deciding to buy out her coauthors' interest in volumes 1 and 2. Her desire to donate copies widely conflicted with her coauthors' expectation of a profit from sales, outlined in the legal partnership they had drawn up back in the 1870s.[146] So Anthony proposed to buy out their shares. She was aided by Gage's tight financial straits. Desperately in need of money, Gage agreed to Anthony's proposition. The transaction did not proceed smoothly, however. Before paying her, Anthony demanded a written receipt from Gage for $1,000, the amount stipulated for the sale, which Gage provided. The check Gage received, however, amounted to only $840. An angry Gage complained that Anthony had her receipt "locked up in a safe," leaving Gage "powerless" to press for the additional money owed her. Gage was further outraged when Anthony bought out Stanton, who enjoyed relative material comfort, for twice what she had offered Gage.[147] Anthony now not only claimed to *be* the history of women's rights; she literally owned that history.

Upon completion of the *History*, the authors planned a grand historical pageant for Seneca Falls, unlike any hitherto staged in the United States. Back in 1883, as they headed home from Europe, Stanton and Anthony had discussed having a grand assembly of women from around the world in order to inaugurate an international suffrage movement as well as celebrate the fortieth anniversary of Seneca Falls.[148] Stanton closed the *History*'s final volume on that note: "Now that the volumes are finished, we are at liberty once more, [and] we shall ascertain as soon as possible the feasibility of a grand international conference in New York in 1888, to celebrate the fourth decade of our movement for women's enfranchisement."[149] The 1888 International Council of Women worked to bring the women's movement in line behind the story Stanton and Anthony had given ten exhausting years to constructing.

5. Commemoration and Its Discontents
✛ 1888–1898

"I think we ought to puncture the bubble that the Seneca Falls meeting . . . was the *first* public demand for suffrage," Lucy Stone began.[1] The National Association's 1888 International Council of Women (ICW) called together women from across the globe to celebrate the fortieth anniversary of Seneca Falls, heralded as the fortieth anniversary of the women's rights movement. The scope of the proposed commemoration was unparalleled. A U.S. suffrage organization had never staged anything like it. In anticipation of the event, Stone conspired with her sister-in-law about what to do. Stone could not resist the story by absenting herself from the gathering. She had already tried that by refusing cooperation with her rivals' anniversary celebrations and with their *History of Woman Suffrage.* To absent herself from an event such as this—a weeklong affair, drawing reformers from nearly all women's groups, of all political stripes, from around the world—would be to assent to her marginalization and concede defeat.

Stone and her sister-in-law, the pioneering minister Antoinette Brown Blackwell, who had also been invited to speak at the ICW, debated strategy for dislodging this steadily gathering origins narrative. In response to Stone's suggestion that the pair "puncture" the Seneca Falls "bubble," Brown Blackwell felt hemmed in. She agreed with Stone that Seneca Falls was not what Stanton and Anthony claimed for it. But she worried about decorum with any full-frontal attack on those claims: "nothing could be fittingly said publicly, it seems to me, about what Mrs. Stantons [*sic*] convention was *not.*"[2] It was not, in their view, the beginning of anything. Still, Stone and Brown Blackwell agreed to speak. Neither had any intention of celebrating the narrative under commemoration, however.

Anthony's bewilderment over Stone's proposed talk gave the first indication. "Lucy Stone—is to speak Pioneer's day," Anthony confided to a friend; "her title is to be—'The advance of the last fifty years'—just why she puts 50—instead of 40—I do not know." Clearly Stone meant to underline what

"Mrs. Stantons convention was *not.*" Yet the significance of Stone's appearance at the ICW, organized by the National Association and celebrating a narrative Stone opposed, was not lost on Anthony. Nor was the fact that the ICW might, at long last, be a unified showing of women, Anthony's longtime aspiration. *"All* of the '*seceders*' are coming now upon the invitation of the Old *National* W.S.A.!!!" she cheered.[3]

The stakes were nothing less than the shape and direction of the movement itself, which was about to undergo a seismic shift. Unification negotiations were underway between the National and the American Associations. At the end of 1887, Anthony had met with Stone and her daughter to consider a mutually satisfactory basis for union. Suspicion on both sides colored the discussions. Each side feared being swallowed up by the other. But pressure from various quarters meant those negotiations continued throughout 1888. How that merger might take place depended on the power each could leverage. Being able to claim authenticity as the movement's originator might lend greater strength to Anthony's negotiating power, something Stone seemed keen to avert. Stone could not avert this outcome, however. She had not attended to the making and marketing of collective memories, and it was now working to her detriment. With the 1888 International Council of Women, Stanton and Anthony helped sediment a Seneca Falls story in movement memory—a story that now rapidly gained in strength. The ICW staged the memory the pair had just laid out in their three-volume *History* —in a pageant unlike any yet seen. An important conference in its own right, the International Council of Women also announced a fully mature origins myth and served as a rehearsal for reunion. In those negotiations, the Seneca Falls story as it had cohered during the postwar years not only shaped events to come but also played a role in the fall of one of its architects and the rise of the other.

❖ A Pageant for the Pioneers

The call for the 1888 anniversary began: "The first organized demand for equal educational, industrial, professional, and political rights for women was made in a convention held at Seneca Falls, New York (U.S.A), in the year 1848. To celebrate the fortieth anniversary of this event, an International Council of Women will be convened under the auspices of the National Woman Suffrage Association."[4] But as National Association organizers were quick to explain, the event would not be confined to a discussion of women's political rights. "Formal invitations . . . will be issued to representative organizations in every department of women's work. Literary Clubs, Art and Temperance Unions, Labor Leagues, Missionary, Peace, and Moral Purity Societies, Charitable, Professional, Educational and Industrial Associations will . . . be offered equal opportunity with Suffrage Societies to be represented in what should be the ablest and most imposing body of women ever assembled."[5] Ambitions ran high.

The National Association assumed sole responsibility for the planning, which fell mainly to Anthony, Rachel Foster (Anthony's assistant), and May Wright Sewall (an Indiana suffragist). Originally intended as a platform to create an International Women's Suffrage Association, the ICW now morphed into a celebration of Seneca Falls.[6] Having conceived of the ICW in 1883,[7] Stanton and Anthony first announced the idea to the National Association's annual January meeting the following year.[8] They finally issued a call for the meeting three years later, in June of 1887, just as they finished the *History*.[9] Stanton, however, sailed back to Europe shortly after the third volume's publication, where she remained, returning just in time for the fortieth anniversary.[10] She was of little help with what organizers called "the herculean task" of necessary arrangements.[11] The affair, scheduled for March of 1888, was to be elaborate: a weeklong event drawing as many women from as many different domestic and international reform organizations as they could muster, all "to impress the important lesson that the position of women anywhere affects the position of women everywhere."[12] The event also now depicted all these disparate women, representing different reform organizations, and even different parts of the globe, as the offshoots of a common, shared American origin—a significantly expanded claim.

Almost immediately, Antoinette Brown Blackwell took aim at an early draft of the event's call, which underwent several revisions. She objected to its opening line, which called the meeting at Seneca Falls the first "public" demand for women's rights. Brown Blackwell's own experience challenged this chronology, and she protested.[13] Anthony then changed the language to draw less fire, while still attempting to make the same claim. The published invitation that eventually went forward instead characterized the Seneca Falls meeting as the first "organized" demand.[14] Neither Stone nor Brown Blackwell liked the revision.[15] Stanton's and Anthony's ongoing depiction of Seneca Falls as "first"—and, therefore, preeminent as well as sanctified— did not sit well with either of them. This produced the round of letters in which Stone and Brown Blackwell strategized about how to use their ICW remarks to deflate these claims.

The call underwent a few other notable changes. It was first titled, "The

Fortieth Anniversary of the First Woman Suffrage Convention." Organizers then changed the title into something more comprehensive—and more inviting—the "International Council of Women." The way the meeting at Seneca Falls was described also changed. Originally characterized as "the first public demand for the political rights of women," the meeting became considerably more all encompassing in subsequent rewrites, no doubt to increase the likelihood that more women would identify with the anniversary as well as with the Seneca Falls story itself. The final version extended that reach, depicting the 1848 meeting as "the first public demand for equal education, industrial, professional, and political rights for women."[16]

When the eight-day event opened in Washington, D.C., on Sunday, 25 March 1888, it was a grand showing. Some women's organizations at first refused to send delegates. But upon finding out what an elaborate, comprehensive affair it would be, they, much like Stone and Brown Blackwell, felt obliged to attend.[17] Others participated enthusiastically. In the end, representatives from nearly fifty women's rights organizations and eight different countries assembled.[18] To impose coherence on this tremendous showing, Anthony, Foster, and Sewall devoted each day to a particular topic. The opening day featured nine women from different reform organizations, all speaking on "Education." The second day saw "Philanthropies" in the morning and "Temperance" in the evening. Subsequent days had sessions on "Industries," "Professions," "Organization," "Legal Conditions," "Social Purity" (reserved for "women alone," given is delicate nature), "Political Conditions," as well as some religious observances.[19] (The topic of free love was, not surprisingly, absent.) The event was not the first international women's rights convention; others had occurred in Europe.[20] It was, however, the first international convention held in the United States by any U.S. suffrage organization.[21] The cost alone—over $10,000 (the modern-day equivalent of a quarter of a million dollars)—indicated the scale of the event.[22] Clara Bewick Colby, a Nebraska suffragist, moved her newspaper, the *Woman's Tribune*, from Nebraska to Washington, D.C., to issue daily reports.[23] Reporters from all sorts of organizations and newspapers swarmed the event.[24] Organizers also later published nearly 500 pages of proceedings, bolstering the event's gravitas. The proceedings featured one sole engraving, placed at the beginning to sanctify the assembly: an image of the departed Lucretia Mott.[25]

Celebrations of the 1848 Seneca Falls meeting bookended the ICW and reinforced the mythology now taking shape around it. The proceedings got under way in a "vast auditorium" decorated with flags from every U.S. state and from numerous nations. "The platform was fragrant with evergreens and flowers, brilliant with rich furniture, crowded with distinguished women, while soft music, with its universal language, attuned all hearts to harmony."[26] Anthony then rose and called the meeting's first day to order by announcing the reason for their gathering: "the first convention ever held in the world, by women."[27] (An outright falsity.) Following a hymn, Anthony continued, "The two moving spirits in originating the call and in carrying forward the [1848] meeting were . . . our sainted Lucretia Mott . . . and Elizabeth Cady Stanton, who is with us to-day." Just as Mott would be the only person depicted in the 1888 proceedings, hers was the only picture gracing the stage. Her portrait (likely from the *History*) was draped with sprigs of lily of the valley. Having reduced the Seneca Falls meeting to these two, Anthony proceeded to introduce Stanton, thought to be the only living organizer.[28]

A thunder of applause, a standing ovation, and a sea of waving handkerchiefs greeted Stanton. She looked out over the immense audience, which was standing room only. "We are assembled here to-day to celebrate the fortieth anniversary of the first organized demand made by women for the right of suffrage," she began. That gathering "started the greatest movement for human liberty recorded on the pages of history," she continued, taking clear aim at abolition and emancipation narratives. Although "it has been our custom to mark the passing years" with suffrage commemorations, for this particular anniversary, Stanton explained, "we decided [upon] a broader recognition of all the reform associations that have been the natural outgrowth of the suffrage agitation in the Old World as well as the New." With that, Stanton positioned *all* women's rights activism as arising from the same, shared origin, Seneca Falls, and *all* women's rights work as being mere variations on the most important of all reforms, suffrage. Temperance activists had founding myths of their own, but Seneca Falls was not among them.[29] And working women had rejected suffrage as the preeminent of all reforms, as well as suffragists' paternalism, not to mention suffragists' insistence that women shared a singular, universal identity. But Stanton ignored all this. "The key-note struck in this country in '48 has been echoed round the world," she added, imitating the language of the American Revolution. As proof, she offered the anniversary event itself, which drew persons or letters from "nearly every state in the Union, from Great Britain, France, Germany, Finland, Italy, Sweden, India, Denmark, Norway, and Russia." In her lengthy remarks, she directed listeners to the *History of Woman Suffrage*, buttressing its authority as the arbiter of the ICW's historical claims.[30]

Near the end of her opening address—which underlined women's fitness for self-governance, evinced a faith in U.S. exceptionalism, and offered assurances of success—Stanton urged women to cohere. "Above all things that women need to-day in their reform work is thorough organization, and to this end we must cultivate some *esprit de corps* of sex, a generous trust in each other." Stanton's call for women's "generous trust" surely caused Lucy Stone to shift uncomfortably in her seat. "A difference of opinion on one question," Stanton continued, "must not prevent us from working unitedly on those in which we agree." Stanton was asking women to unite around suffrage work (and by implication a federal amendment) and to put other issues aside—or at least to subsume them. "I think most of us have come to feel that a voice in the laws is indispensible to achieve success; that these great moral struggles for higher education, temperance, peace, the rights of labor . . . are all questions to be finally adjusted by the action of government." Stanton urged women, in essence, to return to the movement's essence, its most sacred object.[31] She expertly expressed Anthony's long-standing hope that women would unite under a single reform agenda, symbolized by Seneca Falls, to push for the vote in order to accomplish all else. Thus began the weeklong event.

The conference's penultimate day, 31 March, was given over to a session titled the "Conference of Pioneers," designed to celebrate the Seneca Falls convention and to honor suffrage movement veterans. The session boiled the *History*'s narrative down to its essence—the demand for the vote at Seneca Falls in 1848 as a genesis story—and it broadcast that story to a large and varied audience. Numerous "pioneers"—all suffragists—sat on the stage. Those identified as such—forty men and women in all—also received purple badges, known as pioneer badges, a lavender ribbon with "1848–1888" embossed in silver.[32] Once again, Anthony presided. After some notes of welcome, she introduced Stanton. Stanton delivered a lengthy reminiscence about the thrilling events surrounding the 1848 meeting. It followed the narrative outlines of the *History* almost exactly. Stanton began in London in 1840, where she and Mott conceived of the convention born of their outrage; and she ended with the fortuitous meeting of Anthony in 1851, once again referred to as "the Napoleon of our movement,"[33] which completed the story's arc. Stanton's account was full of drama and indignation. Stanton spoke at length about how, with Frederick Douglass's help, she carried the resolution for the vote (the only resolution to be mentioned) against great opposition. This ostensible first demand for suffrage was—once again, in this rendition—her accomplishment, nearly alone.[34] Stanton brought this story, and all that inhered within it, to an audience of women who had surely not heard it before, at least not in this detail. The audience's lack of familiarity with the story was underlined when Anthony, at the close of Stanton's speech, added: "I should have informed the audience that the picture on the platform is that of Lucretia Mott."[35]

Following a song, Anthony asked the six women on the stage who had attended Seneca Falls to stand as their names were read.[36] Leading figures in the American Association—Stone, Julia Ward Howe, and Mary Livermore—were also on the stage that day, but, having played no part in the 1848 meeting, they were ineligible to stand for recognition, a slight surely noticed by the large audience and the many members of the press in attendance.[37] Anthony then introduced a few select pioneers who offered prepared remarks.[38] There were about fourteen speakers in all, most aligned with the National Association. There were also references to letters from pioneers unable to attend, most of which were reprinted in Clara Colby's *Woman's Tribune* for general consumption.[39]

Frederick Douglass spoke after Stanton. He had, of course, been at Seneca Falls, but Anthony had not called his name when she asked those who had attended that first convention to stand. Douglass, age seventy, was now an eminent statesman, one of the most famous men in America. He described the Wesleyan Methodist Church in Seneca Falls, where the 1848 convention had taken place, as "the manger in which this organized suffrage movement was born." Describing that day, he added, "there are few facts in my humble life to which I look back with more satisfaction than to the one, recorded in the History of Woman Suffrage." (In his 1880s autobiography, however, Douglass failed to mention the Seneca Falls convention or his attendance.) He then addressed the ongoing feud over matters of priority and the questions of which was the greater insult, sexism or racism, and which movement had done more for human rights, refusing to be drawn into a battle. It was a great thing for friends of temperance, peace, and antislavery to have organized against drunkenness, war, and slavery, he began. "But it was a much greater thing . . . for woman to organize herself in opposition to her exclusion from participation in government." "War, intemperance, and slavery are open, undisguised, palpable evils," whereas the evils of sexism were at first "too occult to be seen." They were taken for granted as the way things were meant to be. Brave women, however, had changed all that, and he was proud to have lent a helping hand. All were necessary branches of human rights, in his view. He then celebrated Stanton and Anthony, with whom he had no open quarrel. He praised Stanton for her foresight in 1848, when she had insisted upon the vote, and he showered Anthony with honorifics. In all these ways, Douglass implicitly endorsed Stanton and Anthony's historical interpretations of the movement, acknowledging them as "eminent," and even preeminent. Whether he so intended or not, perhaps the most famous human rights activist in America cast Stanton and Anthony as the undisputed, universally acclaimed leaders of women since 1848.[40]

Next Anthony introduced Stone, calling her "one of the oldest and most persistent of the pioneers." "We celebrate to-day the fortieth anniversary of the first Woman's Rights Convention," Stone began, "but, long *before* . . . woman's rights was in the air." With that, she threw down the gauntlet. If she and Brown Blackwell had decided they could not explicitly challenge the event under celebration, they did so indirectly. Henry Blackwell, Stone's husband, who spoke next, joined them. "We celebrate the pioneers of the Woman's Suffrage Movement," Blackwell began, but there were "pioneers behind . . . [those] pioneers." And, he continued, "we . . . must place our garlands on the brows of our first parents."[41]

Like so many feminist-abolitionists aligned with the American Association, Stone and Blackwell credited women's oratory—rather than a convention—with beginning a women's rights movement. "Its sure day came, when the sisters Sarah and Angelina Grimké, and Abby Kelly [*sic*] began to speak publicly, in [*sic*] behalf of the slaves," Stone explained. She and Blackwell both recounted the awful persecution these women endured during the late 1830s—bravely surviving even arson, as one of the halls in which Angelina spoke was burned down over her head, so intense was public opposition. Defiantly, these three pioneers had earned women the right of free speech, and this basic right birthed all that had transpired since. This produced a different chronology and a different genealogy than the one Stanton and Anthony presented. Mott did not figure centrally. Stone, moreover, repeatedly referenced the Worcester convention of 1850, one of the few to do so.[42]

Stone offered her own life as a counternarrative as well. Detailing her early women's rights work, lecturing and canvassing, Stone carefully pointed out that she began this work in 1847, a full year *before* 1848. She was also careful to point out that she continued this work without ever having heard of the 1848 meeting in Seneca Falls. That meeting, she emphasized, was very little known in its day, suggesting—although not outright arguing—that it could not have birthed all that Stanton and Anthony claimed for it. It certainly did not account for the trajectory of Stone's life.[43]

Antoinette Brown Blackwell spoke next, and she also offered a different chronology. She recalled her days with Stone at Oberlin College, the first institution of higher learning to coeducate women with men. She described the ferment surrounding women's rights there before 1848—discussions taking place not in "public," harkening to the dispute over the wording of the ICW's call, but in private circles. "I was warned against Lucy Stone," she added, "because she would lead away a young woman by talking woman's rights." She and Stone soon formed a school club dedicated to women's rights—including the right to vote—between 1846 and 1847. "We called it a society," she continued, "but we met for improvement." And, she added, we "were organized *before* the woman's convention" at Seneca Falls. Her choice of the word "organized" was surely not coincidental, given that Brown Blackwell had already sparred with Anthony over that phrasing in the ICW's call. No matter how Anthony parsed Seneca Falls, whether as the first "public" or first "organized" demand, Brown Blackwell, Stone, and Blackwell marshaled facts, rattling off alternative names and earlier dates to underscore what Seneca Falls was *not*.[44]

Given the occasion, Stone, Blackwell, and Brown Blackwell could hardly hope to roll back the ascendant myth of Seneca Falls. They were outdone in the proceedings, as they had been in the pages of the *History*. Stone was an invited guest, not a convention organizer. She had not stood when the names of the original pioneers were called. And taking the stage that day, with Anthony presiding over the fortieth anniversary celebration for an event that Stone had not attended, she appeared subordinate. To compound matters, the daily ICW reporting in Clara Colby's *Woman's Tribune*, an un-official National Association organ, enraged Stone and Brown Blackwell, who felt it made "lies appear the truth." In the annals of women's rights activism, she and other pioneers, including many founders of the American Association, were reclassified as supporting cast members. Stone was no longer equal in stature, at least in the construction of movement memory.[45]

Smoldering tensions over the Fifteenth Amendment, now twenty years old, also crept into the proceedings. When Anthony introduced Robert Pur-vis, she delivered Stone, Blackwell, and Douglass a thinly veiled insult. Anthony introduced Purvis—a prominent northern black abolitionist—as an honorable man, willing to forgo his own voting rights until women's could also be secured.[46] Purvis had opposed the Fifteenth Amendment for its ex-clusion of women, one of the few African Americans to do so.[47] Purvis had not been there in 1848 to support Stanton, Anthony explained, but he stood by Stanton in 1869 when she insisted it was "more important for this Gov-ernment to have a wheelbarrow load of intelligent, native born, educated, tax-paying women than of ignorant plantation men."[48] Anthony implied that just as history had redeemed Stanton's controversial 1848 demand for the vote—evidenced by the grandeur of the 1888 anniversary itself—surely history also redeemed her controversial 1869 stand against the Fifteenth Amendment. That chapter was closed, but Stanton and Anthony had been right, Anthony insisted (and as the pages of their *History* explained). This left Stanton's reputation as originator, moreover, unsullied. Anthony's choice to reference the tensions of 1869 ignored the ongoing fight that Douglass and others had continually waged since 1860 to secure voting rights for black men, and basic civil rights for all black Americans, which the Fifteenth Amendment had by no means delivered.[49]

Although Stanton's pioneer status was supposedly unassailable, the commemorative focus on 1848 left Anthony herself in an awkward position. She was unquestionably a pioneer of the movement yet had not been present at its creation, as the *Washington Star* noted. "An interesting group at the council will be the survivors of those who attended the Seneca Falls meeting, forty years ago." The newspaper listed the names of more than a dozen such women "among these pioneers already here" and went on to name the "four members of the Anthony family here," including her younger sister Mary, who "were among the original pioneers" (conflating the Rochester meeting with that in Seneca Falls). The long paragraph concluded by paraphrasing Mary: "Miss Susan B. Anthony, though probably the best known advocate of woman suffrage in the country, was not, to use her sister's words, born into the movement. She did not come in until two years after the Seneca meeting was held." This bit of gentle, sisterly teasing nevertheless highlighted an underlying irony: Susan was increasingly identified with the growing myth of Seneca Falls. Although she was not "born into the movement," Anthony was not alone in believing that she was born to lead it. Unable to contribute her own memories, she transcended them by once again presiding.[50]

Anthony closed the Pioneer Day celebration by referring the audience to the *History of Woman Suffrage*. "If you want to know about any of these workers," Anthony explained, "this is the place where you will find it."[51] Throughout the weeklong event, speakers reinforced the authenticity of the *History* by using it as a touchstone again and again in reference to how the past had been.[52] The *History* was a tour de force and an invaluable resource. Still, not every woman agreed with the story enacted in its pages and at the ICW, as evidenced by Stone's and others' comments. But while a few would always question the myth of Seneca Falls, many more were becoming less and less aware that it even was a myth. The ICW represented the maturation, and in many ways, the triumph of the memory Stanton and Anthony had been creating for the movement.

✣ Negotiations for Union

On the heels of the ICW, the National Association held its annual convention, where it considered unification with the American Association. It was a historic debate that would produce realignments within the movement—realignments bolstered by the story of Seneca Falls. Pressure for unity had mounted over the 1880s. First, younger activists could not understand the reasons for national division.[53] Organizational division seemed to violate the way the movement, at least as the *History* presented it, was supposed to be, with a shared origin and presumably, then, a singular national body. Second, in January 1887, the U.S. Senate cast a historic vote. It took the first vote by any U.S. congressional body on a federal amendment for woman suffrage. That vote failed.[54] That same year, on the other side of the continent, the Washington territorial court overturned woman suffrage on a technicality. Washington had granted women, black and white, full voting rights in 1883, but the court now reversed that gain.[55] Also in 1887, the U.S. Congress stripped full voting rights from Utah women.[56] All these developments suggested that unity might help sustain the movement over what now promised to be an even longer battle, as gains reversed. Third, local, state, and regional suffragists continued pressure for unification, something many had demanded since national forces divided back in the 1860s.[57] Finally, Stone's daughter wanted unification. She shared her mother's suspicious stance toward Stanton and Anthony, but her mother was almost seventy and in mixed health. Alice Stone Blackwell worried for her. She wanted to relieve her mother of the burden of managing the American Association. She also wanted to prevent its management falling upon her, once her mother could do it no longer. Stone, who initially opposed the idea of a merger, eventually relented.[58] In the fall of 1887, Stone reached out to Anthony and made an overture for unification.[59]

Stone, her daughter, and Anthony, along with Rachel Foster (Anthony's main lieutenant), met to discuss the idea in December of 1887, a few months before the ICW. There was plenty of wariness on both sides. Because she had suggested the meeting, Stone began by laying out her vision for a united society. She proposed that the two national groups unite under a new name, the United Suffrage Associations (in the plural). All other societies (which were not consulted) would be auxiliary to this new umbrella organization. The National and the American Associations could continue their work as branch societies, each free to pursue state or federal suffrage as they best saw fit. There would be one annual national meeting to end what Stone called "opposition between suffragists." Neither Stanton, Anthony, nor Stone would hold the presidency, in deference to mutual suspicions of self-promotion.[60] Anthony rejected this last provision. Stone further suggested that any united organization pursue the vote in its many forms, including municipal and presidential suffrage, and not simply a federal amendment. Anthony replied that municipal suffrage was fine, but that presidential was a waste of time. The discussions were robust, and they covered much ground. At the conclusion of the meeting, Stone and Anthony each agreed to appoint seven members to a joint committee to enter into negotiations and come up with a nonbinding plan. Once a satisfactory plan was brokered, each seven-member group would bring that proposal to the executive committees of their respective organizations for larger consideration.[61]

There was plenty of internal debate within the National Association around the question of union, some of which turned on where Anthony, a unification supporter, was steering the organization. Stanton threw up her hands, showing her intolerance for organizational politics and her frustration with Anthony's growing acceptance of a suffrage-only stance. "The National Association has been growing politic and conservative for some time," Stanton wrote a friend; "Lucy and Susan alike see suffrage only. They do not see religious and social bondage. Neither do the young women in either association, hence they may as well combine for they have only one mind and one purpose."[62] Gage opposed the idea of union: "Our Association has been steered into an orthodox pit-hole by Miss. Anthony & her aids. . . . Great watchfulness and great circumspection is needed, as . . . orthodoxy and social recognition are our great enemies."[63] Anthony moved ahead despite criticism. "I suppose your feeling of my change is the same as that of Mrs. Gage and Mrs. Stanton," she wrote a friend, "that is because I am not as intolerant of the so-called Christian women as they are—that therefore I have gone, or am about to go over to the popular church."[64] "They say I am eaten up with a desire to make our movement popular."[65]

Over the 1880s, the religious conservatism of the WCTU changed the face of the suffrage movement, as it exerted greater and greater influence. On the ground, it was hard to tell the two movements apart. WCTU recruits expanded the suffrage movement's base and brought it into the mainstream of American politics, but older workers worried about the effect this transformation would have on the movement's ability to pursue and win meaningful change, given the WCTU's deference to gender norms and narrower vision of social and economic reform. Whereas earlier activists had imagined voting as the gateway to a myriad of changes, that conception now narrowed. Focusing on the vote as an end in itself, and less on what it ultimately might do, allowed greater unity across reform interests—many of which did not otherwise see eye to eye. But this suffrage-only orthodoxy that seemed to undergird the pursuit of unification concerned women such as Gage and even Stanton.[66]

The National Association committee of seven brought the newly brokered unification plan to the organization's April 1888 convention, on the heels of the ICW. The main order of business transpired within the executive committee, which met separately from the larger convention. After extensive debates about who had a right to participate and vote in the executive session, the committee of seven made its report. They recommended against unification. They reported being surprised by their own recommendation. And they acknowledged that the executive committee was surely surprised by their recommendation as well. They explained their reasons. They could not accept the American Association's proposal that neither Stanton nor Anthony assume office in the united society, at least for the first year. Second, although the differences in method between the two organizations were not as great as they once were—each conceding to some degree the strategy, or strategies, of the other—they still believed that the suffrage movement would be "impaired instead of strengthened by a union." Unification, they predicted, would be marred by infighting. Better to leave the organizational separation, exhibit good will on all sides, and allow each to work in their own way.[67]

Considerable internal debate followed, in which several women also expressed their unwillingness to overthrow the pioneer and originator of the movement, Stanton. A significant number wanted unification, although they agreed the terms hammered out by the committee of seven were unacceptable. So they appointed a second committee—this time of eight women—to confer with the original committee of seven. That new, expanded committee reversed direction and recommended unification. They rejected everything that had been negotiated to this point, however. They rejected the American Association's proposed constitution, bylaws, and list of proposed officers for the new society. They could not approve of governing methods for a society that did not yet exist, they explained. So they came up with a counterproposal, a brand new idea for unification. They suggested that the officers of both societies "unite in calling a joint convention to consider the terms of union." This convention would be empowered to adopt a constitution and elect officers. The decision of this joint convention should be considered binding, each side acceding to its terms. This was, in some respects, the National Association's way of stalling for more time, being unable to come to agreement within the executive committee about what a new society ought to look like. But because the American Association awaited their reply, they had to send something. So they settled upon this vague endorsement of union, drafting a letter to Blackwell (chair of the American Association's unification committee) outlining this new proposal. Although their reply postponed any decision on the details of unification, it salvaged the possibility.[68]

One particular debate within the National Association's executive session revealed how questions of strategy that had long divided the National and the American Associations were not, by this point, a dead letter. The question of how to pursue suffrage, at the federal or state level, remained vital. But this question was now joined by debates over the type of voting rights to pursue, full versus partial. The American Association and state and local suffragists—along with the WCTU—put partial suffrage goals at the forefront of the campaign. During the ICW session on politics, there had been papers on both municipal and school suffrage, revealing how much partial suffrage strategies now permeated the campaign.[69] The 1888 National Association's annual convention further underscored this. During the executive session, amid discussions about what a new society ought to look like and what work it ought to do, Anthony sparred with members over the type of suffrage it ought to pursue. So many conventioneers were brimming with opinions that speakers were required to keep their comments to one minute. In the end, Anthony salvaged the idea of a federal amendment as an organizational goal, while suggesting "future action in the states," including partial suffrage actions, be left "to the discretion of the members."[70]

Upon receiving the National Association's new terms, the American Association's committee replied within days. They were unanimous. Their seven-person committee had no jurisdiction to effect a union outside the terms endorsed by the American Association's membership at its annual 1887 meeting. The committee had been tasked with negotiating on that basis: outlining a constitution and officers for the first year, to be brought, once negotiated, before the American Association for another vote. Agreeing to the National Association's new proposal would violate procedure, and any action on the National Association's proposal would have to wait until the American Association's next annual convention, when it could be taken up by the membership. This constraint on the committee's power, they continued, had been fully explained in advance to Rachel Foster of the National Association, so the committee expressed some confusion about the National Association's reply. "Hence we regret your rejection," they concluded, "since your action, unless it can be modified, necessarily puts an end to the negotiations for the present year."[71]

The American Association's committee then added several postscripts. The first was perhaps in hopes of rekindling talks. They referred to "a rumor" that they had prohibited either Stanton, Anthony, or Stone from being first president, and they countered that "this was not the case." They thought it desirable that those connected with the original division step aside, in the interest of harmony. For this reason they had proposed Mary Livermore (who had strong temperance ties) for president, but they were more than happy to entertain alternatives. They then sounded a more somber note, expressing concern over making sure union was accomplished through democratic means, with mutual concessions. The National Association's proposal of a joint convention left open the possibility that one society could dominate the other and obliterate it entirely, they pointed out. (There were complicated negotiations as to how voting representation on each side would be counted.) As long as the organizations were separate, unification must be accomplished through a majority vote *within* each. Only then could it be accepted as the legitimate will of both parties, as well as a blending of both societies, rather than the domination of one over the other. This was their only requirement.[72]

For the time being, the proposal died, but it was soon picked up once again. At the end of 1888, the American Association held its annual convention and revisited the question of unification. There, in a smaller business session, they declared themselves to be "in favor of union, on equitable terms." They authorized yet another committee to meet with the National Association in order to hammer out new terms. Two months later, in January of 1889, the National Association convened at its annual convention, and they also appointed a committee to negotiate terms. Their committee, like the American Association's, included most of the original committee members, plus several new faces.[73] The two committees sat down together, with Anthony now presiding, to draw up a provisional constitution and a slate of suggested officers. (Anthony had not been part of the original committee of seven.) The two sides eventually agreed to a new name, the National American Woman Suffrage Association (NAWSA). They hammered out a variety of governing details. And they deferred the election of officers—still a contentious topic—to NAWSA's first annual meeting. Each satisfied, they returned to their respective associations for an internal vote.[74]

Here things began to go awry. National Association members began accusing Anthony and other unionists of underhanded tactics in order to railroad through a favorable vote on unification. A significant contingent within the National Association continued to oppose a merger, agreeing with the original recommendation against union. They worried about the integrity of the National Association's ideological mission. Consequently, disagreements marred the executive session, where Anthony and other unionists sparred with those opposing unification.[75] Anthony became the de facto chair of that session because Gage, who, as chair of the executive committee, should have chaired it, was away in Dakota Territory visiting family. What happened next produced considerable controversy. Unlike the American Association, which put the proposed constitution and question of union to a mail vote of all its members, the National Association voted upon it in executive committee (a smaller, select body) and declared its decision binding. Late into the night, on the convention's last day, after a large number of out-of-town women had departed to catch transportation home, Anthony called the vote. It passed: thirty for unification, and eleven against.[76]

When Gage got word that the executive committee had met to consider and approve union, she was furious. Had she known the question was to be decided, she and others would have approached the annual meeting very differently. Gage would have been present. But she received no notification that the question would be raised, which she fumed violated the association's constitution. Any change to the governing structure of the organization required advance notice, she protested.[77] Together with a handful of other National Association members, Gage drafted a lengthy, heated protest statement, which they had printed and distributed. Signers included Olympia Brown and Harriette Shattuck, who had been members of the original committee of seven (opposing unification), along with signatories Charlotte F. Daley, Marietta M. Bones, and Harriet Robinson (Shattuck's mother, who had sparred with Anthony over the *History*). They titled their protest "A Statement of Facts: Private."

The dissenters raised several distinct issues. They protested unification itself, for merging a federal strategy with a state-level strategy, something they opposed. They especially challenged procedure. "The work of 'union,'" they charged, "was accomplished in a packed committee."[78] Gage and her coauthors alleged that several women who opposed unification were removed from the committee and replaced with supporters. The National Association's governing constitution further required that any radical change in the organization, such as its dissolution, needed advance announcement. Yet none was given. As a result, unification—which was, from their point of view, the dissolution of the National Association—had not received sufficient consideration within the organization, and its members had not consented to this action. Gage and her coauthors further objected to the executive committee's presumption to speak for the entire organization. When Clara Colby, an executive committee member and cosigner to the protest statement, had objected during the proceedings and argued the question ought to be put to a vote of the membership in a written ballot, the "packed committee" had squashed her motion. Debate over the proposal, then, never reached the convention floor, and members were not allowed a voice. That the executive session took a vote at nearly midnight, when many had departed, was further shocking.[79] "The 'thirty,'" Gage and her compeers charged, "violated the principles of a just government, and of the primal woman suffrage demand—individual consent—'the consent of the governed,'—when they thus assumed to control the opinions of the hundreds of individual members of the National Woman Suffrage Association."[80]

Gage had for some time suspected that Anthony was trying to capture control of the association and steer it toward union, but she never imagined that such an important matter would be decided in this fashion.[81] Anthony's sometimes-domineering style was known, but even some of her close allies were astounded. Anthony's "word is the parliamentary law of the meeting," a reporter had earlier and somewhat sardonically noted; "Women . . . are saved any parliamentary discussions such as arise in the meetings of men; they acknowledge that she is an autocrat. All are agreed that no better system than the absolute control of Susan B. Anthony can be devised."[82] Still, Gage was shocked to discover Anthony heralding unification as a fait accompli.[83] "The full extent of the treachery by which we were sold has not yet been fathomed and maybe never will," Gage confided, ". . . unless persons cast aside . . . [a] blind belief in some who were prominent in this 'union.'"[84]

❖ Anthony's Ascent and the New Face of Organizing

The leadership of the newly unified national organization had yet to be decided. That question was deferred for a year, until the two organizations met in 1890 for a joint convention to ratify the union. A number of people suspected Anthony had designs on the presidency. From the beginning of negotiations, Stone had predicted it. When Anthony first rejected Stone's suggestion that none of the three women preside over a unified association, Stone had confided: "She so much wishes to be president herself! To bring her to the top at last would be such a vindication she cannot bear to forgo it."[85] When the National and the American Associations met in February 1890 to formally constitute the new National American Woman Suffrage Association, it became clear that Anthony intended to lead the new organization. Anthony deflected the appearance of self-interest, however, something helped by the origin story she had been laying out over almost two decades. She could not have envisioned her ascent to leadership over a unified campaign when she first began telling that story, or even when she wrote the *History*, but she now deployed that usable past to help reshape the present.

A national organization under a single leadership that set agenda and coordinated policy among state and local workers had long been Anthony's dream. She had felt continually frustrated with the expansion in the suffrage movement during the 1870s, as it headed in myriad different directions. And she had felt frustrated with the inexperience of new recruits. She believed that if suffragists only united behind her and Stanton's experienced lead, suffrage could be won. For all these reasons, she admired the centralized, hierarchical structure of the WCTU. "Your thorough organization is my pride," Anthony told WCTU president Frances Willard; "it is the result of *one head* working to one end."[86] The model of the WCTU's thorough organization enhanced Anthony's wish to remake the suffrage movement in its image. During the initial meeting with Stone, back in December of 1887, Anthony had referenced the WCTU's example. Any unified national organization "really ought to be organized thoroughly, like the W.C.T.U.; every local society paying a portion of its annual fee to the State Association, and the State a part to the National Association," she told Stone.[87] This desire—for a centralized, hierarchical organization, which she believed could usher in victory—helped drive Anthony's desire for unification, and it informed her approach to its leadership.

In February of 1890, both the National and the American Associations met in Washington, D.C., to dissolve themselves and form a new national organization. Both sides had agreed that NAWSA's president would be chosen immediately before the opening of the convention's first day. Before that joint meeting, each association held a final meeting of their respective executive committees in order to conclude organizational business and to officially end their existence. These respective executive committees then met jointly, before the opening day of NAWSA's convention, to formally consummate union and elect the new organization's officers.

As a candidate for president, Anthony ran into trouble. "I have letters which accuse me of having favored the union solely for personal and selfish considerations," she explained. She defended herself by appealing to the now well-established narrative of a singular movement founded at Seneca Falls. Withdrawing her name, she instead urged a strong vote for the undisputed founder. "Now what I want to say to you is, don't you vote for any human being but Mrs. Stanton. . . . I want her elected."[88] Privately, Anthony knew full well that Stanton had no intention of heading the new organization. She disliked organizational politics, and she had a ticket to sail for Europe, where she intended to remain. In fact, neither Stanton nor Stone participated in the deliberations of the executive committees. Stanton exempted herself, and Stone, who had energetically helped run the American Association for twenty years, was too ill to travel. She remained at home in Massachusetts, missing this historic occasion and a crucial chance to influence events and to intervene in how the movement's history was used. This too enhanced Anthony's ability to steer the vote. A Washington, D.C., newspaper noted strife in the proceedings, observing that suffragists might be "of the opinion that serious breaches of parliamentary usage are committed through ignorance or with intent."[89] When it came time for the vote, Anthony strongly encouraged a large turnout among National Association members, so that votes for Stanton might be cast in a larger number. Stanton was elected president; Anthony, vice president; and Stone, chair of the executive committee.[90]

Stone, "choking and breathless" from respiratory problems, waited at home for news from her husband and daughter, both in attendance. She had long believed that if she held the high ground and refused to spar openly with Stanton and Anthony, the "better doings" of the American Association would, over time, become clear to all. Conversely, she believed that time—in essence, history—would prove Stanton and Anthony to be liabilities within the movement. But news of the vote brought a sense of deep foreboding. She regarded her election to chair of the executive committee as nothing more than "complimentary." She understood that Anthony was now in charge of the vast organization she had helped build and lead for twenty years, and she felt dread. Stanton and Anthony's joint election, on the heels of the ICW, where she had been reclassified as a supporting cast member, could only mean trouble for Stone and, she feared, for the American Association's long record of good work. She anticipated with apprehension "the humiliation which will [now] be poured upon our side—only for the cause we would not bear it." For her part, Stanton was not wild about being in close proximity with Blackwell, who continued to sling arrows at her. The merger was anything but harmonious.[91]

On NAWSA's opening day, Anthony presided—both figuratively and literally. Stanton appeared fleetingly, and only because Anthony had pressured her to be present. Although she was elected its president, she had little enthusiasm for the new organization. Stanton spoke briefly at the convention's opening session, to a sea of applause. She then immediately sailed for England (before the convention had even concluded). In Stanton's absence and as NAWSA's vice president, Anthony chaired the meeting and ran the new organization. She presided over it in the coming year, and she steered its course. It was now effectively hers. If Stone had felt confident that history would, over time, prove her right, she had not attended to that history carefully enough. Stanton and Anthony had given the movement a collective memory that cast them as its embodiment, and they now—in no small part due to that memory—stood as its supreme heads.

Anthony's critics within the National Association protested yet again. Gage, Robinson, and Brown boycotted NAWSA's first convention along with Anthony's newfound power. Although NAWSA declared all state organizations to be affiliates of the national parent body, Robinson flatly refused to merge her state chapter, the National Woman Suffrage Association of Massachusetts, into NAWSA. She feared her organization's long-lived autonomy and its own goals would come to an end. Together with her daughter, Harriette R. Shattuck, Robinson kept the National Association of Massachusetts alive and independent for several years, maintaining a robust membership. Anthony, however, kept constant pressure on the group to unite with NAWSA's Massachusetts branch. By 1892, Robinson and her daughter both resigned from the organization. As Robinson's biographer observes, the "union in 1890 . . . marked the beginning of the end of suffrage activity for the Robinson women." Both had been prominent activists for many years. Robinson's women's rights activism dated to the antebellum years, when she had been a Lowell mill girl. Their departure from the movement was the result of what both felt was the narrowing of national policies after the merger.[92]

Gage and Brown, on the other hand, protested by forming a new, rival association, the Woman's National Liberal Union (WNLU). Having advertised well in advance, they held their first national convention in Washington,

D.C., in February 1890, just days after the NAWSA meeting—in an explicit challenge. The Woman's National Liberal Union had a short-lived newspaper, the *Liberal Thinker*, which Gage edited. Its first issue featured numerous articles critical of NAWSA. Opposed to the breaches of democratic procedure and what she viewed as Anthony's self-aggrandizement, Gage was also suspicious of the growing influence of conservative Christian women within organized suffrage ranks—particularly the influence Willard and the WCTU now played within NAWSA. Anthony courted and befriended Willard. That willingness of Anthony and others to sanction the influence of evangelical Christians within the movement led Gage to think that NAWSA could no longer do the work necessary to emancipate women. "The first object of our association is for the purpose of showing the cause why woman has not been enfranchised," Gage began; "It is owing to the teaching of the church." And she called Willard "the most dangerous person upon the American continent today."[93]

Clara Foltz of California also denounced NAWSA for threatening the cause. In contrast, she praised the WNLU for promising to rescue it. "I do think that the women who have had control of the Woman Suffrage movement have led to its defeat; I do think that the course pursued by the women who have assumed its management has brought it to such a condition that but for this brave movement [the founding of the WNLU] it would have been an ignominious and disgraceful pass." This "has been long understood," Foltz continued, "by those who are brave enough to think without the consent of . . . priests." "Mrs Gage in her heroic calling of this convention has shown that she appreciated the situation," Foltz concluded.[94]

Gage's new organization never got off the ground. After a successful inaugural convention, drawing women from around the country, the group faltered, evidently due to a lack of resources. Anthony was a staunch opponent of the group. She did not tolerate divisions in the ostensibly unified suffrage ranks. It went against her goal of a singular movement under "*one head*," which she believed could bring about victory. She actively discouraged women from attending or joining the WNLU. Anthony also absolutely forbade Stanton—who was considering supporting the group because of its attack on conservative Christianity, an interest Gage and Stanton shared— from supporting the WNLU.[95] Anthony needed Stanton firmly in her camp. Stanton was the originator, the pioneer, the legitimator of NAWSA as the restoration of a supposedly unified past, centered in Seneca Falls. Still, Stanton, who always cared more deeply about ideas than movement politics, sent a letter to the *Liberal Thinker* supporting its philosophy.[96] Stanton explained that although she supported the WNLU's positions on religious dogma, she "could not honorably lend my name or influence to what is in the nature of a secession from the suffrage ranks," thereby honoring Anthony's wish that she remain tied to NAWSA.[97] This prompted Gage to call Stanton "a traitor to what she knows is right."[98]

The shape of organizing now looked quite different than it had in the 1870s. NAWSA was the preeminent national organization, and it strove to create a centralized, hierarchical movement. In 1892, NAWSA members elected Anthony its president, a position she would hold until her voluntary retirement in 1900. At that point, she would appoint her successor. NAWSA was very much Anthony's. The younger women within it, who were fast rising through the suffrage ranks, women such as Iowa suffragist Carrie Chapman Catt (also a WCTU member), were known as Anthony's "nieces." She actively trained these recruits, although they did not always do her bidding. The degree to which Anthony could control the new organization is an open question. Yet more than anyone, as one historian points out, she had the stature to keep this large and increasingly disparate coalition together.[99] By the 1890s, NAWSA included not only temperance women but also groups such as the General Federation of Women's Clubs, and many more. It was a sprawling coalition held together by a common goal but not an ideological vision. Anthony had always, even now, held an expansive notion of what the vote could and should do.[100] But it was increasingly eclipsed by the organization's focus on a single goal over a broader vision—a shift Anthony helped oversee.

Stone was only peripherally involved in NAWSA after its creation. She tendered her resignation from the executive committee in 1891. The membership, out of deference, refused to accept it, but she was never very active in NAWSA. She continued to work on her own, but age and illness restricted her activities. When able, she joined her daughter and husband in continuing to edit the *Woman's Journal*, and she traveled, although not much. Stone was able to frustrate one of Anthony's long-standing wishes, however. Ever since having to sell the *Revolution* in 1872, Anthony had dreamt of a single, centralized woman suffrage newspaper under her command. Much to Anthony's chagrin, the *Woman's Journal*, which Anthony presumed would be a NAWSA organ, remained under Stone and Blackwell's ownership, who continued to criticize Stanton and Anthony in its pages—more evidence that at least among movement veterans, unification was a fraught affair.[101]

By the early 1890s, few if any independent state societies still existed.

State societies were made auxiliary to NAWSA, and NAWSA's governing structure made it somewhat impervious to the influence of individual members. This was part of its hierarchical structure. Whereas individuals could have joined the old National Association and voted as a member, without any mediating organization, voting members within NAWSA were now appointed and limited. Activists had to first join a state society, then enter NAWSA as a delegate from that state society. Voting within NAWSA was on a delegate basis, with states appointing delegates to the national organization in the same proportion as that state's congressional representation. This organizational structure reflected that of the old American Association. It meant individual members were disenfranchised, and the old structure of the National Association was obliterated. One could neither join NAWSA directly nor vote in NAWSA as an individual, as was previously possible in the National Association. The state-delegate structure replaced individual representation and vastly narrowed who could participate in NAWSA governance. This worked against the decentralization of the late 1860s and the 1870s, and women such as Gage and other NAWSA dissenters criticized this governing structure for being undemocratic.[102]

Gone too were the independent lecturing women. The vast expansion of the lyceum that had taken place during the Reconstruction years had now collapsed. Over the 1880s, opportunities for suffrage lecturers contracted, as public entertainment shifted to minstrel shows and other acts. Audiences were less and less willing to turn out in large numbers for reform topics. The fervor for that kind of intense political discussion, generated by the Reconstruction-era ferment, had subsided. Women still lectured, but they now needed the independent means to do so or to be among the select few whom suffrage organizations could afford to pay. This underscored another transformation. A woman now had to have either independent wealth or the imprimatur of an organization to find a place in the lecture field. The possibility of earning a living on the lecture circuit during the immediate postwar years meant it was open to all. But this was no longer true. Olympia Brown despaired over the shift. Her business had collapsed, and she had lost her life savings. "As you say," she commiserated with Colby, "one can get nothing by lecturing."[103] Observing the rising star of Carrie Chapman Catt, a popular field agent, Colby noted how Catt's independent wealth allowed her to lecture before audiences—in essence, to be an active suffragist. She is "of course, . . . well fixed and can afford to give her time and expenses for the honor it is," Colby lamented.[104] This too meant that the shape of suffrage organizing in the 1890s underwent a profound transformation. At least in the arena of lecturing, access was no longer democratic, and the groundswell of independent agitation contracted.[105]

A movement fundamentally remade, yet seemingly the same as always: this was the memory work done by the myth of Seneca Falls. By making 1848 into a sacred point of origins, the story had given a persuasive logic to unification, construing it as *reunification*, the mere correction of a fatal error, the return to a righteous path. This mature myth now encompassed disparate women aligned behind a common goal, under a common, centralized leadership. Structurally, the movement was now more centralized and hierarchical, and its focus was considerably narrowed. The full-blown myth of Seneca Falls—carefully laid out in the *History*, as a story of top-down leadership and derivative state satellites—masked how the 1890s movement was radically different than that of just a decade before. That story also concealed the ways in which memory itself had helped to remake the movement. One mid-twentieth-century biographer of Anthony adopted this persuasive if misleading logic, explaining that with the merger, "the continuity of the suffrage movement had been preserved and its descent from Seneca Falls fully established."[106]

In 1891, Stone was still sparring with Stanton and Anthony about where the movement rightfully began, unwilling to concede the dominance of Seneca Falls and 1848 in movement memory.[107] Together with the Massachusetts Woman Suffrage Association, Stone helped organize a fortieth anniversary celebration for the 1850 convention in Worcester.[108] Unable to pull it off in 1890, they held it in the early part of 1891. At the anniversary, Stone told a thrilling narrative about how the original organizers had decided to hold the 1850 convention. She then interpreted its importance: "That was the beginning of the great *movement* for equal rights in any national form." There had previously been conventions at Seneca Falls, Akron, and Rochester, she noted, but those were only "the real beginning of *meetings*," not of a movement.[109] The Worcester anniversary again placed an emphasis on the brave oratory of Abby Kelley and Sarah and Angelina Grimké, while also now nodding to Lucretia Mott—a sign of the changing discourse—by regretting that her early speeches at the first two Worcester conventions, in 1850 and 1851, had not been preserved.[110] The 1891 event was a small meeting, with no particular fanfare. It seemed almost insignificant after the grandeur, scope, and pageantry of the 1888 Seneca Falls anniversary. Worcester seemed, in fact, forgettable. Despite Stone's claims for it over twenty years, however attenuated and episodic, Worcester was not the face of the movement and, partly as a result, neither was Stone.

Anthony's ascent to nearly unrivaled leadership within the pantheon of suffrage "pioneers" was aided by Stone's infirmity over her final years and then by Stone's death in 1893. Despite weakness and frailty, Stone insisted upon addressing the 1893 World's Congress of Representative Women, held in May, in conjunction with the 1893 Chicago World's Fair. Stone again spoke on "The Progress of Fifty Years," and she again referenced the path-breaking work of Abby Kelley Foster and the Grimké sisters. She noted that twenty states now had school suffrage, and women enjoyed municipal suffrage in Kansas. The chronicling of fifty years work exhausted her, and she had to slowly navigate her way back to her seat. It was Stone's last speech. She had hoped to return to Chicago that August, but pain crippled her. A month later, she was diagnosed with advanced stomach cancer. She died within weeks. Anthony's leading rival had departed the earth, helping to further consolidate Anthony's gathering image as the singular, guiding figure of women's rights.[111]

❖ Stanton's Eclipse

Within a few years of Stone's death, Stanton's celebrated role as the movement's mother also died a painful death, although Stanton herself still lived. Her resounding reversal in movement memory soon left Anthony standing alone as the custodian of a memory she had built, despite not having participated in the 1848 meeting itself. The decline in Stanton's reputation began innocuously, resulting from her increasing absence from organizational life. Younger women within the movement, including Anthony's lieutenants, had little opportunity to interact with Stanton. Always more of a philosopher at heart, Stanton attended fewer and fewer suffrage events as her infirmity increased, and she spent more time in the solitary pursuit of writing. By the late 1880s, Stanton was unable to stand long enough to deliver a speech, and she could not navigate stairs. This made attending suffrage conventions difficult and eventually impossible. She had given up her house, and her children now cared for her in their homes. She could not travel unaccompanied, and NAWSA's 1892 annual convention in Washington, D.C., was her last. Anthony, five years Stanton's junior, remained a vagabond, traveling at length and staying on the road for months at a time. She remained able to keep up with the pace of movement life, whereas Stanton could not. The two spent very little time together after finishing the *History*, and they embarked on no major projects together. They remained close, but their interests, priorities, and physical abilities diverged.[112]

Stanton's radical rethinking of the Bible had much more drastic implications for her standing in movement memory. In the early 1880s, Stanton began penning critiques of organized religion's misogyny. Those attacks accelerated over the 1880s and into the 1890s. Although Stanton wanted distance from the day-to-day operations of the organized movement, she did not want to see it captured by devout and conservative Christians, whose influence within the suffrage ranks continued to grow. Over the 1880s, attacks on the gains of the postwar women's rights movement relied heavily on biblical justifications, and this too motivated Stanton's renewed investigation into religion. Stanton's intellectual life also brought her into close contact with free thinkers and the anticlerical movement, who helped inform her thinking. All these influences produced a profound reorientation on Stanton's part.[113]

Stanton's continued disinterest in organizational suffrage politics was now enhanced by her waning faith in the power of the vote. A nominal suffragist to her final days, she had an epiphany in her later years. "I have passed from the political to the religious phase of this question," she wrote a friend, "for I now see more clearly than ever that the arch enemy of woman's freedom sulks behind the altar."[114] She was impatient for change, and she felt betrayed, one historian notes, "both by politicians and by a political process" that met women with sharp indifference and "that fed upon women's energies without ever compensating them with full citizenship."[115] "I am sick of the song of suffrage," she told Gage. "To rouse woman to a sense of her degradation under the canon law and church discipline, is the work that interests me most, and to which I prepare to devote the sunset of my life."[116]

In 1895 Stanton resumed work on what she considered the crowning work of her career, her *Woman's Bible*.[117] In the first part of that year, NAWSA held the first national suffrage convention ever convened below the Mason-Dixon Line. NAWSA's choice to convene in Atlanta represented, to a degree, the ways in which the suffrage movement was exchanging principle for expediency.[118] To appease the white South—which NAWSA was actively courting as part of its bid for a broader base and congressional votes—Anthony asked Frederick Douglass not to appear at the convention.[119] (Douglass died, quite suddenly, only months later.)[120] Despite Anthony's attempt to avoid the scandal of a black man appearing on stage with white women, unthinkable in the white South, the 1896 convention drew considerable fire nevertheless. While Anthony presided over the affair (which Stanton did not attend), a minister denounced all suffrage women in a speech that was picked up by Atlanta newspapers and subsequently produced an uproar. "When I read of the ferocious attack of the Baptist clergymen on woman," Stanton told a reporter, "it seemed to me the time had come."[121]

A new English-language version of the Bible had recently been published (the first revision in two hundred years), and Stanton proposed to put together a committee to examine this version, which—like all versions before it—she believed perverted original scripture. Stanton selected biblical passages and studied and interpreted them, authoring commentaries on each. Stanton concluded that biblical justifications for women's subordination arose not from divine will but from man's thirst for power. Men had, in other words, used the Bible to justify their desire for domination. In 1895, she began running her commentaries in Clara Colby's *Woman's Tribune*, expecting these early installments would generate enthusiasm for her project. Without securing their permission—or even their cooperation with the project—Stanton also published a list of names, which she called her "Revising Committee," women who were supposedly working with her on the project. This drew the ire of some of the women named, including Mary Livermore, a fervent Christian who was staunchly opposed to the project. In the end, her so-called committee never met and never worked collaboratively, although she did have the support of suffragists such as Colby and Gage, who contributed to the project and shared Stanton's suspicions surrounding the church. Anthony declined cooperation. She thought the project ill conceived, but she supported her friend's intellectual freedom.[122]

Stanton's move to print her biblical commentaries in advance backfired, beginning a long and painful episode. Her installments drew immediate fire from the growing number of evangelical women in the suffrage movement who found her scholarship heretical. Her commentaries were the perversion, they countered, not the Bible. Undeterred, Stanton characteristically believed that if only women would listen to her, she could set their minds free. Even as she withdrew from movement operations, Stanton maintained supreme confidence in her role as the movement's ideological leader. And, like Gage, she thought she was saving it from conservative drift—over which Anthony presided. But ever fewer numbers listened.[123]

Just two weeks before publishing her *Woman's Bible* in 1895, she stood, with assistance, before a crowd of 8,000 to mark her eightieth birthday— one of the last public celebrations of the pioneer NAWSA was about to

THE WOMAN'S BIBLE

A Work That Has Called Forth Much Criticism.

DEBATED BY THE SUFFRAGISTS

Proposed Revision of Scriptural Texts Relating to Women.

TO BE CONSIDERED TOMORROW

Newspaper clipping about Elizabeth Cady Stanton's controversial Woman's Bible *(Susan B. Anthony Papers, Rare Books, Special Collections and Preservation Department, University of Rochester)*

ostracize. Lauded as the mother of the movement, within a year, she was branded an infidel. When the 1896 NAWSA convention opened, Rachel Foster Avery (recently married) issued a report condemning the *Woman's Bible* for bringing opprobrium upon the movement. "[Suffrage] work has been . . . much hindered," she began, "by the general misconception of the relation of the so-called 'Woman's Bible' to our association." She suggested NAWSA condemn its author in order to publicly dissociate the suffrage cause from Stanton's inflammatory work.[124] Debate ensued, and Colby, a *Woman's Bible* contributor, managed to get the proposal tabled.[125] Behind the scenes, discussions continued about a formal censure. Stanton got word and grew alarmed. "I stood alone in demanding suffrage in the first convention," and time proved me right, she reminded a friend—and herself.[126] During a lengthy debate that reached the convention floor, Anthony chimed in along similar lines: "Lucretia Mott at first thought Mrs. Stanton had injured the cause of woman's rights by insisting on the demand for suffrage, but she had sense enough not to pass a resolution about it."[127] Both felt certain history was on their side. Both were wrong. A resolution to censure Stanton passed, with Anthony as the only NAWSA officer voting against.[128] "I shall love [and] honor her to the end," Anthony wrote, "whether her Bible pleases me or not." Stanton expected Anthony to resign in the wake of the censure, but she did not.[129]

And yet, this painful episode revealed how the movement's genesis story could work both against Stanton and, eventually, without Stanton. Even as the ostensible mother and originator of the movement, the story she had helped to create and popularize could not save her from censure. The myth of Seneca Falls celebrated the vote as women's emancipator; for Stanton to now argue otherwise was to blaspheme the gospel of the movement and to lend credence to those who called her a heretic. Stanton had, in some sense, written herself into a corner. Increasingly, the myth of Seneca Falls would have to go on without her and, notwithstanding the facts, to center more on Anthony. It was she, not Stanton, who had been on the platform at the National Council of Women's meeting in February 1895, nearly a year before the censure vote, when May Wright Sewall reminded delegates from many women's organizations with many disparate purposes that "when we consider the origin of the spirit of organization, the muse of history takes us to Seneca Falls in August 1848." Wright got the month wrong, but there was no question who the muse of history was. Anthony became—now more than ever—the story's main keeper, literally and figuratively. She continued to stand at the head of a unified and centralized movement, becoming that story's—and that movement's—principal embodiment.[130]

❖ 1898: A Trilogy

Three years later, Anthony staged yet another anniversary convention, this time for the fiftieth anniversary of Seneca Falls. In 1898, Stanton and Anthony both published book-length accounts of their lives, timed to coincide with the fiftieth anniversary. These three developments so powerfully reinforced one another, as did subsequent histories to come, that alternative memories virtually disappeared—or, at least, it became harder to discern myth from history.

The fiftieth anniversary celebration coincided with NAWSA's annual February meeting in Washington, D.C. Although NAWSA brought together women with very different histories, the 1898 anniversary, like the 1888 anniversary, united them under a suffrage banner with a single origin. NAWSA had been founded in 1890 and was holding its eighth convention in 1898, but as Anthony explained to a *Washington Star* reporter, "it will really . . . be the celebration of the fiftieth anniversary of the first woman's rights convention, which was held in Seneca Falls, N.Y., July 20, 1848." The article further detailed "the causes of the holding of the first convention, as stated by Miss Anthony." She had grown so used to speaking as both a "Pioneer Advocate" (as the *Star*'s headline dubbed her) and an authoritative historian, that it could be hard to discern which was which—especially since fewer and fewer gentlemen of the press (or, indeed, ladies of the NAWSA) had any personal knowledge of the antebellum years, or even of the immediate postwar years. Occasionally, journalists asked for clarification. "Miss Anthony said to a Star reporter, speaking of the founding of the association: I did not become a member until 1850. In 1848, I was teaching school in Canajoharie, N.Y.," she explained. "I heard nothing from my family except the talk of this convention." (Anthony's father, mother, and sister Mary had attended the follow-up meeting in Rochester, two weeks after the gathering in Seneca Falls.) Perhaps it felt almost as if she *had* been there. The 1898 anniversary starkly illustrated how Anthony was becoming the face of the myth. For the first time, Stanton was not present to commemorate the 1848 Seneca Falls meeting. As leadership narrowed to Anthony, so did the origins myth. Anthony hosted the anniversary celebration without her lifelong friend, the only living planner of the first women's rights convention.[131]

For the celebration, Anthony secured the round mahogany table upon which Stanton helped write the Declaration of Sentiments back in 1848. The table had remained in the McClintock family, and Anthony had tried to borrow it for the ICW's "Pioneer Day" in 1888. The McClintocks felt it was too valuable to lend. At the end of 1897, a daughter of the McClintocks sent Stanton the table as a gift. She and Anthony planned to use it for the 1898 anniversary. "All our suffrage daughters," Stanton wrote, "will then have an opportunity of seeing . . . valuable mementos of that eventful occasion."[132] It was the only surviving physical link to that fabled document. The original copy of the Declaration of Sentiments had vanished, likely in 1848. It seems no one had found it valuable enough to preserve. That grand old table, quickly becoming a holy relic, now sat upon the stage, however, and

Declaration of Sentiments Table (Courtesy National Museum of American History, Smithsonian Institution)

the seventy-eight-year-old Anthony used it as her lectern, literally standing behind the myth that she now stood for.[133]

A copy of the Declaration of Sentiments was displayed on the table, while copies were printed in abundance and circulated among those present. Anthony read from it, explaining that in 1848, the world had mocked it.[134] And she told the story, beginning in London and ending in Seneca Falls. It must have vexed Henry Blackwell and Alice Stone Blackwell, both present and both active NAWSA members, to be reorganized under this mythology. The *Woman's Journal,* in fact, omitted mention of the anniversary and Seneca Falls from its extensive convention coverage.[135] Decorations were sparse, save for the table, the declaration, and an association flag with four stars, representing the states that now allowed women full voting rights: Wyoming, Utah, Idaho, and Colorado. It also contained markings to indicate victories for school and municipal suffrage.[136] There was a roll call of pioneers' names, but few were on hand, having either passed away or become unable to travel.[137] Gage was too sick to be present, so she sent an address.[138] Stanton, who no longer attended conventions, calling herself a "free lance," did the same. She traced the progress of fifty years, telling the story of her life, again mapped onto the movement as its collective history. "Let this generation pay its debt to the past," Stanton closed, "by continuing the work until the last vestige of woman's subjection shall be erased."[139] A pall fell over the proceedings when news arrived that Frances Willard, president of the WCTU, had died unexpectedly. Celebration was given over to mourning her passing, a sign of how deeply Willard and the WCTU had penetrated the organized suffrage movement.[140]

Stanton's autobiography formed the second piece of the 1898 trilogy. She had begun serially publishing her life story in Clara Colby's *Woman's Tribune* soon after the 1888 ICW.[141] Now she collected those articles in a single volume (with revisions), entitled *Eighty Years and More*, to coincide with the anniversary. Notably, she ended her account in 1895, with the assembled 8,000 paying her tribute on her eightieth birthday. The painful events of 1896 were missing.[142] And surely Stanton intended her life story as vindication, something that strongly inflected her work on the *History* as well. Her autobiography displayed Stanton's usual stylistic brilliance—being a lively, humorous read. With regard to movement memory, Stanton followed the same structure she had devised in the *History*. After giving some early history, Stanton dove into a chapter on the 1848 women's rights convention, titled "The First Woman's Rights Convention." The details were rather sparse, perhaps because the story told itself at this point. Perhaps they were sparse because Stanton had lost interest in the tale, being tired, as she put it, of "the song of suffrage." She was more interested in religious criticism, and her autobiography reflected her newfound conviction.[143] Still, the usual narrative conventions applied.

After describing the 1848 convention, Stanton followed with not one but two chapters on Anthony, in which it seemed once again, as in the *History*'s first edition, that the two had met in 1848. Whether a deliberate choice on Stanton's part or an accident of memory, it is hard to say. But it was a repeated pattern. Stanton then brought Anthony aboard that founding legend with the chapter's first sentence, and each after that. With the movement inaugurated in Seneca Falls, the pair went forth to spread the good word. Stanton once again called Anthony "the Napoleon of our struggle" (in a passage she recycled from the *History*),[144] surely delighting in the military metaphor, as tales of Civil War generals and soldiers continued to pour forth from the presses, drowning out suffragists' insistence that the postwar peace had been betrayed. Both chapters about Anthony are a moving tribute to a friendship lasting nearly half a century. Stanton also speaks to the inevitable pains accumulated over a long life of activism. "But, whatever may be the imprudent utterances of the one or the impolitic methods of the other," Stanton confides to her reader, "the animating motives of both are evermore as white as the light. The good that they do is by design; the harm by accident."[145]

Reading early installments of Stanton's serialized autobiography in 1891, Gage was once again incredulous. Gage railed privately about the "falsity and injustice" of Stanton's account. Gage then recalled an incident years earlier, when a newspaper report offered the transcripts of different women's remarks: "Susan said to Elizabeth in my hearing, 'No ones speech ought to have been reported but yours and mine.' That is a fair example of what always has been her course—only the 'lying' is a newer feature." Just what Gage felt Stanton was distorting is unclear, but her reactions underscored the power and politics of remembering. The memory Stanton and Anthony had so laboriously constructed was further reinforced by Gage's death. A month after the fiftieth anniversary celebration, Gage collapsed from a massive stroke and never recovered. She was seventy-one.[146]

Anthony's authorized biography was the third piece of a trilogy that completed the maturation of the Seneca Falls myth. Anthony hated composition and was not very good at it. So she commissioned the journalist and young suffragist Ida Husted Harper to write the chronicle of her life. Harper moved into Anthony's house, occupied the guest room, and the two set to work in February of 1897. (When Stanton's daughter asked if her mother might spend the summer with Anthony, Anthony regretted that her guest room was occupied.) Resuming history writing held no special pleasures for Anthony, who by this point had a painful appreciation for its draining effect. "I hate the whole business so absolutely that I want to be done with it as soon as possible," Anthony wrote a friend; "I feel like a caged lion every minute that I am compelled to think and talk and read of the past." "While I love *making* history as much as ever," she added jovially.[147] Yet she *wrote* history again and again, a testament to her understanding that the past was too powerful to be left unattended. While Harper did the composition, Anthony supervised. Anthony then read over everything, making suggestions and revisions. *The Life and Work of Susan B. Anthony* was a fully cooperative undertaking.[148]

Working in Anthony's home, Anthony and Harper surrounded themselves with the first, large-scale women's rights archive. Anthony had been accumulating a massive repository of raw archival material related to the movement since her work on the *History*. That collection had grown so large that she had a third-floor attic built onto her house just to store it. She continued to acquire documents after the *History*, adding material regularly. At the 1888 ICW, Anthony had lamented that the women of forty years ago did not realize their historic importance, and thus, tragically, had not saved the records of the movement. She urged each and every woman there "to make a solemn resolution to-day, that every good thing which a woman does, . . . every organization that you have anything to do with," that "you will send" along notices and records so "that all these things may be preserved." "Woman will never be properly recorded in history," she added, " . . . until they do the work themselves."[149] As Harper began work on Anthony's biography in February of 1897, the pair ran announcements in the women's rights press asking for the return of Anthony's letters.[150] As one example of the collection's eventual size, Harper reportedly consulted more than 20,000 letters, fifty years of Anthony's diaries, the complete runs of multiple reform newspapers, and more.[151] The collection was somewhat of a disorganized jumble, however.[152] As the two sat down to work, Anthony hired assistants to iron letters and newspapers creased with age and then to sort everything into some logical, accessible arrangement.[153] There, on Anthony's third floor, the pair collaboratively authored yet more volumes of women's rights history, amid an archival collection that was unrivaled. Nothing like it existed anywhere.

Anthony's authorized biography dwarfed Stanton's. Whereas *Eighty Years and More* was a modest 470 pages, *The Life and Work of Susan B. Anthony* consumed two thick volumes totaling roughly 1,100 pages. Both volumes were published in 1898 and timed, like Stanton's, to coincide with the Seneca Falls anniversary. Anthony's biography detailed her life up through 1897. (A third volume was published posthumously, covering Anthony's final years.) Like the *History*, the *Life and Work* was a significant achievement. Unlike Stanton's account, which dwelt more specifically on anecdotes from her own life, Anthony's discussed movement history, with herself at its center. The volumes' subtitle—*A Story of the Evolution of the Status of Women*—was itself revealing. Anthony used her life to anchor what she believed was the story of all women. Unlike Stanton's autobiography, Anthony's also followed the compositional style of the *History*—which had long ago heralded itself as "an arsenal of facts"—offering extensive excerpts from original material, including everything from speeches to newspaper stories.[154]

Ida Husted Harper and Susan B. Anthony working in Anthony's attic archive (Harper, The Life and Work of Susan B. Anthony, chap. 48)

The fact of Seneca Falls, or rather the facts of who met there for what in 1848, was not part of Anthony's life and work, but it undergirded her *Life and Work*—and with good reason, given all the writing, speaking, and commemorating she had done to build the myth that had so profoundly shaped the movement. Rather than offering a fully detailed retelling of events at Seneca Falls, the text alludes to "a gathering of the believers in 1848" or "that immortal first Woman's Rights Convention of 1848," all in all nearly a dozen times, including how Anthony's father, mother, and sister Mary attended the follow-up meeting in Rochester and signed the Declaration of Sentiments. As the third piece of the trilogy of 1898, the Anthony-Harper collaboration all but took the myth of Seneca Falls for granted. The competing potential origins that Paulina Wright Davis, Lucretia Mott, Lucy Stone, William Lloyd Garrison's children, Antoinette Brown Blackwell, and Henry Blackwell offered from the antebellum decades forward had all given way to a dominant narrative that appeared to be self-evident.[155]

Harper depicted Anthony's leadership, in turn, not as a position achieved over time, but rather as a constant, foreordained outcome of an alchemical formula involving unusual foresight, superior skill, and general acclaim. Yet traces of that long contested process do appear. "Miss Anthony . . . did many . . . things, not because they were officially her duty, but because they ought to be done and there was no one else ready to undertake them," Harper explained. "For many years she [Anthony] was forced to take the lead in all departments of the suffrage work and when they finally became systematized, with a head at each, she sometimes grew impatient at delay and usurped the functions of others without intending any breach of official etiquette."[156] Given her superior skill, the story suggests, the forces of progress impelled Anthony to the movement's fore, a position she assumed through no design of her own. This type of hagiography is not surprising in a commissioned biography, yet when combined with the other interpretative layers Anthony had already spun, it is sometimes hard to see much beyond what Anthony presents. And it can be hard to see what Stone came to understand before her death—that the story was more than an exaggeration or misplaced emphasis. It had made many movements, seemingly, into one.

The mature myth of Seneca Falls became, like the octogenarian Anthony herself, a veritable monument. The *Washington Evening Star* summed up both in 1900, under the headline, "Work of Susan B. Anthony: Her Name Is Synonymous with the Movement." By the turn of the century, both Anthony and "the Movement" were synonymous with Seneca Falls. When NAWSA convened in Minneapolis in 1901, a local newspaper praised the organization for effecting a half century of "betterment of the social and legal position of woman." The editorial continued, "There is one woman in the association who can look back to the initial convention of women to assert their 'rights,' which was held at Seneca Falls, N.Y., in the autumn of 1848, and has seen the movement carried on in the storm and stress of unreasoning public opposition to the attainment, one by one, of most of the demands made in the Seneca Falls platform." That woman, of course, was "Miss Susan B. Anthony . . . the patriarch of the strenuous and persistent movement."[157] If some details were wrong, the larger point was true. One woman more than any other did "look back" to Seneca Falls, to combine history and myth in order to define that event and achieve its purported platform. By 1901, understandings of that event and the movement that followed it had narrowed dramatically to one major goal, and although neither Elizabeth Cady Stanton nor Susan B. Anthony would live to see its attainment, the myth of Seneca Falls would outlive them both and help to revise another sacred text: the Constitution of the United States.

Epilogue
✥ The Bonfires of History

Residents of Rochester reported seeing fires for weeks. Smoke billowed from Anthony's backyard, as flecks of burnt paper floated through the air. Near the end of her life, Anthony made a shocking decision: to burn large portions of the archive housed in her third-floor attic. It is impossible to know what was destroyed, but for someone as committed to historical preservation as Anthony, the act seems unimaginable. She had the dual instincts of an activist and an archivist, whose visionary and organizational energies had fostered the movement and its memory in equal measure. The resulting social and women's history archive would remain unmatched for decades to come. Yet despite a half-century of collecting, organizing, interpreting, and publishing original documents, Anthony now watched that archive go up in flames.

Ida Husted Harper claimed to have supervised the burning. After she and Anthony concluded their last historical collaboration—and after a sufficient time had elapsed in which "no suits for libel and no challenges of any kind" had been lodged against them—"it seemed safe," Harper reported, "to begin the work of destruction." The pair began going through the "mass of material," with Harper invariably recommending throwing things out and Anthony laying them aside for safekeeping. An exasperated Harper rejoined: "Now there is no use in my wasting my time here [if] you are not going to allow this trash to be burned." Anthony, in turn, pleaded, "I can't over come the habit of a lifetime, which has been to save every scrap of writing." Eventually she relented, however, and the burning began. Harper and Anthony's sister Mary at first threw items into the furnace. But with "large waste-baskets and the big clothes-hamper" filled daily, the furnace became inadequate. They began lighting daily bonfires in the backyard. "The task," Harper recounted, "consumed every working hour for almost a month."[1]

She relayed this story in the posthumous volume of Anthony's biography, and it is hard to gauge its accuracy. The burning clearly took place, on a massive scale, but the motivations behind it are harder to decipher. The consequences were clear, however: the destruction of the original sources meant that Anthony's authorized biography and the *History of Woman Suffrage* would become *the* source. A flyer advertising Anthony's authorized biography explicitly made this point: "This is the only authentic biography of her that ever can be written, as the letters and documents will not be accessible to other historians."[2]

Despite this disturbing decision at the end of her life, Anthony was inarguably the greatest woman historian—and historian of women—in her century. And there was arguably no greater American social historian until the African American intellectual and civil rights leader W. E. B. Du Bois. Indeed, Anthony largely pioneered the now familiar figure of the scholar-activist, and particularly the historian-activist. The public role of the historian has typically been credited to later exemplars like Du Bois or Charles Beard, contemporaries who were among the first professionally trained historians. Scholar Richard Hofstadter famously referred to Beard as a "*historian engagé*" in arguing for the value of history written "by embattled participants." Along with her sometime comrade Frederick Douglass (who kept his own papers but did not systematically collect and preserve those of a whole movement), Anthony embodied that ideal as much or more than the historians of twentieth-century campaigns for justice. And her legacy is one we are still grappling with today—in terms of both the activist past we inherit and the stories we tell about that past. We struggle to balance the two.[3]

Anthony's historical work didn't end with her authorized biography. After Harper and Anthony completed it, they embarked on yet another historical project, a fourth volume of the *History of Woman Suffrage*. Anthony had no other collaborators this time besides Harper. Gage had died in 1898, and Stanton took no part. Harper and Anthony shared authorship (or editorship, as they too billed their role), and the aging leader once again self-published and held sole copyright. This volume—which Anthony conceived of quite a long time after finishing the first three—covered the period from the mid-1880s (where the third volume left off) to the turn of the century. Harper found the work as unremittingly exhausting as Anthony's previous collaborators did, and she too wondered if they might ever emerge from the crushing mounds of material. Eventually, after great labor, they published volume 4 in 1902.[4]

Anthony voluntarily retired from the NAWSA presidency in 1900, freeing up time for the *History*. Although there would have to be an election, she all but appointed her own successor, choosing among her "lieutenants" and "nieces," the younger women she had been grooming for over a decade. Lillie Devereux Blake, a veteran New York suffragist who believed that NAWSA's work was stalled, considered making a run for the presidency but concluded that only Anthony's anointed successor could win. That honor went to Carrie Chapman Catt, a wealthy woman with a college degree from Iowa State, a WCTU member, and a NAWSA organizer. There was no love lost between Catt and Stanton, against whom Catt had led the censure vote back in 1896. For Catt's generation, Anthony now stood alone as the object of their affection. This devotion, together with younger feminists' increasingly open disdain for Stanton, accelerated Stanton's decline in movement memory.[5]

Anthony and Harper opened the *History*'s fourth volume as all good movement stories now began, with a recitation of origins. They alluded to "the memorable convention of Seneca Falls, N.Y., in 1848," on the very first page of their introduction, and in the very first sentence of chapter two: "the first Woman's Rights Convention on record was held in Seneca Falls, N.Y., in July 1848." Neither of these references made any mention of Stanton. Given her general disfavor within the movement, and her self-imposed distance from movement politics over the last decade of her life, suffragists increasingly left her out their founding story. It became unclear, or at least unspoken, in these turn-of-the-century recitations exactly who had called "the memorable convention of . . . 1848."[6]

Writing with distinctly junior collaborators, Anthony now used the story of Seneca Falls to validate and augment her own historical legacy. Her undemocratic maneuvers to accomplish unification in 1890 and assume the presidency of the new organization are completely absent in this fourth volume. Origins myths work to legitimate and unify the messy contingencies of political struggle, making both the outcome and the story of that struggle seem unmanipulated. Hence, dispatching unification in a single paragraph, the narrative insists that the 1890 NAWSA convention simply "belonged to Miss Anthony, 'Saint Susan,' as her followers love to call her." Explicitly rooted in Seneca Falls, from the volume's very first page, Anthony's leadership became a fait accompli, and unification became the necessary restoration of an imagined and supposedly shared origin, rather than a dramatic departure in movement history. Anthony's leadership appears as a kind of foreordained, inevitable fact, rather than something she sought, won, and kept through a contentious and contingent process that lasted for decades. Volume 4 did not recount, and perhaps its coauthors did not fully realize, how consistently, centrally, and strategically Anthony had deployed the myth of Seneca Falls to consolidate her leadership and to impose her particular vision of the movement and its goals.[7]

In 1902, a week after Anthony and Harper completed the new volume, Stanton died quietly at her son's home in New York City. She spent her final decade living in an apartment with her children and grandchildren. Her mind remained razor sharp, and she continued to write up until her death. Her eyesight, however, dimmed, and her prodigious weight restricted her movements. She had been failing all year and in her final week became bedridden and eventually lost consciousness. She died on 26 October, two weeks shy of her eighty-seventh birthday. The next day, a front-page obituary in the *Washington Times* recounted the movement's inspiration during Stanton's life-changing visit to London in 1840. "After returning from England with Susan B. Anthony and others she began to agitate for woman suffrage. . . . The result of this agitation was the foundation at Seneca Falls early in 1848 of the National American Woman Suffrage Association." Every detail here was wrong. A short obituary carried in many papers nationwide listed no survivors except "Miss Anthony," a testament to their fifty years of friendship, before going on to tell the story of Seneca Falls. And the departed's closed casket appeared beneath a blanket of flowers and a single framed portrait of Anthony. "It seems impossible," Anthony responded upon receiving the news of Stanton's death, "that the voice is hushed—that I have longed to hear for 50 years." "She forged the thunderbolts," Anthony added, "and I fired them."[8]

Four years later, in 1906, Anthony died. Upon returning home from a NAWSA convention in Baltimore and from her own eighty-sixth birthday celebration, she felt unwell. A doctor diagnosed pneumonia as she gasped for breath. It seemed the pneumonia might take her life, but then her lungs began to recover. Her heart, however, remained weak. She had suffered heart trouble during her final years, and heart failure likely took her life on the morning of 13 March 1906. That evening's widely circulated Associated Press story, almost inevitably, alleged that "with Elizabeth Cady Stanton and others Miss Anthony called in 1848 the first woman's rights convention, which met at Seneca Falls." Newspapers from Nebraska to New England, when not giving her outright credit for having "called" the meeting, placed Anthony in attendance, as in a much-reprinted statement that "Julia Ward Howe and herself were the only survivors of the famous first women's rights convention held in Seneca Falls 1848." The misconception was so widely held that in the months after Anthony's death, the women's columns in newspapers across the country carried a small feature correcting it.[9]

If Stanton increasingly receded from the myth of Seneca Falls after her death, the reverse was true for Anthony. The memory of Anthony became a powerful weapon in intra-movement politics. Catt's NAWSA presidency had been embattled, particularly by the rivalry of Anna Howard Shaw, another of Anthony's protégées. Although by no means Anthony's favorite, Shaw had been in the right place at the right time to care for Anthony during her final days. Shaw spun that experience into a supposed passing of the torch to the NAWSA presidency. According to Shaw, Anthony begged her to lead the movement, in a deathbed plea: "Promise me that you will keep the presidency of the association as long as you are well enough to do the work." Shaw had forced Catt out of the presidency two years earlier, in 1904. But Catt's supporters continued to oppose Shaw as president and fought to unseat her, in an attempt to return Catt to the office (which happened in 1915). As that battle raged, and Shaw struggled to hold onto the presidency, she repeatedly told, revised, and refined this apocryphal story. Using Anthony's memory for what one historian has called Shaw's own "secular sanctification," Shaw helped further elevate Anthony above all others.[10]

Meanwhile, Alice Paul, a young suffragist who never knew Anthony, decided to resurrect a federal strategy, which NAWSA had largely abandoned. She did so from within NAWSA, but soon, for a variety of reasons, Shaw and Catt had her expelled. Undaunted, Paul formed a rival suffrage organization, the National Woman's Party (NWP). The NWP worked for a federal amendment (while NAWSA stayed focused on the states). Resurrecting a version of the federal amendment written by Stanton and introduced into the Senate by Aaron Sargent in 1878, they strategically dubbed it the "Anthony Amendment." Thus challenging NAWSA directly, they claimed that Anthony (and therefore history) was on their side.[11]

The years leading up to the passage of the Nineteenth Amendment in 1920 were politically dazzling. Catt, as head of NAWSA, helped win key victories in several large states, including women's full suffrage in New York in 1917, putting pressure on party politicians to recognize and uphold women's voting power. Paul and the NWP, meanwhile, began audaciously picketing the White House and putting the issue of woman suffrage before the public in tangible, dramatic ways—including hunger strikes. After failed congressional votes on the amendment, President Woodrow Wilson did something unprecedented: he addressed Congress and urged its passage. The "Anthony Amendment" then passed both houses of Congress in 1919, after significant political wrangling. A difficult ratification fight lay ahead, in which NAWSA and the NWP began a full-court press. The long ratification battle came down to one man in Tennessee, a southern state known for its fierce opposition to women's rights. Harry Burn, the Tennessee legislature's youngest member, opposed the amendment. But upon receiving a telegram from his mother urging his support (in which she instructed him to "be a good boy") he changed his vote. Surprising everyone, the Tennessee legislature approved the amendment by one vote, and the Nineteenth Amendment to the U.S. Constitution was officially ratified on 26 August 1920.[12]

Reporting its passage, newspapers around the country framed this historic moment around Anthony and the myth of Seneca Falls. Although Stanton had written the amendment, headlines and stories construed it as "a living monument to its dead framer, Susan B. Anthony." The United Press syndicate headlined its wire story, sent out to hundreds of subscriber newspapers, the "Outline Story of Suffrage in the United States." Ending with the amendment, the story began predictably. "In 1848 at Seneca Falls, N.Y., Miss Anthony called to order the first national woman's convention. . . . She knew her cause was right, [and] she assumed national control of suffrage matters on the occasion of Seneca Falls." This widely reprinted feature did not mention Stanton, Mott, Douglass, or any of the actual leaders of 1848, or indeed any other veterans from later wings and phases of the movement. When Anthony's lifelong goal was finally achieved, the myth of Seneca Falls not only framed this achievement in the public mind but made it hers alone.[13]

In the aftermath, Stanton's children and Lucy Stone's daughter both tried to bring their mothers out of Anthony's lengthening shadow. Alice Stone Blackwell felt her mother's elision keenly, and she now felt the weight of the *History of Woman Suffrage*—to which Lucy had pointedly refused to contribute. That its many volumes now stood unchallenged, Stone Blackwell lamented, "was our misfortune. It cannot be helped now, for few persons will ever take the trouble to dig out our side from the files of the Woman's Journal." Indeed, almost no one has. Today, there exists no published history of the American Association, despite its energetic work over twenty years, and we still know precious little about Stone herself. "In 1847, she gave her first lecture on woman's rights," her daughter wrote in a 1930 biography of her mother, adding pointedly, "This was the year *before* the first *local* woman's rights convention was held, at Seneca Falls." All movement histories, even dissenting ones, now revolved in some way around 1848. The consequences of Stone's failure to understand the political power of history—and how the myth of Seneca Falls all but erased her from public memory—have been surprisingly lasting.[14]

Stanton's children were also upset about their mother being written out of history. In 1922, Theodore and Harriot published a two-volume collection of Stanton's letters, diary, and reminiscences. Much as she had often done, they took significant editorial liberties, splicing together letters, editing entries, and passing off their own words as if they belonged to Stanton. Her autobiography had not dwelled on either Seneca Falls or her 1848 suffrage resolution. By the end of her life, she had lost considerable faith that winning the vote would liberate women. The myth of Seneca Falls, born of celebrations and writings from 1868 to 1898, had become more Anthony's preoccupation than Stanton's. Again showing how widely held that story now was, when Stanton's children tried to set the record straight, their strategy was not to challenge or diminish the myth of Seneca Falls, but rather to put their mother back into it—and to make her its central figure. Revising the chapter she had titled "The First Woman's Rights Convention," they named all the organizers and the signers of the Declaration of Sentiments, as if to remind readers that Anthony had played no part. Harriot and Theodore then added considerable material about the convention itself. They underscored that it was their mother who had first conceived of the vote as an essential, necessary reform. Inserting words into Stanton's mouth, without capturing anything like her characteristic voice, they make her say, unequivocally: "I was wholly responsible for the IX resolution. . . . My revolutionary sentiment read: 'Resolved, That it is the duty of the women of this country to secure to themselves their sacred right to the elective franchise.'" Against resounding opposition, Stanton prevails alone (Douglass is omitted), depicted as the only one who clearly understood the vote as the most "revolutionary" of all reforms.[15]

They also made substantial cuts to Stanton's two chapters about Anthony, merging them into one and cutting Anthony's name from the chapter title. They downplayed Anthony's role in the movement and reordered text to put distance between her and Seneca Falls. Whereas Stanton had dated her friendship with Anthony to 1848, her children dated it to 1851. And whereas Stanton's chapters on Anthony filled thirty pages, her children edited that material down to only seven. Theodore and Harriot also cut Anthony's photograph, along with any text celebrating her executive skills or emphasizing her early commitment to women's enfranchisement. They waged a determined—if largely unsuccessful—battle against Anthony, whose posthumous reputation nevertheless continued to overshadow their mother's.[16]

The struggle to direct the women's movement in the aftermath of the Nineteenth Amendment almost inevitably led to competing interpretations of and claims to the memory of Anthony and Seneca Falls, which were now entirely conflated. To mark the turning point of 1920, Paul and the NWP commissioned sculptor Adelaide Johnson to create a large memorial, intended for the U.S. Capitol. Atop a hulking, eight-ton block of white Italian marble, Johnson carved the portrait busts of three women, Mott, Stanton, and Anthony. The composition of what Johnson grandiosely called the "Woman Movement" emphasized Anthony's preeminence. "Her whole nature speaks to women," the sculptor said of Anthony, whom she positioned not only at the center of the group but also slightly higher than either Stanton or Mott, who flanked her. The bottom two-thirds of the block, as well as one upright column, remained rough and unfinished, to stand in for the rights that remained to be won. The NWP's request to place the monument in the Capitol, however, was resisted by the relevant joint congressional committee ("too heavy for the rotunda") and by the advisory Commission on Fine Arts ("not of adequate artistic merit"). So, in yet another daring act of political theater, the NWP had it shipped to the Capitol, uncrated, and left in an outdoor alcove beneath the main steps. The finished monument weighed 14,000 pounds and stood seven-and-a-half feet tall. It could hardly be ignored. The NWP had forced Congress's hand. Even before Congress acted to accept the monument and move it inside, the activists publicly announced an unveiling ceremony to be held in the Rotunda and printed up programs scheduling it for 15 February 1921—the 101st anniversary of Anthony's birth.[17]

Congress's acceptance of the Woman Movement—later renamed the Portrait Monument—bestowed formal, national recognition on the myth of Seneca Falls. At the official ceremony, representatives of thirty national women's organizations and other supporters crowded under the dome for a "spectacle of pageantry and color"—with the NWP banners of gold, purple, and white "semi-circling the rotunda" and held aloft by "gaily dressed women." Beside each stood a flower girl attired "in spring colors, soft yellows, greens, and fawns, symbolic of the promise of better things brought by the suffrage victory." Chicago feminist and Settlement House founder Jane Addams presided. Sara Bard Field of California spoke for the NWP and pointedly addressed the Speaker of the House: "If you thought you came here tonight to receive on behalf of Congress merely the busts of three women . . . you were mistaken." Field emphasized that this gift to the nation represented "the likeness of them and all they mean in themselves and in us." Anthony, Stanton, and Mott were now an inseparable historical trio, enshrined in the Capitol Rotunda and literally centered as the lone avatars of all American women, past and present, no longer simply leaders of a specific, bounded movement. The sculpture represented "the body and blood of a great sacrificial host," Bard added, "the body and blood of revolution, the body and blood of freedom herself." The drama reached its climax when the lights were dimmed, and attendants removed the drapery covering the monument. "Suddenly the statue was enveloped in a blaze of light, and the figures of Susan B. Anthony, Elizabeth Cady Stanton, and Lucretia Mott were revealed," one newspaper trumpeted, "between the marble figures of Washington and Lincoln." Next, the delegates of American and foreign women's organizations stepped up and paid "tribute to the three leaders, serpentining through the aisles in a long processional, each one pausing to deposit a wreath at the foot of the monument."[18]

Before the floral tributes had time to wilt, however, congressional leaders banished the Portrait Monument from its place of honor. It had taken herculean efforts (involving a block and tackle and an inclined plane) to haul the colossus up the Capitol steps. Nevertheless, a few days after the unveiling, officials banished it to the basement directly below the Rotunda, into a vacant space that had years earlier been designed as a tomb for George Washington. A dark, dank space shunned by Washington's family, the crypt had become by 1921 a dusty storage area visited mostly for its restrooms. By shoving the Portrait Monument into a corner, officials also made it impossible to read a lengthy inscription Johnson had composed and "purposely placed . . . upon the back of the monument, that it might not divert the spectator's attention as he looked upon the noble faces of the three pioneer women." The 246-word text had thus far only been stenciled onto the marble, not carved into it. Some considered its radical language inappropriate, such as this much-quoted provocation: "Woman, first denied a soul, then called mindless, now arisen declared herself an entity to be reckoned." The NWP publicly complained about the relocation and about the obscuring of the inscription, pointing out that it was "a four-sided memorial, instead of one designed to stand against a wall," but to no avail. By early autumn, the neglected sculpture had become so grimy that several NWP members made headlines when they descended on the Capitol armed with scrub brushes and buckets of soapy water. They went back the next day at dawn, according to national news stories, to meet the charwomen showing up for work and implore them to keep the statue clean. Not long after, one morning in mid-October, it was discovered that during the night someone had painted over the inscription, on orders from "Capitol authorities." Newspapers speculated that Congress had required the removal of the inscription as a condition (purportedly accepted by the NWP) for repositioning the sculpture from its out-of-the-way corner into the center of the crypt. The *Washington Times* lamented, "Now . . . the figures stand there, unexplained." Not even a sign or placard identified the three women by name, and the Portrait Monument soon became better known by a derisive nickname, "Three Ladies in a Bathtub." Notwithstanding these indignities, the statue remained an important rallying point for feminists, who used it for pilgrimages and celebrations.[19]

Barely a week after the inscription's erasure, the "good ladies of the suffrage persuasion" who objected were disparaged in a Texas newspaper editorial for lacking "a sense of humor"—a charge that would become a classic putdown of American feminists. What was lost under that layer of paint, however, was not only a few overweening lines of activist hyperbole but actual historical information that might have educated thousands of tourists, activists, and perhaps even lawmakers who viewed the statue in the coming decades. The second of the inscription's seven short but rambling paragraphs read: "Lucretia Mott and Elizabeth Cady Stanton in the call of that first woman's rights convention of 1848 *initiated* and Susan B. Anthony *marshaling* the latent forces through three generations down more than a half century of time *guided* the only fundamental universal uprising on our planet. *The Woman's Revolution.*" The emphases here, which were in the original text, provided a subtle corrective to the myth of Seneca Falls, specifying who had done what (and when) in the revolution, helping to explain a monument that otherwise literally lumped all together. Anthony may not have been present at the creation, but in this ultimate consecration of the myth of Seneca Falls, she would be forever at the center, elevated and first among equals.[20]

Two years later, in 1923, Alice Paul confirmed Anthony as the face of Seneca Falls when she unveiled her new initiative, the Equal Rights Amendment (ERA), which she argued ought to be the next major feminist push. The ERA read: "Men and women shall have equal rights throughout the United States and every place subject to its jurisdiction." Her proposal proved quite controversial inside the women's movement, however, where it threatened the sex-based legislation that many women's groups had championed. In a calculated bid for legitimacy, Paul decided to unveil the ERA in a ceremony at Seneca Falls on 19 July, the famous meeting's seventy-fifth anniversary. It was among the first times twentieth-century feminists returned to the actual site, marked as sacred ground, in order to celebrate and to agitate in what would become a ritual strategy. The anniversary meeting closed on Sunday, 23 July, with a mass pilgrimage that linked two sacred places. For

The Portrait Monument (Courtesy of the Prints & Photographs Division, Library of Congress, LC-DIG-hec-35259)

several weeks thereafter, newspapers around the nation depicted this moment in a wire photo headlined, "Wreaths for Susan B. Anthony's Grave," with a caption describing "the pilgrimage of some 300 women who had been attending the seventy-fifth anniversary of the first woman's rights convention, from the convention town of Seneca Falls to the grave of the woman who initiated that first convention." This much-publicized pilgrimage encouraged the public to memorize an equation that was already ever more understood: Susan B. Anthony and the myth of Seneca Falls were one and the same, equivalent and inseparable.[21]

NAWSA, which opposed the ERA, claimed that the legacy of Seneca Falls remained with them, and they offered not merely symbolic but tangible evidence: the old mahogany table on which the Declaration of Sentiments had been written. The table had nothing to do with Anthony, of course, but its chain of custody put her right back into the story. After the McClintocks had given it to Stanton, she gifted it to Anthony in 1900, for her eightieth birthday. By the end of her life, Anthony owned the two most important embodiments of the Seneca Falls mythology: the *History* and the table. In NAWSA's hands, the table and the events surrounding it centered on Anthony. A popular Susan B. Anthony calendar issued by NAWSA featured a photograph of the table in its natural habitat—Anthony's sitting room. The caption confused more than it clarified: "The Parlor: Showing Table on which the Call for the First Woman-Suffrage Convention was written in 1848." Neither Stanton nor the other women who sat around it were mentioned. Consulting the calendar, it would be easy to conclude that this was always Susan B. Anthony's table, where she had written the invitation to insurrection. After her death, the table went to NAWSA and became the centerpiece of an exhibit they were asked to create and donate to the Smithsonian Institution to commemorate the 1920 victory. Honored with a place in the nation's attic, the table made a fitting counterpart to the Portrait Monument, especially with the text provided by NAWSA: "Mahogany Table. Owned by Miss Anthony, and used when writing the 'Declaration of Sentiments' for women, in 1848." What were visitors to think?[22]

Stanton's children thought it "a memorial to Miss Anthony," noting that the actual women at the table were (as was becoming usual) unmentioned. Their offer to donate a portrait of their mother was rebuffed. "Susan B. Anthony's name has appeared more frequently than that of any other of the pioneers of Women's Rights; and yet, curiously enough, Miss Anthony took no part in the 1848 meeting," Theodore Stanton wrote in a 1923 feature for *The Independent* magazine, adding for good measure, "Another myth concerning Miss Anthony . . . may be disposed of here, viz., that she was the author of the Nineteenth Amendment." In a letter to the *New York Times*, he was even blunter, demanding that the paper stop repeating such errors. "The facts are," he wrote, "that Miss Anthony had no more to do with the convention of 1848 than did the man in the moon."[23]

Although these objections and corrections were understandable, nobody challenged the most insidious silence in the myth of Seneca Falls: its whiteness and its relentless narrowing of many women's movements to the achievement of suffrage by middle-class reformers. That silence grew louder in 1922, when NAWSA published two final installments of the *History of Woman Suffrage*, volumes 5 and 6, which powerfully reinforced the racial inequities inherent in that guiding story. Catt commissioned Harper to write the volumes in 1919, when chances for women's enfranchisement on a national scale looked hopeful. Harper finished them after the ratification of the Nineteenth Amendment. "The effort of women in the 'greatest republic on earth' to obtain a voice in its government began in 1848 and ended in complete victory in 1920," Harper explained. Like the now well-established origins point, this end point denied the racial dimensions that had challenged the movement for seventy-five years. Catt and Harper's "complete victory" completely overlooked women of color, who still could not vote in most southern states, where white supremacists continued to disenfranchise their race (through poll taxes, literacy tests, and outright intimidation, among other tactics). Black women appealed in vain to the main suffrage organizations for help in securing their own voting rights after 1920. White feminists deemed such "race problems" outside their purview. The ways in which black women had been largely written out of the dominant movement memory encouraged white women to overlook the needs and concerns of black women as the movement evolved. But for all of Stanton and Anthony's animus over women's exclusion from the Fifteenth Amendment after the Civil War, the so-called Negro's Hour did not really arrive until the 1960s, when black women and men won the legislative victories of the modern civil rights movement. Only with the 1965 Voting Rights Act did many women of color win the right to vote. But 1920 rendered the story, if not the victory, "complete."[24]

Yet the myth of Seneca Falls has remained an important rallying point for women's rights work throughout the twentieth century as well as an actor in the ongoing struggle for which it stands. Feminists organizing in the 1960s and 1970s adopted the story readily and used it strategically and productively—to legitimate activism and to attract support from women who may not have considered themselves activists. The story was ready-made—full of drama, compelling personalities, and promises of inevitable victory. When the United Nations declared 1977 the International Women's Year, feminists pressured Congress to allocate money for a national women's congress to mark the occasion. That National Women's Conference, the first federally funded women's rights meeting, opened in Houston, Texas, in 1977. It drew 20,000 women from across the country. Over four days, they deliberated on how to set and pursue a feminist agenda. (Another 10,000 women and men assembled in another Houston convention center to oppose women's rights.)[25]

A torch carried from Seneca Falls to Houston officially opened the ceremonies. Its entrance into the hall proved electric. Organizers anticipated the opening of the Houston convention by meeting first in Seneca Falls, two months before. There, a relative of President Jimmy Carter read a new Declaration of Sentiments written by the noted African American poet Maya Angelou, who obliquely highlighted the myth's racial overtones by proclaiming that "we promise to accept nothing less than justice for *every* woman." The next day, a descendant of one of the signers of the Declaration of Sentiments handed the torch to the first runner. Women took different legs of the journey, sprinting the torch closer and closer to Houston—carrying the torch of Seneca Falls both literally and figuratively. The relay took fifty-one days, crossed fourteen states, and covered 2,600 miles. As it approached the convention hall, roughly a thousand women, including noted feminist leaders Bella Abzug and Betty Friedan, ran with the torch for the last mile. Three first ladies of the United States—Lady Bird Johnson, Betty Ford, and Rosalynn Carter—received the torch inside the hall. With the spirit of Seneca Falls and the energy of the foremothers entering the proceedings, women opened a historic convention that helped set the movement's ongoing agenda.[26]

A year later, feminists transformed Seneca Falls into uncharted commemorative territory: they got the National Park Service to consider establishing a new national historical park dedicated to women's rights. Historic preservation had long centered upon the deeds of great men or the soldiers they sent to die in battle, but now a coalition of feminist groups and female politicians began to make headway. Over the years, the Wesleyan Chapel, where the 1848 meeting took place, had been a car dealership, a movie theater, and a laundromat. New York had much earlier erected a historical marker at the site, and women occasionally assembled there to hold makeshift commemorations for Seneca Falls anniversaries—sometimes with nothing more than a card table and a few folding chairs. Post–World War II deindustrialization hit Seneca Falls as it had the nation's larger cities, and facing a rapidly disappearing industrial base, area citizens began to recognize the economic potential of tourism. Later in 1978, when representatives from the National Park Service visited the area, they were mobbed by enthusiastic supporters, and the next year, they recommended to Congress that Seneca Falls become home to a new national historical park. Support from Stanton's descendants proved important as well. "One fall day," one historian explains, "they arrived in Seneca Falls with a load of books and furniture that had once belonged to Stanton." Stanton's elderly great-granddaughter, who had continued to guard Stanton's memory through her nearly seventy-five years spent in eclipse, declared: "It's time they came home." Stanton was well on her way to being rediscovered, thanks to the historical digging of new generations of feminists, and part of the initiative for the park involved preserving not just the Wesleyan Chapel, but also her home in Seneca Falls.[27]

In 1980, Jimmy Carter declared 8 March the start of women's history

Makeshift commemoration for the 130th anniversary of the Seneca Falls convention, in Seneca Falls, N.Y., July 1978 (Seneca Falls Reveille, 26 July 1978, courtesy of John Siccardi)

week, and U.S. representatives introduced legislation in the House for the creation of a Women's Rights National Historical Park. The measure almost died, but thanks to the unflagging pressure of supporters, President Carter signed the park into law that December. A promise of funding did not accompany it, however. The question of how to proceed was mind-boggling. Moreover, three weeks after Carter signed the park into law, Ronald Reagan took office, and a new conservative ethos arrived in Washington, D.C. This further threatened the park's creation, as Reagan instructed his new secretary of the interior, the inimitable James Watt, to freeze all funding for the acquisition of new park lands. The Elizabeth Cady Stanton Foundation tried to raise enough money to purchase Stanton's former house, which they intended to deed to the National Park Service, thus enabling the park's creation. They could not raise sufficient funds, however. Then, out of the blue, actor Alan Alda called the foundation to say he was sending a check for the balance needed. Celebration was cut short, however, as more obstacles ensued, with politicians and activists having to creatively maneuver around Reagan and Watt. At the end of June 1982, an ominous sign dawned, when the ERA, which Alice Paul had first introduced in Seneca Falls in 1923, again failed to be ratified within the congressionally specified time limit. The political tide of the nation was turning, and women clung nervously to hope for a park. That same spring, historian Gerda Lerner became the Organization of American Historians' first female president in roughly fifty years, and she mobilized the resources of professional historians behind the initiative.[28]

Suddenly and almost miraculously, after four years of constant agitation, the Women's Rights National Historical Park received enough funding to open to visitors. To coincide with the original convention, the park was dedicated on 17 July 1982, complete with a dramatic reenactment of the 1848 meeting. Over time, park officials have acquired additional buildings, including the old chapel where the meeting took place and the nearby homes of its organizers. Today, the Women's Rights National Historical Park remains an important destination for many women's rights supporters.[29] Stanton could never have imagined this in 1848; neither could Anthony have imagined it fifty years later, in 1898, despite her gift for shaping collective memory. The park not only pays tribute to Stanton and Anthony's activism and their skill as storytellers; it ratifies their pioneering assertion that women's history mattered—as both a heritage and a scholarly discipline. This has arguably been the greatest reality achieved by the myth of Seneca Falls.

The seventy-fifth anniversary of the Nineteenth Amendment in 1995 and the sesquicentennial of Seneca Falls in 1998 inspired women to pressure Congress to move the Portrait Monument—Johnson's hulking sculpture of Stanton, Anthony, and Mott—from the crypt back up to the Rotunda. That fight underscored the ongoing challenges of getting women's history deemed worthy of national recognition. Women had demanded for years that the sculpture be moved to a more prominent place. But those efforts had failed repeatedly. In 1995, legislation to move it to the Rotunda passed the Senate. House Speaker, Republican Newt Gingrich, however, managed to kill the bill by refusing to allow it off his desk. The House recessed without being able to take a vote. The issue was revived the following year and managed to pass. But this time Speaker Gingrich, together with several Republican congresswomen, blocked the appropriation of funds necessary to move it. The congresswomen claimed the statue was simply "too ugly" to take a place of honor in the Rotunda, an argument that people had been using for decades to denigrate it (and by implication, the feminist movement).

The nearly $75,000 needed had to be raised from private donors. After an engineering study determined the Rotunda floor could support its weight, the statue was at long last moved in 1997, in anticipation of the 150th anniversary of Seneca Falls. There, in the Capitol's symbolic and physical heart, the Portrait Monument disrupted the Rotunda's all-male statuary. Congresswoman Carolyn Maloney, a Democrat from New York, addressed opponents as Johnson's sculpture parted company with the crypt's restrooms: "It took 72 years for women to get the vote and 76 years to get the statue moved. They said the statue was too ugly to stand in the Rotunda. Have you looked at Abraham Lincoln lately? He wasn't placed in the Rotunda because of his good looks and neither were these women. They are placed here because of their accomplishments."[30]

That same fight, however, exposed the ongoing racial fissures in the myth of Seneca Falls, fissures inherent in the movement's past but also in the stories we choose to celebrate and remember in the present. Underscoring the ways in which Stanton and Anthony built both a movement and a memory centering on white women, the National Congress of Black Women (NCBW) had moved to block the monument's relocation. They objected that black women, active participants in the long struggle for rights, were not represented. "We have been left out of history too much, and we're not going to be left out anymore," explained the organization's president C. DeLores Tucker. When it became clear the monument would be relocated, Tucker—a civil rights activist, women's rights advocate, and politician—urged that the image of Sojourner Truth be carved into the sculpture's unfinished column, thus writing Truth (and black women, more generally) into the heart of women's rights narratives. Legislation toward this end was introduced in 2004, but the bill failed. Yet the group kept up pressure, under the joint leadership of E. Faye Williams, the NCBW's new chair, and Representative Sheila Jackson Lee of Texas. In 2006, they persuaded Congress to accept their donation of a Truth statue, as an antidote to the Portrait Monument, or at least as a companion to it.[31]

Intensive fundraising efforts followed, and a bronze bust of Truth was unveiled at a ceremony in April 2009 in Emancipation Hall in the U.S. Capitol Visitors Center, where it remains on permanent display. Actress Cicely Tyson delivered Truth's famous 1851 "Ar'n't I a Woman" speech, which itself has been handed down to us in problematic form through the pages of the *History*. First Lady Michelle Obama addressed the crowd and underscored the fault lines in inherited narratives. "Just as Susan B. Anthony, Elizabeth Cady Stanton, [and] Lucretia Mott would be pleased to know that we have a woman serving as the Speaker of the House of Representatives, I hope that Sojourner Truth would be proud to see me, a descendant of slaves, serving as the First Lady of the United States of America," Obama began, to rejoinders of "yes" and "amen!"[32]

Perhaps such achievements may give us the courage to ask whether the myth of Seneca Falls is finally becoming obsolete. Stanton and Anthony created it in response to a particular, intensely racialized moment in post–Civil War politics, but what does it mean to tell that story today? Seneca Falls continues to frame almost all present-day stories about early women's rights, whether told in an academic setting or on historical tours. And feminists still employ it shrewdly. Former secretary of state Hillary Clinton, for example, lit up the so-called Twittersphere with this tidbit on 19 July 2013: "Seneca Falls, 165 years ago today, began a movement that remains the unfinished business of the 21st century."[33] An essential actor in the decades of drama leading to the achievement of the Nineteenth Amendment, Seneca Falls may now, a century later, be more of a hindrance than an inspiration—in its whiteness, which ignores the rights of women of color; in its emphasis on the vote, which downplays other kinds of rights strategies; and in its middle-class sensibility, which diverts us away from other radicalizing experiences and theoretical foundations. Myths like Abraham Lincoln as the Great Emancipator or Rosa Parks as a tired seamstress can be useful and play important roles in the quest for universal human rights, but eventually all myths constrain the very causes they promote. Seneca Falls is inextricable from the limitations of nineteenth- and early twentieth-century progressivism. And by continuing to foreground it, we leave ourselves little room to create new founding stories that might better address the challenges of the twenty-first century.

Moreover, the myth of Seneca Falls has created a rigid chronology that scholars have had trouble revising. The years 1848 and 1920 frame the period that historians and activists alike refer to as "first-wave" feminism. "Second-wave" feminism is said to be the next large surge of women's rights activism, that of the 1960s and 1970s. Neither framing has been very useful for understanding the complexity of nineteenth- or twentieth-century feminism. These periodizations narrow the wide continuum of issues championed by activists and the wide array of women involved. The myth of Seneca Falls, which early feminists bequeathed to much later generations, also simply cannot encompass the spectrum of social justice causes not explicitly marked as feminist, but which have nevertheless been important to the evolution of feminist thought and action, both personal and political. In turn, the periodization implied by Seneca Falls obscures points of continuity and discontinuity between the so-called waves. For some time now, scholars have been trying to reconceptualize American women's history outside of these models.[34]

My goal has been to aid those efforts by undoing the master narrative itself. I have sought not to write around that narrative, as so many scholars have effectively done, but rather to dissect that still-powerful story, expose its historical life, and thereby help free the historical record. Because origin narratives promote the forgetting of struggles within the struggle, historicizing those narratives can help us counteract those effects and hopefully move in new directions. I have wanted to contribute to an understanding of why scholars and activists alike have been so constrained by a Seneca Falls periodization along with that story's moral (white political rights above all other rights)—constraints that ultimately limit our imaginations, our abilities to form coalitions, and even our potential.

Anthony's painful decision to burn large portions of her archive underscored an important tension in her role as historian-activist. She wrote the campaign's first and most enduring master narrative as a guide to action, and she intended for it to outlive her. One drastic way of achieving that goal was to deny future generations the chance to examine and reinterpret much of the source material. Although it is impossible to reconstruct the motivations behind the destruction, it could not have taken place against her will. Anthony was not unique in wanting to shape what was bequeathed to future generations. Many statesmen and stateswomen prune and consciously shape the archives to one degree or another. And she was not the only suffragist to destroy records. But given her conscious, long-standing cultivation of that record, perhaps the ultimate irony of her bonfires is that, in protecting the myth of Seneca Falls, she has ended up challenging historians while also constraining activists. As an activist first and foremost, Anthony was less interested in the past for its own sake than in the creation of a usable past that would advance her political work and goals. We cannot understand her historical works or her decision to burn documents outside of that reality. Both underscore the central premise of this book: memory is made, not found, and what we remember matters.

Notes

Abbreviations

Blackwell Family Papers	*Papers of the Blackwell Family* (microfilm) (Washington, D.C.: Library of Congress Photo Duplication Service, 1979).
HWS, 1	Elizabeth Cady Stanton, Susan B. Anthony, and Matilda Joslyn Gage, eds., *History of Woman Suffrage, Vol. 1, 1848–1861* (New York: Fowler & Wells, 1881; reprint, New York: Arno Press & New York Times, 1969).
HWS, 1, 2nd ed.	Elizabeth Cady Stanton, Susan B. Anthony, and Matilda Joslyn Gage, eds., *History of Woman Suffrage, Vol. 1, 1848–1861*, 2nd ed. (Rochester, N.Y.: Charles Mann, 1889; reprint, New York: Source Book Press, 1970).
HWS, 2	Elizabeth Cady Stanton, Susan B. Anthony, and Matilda Joslyn Gage, eds., *History of Woman Suffrage, Vol. 2, 1861–1876* (New York: Fowler & Wells, 1882; reprint, New York: Arno Press & New York Times, 1969).
HWS, 3	Elizabeth Cady Stanton, Susan B. Anthony, and Matilda Joslyn Gage, eds., *History of Woman Suffrage, Vol. 3, 1876–1885* (Rochester, N.Y.: Susan B. Anthony, 1886; reprint, New York: Arno Press & New York Times, 1969).
HWS, 4	Susan B. Anthony and Ida Husted Harper, eds., *The History of Woman Suffrage, Vol. 4, 1883–1900* (Rochester, N.Y.: Susan B. Anthony, 1902; reprint, New York: Arno Press, 1969).
HWS, 5	Ida Husted Harper, ed., *The History of Woman Suffrage, Vol. 5, 1900–1920* (New York: National American Woman Suffrage Association, 1922).
IHH Papers	Papers of Ida Husted Harper, 1841–1919, Huntington Research Library, Manuscripts Division, San Marino, Calif.
LDB Papers	Lillie Devereux Blake Papers, 1847–1986, Missouri History Museum Archives, St. Louis, Mo.
LdFG Papers	Laura [de Force] Gordon Papers, 1856–82, Bancroft Library, University of California, Berkeley.
MFA Papers	Fritz Anneke and Mathilde Franziska Anneke Papers, 1791–1934, Wisconsin Historical Society Library–Archives Division, Madison, Wis.
MJG Papers	Matilda Joslyn Gage Papers (microfilm), *Women's Studies Manuscript Collections from the Schlesinger Library, Series 1: Woman Suffrage*, edited by Anne Firor Scott (Bethesda, Md.: University Publications of America, 1990).
NAWSA Papers	*Records of the National American Woman Suffrage Association* (microfilm) (Washington, D.C.: Library of Congress, 1981).

Robinson and Shattuck Papers	Papers of Harriet Jane Hanson Robinson and Harriette Lucy Robinson Shattuck, 1833–1937, Arthur and Elizabeth Schlesinger Library on the History of Women, Radcliffe College, Archives and Manuscripts, Cambridge, Mass.
SAP	*The Papers of Elizabeth Cady Stanton and Susan B. Anthony: Microfilm Edition*, edited by Patricia G. Holland and Ann D. Gordon (Wilmington, Del.: Scholarly Resources, 1992).
Selected Papers, 1	Ann D. Gordon, Tamara Gaskell Miller, Stacy Kinlock Sewell, Ann Pfau, and Arlene Kriv, eds., *In the School of Anti-Slavery, 1840 to 1866*. Vol. 1 of *The Selected Papers of Elizabeth Cady Stanton and Susan B. Anthony* (New Brunswick, N.J.: Rutgers University Press, 1997).
Selected Papers, 2	Ann D. Gordon, Tamara Gaskell Miller, Susan I. Johns, Oona Schmid, Mary Poole, Veronica A. Wilson, and Stacy Kinlock Sewell, eds., *Against an Aristocracy of Sex, 1866 to 1873*. Vol. 2 of *The Selected Papers of Elizabeth Cady Stanton and Susan B. Anthony* (New Brunswick, N.J.: Rutgers University Press, 2000).
Selected Papers, 3	Ann D. Gordon, Allison L. Sneider, Ann Elizabeth Pfau, Kimberly J. Banks, Lesley L. Doig, Meg Meneghel Mac-Donald, and Margaret Sumner, eds., *National Protection for National Citizens, 1873 to 1880*. Vol. 3 of *The Selected Papers of Elizabeth Cady Stanton and Susan B. Anthony* (New Brunswick, N.J.: Rutgers University Press, 2003).
Selected Papers, 4	Ann D. Gordon, Krystal Frazier, Lesley L. Doig, Emily Westkaemper, and Robin Chapdelaine, eds., *When Clowns Make Laws for Queens, 1880 to 1887*. Vol. 4 of *The Selected Papers of Elizabeth Cady Stanton and Susan B. Anthony* (New Brunswick, N.J.: Rutgers University Press, 2006).
Selected Papers, 5	Ann D. Gordon, Lesley L. Doig, Patricia Hampson, Kathleen Manning, and Shannen Dee Williams, eds., *Their Place Inside the Body-Politic, 1887 to 1895*. Vol. 5 of *The Selected Papers of Elizabeth Cady Stanton and Susan B. Anthony* (New Brunswick, N.J.: Rutgers University Press, 2009).
Selected Papers, 6	Ann D. Gordon, Michael David Cohen, Sara Rzeszutek Haviland, Andy Duane Bowers, and Katherine D. Lee, eds., *An Awful Hush, 1895 to 1906*. Vol. 6 of *The Selected Papers of Elizabeth Cady Stanton and Susan B. Anthony* (New Brunswick, N.J.: Rutgers University, 2013).

Prologue

1. "The Anniversaries," *New-York Daily Tribune*, 11 May 1866; *New York World*, 11 May 1866, *SAP*, 11:519–21; "The Anniversaries," *New York Herald*, 11 May 1866, *SAP* 11:516–18; *Proceedings of the Eleventh National Woman's Rights Convention, 1866*, 49–51.

2. Historian Lori Ginzberg has shown that Stanton's demand was not, in fact, women's first public demand for enfranchisement. Ginzberg, *Untidy Origins*.

3. *Proceedings of the Eleventh National Woman's Rights Convention, 1866*, 49–51.

4. For a story of the park's creation, see Wellman, "'It's a Wide Community Indeed.'"

5. Wellman, *The Road to Seneca Falls*; DuBois, *Feminism and Suffrage*; Isenberg, *Sex and*

Citizenship; McMillen, *Seneca Falls*; Hewitt, "'Seeking a Larger Liberty'"; Flexner, *Century of Struggle*; Gurko, *The Ladies of Seneca Falls*.

6. Savage, *Standing Soldiers, Kneeling Slaves*, 7; Wright, *Origin Stories in Political Thought*, 3–23.

7. Theoharis, *Rebellious Life of Mrs. Rosa Parks*; McGuire, *At the Dark End of the Street*.

8. Daniel Horowitz, *Betty Freidan*.

9. For other works that query some of the central mythologies of American history, see Young, *Shoemaker and the Tea Party*; Loewen, *Lies My Teacher Told Me*; and Nash, *The Liberty Bell*.

10. Sklar, "Women's Rights Emerges"; Lerner, *Grimké Sisters from South Carolina*; Walker, "Women"; Ann D. Gordon and Bettye Collier-Thomas, *African-American Women*; McClymer, *This High and Holy Movement*; Dublin, *Women at Work*; *HWS*, 1:37; Ginzberg, *Untidy Origins*, 5; Alice Stone Blackwell, *Lucy Stone*; Kerr, *Lucy Stone*; Hannah Rosen, *Terror in the Heart of Freedom*; Harriet Jacobs, *Incidents in the Life of a Slave Girl*; Silver-Isenstadt, *Shameless*.

11. Said, *Beginnings*, 5.

12. Wright, *Origin Stories in Political Thought*, 11.

13. Ginzberg, *Untidy Origins*, 5.

14. For an account of Stanton and Anthony's friendship, see Rossi, "A Feminist Friendship." Biographies of Susan B. Anthony include Barry, *Susan B. Anthony*; Lutz, *Susan B. Anthony*; Katharine Anthony, *Susan B. Anthony*; Dorr, *Susan B. Anthony*; and Harper, *Life and Work of Susan B. Anthony*. Biographies of Stanton include Lutz, *Created Equal*; Griffith, *In Her Own Right*; and Ginzberg, *Elizabeth Cady Stanton*. *HWS*, 1:457–58.

15. Eric Foner, *Reconstruction*; Eric Foner, "The Meaning of Freedom"; Blight, *Race and Reunion*.

16. Blight, *Race and Reunion*; Fahs and Waugh, *Memory of the Civil War*; Kachun, *Festivals of Freedom*; Savage, *Standing Soldiers*; Kathleen Clark, *Defining Moments*; Brundage, *Where These Memories Grow*.

17. The words belong to New York suffragist Matilda Joslyn Gage. *HWS*, 3:4.

18. For a discussion of the literature on collective memory and social movements, as well as analyses of storytelling and protest politics, see Green, *Taking History to Heart*; Polletta, *It Was Like a Fever*; Ronald Jacobs, "The Narrative Integration"; Wright, *Origin Stories in Political Thought*; Joseph E. Davis, *Stories of Change*; DuBois, "Making Women's History"; Des Jardins, *Women and the Historical Enterprise*; Kachun, *Festivals of Freedom*; Kathleen Clark, *Defining Moments*; Blight, *Race and Reunion*; Hall, "The Long Civil Rights Movement"; and Romano and Raiford, *The Civil Rights Movement*.

19. For accounts that have integrated Stanton's and Anthony's historical work into an understanding of their activism, see DuBois, "Making Women's History"; Des Jardins, *Women and the Historical Enterprise*; Buhle and Buhle, *Concise History of Woman Suffrage*; Kern, *Mrs. Stanton's Bible*; and Ginzberg, *Elizabeth Cady Stanton*. For further discussion of the development of women's history, see the above, and some additional examples, Baym, *American Women Writers*; Melman, "Gender, History and Memory"; Sklar, "American Female Historians in Context"; Bonnie G. Smith, "Contribution of Women to Modern Historiography"; Bonnie G. Smith, "Women's History: A Retrospective"; Bonnie G. Smith, *The Gender of History*. For a theoretical understanding of how the work of storytellers is both conscious and unconscious, see Bruner, *Making Stories*.

20. There are many scholars who understand Seneca Falls to be a mythology, and many more who don't accept it as a helpful origin for understanding the complicated world of nineteenth-century women's rights. See, for example, Isenberg, *Sex and Citizenship*; Wellman, *The Road to Seneca Falls*; Hewitt, ed., *No More Permanent Waves*; Terborg-Penn, *African American Women*; Painter, "Voices of Suffrage"; and the growing literature critiquing the "wave" metaphor. Despite this, Seneca Falls has a tight hold on how scholars narrate and characterize nineteenth-century feminism.

The scholarship that has perhaps most effectively dealt with these challenges in writing about social movements has been civil rights scholarship, where an earlier focus on an idealized Martin Luther King Jr. has been complicated and blended into a much more comprehensive, complex, and contingent understanding of King, the movement, and its adherents. That scholarship has also squarely grappled with the problem of origins mythologies and the ways in which they are both necessary and useful to activism but challenging and debilitating for scholarly understandings of that activism. The classic statement of this in civil rights scholarship has been Jacquelyn Dowd Hall's 2005 article, "The Long Civil Rights Movement and the Political Uses of the Past."

21. For one scholarly call to pay more attention to suffrage history, see Baker, "Getting Right with Women's Suffrage."

22. Ellen DuBois's 1978 study *Feminism and Suffrage* continues to be the classic account of the postwar years, although it covers little of the postwar period, ending in 1872. More recently, scholars have again turned their attention to the movement's middle decades. See, for example, DuBois, *Woman Suffrage and Women's Rights*; Wagner, *A Time of Protest*; Sneider, *Suffragists in an Imperial Age*; and Dudden, *Fighting Chance.*

The only scholarly biography of Anthony is Kathleen Barry's 1988 study, *Susan B. Anthony*. Barry is a sociologist, and she worked before an important documentary collection became available, the *Elizabeth Cady Stanton and Susan B. Anthony Papers Project*. The collection, overseen since the 1980s by the historian Ann D. Gordon, has more than doubled the amount of material thought available on the two women. Sifting through repositories around the world, the project has collected and published their letters and diaries, speech transcripts, newspaper accounts about the women, and much, much more. The collection consists of forty-five reels of microfilm (published in 1991) and six annotated volumes (published between 1997 and 2013). It is a gem, a treasure trove, and a fitting monument to Stanton and Anthony's own hope that women's social history would one day be preserved. Yet despite the ready availability of sources, and the vast expansion in the documentary base, Anthony awaits her biographer. Meanwhile, scholars are still struggling to understand Stanton, who has been more thoroughly studied of late. On the challenges of writing about Anthony, see Gordon, "Knowing Susan B. Anthony." For recent scholarship grappling with Stanton's complexities, see Ginzberg, *Elizabeth Cady Stanton*; and DuBois and Smith, *Elizabeth Cady Stanton.*

23. Ginzberg, *Elizabeth Cady Stanton*, 40.

24. Ibid., 46–47.

25. *Proceedings of the General Anti-Slavery Convention, 1840*, 1–46; Ginzberg, *Elizabeth Cady Stanton*, 37–38.

26. Faulkner "The Root of the Evil," 385; Faulkner, *Lucretia Mott's Heresy*; Palmer, *Selected Letters of Lucretia Coffin Mott.*

27. Sarah M. Grimké, *Letters on the Equality of the Sexes*; Yellin and Van Horne, *The Abolitionist Sisterhood*; Hersh, *The Slavery of Sex*; Hansen, *Strained Sisterhood*; Jeffrey, *Great Silent Army of Abolitionism*; Lerner, *Grimké Sisters from South Carolina*; Yee, *Black Women Abolitionists*; Yellin, *Women and Sisters*; Zaeske, *Signatures of Citizenship*; Pierson, *Free Hearts and Free Homes*; Salerno, *Sister Societies*; Ginzberg, *Women and the Work of Benevolence*; Robertson, *Hearts Beating for Liberty*; Jeffrey, *Abolitionists Remember.*

28. Tolles, "Slavery and 'The Woman Question.'"

29. Quote from Judith Wellman, *The Road to Seneca Falls*, 186.

30. Ibid., 188.

31. The call is quoted in ibid., 189; see also Wellman, "Seneca Falls Women's Rights Convention."

32. Stanton to Elizabeth W. McClintock, [14? July 1848], *Selected Papers*, 1:69.

33. *Report of the Woman's Rights Convention, 1848.*

34. Wellman, *The Road to Seneca Falls*, 190–204.

35. There is an ongoing debate in the historiography about why the demand for women's voting rights proved so controversial. Previous wisdom held this was because the demand was so radical, the most radical of all the demands made. That interpretation, however, has undergone trenchant revision in recent years. More likely, the demand proved controversial not because it was the most radical, or the most forward thinking, but because Mott and others were Garrisonians, who eschewed participation in politics because of its collaboration with slavery. The idea that the vote was the most important demand, and the most radical, seems itself to be a product of a Seneca Falls mythology built over the postwar decades.

36. There is uncertainty about by what margins the ninth resolution passed. Wellman, *The Road to Seneca Falls*, 278n58.

37. Wellman, *The Road to Seneca Falls*, 193–208; Philip S. Foner, *Frederick Douglass on Women's Rights*; *Report of the Woman's Rights Convention, 1848*.

38. Wellman, *The Road to Seneca Falls*, 213.

39. Rossi, "A Feminist Friendship."

40. For an overview of antebellum women's rights organizing, see *HWS*, 1; Isenberg, *Sex and Citizenship*; and Hoffert, *When Hens Crow*; Hewitt, *Women's Activism and Social Change*; Boylan, *Origins of Women's Activism*; Ginzberg, *Untidy Origins*; Wellman, *The Road to Seneca Falls*; McClymer, *This High and Holy Moment*; and Anderson, *Joyous Greetings*. On Ernestine Rose, see Doress-Worters, *Mistress of Herself*; and Kolmerten, *The American Life of Ernestine L. Rose*. On Maria Stewart, see Richardson, *Maria W. Stewart*.

41. Alice Stone Blackwell, *Lucy Stone*; Kerr, *Lucy Stone*, 52, 86–87; Million, *Woman's Voice, Woman's Place*; Lasser and Merrill, *Friends and Sisters*.

42. In 1848, Stanton informed Mott that she and Elizabeth McClintock were preparing a history of the movement. Stanton made no reference to the history again until 1855, when Stanton wrote Mott asking for details about women's activism. By 1858, she had written a short historical address, which Anthony read to the 1858 National Woman's Rights Convention. It was never published, and no manuscript version remains, only Anthony's reading copy. Mott to Stanton, 3 October 1848, *Selected Papers*, 1:127–28, 129n5; address by Stanton to the Eighth National Woman's Rights Convention, [13 May 1858], *Selected Papers*, 1:361–72.

43. Lucretia Mott to Elizabeth Cady Stanton, 16 March 1855, Palmer, *Selected Letters of Lucretia Coffin Mott*, 233; and Faulkner, *Lucretia Mott's Heresy*, 72.

44. *Proceedings of the National Women's Rights Convention, 1853*, 67–94.

45. J. Elizabeth Jones, unidentified newspaper clipping, [1861], annotated by Anthony, and bound before #18 in a collection of pamphlets Anthony compiled, labeled "Reports of Woman's Rights Conventions, 1848–1870," Susan B. Anthony Collection.

46. Lucretia Mott to Elizabeth Cady Stanton, 16 March 1855, Palmer, *Selected Letters of Lucretia Coffin Mott*, 236; Ginzberg, *Elizabeth Cady Stanton*, 41.

47. Lucretia Mott to Elizabeth Cady Stanton, 16 March 1855, Palmer, *Selected Letters of Lucretia Coffin Mott*, 236.

Chapter 1

1. "Meeting of the American Equal Rights Association in New York," 10 May 1867, *Selected Papers*, 2:63; "The Anniversaries," *New York Times*, 11 May 1867, *SAP*, 12:197–99. "Meeting of the American Equal Rights Association in New York," 10 May 1867, *Selected Papers*, 2:64. For a discussion of Stanton's support for educated suffrage, see Kern, *Mrs. Stanton's Bible*; Mitchell, "'Lower Orders.'" For a rebuttal, see Ann D. Gordon, "Stanton and the Right to Vote." "Meeting of the American Equal Rights Association in New York," 10 May 1867, *Selected Papers*, 2:65, 66, 71n. One newspaper identified the woman shouting "shame!" as Abby Kelley Foster. "The Anniversaries," *New York Times*, 11 May 1867, *SAP*, 12:198.

2. The standard account for these developments is DuBois, *Feminism and Suffrage*.

3. For discussions on freedpeople's definitions of freedom, see Hannah Rosen, *Terror in the Heart of Freedom*, 2–6; Laura F. Edwards, *Gendered Strife and Confusion*, 46–54, 92–100; Hunter, *To 'Joy My Freedom*, 21–43; Stanley, *From Bondage to Contract*, 35–59; Schwalm, *A Hard Fight for We*, 147–86; Eric Foner, *Reconstruction*, 78–128; Eric Foner, *The Story of American Freedom*, 95–113; Saville, *The Work of Reconstruction*, 5–31.

4. Quotation from Keyssar, *The Right to Vote*, 184.

5. Quoted in Ann D. Gordon, "Woman Suffrage (Not Universal Suffrage)," 5.

6. Keyssar, *The Right to Vote*.

7. DuBois, *Feminism and Suffrage*, 63–65, 67–68; Ginzberg, *Elizabeth Cady Stanton*, 119; Terborg-Penn, *African American Women*, 24–35, and Terborg-Penn, "African American Women and the Vote"; Painter, "Voices of Suffrage"; Collier-Thomas, "Frances Ellen Watkins Harper"; Porter, "The Remonds of Salem, Massachusetts." For discussions on antebellum feminist-abolitionism, see Yellin and Van Horne, *The Abolitionist Sisterhood*; Hersh, *The Slavery of Sex*; Hansen, *Strained Sisterhood*; Jeffrey, *The Great Silent Army of Abolitionism*; Lerner, *The Grimké Sisters from South Carolina*; Yee, *Black Women Abolitionists*; Yellin, *Women and Sisters*; Zaeske, *Signatures of Citizenship*; Pierson, *Free Hearts and Free Homes*; Salerno, *Sister Societies*; Robertson, *Hearts Beating for Liberty*. For a discussion on the ideal role of middle-class women in the antebellum era, see Welter, "The Cult of True Womanhood."

8. "Meeting of the American Equal Rights Association in New York," 9 May 1867, *Selected Papers*, editorial note, 2:61–62.

9. Stanton to the Editor, National Anti-Slavery Standard, 26 December 1865, *Selected Papers*, 1:565n1. The phrase was in use from May 1865 on, first used by Wendell Phillips at the Thirty-Second Anniversary meeting of the American Anti-Slavery Society. "Thirty-Second Anniversary of the American Anti-Slavery Society," *Liberator*, 19 May 1865, 78; "The Anniversaries," *New York Times*, 10 May 1865; Ginzberg, *Elizabeth Cady Stanton*, 215n47.

10. DuBois, *Feminism and Suffrage*, 64–71.

11. Martha S. Jones, *All Bound Up Together*, 119–49.

12. Ibid., 141.

13. Painter, "Voices of Suffrage"; Martha S. Jones, *All Bound Up Together*; Sumler-Edmond, "The Quest for Justice"; Terborg-Penn, *African American Women*, 36–53. Debates about black women's rights in the South took a different form. See Elsa Barkley Brown, "Negotiating and Transforming the Public Sphere"; Schwalm, *A Hard Fight for We*; Hunter, *To 'Joy My Freedom*.

14. Gillette, *The Right to Vote*, 25–29; Wang, *The Trial of Democracy*, 21–23.

15. On the Fourteenth Amendment, see Eric Foner, *Reconstruction*, 251–61; Dudden, *Fighting Chance*, 77–80; Wang, *The Trial of Democracy*, 18–28, 40; Epps, *Democracy Reborn*. For an interpretation of how "male" ended up in the Fourteenth Amendment, see Sandage, *Born Losers*, 212–15. For discussion on AERA's focus on Kansas, see Dudden, *Fighting Chance*, 108–32; Dubois, *Feminism and Suffrage*, 79–104.

16. Train, *The Great Epigram Campaign of Kansas*, 58.

17. Dudden, *Fighting Chance*, 108–32; Train, *The Great Epigram Campaign of Kansas*; and Anthony to Anna E. Dickinson, 23 September 1867, *Selected Papers*, 2:92–95n11; speech by Anthony in St. Louis, Missouri, [25 November 1867], Anthony to Anna E. Dickinson, 28 November 1867, Stanton to Edwin A. Studwell, 30 November [1867], and Stanton to the editor of the *New York World*, [before 19 December 1867], *Selected Papers*, 2:104–17, 119–21; Harper, *Life and Work*, 1:286–94.

18. "Woman and the Ballot," *Daily Missouri Democrat*, 16 November 1867, *SAP*, 12:583; "The Suffrage Question," *Chicago Tribune*, 23 November 1867, *SAP*, 12:590–91; "Woman Suffrage," *St. Louis Daily Times*, 26 November 1867, *SAP*, 12:592; "Woman Suffrage and Greenbacks," unidentified clipping, 28 November 1867, *SAP*, 12:595–97; "Female Suffrage and Equal Rights," *Cincinnati Daily Gazette*, 29 November 1867, *SAP*, 12:607–8; "Female Suffrage," *Hartford Daily Courant*, 11 December 1867, *SAP*, 12:641.

19. Stanton to Ellen D. Eaton, 17 December [1867], *Selected Papers*, 2:117–19n2.

20. The first issue stated, "The *Revolution* will advocate: 1. In Politics—Educated Suffrage, Irrespective of Sex or Color," *Revolution,* 8 January 1868, 1.

21. Lucy Stone to William Lloyd Garrison, 6 March 1868, William Lloyd Garrison Correspondence, 1823–79, Ms. A.1.2, vol. 36, p. 11b, Rare Books and Manuscripts Division, Boston Public Library, Mass.

22. "Editorial from the *Revolution,*" 6 August 1868, in *Selected Papers,* 2:159n3; DuBois, *Feminism and Suffrage,* 145–47; Ray, "Representing Working Class in Early U.S. Feminist Media."

23. On Stanton's thought, see Ginzberg, *Elizabeth Cady Stanton*; Sue Davis, *Political Thought of Elizabeth Cady Stanton*; Gornick, *The Solitude of Self*; DuBois, *Feminism and Suffrage,* 103–4, 106–8, 116–18; Dubois and Smith, *Elizabeth Cady Stanton.* On divorce, see Cott, *Public Vows,* 24–67; Stanton to John Hooker, 22 February [1870], *Selected Papers,* 2:305–6; Speech by Stanton to a Mass Meeting of Women in New York, [17 May 1870], *Selected Papers,* 2:336–56; and "Mrs. Stanton's Radical Views," *Revolution,* 17 November 1870. Stanton also had a speech titled "Marriage and Divorce," Anthony Diary, 17 October 1870, *Selected Papers,* 2:367. The *Woman's Journal* criticized her lectures on divorce, claiming divorce would "destroy the purity and stability of marriage," *Woman's Journal,* 5 November 1870. On the *Revolution,* see Dow, "The *Revolution*"; Walters, "Their Rights and Nothing Less"; and Walters, "To Hustle with the Rowdies."

24. Quoted in DuBois, *Feminism and Suffrage,* 164.

25. Ibid., 180.

26. Gillette, *The Right to Vote*; Wang, *The Trial of Democracy,* 39–48; Keyssar, *The Right to Vote,* 93–104.

27. "Women of the Period," *New York World,* 13 May 1869, *SAP,* 13:501–2. For a discussion of the racism in the postwar suffrage movement, see Angela Davis, "Racism in the Woman Suffrage Movement"; Ginzberg, *Elizabeth Cady Stanton*; Mitchell, "'Lower Orders'"; and Newman, *White Women's Rights*; Terborg-Penn, *African American Women*; Painter, "Voices of Suffrage"; Martha S. Jones, *All Bound Up Together.*

28. "Women of the Period," *New York World,* 13 May 1869, *SAP,* 13:503.

29. Ibid., 504–5.

30. DuBois, *Feminism and Suffrage,* 188–89; "Women of the Period," *New York World,* 13 May 1869, *SAP,* 13:504; "Equal Rights," *New York Times,* 13 May 1869, *SAP,* 13:517.

31. "Equal Rights," *New York Times,* 14 May 1869, *SAP,* 13:519.

32. "The Women in Council," *Methodist, SAP,* 13:524.

33. "The Women in Council," *Methodist, SAP,* 13:524.

34. Ibid.

35. Blackwell later charged that Stanton had told him the day prior to the reception "that all idea of forming a new society or taking any steps towards doing so were for the present abandoned," so he and Stone had left town. Stanton, "National Woman's Suffrage Association," *Revolution,* 20 May 1869, *Selected Papers,* 2:241–43n1; "The Woman Suffrage Movement," 9 April 1870, *Woman's Journal.*

36. Stanton, "National Woman's Suffrage Association," *Revolution,* 20 May 1869, *Selected Papers,* 2:241–42.

37. "The Woman's Suffrage Association," *New York Times,* 18 May 1869, *SAP* 13:538.

38. Stanton, "National Woman's Suffrage Association," *Revolution,* 20 May 1869, *Selected Papers,* 2:241–42.

39. "The Fifteenth Amendment," *Revolution,* 20 May 1869, 313; "The Fifteenth Amendment," *Revolution,* 3 June 1869, 344; "Paula Wright Davis on the Fifteenth Amendment," *Revolution,* 17 June 1869, 374; "The Fifteenth Amendment," *Revolution,* 1 July 1869, 408. "Woman Suffrage," *Toledo Blade,* 6 March 1869, *SAP,* 13:417; "Suffrage," *Chicago Republican,* 12 February 1869, *SAP,* 13:328–30; "The Woman Suffrage Convention," *Buffalo Commercial Advertiser,* 6 July 1869, *SAP,* 13:591. Also see DuBois, *Feminism and Suffrage,* 174–85.

40. Keyssar, *The Right to Vote*; Gillette, *The Right to Vote*; Wang, *Trial of Democracy.*

41. Quoted in Stanton, "The Sixteenth Amendment," 29 April 1869, *Revolution, Selected Papers*, 2:236–38; and Keyssar, *The Right to Vote*, 185.

42. Ann D. Gordon, "Introduction," *Selected Papers*, 2:xxv–xxvii; Ginzberg, *Elizabeth Cady Stanton*, 141–42.

43. Stanton, "National Woman's Suffrage Association," *Revolution*, 20 May 1869, *Selected Papers*, 2:241–42; and Lucy Stone unpublished manuscript, 4 February 1882, AERA File, *NAWSA Papers*, 26:25–42, transcribed by Ida Porter Boyer.

44. DuBois, *Feminism and Suffrage*, 195.

45. Ibid.

46. Ibid.

47. Stone to Ester Pugh, 30 August 1869, Papers of Ida Husted Harper, 1841–1919, box 1.

48. "Woman Suffrage," *Cleveland Leader*, 25 November 1869, *SAP*, 14:93.

49. *SAP*, 14:96; "Woman Suffrage," *Cleveland Plain Dealer*, 25 November 1869, *SAP*, 14:108.

50. "Woman Suffrage," *Cleveland Plain Dealer*, 25 November 1869, *SAP*, 14:108.

51. For a discussion of the creation of the American Woman Suffrage Association, see Kerr, *Lucy Stone*, 138–59; "Woman Suffrage," *Cleveland Leader*, 25 November 1869, *SAP*, 14:93–98; "Woman Suffrage," *Cleveland Plain Dealer*, 25 November 1869, *SAP*, 14:105–8; "Woman Suffrage," *Cleveland Daily Leader*, 26 November 1869, *SAP*, 14:99–104; "Woman Suffrage," *Cleveland Plain Dealer*, 26 November 1869, *SAP*, 14:109; "Woman Suffrage," *New York World*, 27 November 1869, *SAP*, 14:110–12. For the allegiances of African American women, see Terborg-Penn, *African American Women*, 34.

52. On the American Association's state strategy, see *Constitution of the American Woman Suffrage Association*, 3. Anthony to Laura de Force Gordon, 9 February 1871, *Selected Papers*, 2:418n4; "To Woman Suffragists," *Woman's Journal*, 24 November 1877; Flexner, *Century of Struggle*, 146–47, 167–69; DuBois, *Feminism and Suffrage*, 195–200. On Americans' belief that states regulated voting, see Wang, *The Trial of Democracy*, 13–14, 43, 62; Keyssar, *The Right to Vote*, 99; Gillette, *The Right to Vote*, 88–90. Mead, *How the Vote Was Won*, 35–44; "American Woman Suffrage Association, Mass Convention," *Woman's Journal*, 28 May 1870.

Because the American Association supported gaining suffrage through state-level politics, its officers also conceived of themselves differently than those of the National Association did. They viewed the American Association as a coordinating body, something to aid and help coordinate suffrage efforts in the states. They wanted "to create local centres [*sic*] of activity, each supreme within its own jurisdiction," to make these "local centres the real source of power." (Henry Brown Blackwell, "Political Organization," *Woman's Journal*, 8 January 1870.) They did not see themselves as setting movement agenda. And rather than being an open body, inviting all, and giving all voting rights, as did the National Association, they organized themselves on a delegate basis. Each state had voting representatives in the same proportion as their numbers in the U.S. House of Representatives.

53. The editors are listed on the first page of its first issue, *Woman's Journal*, 8 January 1870. The editors evolved and changed over the years.

54. Henry Brown Blackwell, "American Woman Suffrage Association," *Woman's Journal*, 8 January 1870.

55. Blackwell, "Political Organization," *Woman's Journal*, 8 January 1870.

56. Walters, "A Burning Cloud by Day"; Walters, "To Hustle with the Rowdies"; Huxman, "The Woman's Journal."

57. "Letter from Miss Anthony," *Revolution*, 14 April 1870, 235; "A Good Movement," *Revolution*, 21 April 1870; "Meeting to Dissolve the National Woman Suffrage Association in New York," *Selected Papers*, 2:333n3.

58. Parker Pillsbury, "The Two Associations," *Revolution*, 24 March 1870.

59. "Remarks by Anthony to the American Woman Suffrage Association in Cleveland," [23 November 1870], *Selected Papers*, editorial note, 2:376; for Mott, see "Peace on Earth,

and Good Will to Women," *Independent*, 14 April 1870; for another demand for union, see Martha Coffin Wright to Anthony and Stone, 4 November 1869, *SAP*, 14:67–68.

60. "The Peace Conference," *Revolution*, 14 April 1870, 233–34.

61. For Tilton's petition, see "The Enfranchisement of Woman," *Revolution*, 24 March 1870, 189.

62. Anthony to Hooker, 21 March 1870, *SAP*, 14:652; Anthony to Stanton, [21 March 1870], *SAP*, 14:660; Anthony to Anna Dickinson, 22 March 1870, *SAP*, 14:663.

63. Pillsbury, "An Olive Branch," *Revolution*, 31 March 1870.

64. William Lloyd Garrison, Julia Ward Howe, Henry B. Blackwell, Mary A. Livermore, "The Woman Suffrage Movement," *Woman's Journal*, 9 April 1870.

65. Garrison et al., "The Woman Suffrage Movement," *Woman's Journal*, 9 April 1870; and "Peace on Earth and Good Will to Women," *Independent*, 14 April 1870. In the *Journal's* next issue, its editors angrily charged that Tilton had refused to print their letter of opposition to the plan, "A One-Sided Method of Effecting Peace," *Woman's Journal*, 16 April 1870.

66. Anthony to Isabella Beecher Hooker, 21 March 1870, *SAP*, 14:653.

67. Anthony to Hooker, 2 May 1870, *SAP*, 14:699–700.

68. For the list of those elected to represent the National Association, see "The Peace Conference," *Revolution*, 7 April 1870, 219.

69. "Peace on Earth and Good Will to Women," *Independent*, 14 April 1870; Pillsbury, "The Peace Conference," *Revolution*, 14 April 1870, 233–34; "Mr. Tilton's Meeting," *Woman's Journal*, 9 April 1870.

70. "Woman Suffrage," *New York Times*, 11 May 1870, *SAP*, 14:720; "Woman Suffrage," *New York Times*, 12 May 1870, *SAP*, 14:721–22; "The Disenfranchised Sex," *New York World*, 12 May 1870, *SAP*, 14:723; "Woman Suffrage," *New York Tribune*, 11 May 1870, *SAP*, 14:716–17; "Miss Anthony's Convention," *New York Tribune*, 12 May 1870, *SAP*, 14:718–19; and "Anniversary of the National Woman Suffrage Association," *Revolution*, 19 May 1870, 305–9, and 26 May 1870, 321–23. For a biting *Woman's Journal* column denouncing the Union Association, see "Mr. Tilton's Movement," *Revolution*, 21 April 1870, 250. For a good account of the debate over unification that engulfed the American Association's November convention, where Anthony appeared to apply pressure, see "Woman Suffrage," *Cleveland Daily Leader*, 24 November 1870, *SAP*, 14:1081–85.

71. Lucy Stone, unpublished manuscript, 4 February 1882, AERA File, *NAWSA Papers*, 26:29–33. Transcribed by Ida Porter Boyer. Blackwell, "American Equal Rights Association," *Woman's Journal*, 28 May 1870; "Important Transfer," *Revolution*, 19 May 1870, 312–13; and Anthony Diary, [13–14 May 1870], *Selected Papers*, 2:333–34; and Stone to Antoinette Brown Blackwell, 22 March 1870, Lasser and Merrill, *Friends and Sisters*, 177.

72. "Its Work Accomplished," *Chicago Tribune*, 10 April 1870, 2; "The Anti-Slavery Society," *New York Times*, 10 April 1870, 8; "Woman Suffrage," *New York Times*, 11 May 1870, 1; "Woman Suffrage, " *New York Times*, 12 May 1870, 5; "Anniversaries," *New York Times*, 13 May 1870, 5; "The Anniversaries," *Chicago Tribune*, 12 May 1870, 4; "A Divided House," *New York Times*, 14 May 1870, 4; "Woman Suffrage—Concentrating Forces," *New York Times*, 15 May 1870, 6.

73. "The Decade Meeting," *Revolution*, 8 September 1870, 153.

74. Stanton briefly referred to the Seneca Falls anniversary in her remarks to the 1868 AERA meeting. She simply stated, as one newspaper reported it, "that it was just twenty years since the initiation of the movement for equal wages and work, and equal representation." "Equal Rights," *New York World*, 15 May 1868, *SAP*, 12:896.

75. Jeffrey, *Abolitionists Remember*, 99.

76. Ibid., 1; Kachun, *Festivals of Freedom*; Kathleen Clark, *Defining Moments*; Blight, *Race and Reunion*; Brundage, *Where These Memories Grow*; Fahs and Waugh, *The Memory of the Civil War*; Savage, *Standing Soldiers, Kneeling Slaves*.

77. Blight, *Race and Reunion*.

78. Kachun, *Festivals of Freedom*; Kathleen Clark, *Defining Moments*; Blight, *Race and Reunion*; Savage, *Standing Soldiers, Kneeling Slaves*; Eric Foner, *The Story of American Freedom*.

79. Kachun, *Festivals of Freedom*; Kathleen Clark, *Defining Moments*; Blight, *Race and Reunion*; Savage, *Standing Soldiers, Kneeling Slaves*; Fahs and Waugh, *The Memory of the Civil War*.

80. Berlin, "Who Freed the Slaves?"; Masur, "'A Rare Phenomenon of Philological Vegetation.'"

81. Quoted in Jeffrey, *Abolitionists Remember*, 102. Yellin and Van Horne, *The Abolitionist Sisterhood*; Hersh, *The Slavery of Sex*; Hansen, *Strained Sisterhood*; Jeffrey, *The Great Silent Army of Abolitionism*; Lerner, *The Grimké Sisters from South Carolina*; Yee, *Black Women Abolitionist*; Yellin, *Women and Sisters*; Zaeske, *Signatures of Citizenship*; Pierson, *Free Hearts and Free Homes*; Salerno, *Sister Societies*; Robertson, *Hearts Beating for Liberty*.

82. Lederman, "Davis, Paulina Kellogg Wright"; and McClymer, *This High and Holy Moment*.

83. Paulina Wright Davis, *History of the National Woman's Rights Movement*, 5–6.

84. "The Disenfranchised Sex," *New York World*, 12 May 1870, *SAP*, 14:723.

85. "The Decade Meeting," *Revolution*, 8 September 1870.

86. Ibid.

87. Anthony Diary, 1 October 1870, *Selected Papers*, 363–64n3; "The Decade Meeting Again," *Revolution*, 13 October 1870, 233; "Woman Suffrage Celebration," *Revolution*, 20 October 1870, 252.

88. "Second Decade Celebration," *Revolution*, 27 October 1870, 265.

89. There was a Unitarian conference in New York City those same days, and a popular English lecturer, Thomas Hughes, spoke at Cooper Institute that evening. Ibid.

90. Ibid.

91. Stanton was reading from the call. Paulina Wright Davis, *History of the National Woman's Rights Movement*, 5.

92. Paulina Wright Davis, *History of the National Woman's Rights Movement*, 6.

93. Unidentified column, MJG Papers, Part A, Gage Scrapbook, 4:448–49; "Newport Convention," *Revolution*, 9 September 1869, 147–49.

94. "Newport Convention," *Revolution*, 9 September 1869, 147.

95. Paulina Wright Davis, *History of the National Woman's Rights Movement*, 13.

96. "Newport Convention," *Revolution*, 9 September 1869, 147.

97. Paulina Wright Davis, *History of the National Woman's Rights Movement*, 6.

98. Ibid.

99. "Second Decade Celebration," *Revolution*, 27 October 1870, 265.

100. Ibid.

101. Paulina Wright Davis, *History of the National Woman's Rights Movement*, 6.

102. Ibid., 8–9.

103. Paulina Wright Davis, *History of the National Woman's Rights Movement*, 23.

104. "What the Papers Said about the Second Decade Celebration," *Revolution*, 27 October 1870.

105. Paulina Wright Davis, *History of the National Woman's Rights Movement*, 6–31

106. Ibid., 23, 25.

107. Ibid., 24.

108. *Proceedings of the National Woman's Rights Convention, 1853*; Anthony Diary, [early November 1853], *Selected Papers*, 1.

109. Stanton did send a letter to the 1850 convention; see McClymer, *This High and Holy Moment*, 121, 123–26; Ginzberg, *Elizabeth Cady Stanton*, 75; *Proceedings of the Tenth National Woman's Rights Convention, 1860*.

110. The signers to the 1870 convention call were Lucretia Mott, Sarah Pugh, Stanton, Ernestine Rose, Samuel May, and Clarina I. H. Nichols. All but one, Ernestine Rose, having signed the original call for Worcester in 1850.

111. "What the Papers Said about the Second Decade Celebration," *Revolution*, 27 October 1870, 266.

112. Paulina Wright Davis, *History of the National Woman's Rights Movement*, 8, 12; "What the Papers Said about the Second Decade Celebration," *Revolution*, 27 October 1870, 266.

113. "Mrs. Elizabeth Cady Stanton's Address at the Decade Meeting on Marriage and Divorce," in Paulina Wright Davis, *History of the National Woman's Rights Movement*, 60–83.

114. Stanton, "The Woman's Rights Movement."

115. Ibid., 377–79.

116. Ibid., 392.

117. Theodore Tilton, "Mrs. Elizabeth Cady Stanton," in Parton, *Eminent Women of the Age*, 346.

118. Stanton was reading from the call. Paulina Wright Davis, *History of the National Woman's Rights Movement*, 5.

Chapter 2

1. "Woman's Rights," *New York Herald*, 7 May 1873, *SAP*, 17:63; Woman Suffragists," *New York World*, 7 May 1873, *SAP*, 17:60.

2. For an account of the Seneca Falls commemorations, see Rose et al., "Remembering Seneca Falls"; and Rose, "Seneca Falls Remembered." For a general discussion of ritual commemoration, see Connerton, *How Societies Remember*.

3. In Paulina Wright Davis's 1871 published history, she comments on the vast expansion in the movement after the war. Paulina Wright Davis, *History of the National Woman's Rights Movement*, 27–30.

4. DuBois, *Feminism and Suffrage*, 181.

5. Stanton spoke of the people showing up at the new National Association's weekly meetings in New York City. The National Association eventually suspended these weekly meetings, which were short lived, partly because organizers could not control the agenda. Stanton interview with the *Cincinnati Daily Enquirer*, October 1869; *New York World*, 15 October 1869.

6. "The Suffrage Movement," *New York Times*, 31 December 1869, *SAP*, 14:161. After shutting down the meetings as one way to control them, they reopened them with tighter controls on who could speak. See reports from "Woman Suffrage," *New York Times*, 7 January 1870, *SAP*, 14:514; and "Woman Suffrage," *New York Tribune*, 7 January 1870, *SAP*, 14:515–16.

7. This trend has dominated the scholarship for a long time. For an early account, see Flexner, *Century of Struggle*; and, most recently, McMillen, *Seneca Falls and the Origins of the Women's Rights Movement*.

8. Most suffrage scholarship continues to emphasize the preeminence of national figures, particularly Stanton and Anthony. Most recently, see Dudden, *Fighting Chance*. For a helpful discussion of the political costs of overlooking the importance of movement work at the grassroots, albeit in a different context, see Payne, *I've Got the Light of Freedom*; and Dittmer, *Local People*.

9. Walter, "Woman Suffrage in Missouri," 42; and Monia Cook Morris, "History of Woman Suffrage in Missouri," 37.

10. Noun, *Strong-Minded Women*, 116, 119.

11. Papers of Elizabeth Boynton Harbert.

12. "The Lafayette Convention," *Woman's Advocate* (Dayton, Ohio), 20 November 1869.

13. "Woman Suffrage Association," *Pioneer*, 22 January 1870.

14. Ann Smith, "Ann Martin," 10.

15. Beeton, *Women Vote in the West*; Sarah Barringer Gordon, *The Mormon Question*; Mead, *How the Vote Was Won*; and Heather Cox Richardson, *West from Appomattox*.

16. Paul E. Fuller, *Laura Clay*, 22.

17. Elsa Barkley Brown, "To Catch the Vision of Freedom"; Gatewood, "'The Remarkable Misses Rollin.'"

18. Scott, *The Southern Lady*, 172.

19. "The Ballot," *Daily Morning Chronicle*, 13 January 1871, *SAP*, 15:329. Corroborating Davis's observations, Elaine Frantz Parsons has argued that in the early years of Reconstruction, there existed "a small flurry of [woman suffrage] activity in many Southern states . . . as [white] Southern strategists contemplated their response to the enfranchisement of freedmen." Parsons, "Elizabeth Avery Meriwether."

20. Paulina Wright Davis also observed this harassment during her southern travels, where she witnessed black women shaping black men's voting through pressure tactics and collective collusion. "The Ballot," *Daily Morning Chronicle*, 13 January 1871, *SAP*, 15:329. See also Saville, *The Work of Reconstruction*; and Elsa Barkley Brown, "To Catch the Vision," and "Negotiating and Transforming the Public Sphere," 125.

21. The committee chair was Mary Ann Shadd Cary, the first African American woman to cast a vote in the United States. Rhodes, *Mary Ann Shadd Cary*, 191–96; and Martha S. Jones, *All Bound Up Together*, 147.

22. Terborg-Penn, *African American Women*, 38–42, 47; "Unusual Scene at the Board of Registry in Washington," 22 April 1869, *Washington (D.C.) Tribune*, in Matilda Joslyn Gage Scrapbooks, vol. 1.

23. "Woman's Rights," *Daily Missouri Republican*, 21 December 1868.

24. Speakers included "Mrs. Augusta Lilienthal, Mrs. Clara Neymann and Dr. A. Donal." "New York," *New York Times*, 21 March 1872, 8.

25. Lillie Devereux Blake, diary, 9 September 1874, 27 January and 24 June 1875, Lillie Devereux Blake Papers, 1847–1986. Blake spoke to this group on several occasions. Its meetings were also regularly reported in the *New York Times*: see "Woman Suffrage," 10 September 1874, 7; "Woman Suffrage: Meeting of the Young Men's Woman Suffrage Association at Plimpton Hall," 24 September 1874, 10; "The Young Men's Woman's Suffrage League: The Proceedings Last Night," 19 November 1874, 8; "City and Suburban News," 4 March 1875, 10; "City and Suburban News," 21 April 1875, 12; and "Female Citizenship: An Address by Mrs. Lilie [*sic*] Devereux Blake before the Young Men's Woman's Suffrage Association," 24 June 1875, 7.

26. William Lloyd Garrison to Elizabeth Pease Nichol, 26 September 1869, William Lloyd Garrison Correspondence, Ms. A.1.1, vol. 7, p. 104.

27. Stanton to Anthony, 2 January 1871, *Selected Papers*, 2:401–2. Isabella Beecher Hooker, sister of the famous Beecher siblings, and a new suffrage recruit after the Civil War, took charge of the 1870 Union Association convention.

28. Anthony to Stanton, 2 January 1871, *Selected Papers*, 2:402n3.

29. For biographies of the pair, in which their individual work is discussed, see Lutz, *Created Equal*; Griffith, *In Her Own Right*; Ginzberg, *Elizabeth Cady Stanton*; Barry, *Susan B. Anthony*; Lutz, *Susan B. Anthony*; Katharine Anthony, *Susan B. Anthony*; Dorr, *Susan B. Anthony*; Harper, *Life and Work of Susan B. Anthony*. Their work is best traced, however, through the magisterial *Elizabeth Cady Stanton and Susan B. Anthony Papers Project*, on microfilm and in print, cited throughout.

30. This wealth of journalistic activity, only cursorily sampled here, supported a host of postwar woman suffrage newspapers, their titles being astonishingly numerous. These included the *Universe* (1869); Mary Livermore's *Agitator* in Chicago (1869); Emily Pitts Stevens's *Pioneer* in San Francisco (1869–73); Abigail Scott Duniway's *New Northwest* in Portland, Oregon (1871–87); Emmeline B. Wells's *Woman's Exponent* in Salt Lake City, Utah (1872–1914); Nettie Stanford's *Ladies Bureau* in Marshalltown, Iowa (1875–77); the Toledo Woman Suffrage Association's *Ballot Box* in Toledo, Ohio (1876–77); A. J. Boyer's *Woman's Advocate* in Dayton, Ohio (1868–70), not to be confused with William P. Tomlinson's *Woman's Advocate* published in New York City (1869); *Die Neue Zeit*, a German suffrage

paper in New York City (1869); *L'Amérique*, a French suffrage paper in Chicago (1869); and yet another French woman suffrage newspaper in Detroit—all beginning publication sometime between 1868 and 1877.

Most of these periodicals are extant. Complete runs, however, are not always available, and the publication dates are therefore sometimes approximate. Other titles appear to be lost. I was not able to locate extant copies of the *Universe, Die Neue Zeit,* or *L'Amérique.* Contemporary sources, however, cite these papers as examples of women's rights publishing. The *Woman's Advocate* (Dayton, Ohio), 4 September 1869, for example, identifies the *Universe* as an important and vital women's rights paper in 1869, but I have not seen mention of it elsewhere. In advance of the creation of *Die Neue Zeit,* the German women of New York requested that the St. Louis woman suffrage association purchase five-dollar shares to help with the cost of establishing the paper. See the *Daily Missouri Republican,* 26 April 1869, cited in Walter, "Woman Suffrage in Missouri," 59. For additional mention of *Die Neue Zeit* and also of *L'Amérique,* both published in 1869, and perhaps later, see *HWS,* 1:47. For a general discussion of the western women's rights newspapers, see Bennion, *Equal to the Occasion.*

The vibrancy of woman suffrage activity along with general public interest in the question also spawned a dramatic expansion in a new type of woman suffrage publishing, the "woman's column." Mainstream newspapers from around the country began a regular weekly feature, often known as the "woman's department," which was sometimes compiled by a local suffragist who gave news about women's rights activity in the area and around the country. These columns were not new, but their content was. In the antebellum decades, these were largely fluff pieces, full of domestic advice. But in the postwar period, large numbers of newspapers turned these columns over to women's suffrage advocates. For a fuller discussion of women's rights publishing in this period, see Tetrault, "Memory of a Movement," 89–101, 146–47.

31. Quoted in Greef, *Public Lectures,* 23. Tetrault, "The Incorporation of American Feminism."

32. Tetrault, "The Incorporation of American Feminism."

33. Livermore, *The Story of My Life,* 493.

34. For some of these women's names and audience sizes, see Tetrault, "The Incorporation of American Feminism"; Hindman, "Notes from the Lecture Field," *Woman's Journal,* 21 October 1876, and 18 November 1876. When suffragists recorded their own histories, they frequently devoted a chapter to the lecture circuit, underscoring its prominence in their lives and imaginations. Robinson, *Massachusetts in the Woman Suffrage Movement,* 155; Elizabeth Cady Stanton, *Eighty Years and More,* 259–82; Livermore, *The Story of My Life,* 487–521; Hanaford, *Daughters of America,* 305–30.

35. Gallman, *America's Joan of Arc,* 97–99; and "Woman Suffrage," *New York Tribune,* 14 May 1870, *SAP,* 14:765.

36. Anthony to Lepha Johnson Canfield, 2 January 1871, *Selected Papers,* 2:399.

37. Anthony to Hooker, [28? December 1869], *SAP,* 14:149–50; Stanton to Hooker, 1 December [1870], *SAP,* 14:1126–32; Stanton to Martha Coffin Wright, 27 December 1870, *SAP,* 14:1160; Stanton to Wright, 28 January 1873, *SAP,* 16:1006; Stanton to Martha Coffin Wright, 8 March [1873], *Selected Papers,* 2:597–98. In her biography of Anthony, Barry also notices this phenomenon. Barry, *Susan B. Anthony.*

38. Stanton to Wright, 27 December 1870, *SAP,* 14:1160.

39. Stanton to Hooker, 1 December [1870], *SAP,* 14:1128.

40. Second Decade Celebration," *Revolution,* 27 October 1870, 265.

41. Tetrault, "Incorporation of American Feminism."

42. Virginia L. Minor to Stanton, 4 May 1868, *Selected Papers,* 2:134–35.

43. Monia Cook Morris, "Woman Suffrage in Missouri," 65.

44. Noun, *Strong-Minded Women,* 133–39, 148.

45. Anthony to Matilda Joslyn Gage, 21 October 1875, *Selected Papers*, 3:3:207n4; and *HWS*, 3:754.

46. *HWS*, 3:535.

47. Stone to M. C. Callanan, 24 November 1878, *Blackwell Family Papers*, 62:390.

48. Peckham was also angry that her name was originally listed on the call to the American Association's founding convention. Apparently, she had not authorized its inclusion, and she wrote insisting that it be removed, suggesting that even those listed as calling the meeting did not necessarily always endorse it. Peckham to Matilda Franz Anneke, 28 October 1869, and Anthony to Anneke, 8 November 1869, MFA Papers, box 5, folder 4.

49. Fanny Russell, "Unauthorized Use of Names," *Woman's Journal*, 2 November 1872.

50. *Saturday Evening Mercury*, 26 June 1869, 1.

51. For the call to this convention, see "Western Woman Suffrage Association," *Woman's Advocate* (Dayton, Ohio), 4 September 1869, 16. For lengthy daily reports of the proceedings and editorials, see the *Chicago Times*, 10–14 September 1869.

52. *Woman's Advocate* (Dayton, Ohio), 4 September 1869, 16.

53. Walter, "Woman Suffrage in Missouri," 75, 79.

54. There is some competing information about the Northwestern Woman Suffrage Association's allegiance. It was formed in May, with Anthony's participation. See Stanton to Martha Coffin Wright, [c. 15 May 1870], *Selected Papers*, 2:334–35n1; and Meeting to Dissolve the National Woman Suffrage Association in New York, [10 May 1870], *Selected Papers*, 2:333n3. For reports of their meeting, see "Woman Suffrage," *Detroit Advertiser and Tribune*, 30 November 1870 and 1 December 1870, *SAP*, 14:1105–11.

55. Anthony to Isabella Beecher Hooker, 2 December 1870, *Selected Papers*, 2:385n4.

56. The first Pacific Slope Convention took place 16–19 May 1871. It was held again in 1872. "The Sixteenth Amendments: Pacific Slope Woman Suffrage Convention," *San Francisco Chronicle*, 16 May 1871, 3; "Strong Minded," *San Francisco Chronicle*, 17–20 May 1871, 3; and "Pacific Slope Woman Suffrage Convention," *Pioneer*, 23 and 30 May 1872, 1, 5.

57. "Woman Suffrage Organizations," unidentified clipping in Matilda Joslyn Gage Scrapbooks, vol. 2.

58. For examples of some of the divisions in California, see Anthony to L. C. Canfield, 2 January 1871, *Selected Papers*, 2:400nn4–5; Anthony Diary, 9–15 July 1871, *Selected Papers*, 2:433n2; Anthony to Gage, 21 October 1875, *Selected Papers*, 3:207n4. Schuele, "None Could Deny the Eloquence," 176–84.

59. Lucretia Coffin Mott to Stanton, 25 March 1872, *Selected Papers*, 2:488n4; "Red Flag," unidentified column in Matilda Joslyn Gage Scrapbooks, vol. 3; Anthony Diary, 18 February 1873, *Selected Papers*, 2:593n1.

60. Virginia L. Minor and Francis Minor to Anthony, 7 May 1874, *Selected Papers*, 3:75n2.

61. For the omission of the "People's Convention" from Stanton, Anthony, and Gage's account, see *HWS*, 3:570–71. The People's Convention, dedicated to universal suffrage and human rights, called its state organization, the "Universal Suffrage Association of the State of Illinois." It is not clear what happened to this organization, but scholar Steven Buechler claims it faded from the political scene within the year. Buechler, *Transformation of the Woman Suffrage Movement*, 67–76. Livermore and others called their state organization the "Illinois Woman Suffrage Association." For reports about these two events, including the convention's proceedings, see the many reports in the *Chicago Times* and the *Chicago Tribune*, 4–13 February 1869, *SAP*, 13:331–52.

62. Antoinette Brown Blackwell to Stanton with Stanton to Anthony, 21 December 1874, *Selected Papers*, 3:131–32.

63. Anthony to Martha Coffin Wright, 1 January 1873, *Selected Papers*, 2:547.

64. Gabriel, *Notorious Victoria*, 4; Braude, *Radical Spirits*.

65. Frisken, *Victoria Woodhull's Sexual Revolution*, 7, 14, 31; Gabriel, *Notorious Victoria*, 30–31, 101–2. For additional information of the life of Victoria Woodhull, also see Under-

hill, *Woman Who Ran for President*; Goldsmith, *Other Powers*; Helen Lefkowitz Horowitz, "Victoria Woodhull"; Passet, *Sex Radicals*; Cott, "Passionlessness."

66. Frisken, *Victoria Woodhull's Sexual Revolution*, viii, 8. Woodhull's invitation to address the congressional committee materialized out of her friendship with Massachusetts representative Benjamin Butler. Anthony Diary, 10 January 1871, *Selected Papers*, 2:403–4n2; Gabriel, *Notorious Victoria*, 69–70.

67. DuBois, "Taking the Law."

68. Historian Benjamin Quarles has found that in certain districts in South Carolina during the election of 1870, "colored women, under the encouragement of Negro election officials, exercised the privilege of voting." DuBois, "Taking the Law," 88; Quarles, "Frederick Douglass and the Woman's Rights Movement"; and Terborg-Penn, *African American Women*, 36–42.

69. DuBois, "Taking the Law," 88–89; *SAP*, 15:330.

70. Ibid., 89; "Woman's Demands," *Daily Morning Chronicle*, 12 January 1871, *SAP*, 15:326; "The Ballot," *Daily Morning Chronicle*, 13 January 1871, *SAP*, 15:330; "The Ballot," *Daily Morning Chronicle*, 13 January 1871, *SAP*, 15:330.

71. "The Ballot," *Daily Morning Chronicle*, 13 January 1871, *SAP*, 15:330.

72. Anthony to Laura de Force Gordon, March 1871, quoted in Mead, *How the Vote Was Won*, 37.

73. "The Campaign Opened," *National Republican*, 12 January 1871, in *SAP*, 15:332.

74. The House Judiciary Committee issued a minority report in favor of Woodhull's memorial.

75. Anthony to Stanton and Isabella Beecher Hooker, 13 March 1872, *Selected Papers*, 2:485.

76. ECS to Isabella Beecher Hooker, 15 October [1871], *Selected Papers*, 2:454n7.

77. Messer-Kruse, *Yankee International*; and Montgomery, *Beyond Equality*.

78. For discussions of Stanton's political philosophy, see DuBois, "On Labor and Free Love"; Tetrault, "The Incorporation of American Feminism"; Ginzberg, *Elizabeth Cady Stanton*; Dubois and Smith, *Elizabeth Cady Stanton*; Sue Davis, *Political Thought of Elizabeth Cady Stanton*.

79. "Announcement of A People's Convention," March 1872, *Selected Papers*, 2:489–90.

80. Anthony Diary, 6–14 May 1872, *Selected Papers*, 2:492–94.

81. It was common for suffrage conventions to charge admission, but it was done generally only for the evening sessions, when long lectures were given by prominent names. The transaction of organizational business, which took place during the morning and afternoon sessions, generally involved no admission fee. "Official Report of the Equal Rights Convention, Held in New York City, on the Ninth, Tenth and Eleventh of May, 1872," *Woodhull and Claflin's Weekly* (New York), 25 May 1872, *SAP*, 16:104.

82. Ibid.

83. "Announcement of A People's Convention," March 1872, *Selected Papers*, 2:490n2, n3.

84. "Official Report of the Equal Rights Convention . . . ," *Woodhull and Claflin's Weekly* (New York), 25 May 1872, *SAP*, 16:105.

85. "The Woman Suffragists," *New York World*, 10 May 1872, *SAP*, 16:102; "Official Report of the Equal Rights Convention . . . ," *Woodhull and Claflin's Weekly* (New York), 25 May 1872, *SAP*, 16:105–6.

86. We are in great need of research into Anthony's intellectual life, which has been woefully under-researched. The best insights into her thinking can be found in the documentary collections associated with the invaluable *SAP*.

87. "The National Woman Suffrage Association at Steinway Hall," *New York Times*, 11 May 1872, *SAP*, 16:110; "Lady Reformers on the Alert," unidentified clipping, *SAP*, 16:111.

88. Frisken, *Victoria Woodhull's Sexual Revolution*, 21, 55–56, 80.

89. Anthony Diary, 8 May 1872, *Selected Papers*, 2:493.

90. Anthony Diary, 10–11 May 1872, *Selected Papers*, 2:493–94.

91. Interview with Anthony by Anne E. McDowell in Philadelphia, c. 11 June 1872, *Selected Papers*, 2:510.

92. Stanton to Isabella Beecher Hooker, 14 June 1872, *Selected Papers*, 2:511–13n6.

93. Anthony Diary, 12 May 1872, *Selected Papers*, 2:494.

94. Ibid.

95. Anthony to Martha Coffin Wright, 22 May 1872, *Selected Papers*, 2:496.

96. The issue of *Woodhull & Claflin's Weekly* was dated 2 November 1872, but it was available on 28 October. *Selected Papers*, 2:535n2.

97. Frisken, *Victoria Woodhull's Sexual Revolution*; Goldsmith, *Other Powers*; Gabriel, *Notorious Victoria*; Underhill, *Woman Who Ran for President*; Helen Lefkowitz Horowitz, "Victoria Woodhull"; Passet, *Sex Radicals*; Cott, "Passionlessness"; Fox, *Trials of Intimacy*.

98. Fox, *Trials of Intimacy*, 128, 16, 41.

99. Underhill, *Woman Who Ran for President*, 233–35; Gabriel, *Notorious Victoria*, 194–203.

100. Blackwell, who along with Anthony, had been present at the Republican Party's convention in Philadelphia in order to pressure for women's inclusion, leaned on Anthony to join with him in a grand push to reelect Grant. He argued that if women could make their influence felt in this election, the Republicans (the party in power) would certainly enfranchise women by the next presidential election in 1876, if not sooner. He also wrote Stanton a confidential letter, urging her to learn from the mistakes of the past, including collaboration with George Francis Train and now Woodhull's "egotism," and to seize this "propitious moment" for a meaningful "new depart[ure]," wherein the National Association would unite with the American Association to hold "a Conv[ention] of Loyal Republican Women to ratify the nom[ination] of Grant." Stanton considered union with Boston, and suffragists, sometimes including Stanton and Anthony, did organize a slate of mass women's campaign rallies as per Blackwell's plan, but the strategy brought no grand unification in forces. Henry B. Blackwell to Stanton, 8 June 1872, *Selected Papers*, 2:504–5.

101. The fourteenth plank read: "The Republican party is mindful of its obligations to the loyal women of America for their noble devotion to the cause of freedom. Their admission to wider fields of usefulness is viewed with satisfaction, and the honest demand of any class of citizens for additional rights should be treated with respectful consideration." "The Republican Party Platform of 1872"; and Henry B. Blackwell to Stanton, 8 June 1872, *Selected Papers* 2:505n2.

102. Lucy Stone, unpublished manuscript, 4 February 1882, in AERA File, *NAWSA Papers*, 26:25–42; Henry Blackwell, unpublished manuscript, n.d. [1887], in AERA File, *NAWSA Papers*, 26:42–60. Both transcribed by Ida Porter Boyer. Alice Stone Blackwell to Mrs. Mary Hunter, 13 August 1938, in AWSA File, *NAWSA Papers*, 26:147.

103. Anthony to Isabella Beecher Hooker," 16 November 1872, *Selected Papers*, 2:533–34, 535n2, 4; Stanton to Isabella Beecher Hooker, 19 November 187[2], *Selected Papers*, 2:535–56; Anthony to Isabella Beecher Hooker, 13 October 1873, *Selected Papers*, 3:3n8; Stanton to Isabella Beecher Hooker, 3 November 1873, *Selected Papers*, 3:12–15n2–3.

104. Anthony to Isabella Beecher Hooker, 13 October 1873, *Selected Papers*, 3:3n8.

105. Anthony to Stanton, 5 November 1872, *Selected Papers*, 2:524.

106. DuBois, "Taking the Law," 94.

107. Anthony to Stanton, 5 November 1872, *Selected Papers*, 2:524–29; DuBois, "Taking the Law," 94.

108. Technically, Anthony was charged with violating the Enforcement Act. DuBois, "Taking the Law," 94.

109. Ibid., 94.

110. For the most complete list of those who voted, see "Appendix C: Women Who Went to the Polls, 1868–1873," *Selected Papers*, 2:645–54.

111. Stanton to Isabella Beecher Hooker, 14 June 1872, *Selected Papers*, 2:511.

112. DuBois, "Taking the Law," 94.

113. Anthony also lectured to raise money for her defense, see Anthony to Edward M. Davis, 19 December 1872, *Selected Papers*, 2:541–42n; Anthony to Martha Coffin Wright, 1 January 1873, *Selected Papers*, 2:548; Anthony to Mathilde Franziska Anneke, 6 January 1873, *Selected Papers*, 2:551. Anthony, "Is It a Crime for a U.S. Citizen to Vote?" *Selected Papers*, 2:554–83.

114. Harper, *Life and Work*, 1:436; Wagner, *Matilda Joslyn Gage*.

115. M. M. Cole, *Woman's Journal*, 18 January 1873.

116. Thomas Wentworth Higginson, *Woman's Journal*, 8 December 1877.

117. Anthony to Martha Coffin Wright, 1 January 1873, *Selected Papers*, 2:547.

118. Paulina Wright Davis, *A History of the National Woman's Rights Movement*, 5.

119. "Woman's Rights," *New York Herald*, 7 May 1873, *SAP*, 17:63; "Woman Suffragists," *New York World*, 7 May 1873, *SAP*, 17:60.

120. Stanton to Martha Coffin Wright, 8 March [1873], *Selected Papers*, 2:597.

121. The newspaper reports, at least, do not indicate that Stanton offered recollections. For the call, see "Woman Suffrage Anniversary," *SAP*, 17:49.

122. "The Woman Suffrage Cause," *New York Tribune*, 7 May 1873, *SAP*, 17:68.

123. Mott continued to work with and encourage Stanton and Anthony, but she did not formally endorse one society over another. For a discussion of her alignment and of her sanctification, see Faulkner, *Lucretia Mott's Heresy*. Historian Nancy Isenberg has also discussed the ways in which Mott was transformed into women's rights "prophet and oracle" in the postwar period. Isenberg, *Sex and Citizenship*, 3.

124. "Woman's Rights," *New York Herald*, 7 May 1873, *SAP*, 17:63.

125. Woman's Rights Convention, Held at Seneca Falls, 19–20 July 1848, *Selected Papers*, Preface to Notes, 1:83; Wellman, "Seneca Falls Women's Rights Convention," 30n4.

126. Tilton, "Mrs. Elizabeth Cady Stanton," 346.

127. The database WorldCat of the Online Computer Library Center (OCLC), lists only nineteen repositories that hold an original printing of the Seneca Falls report.

128. Stanton and Amy Post prepared the 1870 report for publication. "Proceedings of the Woman's Rights Conventions at Seneca Falls and Rochester, N.Y., July and August, 1848." For additional information about the printings of proceedings from the 1848 Seneca Falls meeting, see "Woman's Rights Convention held at Seneca Falls, 19–20 July 1848," *Selected Papers*, 1:83; Address by Stanton on Woman's Rights, September 1848, *Selected Papers*, editorial note, 1:94–95; and SBA to Mary Post Hallowell, 11 April 1867, *Selected Papers*, 2:52–53n4.

129. "Woman-Suffrage," *Pioneer*, 29 May 1873, *SAP*, 17:66.

130. This 1870 reprint did not match the original exactly. In this 1870 reprint, most notably, Stanton added one of her antebellum women's rights speeches, reprinting it along with the original report. She claimed to have delivered it at the 1848 meeting, only this was incorrect. She first delivered it much later, which she knew. But for whatever reasons, she included it as her speech delivered at the Seneca Falls meeting. For additional information about the printings of the proceedings from the 1848 Seneca Falls meeting, see "Woman's Rights Convention Held at Seneca Falls, 19–20 July 1848," *Selected Papers*, Preface to Notes 1:83; Address by Stanton on Woman's Rights, September 1848, *Selected Papers*, editorial note, 1:94–95; and Anthony to Mary Post Hallowell, 11 April 1867, *Selected Papers*, 2:52–53n4.

131. "Woman's Rights," *New York Herald*, 7 May 1873, *SAP*, 17:63.

132. Bruner, *Making Stories*, 5–6.

133. "Woman-Suffrage," *Pioneer*, 29 May 1873, *SAP*, 17:65.

134. Martha Coffin Wright was further sidelined in this commemorative convention by giving no remarks or reminiscences of her own. The reports from the convention, at least, offer no evidence that she did.

135. "Woman Suffragists," *New York World*, 7 May 1873, *SAP*, 17:60; "Woman's Rights,"

New York Herald, 7 May 1873, *SAP*, 17:63; and "National Woman Suffrage Convention," *Woodhull and Claflin's Weekly*, 24 May 1873, *SAP*, 17:60–63.

136. "National Woman Suffrage Convention," *Woodhull and Claflin's Weekly*, 24 May 1873, *SAP*, 17:62; "Woman Suffragists," *New York World*, 7 May 1873, *SAP*, 17:60; "Woman's Rights," *New York Herald*, 7 May 1873, in *SAP*, 17:63.

137. Venet, *A Strong-Minded Woman*; Anthony to Barbara Binks Thompson, 18 August 1881, *Selected Papers*, 4:104–7.

138. "Remarks by SBA in the Circuit Court of the United States for the Northern District of New York," 19 June 1873, *Selected Papers* 2:612–16; and Anthony, *An Account of the Proceedings on the Trial of Susan B. Anthony*.

139. Women still committed civil disobedience and voted illegally in elections for the remainder of the century. On the *Minor* decision, see *Minor v. Happersett*, 88 U.S. 162 (1875); Weatherford, "Postwar Politics"; Basch, "Reconstructing Female Citizenship."

140. Eric Foner, *Reconstruction*; and DuBois, "Taking the Law."

Chapter 3

1. Eric Foner, "The Meaning of Freedom"; Berthoff, "Conventional Mentality."

2. On WCTU membership, see Gusfield, "Social Structure and Moral Reform," 221–32, esp. 222; Blocker, "Separate Paths."

3. *HWS*, 1:376, 379.

4. Merk, "Massachusetts in the Woman Suffrage Movement."

5. Keyssar, *The Right to Vote*.

6. Klinghoffer and Elkis, "'The Petticoat Electors.'"

7. McCammon and Campbell, "Winning the Vote in the West."

8. *Debates and Proceedings of the Convention Which Assembled at Little Rock, 1867*, 701–25; Stapler, *The Woman Suffrage Year Book*, 32–38; Ann D. Gordon, "Conversation"; and Mrs. Abigail Scott Duniway, "Memorial Address," *National Citizen and Ballot Box*, August 1878, 8.

9. How woman suffrage resonated in the federally mandated state constitutional conventions of the former Confederate states awaits its historian, but preliminary findings suggest that woman suffrage received a respectful and supportive hearing among some delegates, particularly black men. Elsa Barkley Brown, "To Catch the Vision of Freedom"; and *Debates and Proceedings of the Convention Which Assembled at Little Rock, 1867*, 701–25.

10. Quoted in Coulter, "History of Woman Suffrage in Nebraska," 19–21, quotation from 20.

11. Quoted in Keyssar, *The Right to Vote*, 183.

12. Keyssar, *The Right to Vote*, 187.

13. Dudden, *Fighting Chance*, 144; Caruso, "History of Woman Suffrage in Michigan," 40–50; *Debates and Proceedings of the Constitutional Convention of the State of Michigan*, 2:252–78, 284–89, 766–75.

14. Margaret Campbell to Lucy Stone, 30 March 1874, *Blackwell Family Papers*, 66:432.

15. Stone to Campbell, 13 June 1874, *Blackwell Family Papers*, 66:442.

16. Campbell to Stone, 8 June 1874; Stone to Campbell, 13 June 1874; Campbell to Stone, 30 September 1874, *Blackwell Family Papers*, 66:440, 442, 461.

17. Campbell to Stone, 2 July 1874; and Stone to Campbell, 6 July 1874, *Blackwell Family Papers*, 66:447, 450.

18. Anthony to Isabella Beecher Hooker, 12 Oct. 1875, *Selected Papers*, 3:204.

19. Ibid.

20. Anthony Diary, 24–27 September 1874, *Selected Papers*, 3:111n4.

21. Anthony Diary, 20–21 October 1874, *Selected Papers*, 3:122n7; and Anthony Diary, 21 October 1874, *Selected Papers*, 3:121.

22. For the few mentions of Anthony's name, see "Michigan Items," *Woman's Journal*, 17

October 1874, 335; "Michigan Items," *Woman's Journal*, 24 October 1874, 342; "The Michigan Campaign," *Woman's Journal*, 7 November 1874, 359.

23. Stanton to Anthony, 1 June 1874, *Selected Papers*, 3:86.

24. Ibid., 3:86, 87n4; Anthony Diary, 20–21 October 1874, *Selected Papers*, 3:122n7; Anthony to Isabella Stanton Hooker, 20 January 1875, *Selected Papers*, 3:146.

25. Stanton's mixed reception in Michigan not only infused the local papers but made national news as well, a *New York Evening Post* piece being picked up and reprinted. See "Woman Suffrage in Michigan," *Daily Evening Bulletin*, 12 June 1874.

26. "The Results in Michigan," *Woman's Journal*, 5 December 1874, 390. One newspaper estimated that while eligible voter turnout had been 79 percent, only 58 percent voted in the woman suffrage referendum. "Defeated But Not Destroyed," *Christian Union*, 9 December 1874, 458; see also "The Results in Michigan," *Woman's Journal*, 5 December 1874, 390.

27. "MI Campaign—Letter from Miss Hindman" *Woman's Journal*, 10 October 1874, 330; Matilda Hindman, "Matilda Hindman in Michigan," ibid., 14 November 1874, 366; "Michigan Items," ibid., 14 November 1874, 367; and Anthony Diary, 4 November 1874, *Selected Papers*, 3:127–28n1.

28. Anthony Diary, 4 November 1874, *Selected Papers*, 3:127n1.

29. Ibid., 3:127.

30. Ibid., 3:127n1.

31. Anthony to Isabella Beecher Hooker, 20 January 1875, *Selected Papers*, 3:146.

32. Stapler, *The Woman Suffrage Year Book*, 34.

33. *California Evening Mercury*, 12 June 1869, 1.

34. Stapler, *The Woman Suffrage Yearbook*, 35; and *Pioneer*, 4 December 1869.

35. Stapler, *The Woman Suffrage Year Book*, 39, 41; and *California Evening Mercury*, 14 August 1869, 1.

36. Stapler, *The Woman Suffrage Year Book*, 33.

37. *Pioneer*, 22 January 1870, 2.

38. Stapler, *The Woman Suffrage Year Book*, 37. A similar measure passed in 1885, but was then vetoed by North Dakota's territorial governor. Ibid.

39. Elsa Barkley Brown, "To Catch the Vision," 77.

40. Anthony to Isabella Beecher Hooker, 11 November 1877, *Selected Papers,* 3:339–40n9.

41. The Massachusetts legislature did not vote upon woman suffrage in 1874, however. Stapler, *The Woman Suffrage Yearbook*, 32.

42. The votes in the Massachusetts legislature were: 1868, 74:199; 1869, 84:111; 1870, 68:133; 1871, 68:68; 1872, 78:135; 1873, 83:98; 1874, no vote taken; 1875, 75:120; 1876, 77:127; 1877, 83:22; 1878, 93:127; 1879, 82:85; 1880, 60:138; 1881, 76:122; and 1882, 66:107. Numbers of votes for woman suffrage are listed first. Stapler, *The Woman Suffrage Year Book*, 32.

43. Ibid., 31.

44. Ibid., 30.

45. The Iowa legislature voted on woman suffrage in 1868, 1870, 1872, 1874, and 1876. The Iowa legislature also voted on woman suffrage every other year throughout the 1880s. Ibid., 30.

46. Anthony to Isabella Beecher Hooker, 20 January 1875, *Selected Papers*, 3:146.

47. Noun, *Strong-Minded Women*, 203.

48. Noun, *Leader and Pariah*.

49. Tutt, "'No Taxation without Representation.'"

50. "Conditional Suffrage," *Philadelphia North American & United States Gazette,* 12 November 1878.

51. Both Virginia Minor and Victoria Woodhull protested women's taxation without representation in their defenses of the New Departure. Kerber, *No Constitutional Right*, 102–4.

52. Ibid., 95–97, 104; Keyssar, *The Right to the Vote*, 129–36, 182.

53. Quoted in "Before the New York Legislature," *Woman's Journal*, 21 February 1874.

54. Mary B. Willard, "Social Taxation," *Woman's Journal*, 7 October 1871, 319; quoted in Carolyn C. Jones, "Dollars and Selves," 307. Anthony was persuaded by all this action, writing a friend: "I more & more feel that we *must combine* & *refuse* to pay taxes." Anthony to Isabella Beecher Hooker, 6 February [1872], *Selected Papers*, 2:481.

55. Kerber, *No Constitutional Right*, 81, 99; Carolyn C. Jones, "Dollars and Selves."

56. Speech by Anthony to the Centennial of the Boston Tea Party in New York City, [16 December 1873], *Selected Papers*, 3:22–25.

57. Kerber, *No Constitutional Right*, 100.

58. The sisters' case wound its way through the courts for eleven years, finally being settled for the Smiths on a technicality in 1880, two years after Abby's death. Kerber, *No Constitutional Right*, 88, 110–12; Julia E. Smith, *Abby Smith and Her Cows*. See also Carolyn C. Jones, "Dollars and Selves," and Cartledge, "Seven Cows on the Auction Block."

59. Bowditch, *Taxation of Women in Massachusetts*.

60. Carolyn C. Jones, "Dollars and Selves," 279–80.

61. And by the mid-1870s, in New York State, women had formed the Monroe County New York Tax Payer's Association, based in Rochester, N.Y.

62. "Woman's Anti-Tax League of San Francisco," *Woman's Journal*, 13 December 1873.

63. A sympathetic Susan B. Anthony does not appear to have been a member. Anthony to Lydia C. Smith, 3 September 1873, *SAP*, 17:276.

64. Terborg-Penn, *African American Women*, 38–42.

65. Welch, "Local and National Forces," 56.

66. Smedley, "Martha Schofield," 199.

67. Welch, "Local and National Forces," 61–63; Speech by Anthony to the Centennial of the Boston Tea Party in New York City, *Selected Papers*, editorial note, 3:22. In May of 1873, a body of the New York legislature was considering granting suffrage to tax-paying women, and the proposed bill split New York suffragists, with Lillie Devereux Blake opposing it and Stanton supporting it. "Woman Suffrage," *New York Times*, 7 May 1873, *SAP*, 17:59; "Woman Suffragists," *New York World*, 7 May 1873, *SAP*, 17:60. Taxation ultimately lost sway as an argument by the century's end. As the century wore on, legal theorists increasingly insisted that if the Supreme Court in the *Minor v. Happersett* decision had decided that there was no link between citizenship and voting (that voting was not a right of citizenship), then there was no link between taxation and representation (that voting was not a requirement for taxation). Kerber, *No Constitutional Right*, 104–7, 115–17.

68. "Memorials Adopted by the National Woman Suffrage Association," 15 January 1874, *Selected Papers*, 3:33.

69. "Resolutions Adopted by the National Woman Suffrage Association," 14–15 January 1875, *Selected Papers*, 3:136, 3:138n1–2.

70. "Memorials Adopted by the National Woman Suffrage Association," 15 January 1874, *Selected Papers*, 3:32–34.

71. For accounts of the remarks by the Misses Smith from Glastonbury, Connecticut, see "Woman Suffrage," *New York Herald*, 11 May 1876, *SAP*, 18:768; "Woman Suffrage Convention," *New York Herald*, 12 May 1876, *SAP*, 18:769; "The Woman Suffragists," *New York World*, 12 May 1876, *SAP*, 18:771. For the reception held in honor of Julia Smith, see *HWS*, 3:98.

72. Stanton, Lecture on "Taxation," 1877, in *SAP*, 19:726–27.

73. Memorials Adopted by the National Woman Suffrage Association, 15 January 1874, *Selected Papers*, 3:32–33, 34n1.

74. Welch, "Local and National Forces," 36–39; "An Entering Wedge," *Woman's Journal*, 13 May 1871, 145. Women would not be able to vote in presidential elections until the 1910s, when seventeen states extended this partial voting right before 1920. For a list that excludes states with full suffrage, see Keyssar, *The Right to Vote*, table A.19. For what presidential

suffrage entailed, see Minutes of Informal Conference Between Lucy Stone and Anthony, 21 December 1887, *Selected Papers*, 5:66n6.

75. DuBois, "Taking the Law"; and Masur, *An Example for All the Land.*

76. *HWS*, 3:809. The U.S. senator was Samuel C. Pomeroy, on whom see Anthony to Samuel N. Wood, 21 April 1867, *Selected Papers*, 2:56n8. And see also Wang, *The Trial of Democracy.*

77. Welch, "Local and National Forces," 94–96; and Merk, "Massachusetts in the Woman Suffrage Movement."

78. Welch, "Local and National Forces," 94–99; and Merk, "Massachusetts in the Woman Suffrage Movement." For states that gave women voting rights in municipal elections, see Keyssar, *The Right to Vote*, table A.18.

79. School suffrage is under-researched and in desperate need of a historian. Perhaps the most knowledgeable person on this topic is T. J. Mertz, of Madison, Wisconsin, whose work remains unpublished. Welch, "Local and National Forces," 68–112, Stone and Blackwell quotations from 80; Caruso, "History of Woman Suffrage in Michigan," 55, 72; Thomas, "School Suffrage"; Marilyn Schultz Blackwell, "The Politics of Motherhood"; and for a list of school suffrage laws and corresponding dates, see Keyssar, *The Right to Vote*, table A.17.

80. Anthony, Speech by Anthony to the Pennsylvania Yearly Meeting of Progressive Friends, 6 June 1885, *Selected Papers*, 4:420–29.

81. This phenomenon is wonderfully described by Welch, "Local and National Forces," 68–112; see also, Higginson, "The Worcester Convention," *Woman's Journal*, 6 November 1880; Robinson, *Massachusetts in the Woman Suffrage Movement*, 108; Speech by Anthony to the Pennsylvania Yearly Meeting of Progressive Friends, 6 June 1885, *Selected Papers*, 4:425; Minutes of Informal Conference Between Stone and Anthony, 21 December 1887, *Selected Papers*, 5:62; Kerr, *Lucy Stone*, 202.

82. Bordin, *Woman and Temperance*, 19. The classic statement on the separate spheres ideology is Welter, "The Cult of True Womanhood."

83. Bordin, *Woman and Temperance*, 15–33.

84. Stanton, "Woman's Whiskey War," [25 February 1874], *Selected Papers*, 3:54–59.

85. Anthony to Daniel R. Anthony, [before 5 May 1874], *Selected Papers*, 3:73–74.

86. Bordin, *Woman and Temperance*, 4.

87. Levenson, *Women in Printing*, dedication page, and 93.

88. Anthony to Lepha Johnson Canfield, 2 January 1871, *Selected Papers*, 2:400n4.

89. Venet, *A Strong-Minded Woman*; and "The Woman's Column," *Rocky Mountain News*, 24 September 1876.

90. It is worth remembering that temperance women achieved their ultimate goal before suffragists did, culminating in the Eighteenth Amendment, which was ratified by forty-five states in 1919, within a year of its passage. Willard, *Home Protection Manual*, 5; Willard, *Let Something Good Be Said*, 200–201.

Although there were lots of exceptions to the rule, temperance women upheld the idea that God had assigned women to be the guardians of the home, or the private sphere, whereas men were fitted for the public sphere. Midcentury suffrage organizations, by contrast, squarely challenged the idea that women and men belonged to different social spheres, and asserted that women were just as fitted for the public, political world as men. See Bordin, *Woman and Temperance*; and Giele, *Two Paths to Women's Equality.*

91. Passet, *Sex Radicals*, 101–7, 111; Friskin, *Victoria Woodhull's Sexual Revolution*, 9; Gabriel, *Notorious Victoria*, 256.

92. Frisken, *Victoria Woodhull's Sexual Revolution*, 18, 38; and Passet, *Sex Radicals*, 68–74.

93. Cott, "Passionlessness"; Passet, *Sex Radicals*, 74–77; Dubois and Gordon, "Seeking Ecstasy on the Battlefield."

94. Passet, *Sex Radicals*, 104.

95. Ibid., 99–100.

96. Quoted in ibid., 110.

97. Ibid., 100.

98. Ibid., 100, 116–17.

99. The law was officially titled "The Act for the Suppression of Trade in, and Circulation of Obscene Literature and Articles of Immoral Use." Ibid., 95.

100. The 1973 U.S. Supreme Court decision, *Roe v. Wade*, legalizing abortion, would overturn the criminalization Comstock and others successfully pursued at midcentury. Ibid., 95–96; Brodie, *Contraception and Abortion*; Brodie, "Reproductive Control"; Helen Lefkowitz Horowitz, "Victoria Woodhull," and *Rereading Sex*; Beisel, *Imperiled Innocents*.

101. Eric Foner, *Reconstruction*, 461–62.

102. Ibid., 460–511; Montgomery, *Beyond Equality*; Messur-Kruse, *The Yankee International*.

103. Messer-Kruse, *The Yankee International*, 1; Stowell, *The Great Strikes of 1877*.

104. DuBois, *Feminism and Suffrage*, 134; Vapnek, *Breadwinners*, 25; Hattam, *Labor Visions and State Power*; Hattam, "Economic Visions and Political Strategies."

105. Vapnek, *Breadwinners*, 14, 23.

106. Ibid., 25.

107. DuBois, *Feminism and Suffrage*, 133.

108. Quoted in ibid., 134.

109. Ibid., 134.

110. Ibid., 141, 135.

111. Vapnek, *Breadwinners*, 11–33, quotation from 28; DuBois, *Feminism and Suffrage*, 133–41, 160; Balser, *Sisterhood and Solidarity*, 43–86; Blewett, *Men, Women, and Work*, 142–220.

112. Blair, *The Clubwoman as Feminist*, 29.

113. Blair, "Women's Club Movement," 835.

114. Blair, *The Clubwoman as Feminist*, 4–5, 17.

115. Bordin, *Woman and Temperance*, 43; Blair, *The Clubwoman as Feminist*, 43–44.

116. Quoted in Blair, *The Clubwoman as Feminist*, 43.

117. Kerr, *Lucy Stone*, 180.

118. Anthony to Isabella Beecher Hooker, 13 October 1873, *Selected Papers*, 3:1–3.

119. Stanton to Isabella Beecher Hooker, 3 November 1873, *Selected Papers*, 3:16–17n18; Henry B. Blackwell, "Woman's Congress," *Woman's Journal*, 13 December 1873.

120. Blair, *The Clubwoman as Feminist*, 44.

121. Quoted in ibid., 45.

122. Ibid., 39.

123. Ibid., 45.

124. Mary F. Eastman was the only speaker to deliver remarks on women's suffrage. *Papers and Letters Presented at the First Woman's Congress of the Association for the Advancement of Woman*, 121–32.

125. Ibid., 4.

126. Blair, *The Clubwoman as Feminist*, 39–56.

127. Martha S. Jones, *All Bound Up Together*, 119–49, quotation from 121; and Hunter, *To 'Joy My Freedom*; Schwalm, *A Hard Fight for We*.

128. Martha S. Jones, *All Bound Up Together*, 119–49, quotation from 133; Higginbotham, *Righteous Discontent*; Cooper, *A Voice from the South*; Gilmore, *Gender and Jim Crow*; Hunter, *To 'Joy My Freedom*; Terborg-Penn, *African American Women*; Stephanie Shaw, *What a Woman Ought to Be*; Stephanie Shaw, "Black Club Women"; Painter, "Voices of Suffrage"; Hine, "Rape and the Inner Lives of Black Women"; Higginbotham, "African-American Women's History"; Elsa Barkley Brown, "'What Has Happened Here'"; and Elsa Barkley Brown, "Womanist Consciousness."

129. Vapnek, *Breadwinners*, 28.

130. Resolutions Adopted by the National Woman Suffrage Association, [14–15 January 1875], *Selected Papers*, 3:137.

131. Stanton to the Editor, *Ballot Box*, 24 January [1877], *Selected Papers*, 3:286.

132. "Appeal by the National Woman Suffrage Association, with Petition," 10 November 1876, *Selected Papers*, 3:268.

133. As one example of this interference, in the mid-1870s, Congress was considering taking the vote away from women in Utah. "Call to the Washington Convention of the National Woman Suffrage Association," 10 November 1876, *Selected Papers*, 3:270; and Sarah Barringer Gordon, *The Mormon Question*.

134. Appeal by the National Woman Suffrage Association, with Petition, 10 November 1876, *Selected Papers*, 3:268.

135. "Introduction," *Selected Papers*, 3:xxii.

136. Blight, *Race and Reunion*; Eric Foner, *Reconstruction*; Keller, *Affairs of State*; Cohen, *The Reconstruction of American Liberalism*.

137. *HWS*, 3:2, 4.

138. U.S. Centennial Commission, *International Exhibition, 1876*, 159; Paine, "The Woman's Pavilion of 1876." For Stanton and Anthony's critique of exhibits in the Woman's Pavilion, see *HWS*, 3:54–56.

139. Cordato, "Toward a New Century," 130; and Paine, "The Woman's Pavilion of 1876."

140. *HWS*, 3:21–22.

141. *HWS*, 3:22.

142. The National Association circulated a statement calling upon women to protest their political slavery (a metaphor they used repeatedly). *HWS*, 3:22; "Centennial Protest," *Milwaukee Daily Sentinel*, 4 July 1876, 1; and B.A.U. to the editor, "A Second Declaration of Independence," *Chicago Inter Ocean*, 30 August 1876, 3.

143. *HWS*, 3:21–22; Gage also announced the forthcoming declaration in her speech at the National Association's annual meeting in May in New York City. "Declaration of the Rights of the Women of the United States," 4 July 1876, *Selected Papers*, 3:234–41; and Anthony to Mathilde Franziska Geister Anneke, 1 July 1876, *SAP*, 18:843.

144. *HWS*, 3:27; "Woman Suffrage at the Centennial," *National Republican*, 3 July 1876, 1.

145. On Stone and the American Association, see "Woman's Suffrage Association," *Arkansas Daily Gazette*, 4 July 1876; and see also untitled item in *National Republican*, 4 July 1876, 1. Both the American program and the National's program at the First Unitarian Church are discussed in "A Woman Suffrage Declaration," *Galveston (Tex.) News*, 4 July 1876. *HWS*, 3:27–30, quotations from 28–29; accompanying Anthony were Matilda Joslyn Gage, Sarah Spencer, Lillie Devereux Blake, and Phoebe W. Couzins. Mires, *Independence Hall*, 133–34.

146. "Woman Suffrage at the Centennial," *National Republican*, 3 July 1876, 1. U.S. Centennial Commission, *International Exhibition, 1876*, 47–76. "The Nation's Jubilee," *Evening Star*, 5 July 1876, 1. "Dawn of a New Century; A Day of Glorious Festivity at Philadelphia," *New York Tribune*, 5 July 1876, 1. On Ferry, see Roy Morris Jr., *Fraud of the Century*, 126–27, 200. Couzins is quoted in *HWS*, 3:36.

147. Anthony's full statement in handing over the scroll was, "Mr. President, we present this Declaration of Rights of the women citizens of the United States." "The Woman's Suffrage Movement," *Leavenworth (Kans.) Daily Times*, 20 July 1876; and "The Woman's Declaration of Rights," *The New Northwest*, 28 July 1876.

148. *New-York Daily Tribune*, 20 July 1876, 4, quoted in *HWS*, 3:42–43.

149. Sources disagree about where Anthony stood for the public reading of the women's declaration. Phoebe Couzins, who took part in the action and described it that same afternoon in a speech at the First Unitarian Church, placed Anthony reading the declaration "from the steps of Independence Hall"; *HWS*, 3:36. In an article dated 13 July, the pseudonymous journalist "Aunt Fanny" (Lewise Oliver) reported, "afterward on the steps of Independence Hall she read it to an assembled multitude"; *HWS*, 3:41; see Lewise Oliver, "From Bradford, Penn.," *The New Northwest*, 23 September 1880. Later in July, an anonymous, sympathetic eyewitness from Bristol, Pennsylvania (twenty miles from Philadelphia), wrote: "Miss Anthony read the Declaration of Rights from the steps in front of the Hall," in J.B.N., "Centennial Letter," in *The Grange Advance*, 26 July 1876, 4.

These three quite contemporary sources might be persuasive but for the fact that they are contradicted by three accounts that were in Anthony's direct or indirect control. Her brother Daniel R. Anthony's Kansas newspaper reprinted a *Philadelphia Bulletin* report that "the delegation retired to the front of Independence Hall, where Miss Anthony read it from the stand," in "The Woman Suffrage Movement; The Declaration of Rights—Presenting the Document," *Leavenworth (Kans.) Weekly Times*, 20 July 1876, 1. Two years after the event, her own account in an encyclopedia specified that "the ladies retired to a rostrum in front of Independence Hall," in Anthony, "Woman's Rights," 1477–80, esp. 1480. Finally, the *HWS*, 3:32, reports that Anthony read the declaration from "a platform erected for the musicians in front of Independence Hall."

150. "Declaration of the Rights of the Women of the United States," 4 July 1876, *Selected Papers*, 3:234–41; "The Woman Suffrage Movement," Philadelphia Evening Bulletin, 5 July 1876, *SAP*, 18:859–60.

151. Stanton and Gage authored the declaration, and numerous women signed it as a pledge of support. Stone refused to sign it. For authorship, see Anthony to Elizabeth Boynton Harbert, 19 June 1876, *Selected Papers*, 3:231; NWSA, "Declaration of Rights of the Women of the United States," [4 July 1876], *Selected Papers* 3:234–41; for Stone's refusal, see Stone to Stanton, 3 August 1876, *Selected Papers*, 3:249–50; and for signers, see "The Woman's Suffrage Movement," *Philadelphia Evening Bulletin*, *SAP*, 18:860. Among many newspapers that printed the entire declaration verbatim, see "The Woman Suffrage Movement," *Philadelphia Evening Bulletin*, *SAP*, 18:859–60; and "Declaration and Protest of the Women of the United States by the National Woman Suffrage Association," *Rocky Mountain News*, 23 July 1876, 1.

The plan had been in the works for well over a year. Resolutions Adopted by the National Woman Suffrage Association, [14–15 January 1875], *Selected Papers*, 3:137–38; Anthony to Hooker and Theodore W. Stanton, 20 January 1875, *SAP*, 18:286; Stanton to Edward M. Davis, Radical Club Meeting of Philadelphia, unidentified clipping, 18 January 1875, *SAP*, 18:292. When NWSA members were denied the right to present their protest, Stanton and Mott resigned their seats on the platform and gave them to younger members of NWSA. "Letter from Mrs. Stanton," *Ballot Box*, October 1876, *SAP*, 18:999. Stanton to Joseph Roswell Hawley [ca. 1 July 1876], *Ballot Box*, August 1876, *SAP*, 18:848; "The Woman's Suffrage Movement," *Philadelphia Evening Bulletin*, *SAP* 18:859.

152. *HWS*, 3:34–38; J.B.N., "Centennial Letter," *The Grange Advance*, 26 July 1876, 4. Variations of the "women of 1976" quotation also appear in HWS 3:30, 42, and in "Equality of Rights," *Jackson Sentinel*, 27 July 1876, 1, which reprints a detailed account of the day from the *Philadelphia Bulletin*.

153. *HWS*, 3:27–30, 42; Harper, *Life and Work*, 1:475. The earliest surviving mention of the proposed history was in November 1875, when Anthony anticipated going through the personal papers of Martha Coffin Wright, recently deceased, thinking them useful for "our history." Anthony to Matilda Joslyn Gage, 3 November 1875, *Selected Papers*, 3:208–9. Stanton indicated they planned to finish by year's end. Stanton to Henry Browne Blackwell, 31 July 1876, *SAP*, 18:947; and "Announcement of National Woman Suffrage Parlors at Philadelphia," Centennial Circular advertising the History of Woman Suffrage, 1876, *SAP*, 18:790.

154. In anticipation of the centennial, the National Association had planned to hold a mass reunion meeting to celebrate Seneca Falls over the days of July when the 1848 convention had taken place. But they cancelled the event due to the heat. They did hold a smaller, local meeting with the National Association–aligned and Philadelphia-based Citizen's Suffrage Association, chaired by Mott's son-in-law, Edward M. Davis, an active area suffragist. Letters of support celebrating 1848 and making connections between it and 1876 were read and later reprinted. *HWS*, 3:21–22, 44–51.

155. Appeal by the National Woman Suffrage Association, with Petition, 10 November 1876, *Selected Papers*, 3:266–70.

156. Anthony to Laura de Force Gordon, 18 March 1877, *Selected Papers*, 3:294.

157. The *Woman's Journal* continued its silence on the petition drive until late 1877, when the publishers grudgingly mailed out Sixteenth Amendment petitions to every *Woman's Journal* subscriber. They tacitly condemned the strategy, however, by also including petitions for state legislative action and requesting recipients "give special prominence" to the state petitions. "To Woman Suffragists," *Woman's Journal*, 24 November 1877, 372. Higginson also explained to *Woman's Journal* readers in a front-page column two weeks later that a proper balance between state and federal power was essential, lest the nation descend into "despotism." *Woman's Journal*, 8 December 1877. The *Woman's Journal* did nevertheless receive 120 petitions for a federal amendment with roughly 6,000 signatures. George Hoar, senator from Massachusetts, presented them to Congress on 5 February 1878; *Selected Papers*, 3:339n8.

158. "To Woman Suffragists," *Woman's Journal*, 24 November 1877, 372.

159. William Lloyd Garrison to Anthony, 4 January 1877, IHH Papers.

160. *HWS*, 3:72.

161. Stanton to the editor of the *Ballot Box*, 24 January [1877], *Selected Papers*, 3:286, 289–90n15.

162. Anthony Diary, 6–22 January 1877; and Stanton to the Editor of the *Ballot Box*, 24 January [1877], both in *Selected Papers*, 3:281–90.

163. Mead, *How the Vote Was Won*, 54–60; Beeton, *Women Vote in the West*, 104–8; and Jensen, "Colorado Woman Suffrage Campaigns of the 1870s."

164. Congress. Senate. 45th Cong., 1st sess., S.R. 12, *Congressional Record* 7, 252–55 (10 January 1878); quoted in Keyssar, *The Right to Vote*, 185. This language would remain unchanged until its eventual ratification, as the Nineteenth Amendment, in 1920. The text of the proposed Sixteenth Amendment does not appear in the *Congressional Journal* until 19 January 1880, when Senator Ferry introduced joint resolution S.R. No. 65: "Article XVI. Section 1. The right of suffrage in the United States shall be based on citizenship, and the right of citizens of the United States to vote shall not be denied or abridged by the United States, or by any State, on account of sex, or for any reason not equally applicable to all citizens of the United States. Sec. 2. Congress shall have power to enforce this article by appropriate legislation." Congress. Senate. 46th Cong., 2nd sess., S.R. 65, *Congressional Record* 10, 380 (19 January 1880); *HWS*, 3:97

165. Stanton is quoted in the Editorial Note to Stanton, "National Protection for National Citizens," Speech to the Senate Committee on Privileges and Elections, 11 January 1878, *Selected Papers*, 3:345, 346–73. For the names and remarks of the other women who spoke, see also *HWS*, 3:70–106. Committee on Privileges and Elections, *Arguments before the Committee on Privileges and Elections of the United States Senate on behalf of a Sixteenth Amendment to the Constitution of the United States*, 45th Cong., 1st Sess., 11–12 January 1878. The federal amendment for woman suffrage first introduced in Congress by the Radical Republican George Julian in 1869, differed from the 1878 version. See Keyssar, *The Right to Vote*, 185. On 14 June 1878, the Committee on Privileges and Elections submitted an unfavorable report on S.R. 12 and recommended that the resolution "be indefinitely postponed." Committee on Privileges and Elections, Report No. 523, 45th Cong., 2nd Sess., 14 June 1878.

166. The National Association had proposed a Seneca Falls commemoration convention, for July, at the 1876 Centennial. It never took place, however, due to the heat. The first to follow the 1873 commemoration was the 1878 celebration. "The 19th of July—Woman's Independence Day," *Democrat and Chronicle*, 8 July 1878, *SAP*, 20:310.

167. "The National Woman Suffrage Association" and "The 19th of July—Woman's Independence Day," *Democrat and Chronicle*, 8 July 1878, *SAP* 20:310; and [no title], *National Citizen and Ballot Box*, August 1878, 4.

168. U.S. Bureau of Census, *Seventh Census*, 107; Department of the Interior, *Compendium of the Tenth Census, 1880*, 396.

169. The church held participants for the daytime conference sessions, but the evening celebrations—when major speakers appeared—drew so many spectators that they had to be moved to nearby Corinthian Hall, a 1,200-seat auditorium, Rochester's largest and finest. Editorial note to "Third Decade Celebration at Rochester, New York," *Selected Papers*, 3:386. *National Citizen and Ballot Box*, August 1878, 4.

170. "Notes and News," 1 June 1878, *Woman's Journal*, emphasis added.

171. "The First Woman's Rights Convention," *National Citizen and Ballot Box*, August 1878, 4.

172. Frances D. Gage, "The Early Woman's Rights Conventions," *Woman's Journal*, 15 June 1878. The evidently widespread error may have derived from Appleton's 1876 *American Cyclopaedia*, which reported that "the first conventions were held at Seneca Falls and Rochester in 1848, under the auspices of Elizabeth Cady Stanton, Amelia Bloomer, Mrs. Stebbins, and Frederick Douglass. Anthony, "Woman's Rights," 16:701.

173. "The First Woman's Rights Convention," *National Citizen and Ballot Box*, August 1878, 4.

174. Ibid. A reporter also asked Stanton if Anthony had been there, and Stanton explained she had not. See, "Thirty Years Agitation," *New York World*, 18 July 1878, *SAP*, 20:312.

175. Hewitt, *Women's Activism and Social Change*, 130. Because Post's voice was weak, Lucy Coleman read Post's reminiscence. "Woman Suffrage. Meeting of the National Association in Rochester," *National Citizen and Ballot Box*, August 1878, *SAP*, 20:316–17.

176. "Woman Suffrage. Meeting of the National Association in Rochester," *National Citizen and Ballot Box*, August 1878, *SAP*, 20:315.

177. "Woman Suffrage in America. Third Decade Celebration in Rochester," *Woman's Words*, 2 August 1878, *SAP*, 20:333.

178. "Woman Suffrage. Meeting of the National Association in Rochester," *National Citizen and Ballot Box*, August 1878, *SAP*, 20:317; and Stanton to Theodore Weld Stanton, 28 July 1878, *SAP*, 20:359. See also, Painter, *Sojourner Truth*, 197–99.

179. "Woman Suffrage. Meeting of the National Association in Rochester," *National Citizen and Ballot Box*, August 1878, *SAP*, 20:317.

180. Philip S. Foner, *Frederick Douglass*.

181. Anthony to Stone, 9 August 1878, *SAP*, 20:372–73.

182. "America's Women," *Democrat and Chronicle*, 20 July 1878, *SAP*, 330–31; "Woman Suffrage. Meeting of the National Association in Rochester," *National Citizen and Ballot Box*, August 1878, *SAP*, 20:316.

183. "Woman Suffrage. Meeting of the National Association in Rochester," *National Citizen and Ballot Box*, August 1878, *SAP*, 20:315; "America's Women," *Democrat and Chronicle*, 20 July 1878, *SAP*, 20:327.

184. Faulkner, *Lucretia Mott's Heresy*, 209; *HWS*, 3:125; "Woman Suffrage. Meeting of the National Association in Rochester," *National Citizen and Ballot Box*, August 1878, *SAP*, 20:315.

185. On the 18th, the day of the National Association's Annual Meeting, Mott also spoke about the gains of women in literature. "Woman Suffrage in America. Third Decade Celebration in Rochester," *Woman's Words*, 2 August 1878, *SAP*, 20:332; "America's Women," *National Citizen and Ballot Box*, August 1878, *SAP*, 20:313, 316.

186. "America's Women," *National Citizen and Ballot Box*, August 1878, *SAP*, 20:316.

187. Anthony to Stone, 9 August 1878, *SAP*, 20:374.

188. "Celebration of the 30th W. S. Anniversary," *National Citizen and Ballot Box*, August 1878, 8.

189. Stone, "The Thirtieth Anniversary," and "The Proceedings at Worcester," *Woman's Journal*, 30 October 1880, 348.

190. Anthony, "The History," *Ballot Box*, February 1877, SAP, 1:469.

191. Anthony to Laura de Force Gordon, 15 May 1876, *Selected Papers*, 3:225–26n3. The

editors-in-chief, associate editors, and assistant editors are listed, with academic degrees and affiliations, on the title page of *Johnson's New Universal Cyclopaedia*.

192. For joint authorship, see Anthony to Laura de Force Gordon, 15 May 1876, *Selected Papers*, 3:225–26n3. Only Anthony's name appeared on the entry as author, however.

193. Although volume four of the *Cyclopaedia* was published in 1878, it appears Anthony wrote most, if not all, of the entries in 1876. For authorship in 1876, when Anthony calls "now (1876)," see Anthony, "Elizabeth Cady Stanton," *Johnson's New Universal Cyclopaedia*, 4:459.

194. Anthony to Laura de Force Gordon, 15 May 1876, *Selected Papers*, 3:225.

195. Ibid., 3:224. Anthony, "Woman's Rights," *Johnson's New Universal Cyclopaedia*, 4:1477.

196. Anthony, "Woman's Rights," *Johnson's New Universal Cyclopaedia*, 4:1477.

197. Ibid., 4:1477–78.

198. Anthony began using this secessionist language very early. In 1870, she had referred to Woodhull as a secessionist, after becoming angry with Woodhull for attempting to form a "People's Party." Anthony to Anna Dickinson, 22 March 1870, *SAP*, 14:663–64. Anthony, "Woman's Rights," *Johnson's New Universal Cyclopaedia*, 4:1477–79.

199. Stanton's 1898 autobiography revised the entry's claim that "many withdrew their names," stating "that most of the ladies who had attended the convention and signed the declaration, one by one, withdrew their names and influence and joined our persecutors." Elizabeth Cady Stanton, *Eighty Years and More*, 149. As Lori Ginzberg points out, "There is not an iota of evidence for this." Ginzberg, *Elizabeth Cady Stanton*, 67. Judith Wellman notes, "the majority of newspapers throughout the country provided either positive support or relatively neutral reactions to the Seneca Falls convention." Wellman, *Road to Seneca Falls*, 210; and see 279n65 for Wellman's interpretation of claims that some signers withdrew their names.

200. Anthony, "Woman's Rights," *Johnson's New Universal Cyclopaedia*, 4:1480.

Chapter 4

1. Stanton had helped earn her children's tuition expenses on the lecture platform. Matilda Joslyn Gage to Laura de Force Gordon, 29 December 1880, LdFG Papers, Box 1; Lutz, *Created Equal*, 193; and Tetrault, "The Incorporation of American Feminism."

2. Stanton was helped in her persuasive efforts by another suffragist, Sarah Pugh. Anthony to Harriet Hanson Robinson, 24 October 1880, *Selected Papers*, 4:9n2.

3. Anthony to Harriet Hanson Robinson, 24 October 1880, *Selected Papers*, 4:6–9n2.

4. In her autobiography, Stanton incorrectly remembered the simultaneous arrival of Anthony and Gage on 20 November 1880. Anthony to Harriet Hanson Robinson, 24 October 1880, *Selected Papers*, 4:9n2; Elizabeth Cady Stanton, *Eighty Years and More*, 326.

5. *HWS*, 1:7.

6. Fahs and Waugh, "Introduction," *Memory of the Civil War*, 2; and Waugh, "Ulysses S. Grant: Historian," 9.

7. Newell and Shrader, *Of Duty Well and Faithfully Done*, 89–90.

8. For a discussion of these various forms, see Fahs and Waugh, *Memory of the Civil War*; Jeffrey, *Abolitionists Remember*; Blight, *Race and Reunion*. Waugh, "Ulysses S. Grant," 9.

9. For more of the outpouring of Civil War publishing, see Blight, *Race and Reunion*; Fahs and Waugh, *Memory of the Civil War*; Fahs, "The Feminized Civil War."

10. *HWS*, 1:13, 747.

11. *HWS*, 1:429.

12. Blight, *Race and Reunion*.

13. *HWS*, 3:36, 42, 58; Van Tyne and Leland, *Guide to the Archives*, v–ix; and James D. Richardson, *Messages and Papers of the Presidents, 1787–1897*.

14. Women's history did exist, albeit not as a recognizable field. See, for example, Ellett, *Pioneer Women of the West*; Ellett, *The Women of the American Revolution*; Sarah Margaret Fuller, *Woman in the Nineteenth Century*; Child, *The History of the Condition of Women*; Hurlbut, *Essays of Human Rights and Their Political Guaranties*; and Des Jardins, *Women and the Historical Enterprise in America*.

15. *HWS*, 3:42, 58. See also Blouin and Rosenberg, *Contesting Authority*, chap. 2; Steedman, *Dust*; Mayhall, "Creating the 'Suffragette Spirit'"; and the essays in Buss and Kadar, *Working in Women's Archives*.

16. What would eventually become the *History*'s first chapter, "Preceding Causes," debuted in the *National Citizen*'s September 1878 issue. The "especial object of the publication of the Woman Suffrage History by its editors in a newspaper," they explained, "is that all dropped facts may be picked up, all mistakes corrected, and everything made right before it is put into book form." Additional draft chapters appeared in serialization over the next four years—eight chapters in all—with the final one appearing in February 1881.

17. *Selected Papers*, 3:xxiv; and Matilda Joslyn Gage to Laura de Force Gordon, December 29, 1880, LdFG Papers, box 1.

18. Stanton nevertheless found time to vote illegally in the fall elections, striding to the polls with Anthony on her arm. Stanton to Theodore Stanton, 2 November 1880, *Selected Papers*, 4:14–15; Elizabeth Cady Stanton, *Eighty Years and More*, 326–27.

19. Stanton to Elizabeth Boynton Harbert, September 29, [1876], *Selected Papers*, 3:264.

20. Stone to Stanton, 30 August 1876, IHH Papers, box 1.

21. *HWS*, 1:7.

22. Elizabeth Cady Stanton, *Eighty Years and More*, 326.

23. Matilda Joslyn Gage to Laura de Force Gordon, 29 December 1880, LdFG Papers, box 1.

24. Ibid.

25. For one interpretation of Gage's role, see Corey, "Matilda Joslyn Gage," 103–60.

26. Matilda Joslyn Gage to Laura de Force Gordon, 29 December 1880, LdFG Papers, box 1. For a similar description of the chaos in Tenafly, see Stanton to Mathilde Franz Anneke, 20 October [1876 or 78], MFA Papers, box 5, folder 4.

27. *The Elizabeth Cady Stanton and Susan B. Anthony Papers Project*, overseen since the 1980s (and recently completed) by Ann D. Gordon, now arguably holds that distinction. The collection consists of forty-five reels of microfilm (published in 1991) and six annotated volumes (published between 1997 and 2013). But unlike the *HWS*, they are not also one long narrative, making them distinctly different. The Schlesinger Library's microfilmed collection of documents relating to their suffrage collection is also a massive, readily accessible collection.

28. Anthony to Barbara Binks Thompson, 18 August 1881, *Selected Papers*, 4:105.

29. *Selected Papers*, 4:xxv; Harper, *Life and Work*, 2:529–31.

30. Anthony to Elizabeth Boynton Harbert, 20 March 1881, *Selected Papers*, 4:53–54.

31. Elizabeth Cady Stanton, *Eighty Years and More*, 329.

32. Novick, *That Noble Dream*, 21, 33, 48.

33. *HWS*, 1:7.

34. The Senate Committee on Woman Suffrage was created in January 1882, and Stanton spoke before it in a hearing several weeks after its creation in conjunction with the National Woman Suffrage Association's annual 1882 January convention in Washington, D.C. Stanton to Olympia Brown, 29 January [1882], *Selected Papers*, 4:145.

35. "The ridicule of fact," the authors remind opponents, "does not change their character. Many who study the past with interest and see the importance of seeming trifles in helping forward great events, often fail to understand some of the best pages of history made under their own eyes. Hence the woman suffrage movement has not yet been accepted as the legitimate outgrowth of American ideas—a component part of the history of our republic—but is falsely considered the willful outburst of a few unbalanced minds." *HWS*, 1:51.

36. This same dynamic was emerging within the African American community, where remembering and history were explicitly understood to be forms of social activism. This informed efforts to build some of the first black archives after the Civil War. See Julie Des Jardins, *Women and the Historical Enterprise*; Kathleen Clark, *Defining Moments*; Blight, *Race and Reunion*; and Novick, *That Noble Dream*.

37. *HWS*, 1:7–8. Not until the advent of progressive historians in the 1920s and new social historians in the 1970s would many scholars explicitly consider how their historical and social standpoint shaped how they presented the past—or argue that this was not only inevitable but was perhaps a good thing. Novick, *That Noble Dream*, 92–97, 439–45, 458.

38. *HWS*, 1:7–8.

39. The question of subjectivity is an ongoing debate among historians. Blouin and Rosenberg, *Archives, Documentation and Institutions of Social Memory*; Novick, *That Noble Dream*; and Appleby, Hunt, and Jacob, *Telling the Truth about History*.

40. Gage reprinted many of the press reviews in the *National Citizen and Ballot Box*. Its August 1881 issue, for example, was devoted to a promotion of the *History's* first volume, and the issue included pages of excerpted reviews from periodicals across the country. "History of Woman Suffrage: Press Notices," *National Citizen and Ballot Box*, August 1881, 1–2; and "History of Woman Suffrage," *Nation*, 19 May 1887, 432–33.

41. Stone, "The History of Woman Suffrage," *Woman's Journal*, 11 June 1881, 188; *HWS*, 1:7.

42. Blouin and Rosenberg, *Archives, Documentation and Institutions of Social Memory*, 1–3; see Geary, "Medieval Archivists as Authors"; Eiss, "Redemption's Archive"; McAdams, *The Redemptive Self*; Polletta, *It Was Like a Fever*; Ronald Jacobs, "The Narrative Integration"; Joseph E. Davis, *Stories of Change*.

To this day, historians generally consult the *History* as a compendium of primary material, and only rarely as a monograph with clear interpretative lines. For scholars who consider the constructedness of the story told, see DuBois, "Making Women's History"; Buhle and Buhle, *Concise History of Woman Suffrage*; Isenberg, *Sex and Citizenship*; Des Jardins, *Women and the Historical Enterprise*; and Terborg-Penn, *African American Women*.

43. *HWS*, 1:29, 32, 34–35, 39.

44. *HWS*, 1:51–52, 61, emphases added.

45. *HWS*, 1:61–62. Stanton similarly underplays the antislavery movement's influence on woman suffragists in the eulogistic biographical sketch of Mott (who died in November 1880) she wrote for volume 1, chapter 11. Mott's formative and significant antislavery activism barely figures in the chapter, further reflecting Stanton's ambivalence about that movement. As in the London chapter, she instead belabors Mott's exclusion from the 1840 convention—a story that Mott, an ardent abolitionist, never told about herself. Lucretia Mott to Elizabeth Cady Stanton, 16 March 1855, Palmer, *Selected Letters of Lucretia Coffin Mott*, 233–36.

Carol Faulkner, Mott's biographer, discusses how various constituencies used Mott after her death to lend authority to their agendas, turning Mott into a sainted hero rather than a three-dimensional figure. Faulkner, *Lucretia Mott's Heresy*. For more on how Mott operated as a sainted symbol within the women's rights movement, see Isenberg, *Sex and Citizenship*, 96–97; Stanton, "Lucretia Mott," Chapter 11, *HWS*, 1:407–40.

46. *HWS*, 1:67, 472.

47. It also borrows in important ways from Stanton's 1850s historical account, which was never published. "Address by Stanton to the Eighth National Woman's Rights Convention," 13 May 1858, *Selected Papers*, 1:361–72.

48. *HWS*, 1:67–68. Oddly, this passage omits Jane Hunt as one of the women around "the tea-table of Richard Hunt," her husband.

49. *HWS*, 1:68. The theme of earnest innocence, inexperience, and lack of preparation anticipates an origins myth of the mid-twentieth-century civil rights struggle: the story of an exhausted seamstress who sat down on an Alabama bus and sparked a movement. See Theoharis, *Rebellious Life of Mrs. Rosa Parks*.

50. *HWS*, 1:67–68.

51. *HWS*, 1:68–73, emphasis added.

52. *HWS*, 1:74.

53. *HWS*, 1:88, 355, 124, 73.

54. *HWS*, 1: 456 (the Napoleon analogy originated in a remark by William Ellery Channing). Stanton's reminiscence (chapter 13) is not the first mention of Anthony in volume one. She receives mention in earlier chapters as well—identified, for example, as a central figure in some of the early "preceding causes," such as the temperance and teacher's movements. She is also discussed after the Seneca Falls chapter in several state overviews, as a leading figure in some of the early women's rights conventions throughout the 1850s. But she remains a tangential character in volume one until Stanton introduces her in the thirteenth of the work's fifteen chapters.

55. *HWS*, 2nd ed., 1:456. In her biography of Stanton, Elisabeth Griffith says that Stanton frequently misremembered the date when she and Anthony first met. Griffith, *In Her Own Right*, 73, 245n29. However, Stanton had gotten it right in a separate biographical sketch of Anthony; see Stanton, "The Woman's Rights Movement," 397. The frequency of the error noted by Griffith was, I suspect, due less to forgetfulness than to the different ways in which Stanton told and deployed the story over the years. See also Ann D. Gordon, "Afterword," in Elizabeth Cady Stanton, *Eighty Years & More*, 476. Anthony, however, said of Stanton: "She can tangle up chronology to beat any other one who puts pen to paper." So it may well have been an error. Quoted in Kern, *Mrs. Stanton's Bible*, 21.

56. *HWS*, 1:459–60.

57. *HWS*, 1:456, 472.

58. *HWS*, 1:802–10, 859.

59. "Preface," *HWS*, 1:7.

60. Anthony to Amelia Jenks Bloomer, 1 August 1885, *Selected Papers*, 4:437–38.

61. Anthony to Amelia Jenks Bloomer, 4 August 1881, *Selected Papers*, 4:103.

62. *Selected Papers*, 4:xxv.

63. State chapters were often collaborative enterprises, with various people contributing pieces that Stanton and Anthony made into a whole. Gage to Gordon, 29 December 1880, LdFG Papers, box 1.

64. Anthony to Harriet Hanson Robinson, 24 October 1880, *Selected Papers*, 4:6–11; Bushman, *"A Good Poor Man's Wife"*; and Robinson, *Massachusetts in the Woman Suffrage Movement*. This was reprinted again in 1883. Dublin, *Women at Work*.

65. Fischer, *Pantaloons and Power*. Griffith, *In Her Own Right*, 71–73.

66. Rose was a Jewish Polish immigrant living in New York who campaigned for a variety of reforms throughout the 1840s, including married women's property reform. Stanton to Amelia Jenks Bloomer, 30 July [1881], *Selected Papers*, 4:101–2n1; Doress-Worters, *Mistress of Herself*; Kolmerten, *American Life of Ernestine L. Rose*.

67. Stanton to Amelia Jenks Bloomer, 30 July [1881], *Selected Papers*, 4:101; Anthony to Amelia Jenks Bloomer, 4 August 1881, *Selected Papers*, 4:102–3.

68. Stanton and Anthony did not use Bloomer's newspaper the *Lily* to reconstruct and document antebellum temperance work but instead used Paulina Wright Davis's *Una*, and this further angered Bloomer. Stanton to Amelia Jenks to Bloomer, 30 July [1881]; Anthony to Amelia Jenks Bloomer, 4 August 1881, *Selected Papers*, 4:101–4.

69. Amelia Bloomer to Mary Jane Coggeshall, 29 June 1885, quoted in Noun, *Strong-Minded Women*, 264–65.

70. Anthony to Amelia Bloomer, 4 August 1881; Stanton to Harriet Hanson Robinson, 26 October [1881], *Selected Papers*, 4:103, 118–19; Harper, *Life and Work*, 2:537; and Stanton to Robinson, 26 October [1881], *Selected Papers*, 4:118–19. Acknowledging that Stanton would be slow to recover, the August 1881 issue of the *National Citizen and Ballot Box* informed readers that "her illness will somewhat delay the second volume of the History."

71. The paper, already strapped for cash, was losing money because of the *History*'s production. Anthony's decision to stop lecturing the previous winter had had a devastating effect on the paper's fortunes. An important portion of the paper's income came from sales Anthony generated during her lecture tours. Adding the prospect of resuming work on volume two sealed the paper's fate. "I find it impossible to subject myself to the same draught upon my health and strength that I did last year," Gage told readers. The paper never resumed. "Executive Session of the National Woman Suffrage Association," 17 and 21 January 1882, *Selected Papers*, 4:139n; and Gage, "To Subscribers of the National Citizen," *National Citizen and Ballot Box*, October 1881, 2. On Gage's personal financial troubles that continued over the last two decades of her life, see Tetrault, "The Incorporation of Feminism"; and Brammer, *Excluded from Suffrage History*, 13–15.

72. Stanton to Frederick A. Hinckley, 30 January [1882], *Selected Papers*, 4:148.

73. The authors had decided upon a third volume by January of 1882. Stanton to Olympia Brown, 29 January 1882; and Anthony to Elizabeth Boynton Harbert, 8 March 1882, *Selected Papers*, 4:145–46, 161–62.

74. *HWS*, xxi, 1; Anthony to Robinson, October 24, 1880, *Selected Papers*, 4:8.

75. Anthony to Elizabeth Boynton Harbert, 10 May 1882, *Selected Papers*, 4:166–67.

76. *HWS*, 2:288, 99, 322–23, emphasis mine.

77. *HWS*, 2: 66, 892, 895, 153.

78. *HWS*, 2:v–vii.

79. *HWS*, 2:1–3, 87–88. When the authors decided to defer wartime history to volume two, Anthony explained in an eloquent letter to Clara Barton, "What we want, is, to open our *2d Volume* with this grand work of women to save . . . *Liberty*. . . . Sacrificing everything—holding woman's own *claim for rights* in abeyance even—and then after all this herculean work—*we shall* charge back on man his ingratitude & injustice in *denying to women* their *equal share* in the *new* powers—the new guarantees for freedom & the franchise—They fought for national supremacy *over* the states to enslave & disenfranchise people—and then refused to exercise that new power in behalf of the people—It was—and is—the crime of the ages." Anthony to Clara Barton, 14 February 1881, *Selected Papers*, 4:49.

80. *HWS*, 2:89. The most important book on this question of Civil War memory is Blight's *Race and Reunion*, which, while masterful, overlooks questions of gender beyond questions of manhood. More recently, scholars are beginning to ask questions about women's roles in the creation the postwar memory culture. The most recent work is "Women and Reconciliation, 1880s–1910s," in Janney, *Remembering the Civil War*, 232–65.

81. *HWS*, 2:91.

82. *HWS*, 2:172, 190.

83. *HWS*, 2:88.

84. For the fullest account to date of the ubiquity of Stanton's racism, and the complex interplay of that racism throughout her career, see Ginzberg, *Elizabeth Cady Stanton*.

85. *HWS*, 2:391.

86. *HWS*, 2:353, 382, 365. For other instances of Stanton's "Sambo" statement, see 2:94, 270, and 508. For its quotation by another suffragist, see 2:944.

87. *HWS*, 2:316. Claims about educated white women's superior claims to the ballot are found throughout the volume. See, for example, *HWS*, 2:245, 266, 322–23.

88. The *History*'s authors do not indicate what or whom they are quoting in this passage. *HWS*, 1:8.

89. "Preface," *HWS*, 1:7

90. *HWS*, 2:319, 321, 324.

91. *HWS*, 2:888.

92. *HWS*, 2:391.

93. *HWS*, 1:114–17. This important reading of Truth's speech belongs to Painter, *Sojourner Truth*. See also Painter, "Representing Truth" and "Voices of Suffrage."

94. *Proceedings of the Eleventh National Woman's Rights Convention, 1866*, 45–48; Painter, "Voices of Suffrage."

95. *HWS*, 2:171.

96. Terborg-Penn, *African American Women*, 15, also makes this observation.

97. *HWS*, 2:179.

98. This problem did not begin with Stanton and Anthony, and it has extended well past them, plaguing feminism as well as civil rights into the twenty-first century. For more on the so-called woman question in black discourse and black politics in the mid- to late nineteenth century, see Martha S. Jones, *All Bound Up Together*; Painter, "Voices of Suffrage"; Terborg-Penn, *African American Women*; Gordon and Collier-Thomas, *African-American Women*; Elsa Barkley Brown, "Negotiating and Transforming the Public Sphere"; Hine, "Rape and the Inner Lives of Black Women"; Higginbotham, *Righteous Discontent*; Cooper, *A Voice from the South*; Gilmore, *Gender and Jim Crow*; Hannah Rosen, *Terror in the Heart of Freedom*.

99. *Constitution of the American Woman Suffrage Association, The Gerritsen Collection of Women's History*, microfiche, no. 69.

100. *HWS*, 2:323. Lucy Stone, unpublished manuscript, 4 February 1882, in AERA File, *NAWSA Papers*, microfilm, 26:25–42; Henry Blackwell, unpublished manuscript, n.d. [1887], in AERA File, *NAWSA Papers*, 26:42–60. Both transcribed by Ida Porter Boyer. Quotation from Blackwell, 26:57.

101. Lucy Stone, unpublished manuscript, 4 February 1882, in AERA File, *NAWSA Papers*, 26:25–42; Henry Blackwell, unpublished manuscript, n.d. [1887], in AERA File, *NAWSA Papers*, 26:42–60, quotation from 57. Both transcribed by Ida Porter Boyer.

102. Lucy Stone, unpublished manuscript, 4 February 1882, in AERA File, *NAWSA Papers*, 26:25–42; Henry Blackwell, unpublished manuscript, n.d. [1887], in AERA File, *NAWSA Papers*, 26:42–60. Both transcribed by Ida Porter Boyer. Quotation from Romano and Raiford, "Introduction," *Civil Rights Movement in American Memory*, xxi.

103. *HWS*, 2:406.

104. Stanton and Anthony only agreed to include a chapter about the American Association after pressure from Stanton's daughter. The *History*'s authors did not quite know what to do with the American Association. Once Harriet Hanson Robinson had published her *Massachusetts in the Woman Suffrage Movement* in 1881, they decided to forgo trying to write a history of the American Association, arguing that Robinson's work (a work Stone disliked) covered that ground. Harriot disagreed. Stanton had summoned her home from England to help with the *History*'s crushing labor. Harriot argued that because the *History*'s authors had marketed the book "to be a history of the suffrage movement and not merely of the National," and because "it would . . . do credit to the authors if they rose above the roar of battle," Stanton and Anthony must give "space . . . [to] their antagonists." Otherwise, Harriot feared, the *History* would be swamped with "a deluge of adverse comment." Stanton rejoined that she was "too fagged out" and "too prejudiced," while Anthony pled "she was no writer, and would not undertake this task if she could." The pair agreed to relent if Harriot would write the chapter, which she did. SBA to Harriet Hanson Robinson, 24 October 1880, *Selected Papers*, 4:8; Stanton to Harriet Hanson Robinson, 26 October [1881], *Selected Papers*, 4:118–19; and Blatch and Lutz, *Challenging Years*, 61–63.

105. Higginson, "The Reverse of the Picture," *Woman's Journal*, 23 September 1882.

106. Stone, "Woman Suffrage History," *Woman's Journal*, 10 March 1883.

107. This alternate movement origin, rooted in abolitionist women's oratory, was not something the Garrison children invented whole cloth. Rather it appears to have originated with fellow feminist-abolitionist Abby Kelley Foster, who had tangled with Stanton and Anthony in the 1860s, and who despised their position on the Fifteenth Amendment—a position that the *History* enshrined as the movement's position. Kelley Foster had dictated her memoirs to her daughter before her death, but never managed to publish them. The

Garrisons evidently used Kelley Foster's unpublished account to offer a dissenting narrative about when and where women's rights had begun. Wendell Phillips Garrison and Francis Jackson Garrison, *William Lloyd Garrison, 1805–1879*, see especially 2:204, 380–1, and 3:262; Alla W. Foster, Reminiscence of her Mother Abby Kelley Foster, untitled, undated [1881], and unpublished manuscript, in Abby Kelley Foster Papers, box 2, folder 30, American Antiquarian Society, Worcester, Mass.

108. Stanton to the Editor, *Ballot Box*, 24 January [1877], *Selected Papers*, 3:285.

109. *Selected Papers*, 4:xxv.

110. The minimization of Gage's role continued after her 1898 death, when the advertisements and preface to a fourth volume, produced by Anthony and Ida Husted Harper, either omitted Gage altogether as an author of earlier volumes or cast her as a mere assistant, causing her children to angrily object. Matilda Joslyn Gage to Laura de Force Gordon, 29 December 1880, LdFG Papers, box 1; Anthony to Thomas Clarkson Gage, 1903, and Anthony to Helen Leslie Gage, 16 June 1903, MJG Papers, microfilm, reel 1, images 531–32.

111. When published, the title became "Trials and Decisions." Anthony to Elizabeth Boynton Harbert, 8 March 1882, *Selected Papers*, 4:162; and *HWS*, 2:586–755.

112. The efforts of women to vote in other states would find their way into the state chapters of volume three. "Trials and Decisions," *HWS*, 2:586–755.

113. Matilda Joslyn Gage to Lillie Devereux Blake, 8 July 1884, LDB Papers, box 6, folder 21.

114. Blake's trouble was over Anthony's work on the steel portrait engravings that appeared on the pages of the *History*, and particularly over the payment for Blake's own engraving. Gage too had trouble with how Anthony dealt with Gage's engraving. [Matilda Joslyn Gage] to Lillie Devereux Blake, 13 July 1881, LDB Papers, box 6, folder 18.

115. [Matilda Joslyn Gage] to Lillie Devereux Blake, 13 July 1881, LDB Papers, box 6, folder 18.

116. Matilda Joslyn Gage to Lillie Devereux Blake, 14 March 1891, LDB Papers, box 7, folder 6.

117. Stanton to Frederick A. Hinckley, 30 January [1882], *Selected Papers*, 4:148.

118. My thinking here has been aided by Eiss, "Redemption's Archive."

119. Anthony to Amelia Jenks Bloomer, 23 June 1885, *Selected Papers*, 4:429–30.

120. *Selected Papers*, 4:xxvi–xxvii.

121. Nebraska women shifted from full suffrage to a battle for municipal suffrage after the 1882 defeat. Bloomberg, "'Striving for Equal Rights for All'"; Wilhite, "Sixty-Five Years till Victory"; Welch, "Local and National Forces," 113–53.

122. "Interview with Anthony in Philadelphia," *Philadelphia Evening News*, [22 February 1883], *Selected Papers,* 4:222–23; Dorr, *Susan B. Anthony*, 291.

123. "Interview with Anthony in Philadelphia," *Philadelphia Evening News*, [February 22, 1883], *Selected Papers*, 4:222–23; Dorr, *Susan B. Anthony*, 291.

124. Anthony had told reporters they would sail back that September, but they did not return until November. They likely delayed their return because Harriot expected her first child in October 1883. "Interview with Anthony in Philadelphia," *Philadelphia Evening News*, [February 22, 1883], *Selected Papers*, 4:222–23; Stanton to Anna M. Preistman et al., 30 October [1883], *Selected Papers*, 4:291–92.

125. Partnership agreement for preparation and publication of the *History of Woman Suffrage*, 15 November 1876, SAP, 18:1081–84.

126. Harper, *Life and Work*, 2:613. For an account of how Anthony funded the *History*, see Tetrault, "We Shall Be Remembered."

127. Anthony to Amelia Jenks Bloomer, 23 June 1885, *Selected Papers*, 4:429–30n1.

128. Ibid.

129. Harper, *Life and Work*, 2:601–2.

130. Ibid.

131. Anthony to Lillie Devereux Blake, 27 October 1885, *Selected Papers*, 4:444.

132. Harper, *Life and Work*, 2:608–9.

133. Anthony to Elizabeth Boynton Harbert, 3 June 1886, *Selected Papers*, 4:506.

134. Ibid., 4:506–8n3; Harper, *Life and Work*, 2:613. The indexing cost $250—translating to roughly $5,800 today.

135. Anthony to John W. Weinheimer, 13 August 1886, *Selected Papers*, 4:508.

136. Harper reported that volume three was published in December, but Stanton reported the books available in November 1886. Harper, *Life and Work*, 2:612; Stanton to Victoria Woodhull Martin, 12 November [1886], *Selected Papers*, 4:525.

There would be three more volumes added in the early twentieth century, but their authors had not yet conceived of them. These first three—the only ones Stanton, Anthony, and Gage authored together—were understood by their authors to be a complete project.

137. *HWS*, 3:iv.

138. *HWS*, 3:iii.

139. *HWS*, 1:51.

140. Contemporary biographical compendiums included Parton, *Eminent Women of the Age*; Hanaford, *Daughters of America*; Willard and Livermore, *A Woman of the Century*.

141. Anthony to Elizabeth Boynton Harbert, 3 June 1886, *Selected Papers*, 4:507.

142. Harper, *Life and Work*, 2:614. Whether those who pledged their five dollars back in 1876 ever received a copy is a mystery.

143. Ibid.; *HWS*, 4:viii.

144. Dorr, *Susan B. Anthony*, 329; Andrew Dickson White to Anthony, 15 October 1881, *SAP*, 22:107–8. Later, in the early twentieth century, Harvard reversed course and asked Anthony for a complete set, offering payment in advance. Cornell University, by contrast, warmly welcomed Anthony's initial gift of volume one.

145. Harper, preface to *HWS*, 4:viii; Harper, *Life and Work*, 2:614. The Sewall-Bellmont House, in Washington, D.C., for example, holds a copy originally belonging to the American Federation of Labor.

146. Buhle and Buhle, "Preface," *Concise History of Woman Suffrage*, xix.

147. The dispute over the $160 difference turned on a long-standing dispute between Gage and Anthony over money owed for *History* advertising in the *National Citizen and Ballot Box*. Matilda Joslyn Gage to Lillie Devereux Blake, n.d., 1890, LDB Papers, box 7, folder 5.

148. Anthony Diary, 16 November 1883, *Selected Papers*, 4:299–300n1; and Sewall, *Genesis of the International Council of Women*, 1–3; and *Report of the International Council of Women, 1888*, 9.

149. *HWS*, 3:952.

Chapter 5

1. Lucy Stone to Antoinette Brown Blackwell, n.d. [winter 1888], *Friends and Sisters*, 255.

2. Brown Blackwell to Stone, 10 February 1888, in Lasser and Merrill, *Friends and Sisters*, 256.

3. Anthony to Frederick Douglass, 6 February 1888, *Selected Papers*, 5:83–84.

4. *Report of the International Council of Women, 1888*, 10.

5. Ibid., 11.

6. Ibid., 9–11.

7. Anthony Diary, 16 November 1883, *Selected Papers*, 4:299–300n1; and Sewall, *Genesis of the International Council of Women*, 1–3; and *Report of the International Council of Women, 1888*, 9.

8. Anthony Diary, 16 November 1883, *Selected Papers*, 4:299–300n1; Stanton and Anthony, *Report of the Sixteenth Annual Washington Convention, 1884*, 25–26, 43, 53–55, 96–116.

9. "Call to the International Council of Women," 1 June 1887, *Selected Papers*, 5:27–29.

10. Stanton sailed to Europe in 1886 and did not return to the United States until early 1888. Ginzberg, *Elizabeth Cady Stanton*, 168.

11. *Report of the International Council of Women, 1888*, 10.

12. Quoted in ibid., 10.

13. This early draft was also titled, "The Fortieth Anniversary of the First Woman Suffrage Convention," but that title was later changed to the "International Council of Women." Early Text of the Call to the International Council of Women, [19? April? 1887], and Call to the International Council of Women, 1 June 1887, *Selected Papers*, 5:24–26, 27–29; Brown Blackwell to Stone, 10 February 1888, in Lasser and Merrill, *Friends and Sisters*, 256.

14. The final draft was titled, "International Council of Women." "Call to the International Council of Women," 1 June 1887, *Selected Papers*, 5:27–29.

15. Brown Blackwell to Stone, 10 February 1888, in Lasser and Merrill, *Friends and Sisters*, 256.

16. The irony of the focus on suffrage that would characterize the event was that the original 1848 call omitted the word "political" from its language. "Early Text of the Call to the International Council of Women," [19? April? 1887], and "Call to the International Council of Women," 1 June 1887, *Selected Papers*, 5:24–26, 27–29. The original call from 1848 read: "Woman's Rights Convention.—A Convention to discuss the social, civil, and religious condition and rights of woman, will be held in the Wesleyan Chapel, at Seneca Falls, N.Y., on Wednesday and Thursday, the 19th and 20th of July, current; commencing at 10 o'clock A.M. During the first day the meeting will be exclusively for women, who are earnestly invited to attend. The public generally are invited to be present on the second day, when Lucretia Mott, of Philadelphia, and other ladies and gentlemen, will address the convention." *HWS*, 1:67.

17. Harriet Hanson Robinson Diary, 1 April 1888, Robinson and Shattuck Papers.

18. "The Twentieth Annual Convention of the National Woman Suffrage Association, Minutes of the meeting of the Executive Committee and Executive Session," 3–4 April 1888, NWSA File, *NAWSA Papers*, 47:334.

19. *Report of the International Council of Women, 1888*, 12–18.

20. Anderson, *Joyous Greetings*; McFadden, *Golden Cables of Sympathy*; Rupp, *Worlds of Women*, and "Constructing Internationalism."

21. Bonnie Anderson, *Joyous Greetings*; Rupp, *Worlds of Women*.

22. *Report of the International Council of Women, 1888*, 455. The monetary translation was derived by using measuringworth.com.

23. Olympia Brown, *Democratic Ideals*, 32–33, 82.

24. "Council of Women," *New York Times*, 25 March 1888, 4; "Women in Council," *New York Times*, 29 March 1888, 5; "The International Council of Women," *Friends' Intelligencer*, 14 April 1888, 237; "The Women in Council," *Chicago Daily Tribune*, 29 March 1888, 2; "The Women's Council Ended," *New York Times*, 2 April 1888, 1; "Woman's International Council," *Christian Advocate*, 12 April 1888, 248; "About the Women," *Zion's Herald*, 18 April 1888, 126; "Close of the Big Council," *Chicago Daily Tribune*, 2 April 1888, 2; "Women on the Platform," *New York Times*, 31 March 1888, 3; "First Gun of the Council," *Chicago Daily Tribune*, 26 March 1888, 1; "The Woman's Movement," *Christian Union*, 5 April 1888, 423; "Closing Session of the Council," *Chicago Daily Tribune*, 2 April 1888, 2; "International Council of Women," *Harpers Bazaar*, 28 April 1888, 278; "International Council of Women at Washington," *The Leeds Mercury*, 11 April 1888.

25. *Report of the International Council of Women, 1888*. Mott's image is in the proceeding's front matter.

26. Ibid., 30.

27. Ibid.

28. Ibid., 30–31. For a time Anthony worried that Stanton would not return for the anniversary. When she received a cable from Stanton in mid-February reading simply, "Coming,"

she reported enormous relief. Anthony Diary, 14 February 1888, *Selected Papers*, 5:85. One other original organizer lived, Jane Hunt, who would die the following year.

29. *Report of the International Council of Women, 1888*, 31–32. For temperance founding myths, see Stebbins, *Fifty Years History of the Temperance Cause*; Lewis, "A Brief History of the Woman's Crusade"; Wittenmeyer, *History of the Woman's Temperance Crusade*; Steel, *The Woman's Temperance Movement*; Stewart, *Memories of the Crusade*; Carpenter, *The Crusade*.

30. *Report of the International Council of Women, 1888*, 31–36, quotation from 32.

31. Ibid., 31–39, quotation from 37, 34.

32. Harriet Hanson Robinson Diary, 31 March 1888, Robinson and Shattuck Papers; *Report of the International Council of Women, 1888*, 352.

33. *Report of the International Council of Women, 1888*, 324.

34. 1848 was not, despite Stanton's claims for it, and for herself, women's first organized demand for the vote. In 1846, women in New York petitioned for the right to vote. Ginzberg, *Untidy Origins*.

35. *Report of the International Council of Women, 1888*, 325.

36. They were Stanton, Catharine Stebbins, Sarah Burtis, Amy Post, Mary Hallowell, and Sarah Willis. Ibid., 327.

37. Harriet Hanson Robinson Diary, 31 March 1888, Robinson and Shattuck Papers; and *Report of the International Council of Women, 1888*, 17, 331.

38. *Report of the International Council of Women, 1888*, 322–53.

39. Ibid., 355–68.

40. Douglass's remarks appear in the 1 April 1888 issue of the *Woman's Tribune*, 11–12, and *Report of the International Council of Women, 1888*, 327–31, quotations from 328, 329. Douglass, *Life and Times*.

41. *Report of the International Council of Women, 1888*, 331, emphasis mine; and Stone and Blackwell's remarks, 1 April 1888, *Woman's Tribune*, 12–13.

42. *Woman's Tribune*, 1 April 1888, 12–131; and *Report of the International Council of Women, 1888*, 331–35, 335–39.

43. *Woman's Tribune*, 1 April 1888, 12; and *Report of the International Council of Women, 1888*, 331–35.

44. Brown Blackwell's comments are in the 1 April issue of the *Woman's Tribune*, 13, emphasis mine; and *Report of the International Council of Women, 1888*, 340–42.

45. Stone and Brown Blackwell were both upset over the reporting of the ICW in Clara Bewick Colby's *Woman's Tribune*. Colby, a Nebraska suffragist, sided with Stanton and Anthony's National Association. She had moved her paper from Nebraska to Washington, D.C., for the ICW, in order to issue daily reports. Brown Blackwell felt her comments were distorted, and she complained to Colby. Stone, meanwhile, lambasted the *Woman's Tribune* for its ability to make "lies appear the truth." Stone to Brown Blackwell, 20 August 1888, in Lasser and Merrill, *Friends and Sisters*, 257–58. After Stone's speech, she and Harriet Hanson Robinson, another suffragist from Massachusetts who was rare for her support of Stanton and Anthony, sparred. Stone did not like Robinson's history, titled *Massachusetts in the Woman Suffrage Movement*, as she thought it too partisan, and she delivered a jibe at the work in her ICW remarks. Robinson then issued a rejoinder in Colby's *Tribune*. See Robinson, "A Correction," 5 May 1888, *Woman's Tribune*.

46. Anthony used pointedly racist language: "I believe in universal suffrage for all men and all women: still, if the Republican party will insist upon taking a wheelbarrow full of people at a time into the body politic, I insist that it is more important for this Government to have a wheelbarrow load of intelligent, native born, educated, tax-paying women than of ignorant plantation men." Anthony's comment was not entered into the official proceedings. *Woman's Tribune*, 1 April 1888, 14.

47. Terborg-Penn, *African American Women*.

48. *Woman's Tribune*, 1 April 1888, 14; *Report of the International Council of Women, 1888*, 342.

49. Blight, *Race and Reunion*; and Wang, *The Trial of Democracy*.

50. "The Women Assembling; Delegates Who Arrived To-Day—The Pioneers Who Are In Town," *Washington Evening Star*, March 24, 1888, 5. Colby also ran sketches of pioneers in her newspaper, including some of Anthony and notably one about her arrest and trial for voting in 1872 that was paired with accounts of Pioneer Day. Colby, "Susan B. Anthony," *Woman's Tribune*, 17 March 1888, 1–2, and 1 April 1888.

51. Anthony, *Woman's Tribune*, 1 April 1888, 16.

52. Ibid.

53. Olympia Brown, Charlotte F. Daley, Marietta M. Bones, Matilda J. Gage, Harriette R. Shattuck, and Harriet H. Robinson, "A Statement of Facts: Private," p. 4, in MJG Papers, Part A: National Leaders, 4:342.

54. Ann D. Gordon suggests that this vote, and its failure, produced transformations in the movement over the long term. *Selected Papers*, 5:xxii–xxvii. For an account of why the federal amendment came to a vote, see Sneider, *Suffragists in an Imperial Age*.

55. Mead, *How the Vote Was Won*, 47–48.

56. Sarah Barringer Gordon, *The Mormon Question*.

57. Editorial note on the reasons for unification, *Selected Papers*, 5:54–56.

58. Stone to Brown Blackwell, n.d. [winter 1888], in Lasser and Merrill, *Friends and Sisters*, 255.

59. *NAWSA Papers*, 26:200; Stone to Anthony, 7 November 1887, *Selected Papers*, 5:52–53, 54–57. To date, far too little is known about why and how the American Association decided to propose union. For one interpretation, see Ann D. Gordon's editorial note on the reasons for unification, *Selected Papers*, 5:54–56.

60. Stone to Brown Blackwell, 23 July 1887, in Lasser and Merrill, *Friends and Sisters*, 253–54.

61. Anthony to Stone, 13 December 1887, *Selected Papers*, 5:57; Minutes of the Informal Conference between Stone and Anthony, [21 December 1887], *Selected Papers*, 5:59–67; Stone to Anthony, 23 December 1887, *Selected Papers*, 5:68–69; and Appendix A: Alice Blackwell's Memorandum on Discussions About Union, 25 December 1887, *Selected Papers*, 5:733–34; "Negotiations for Union," *Woman's Journal*, 5 May 1888, 139–40, 142–43, 146; Anthony to Rachel Foster, 24 December 1887, *Selected Papers*, 5:569–70.
The National Association committee members were May Wright Sewall (chair), Laura M. Johns, Harriet Robinson Shattuck, Clara B. Colby, Rachel Foster, Olympia Brown, and Helen M. Gougar. Minutes of the Informal Conference between Stone and Anthony, [21 December 1887], *Selected Papers*, 5:59–67. The American Association committee members were Julia Ward Howe, William Foulke, Hannah Cutler, Margaret Campbell, Mary Thomas, Anna Howard Shaw, and Henry Blackwell. Stone to Anthony, 23 December 1887, *Selected Papers*, 5:69n2. See also, "The Twentieth Annual Convention of the National Woman Suffrage Association, Minutes of the meeting of the Executive Committee and Executive Session," 3–4 April 1888, NWSA File, *NAWSA Papers*, 47:406–7.

62. Stanton to Olympia Brown, 8 May 1888, Olympia Brown Papers, 1849–1963, Arthur and Elizabeth Schlesinger Library on the History of Women, Radcliffe College, Archives and Manuscripts, Cambridge, Mass.

63. M. J. Gage to Thomas Clarkson Gage, 26 May 1888, MJG Papers.

64. Anthony to Brown, 11 March 1889, Olympia Brown Papers, 1849–1963, Arthur and Elizabeth Schlesinger Library on the History of Women, Radcliffe College, Archives and Manuscripts, Cambridge, Mass.

65. Anthony to Frances Willard, 23 August 1888, quoted in Kern, *Mrs. Stanton's Bible*, 127.

66. For a discussion of the growing influence of the WCTU within the organized suffrage movement and Stanton's concerns about it, see Kern, *Mrs. Stanton's Bible*, 121–25.

67. "The Twentieth Annual Convention of the National Woman Suffrage Association, Minutes of the meeting of the Executive Committee and Executive Session," 3–4 April 1888, NWSA File, *NAWSA Papers*, 47:342–47, quotation from 346.

68. Ibid., 47:342–64, 404–7. For the text of the reply letter, see "Twentieth Annual Convention of the National Woman Suffrage Association," *Woman's Tribune*, 21 April 1888.

69. Rev. Anna Howard Shaw, superintendent of the Franchise Department of the National WCTU spoke on school suffrage, and Laura M. Johns—who would serve on the unification committee for the National Association—spoke on municipal suffrage. *Report of the International Council of Women, 1888*, 16, 309–21.

70. "Twentieth Annual Convention of the National Woman Suffrage Association," *Woman's Tribune*, 21 April 1888.

71. There was one member of the American Association's committee of seven that did not weigh in on the National Association's reply. Julia Ward Howe was in California and could not be consulted. William Dudley Foulke, H. M. Tracy Cutler, Margaret W. Campbell, Mary F. Thomas, Annie H. Shaw, Henry B. Blackwell to the Conference Committee of the National Suffrage Association, 2 May 1888, *NAWSA Papers*, 26:82–88, quotation from 87–88. For additional details about what the American Association approved, see "The Question of Union," 1 December 1888, *NAWSA Papers*, 26:95–97. All transcribed in the hand of Ida Porter Boyer.

72. [Blackwell] to the Conference Committee of the National Suffrage Association, 2 May 1888, *NAWSA Papers*, 26:88–92, quotation from 88–89; and "The Question of Union," 1 December 1888, *NAWSA Papers*, 26:97–99. All transcribed in the hand of Ida Porter Boyer.

73. The American Association's committee of eleven consisted of Foulke, Shaw, Clay, Campbell, W. H. Carruth, Stone Blackwell, Mary Grew, Brown Blackwell, Sarah C. Schrader, C. V. Waite, and May S. Knaggs. List from the *Woman's Journal*, 1 December 1888, 382, in AWSA File, *NAWSA Papers*, 26:141. The National Association committee consisted of Anthony, Isabella Beecher Hooker, Sewall, Johns, Brown, S. M. Perkins, Virginia Minor, Jane H. Spofford, Abigail Scott Duniway, Lillie Devereux Blake, Helen Gougar, and Rachel Foster Avery. Colby had been appointed to the committee but resigned so that the South might have greater representation, and Caroline Hallowell Miller was appointed in her place. "United We Stand," 2 February 1889, in *NAWSA Papers*, 26:106–8; "Executive Sessions of the National Convention," *Woman's Tribune*, 16 February 1889, 76.

74. Not knowing what to expect of the meeting, the American Association did not send its entire committee, only Stone Blackwell and Shaw. The assembled agreed that the two women could represent the interests of the whole committee, to which they would bring any agreement reached for a vote. "United We Stand," 2 February 1889, in *NAWSA Papers*, 26:106–26. The *Woman's Journal* for 2 March 1889, 71, printed the tentative constitution.

75. *Woman's Tribune*, 16 February 1889.

76. Gage et al., "A Statement of Facts, MJG Papers, 4:342. The tally of the votes was reported in the *Woman's Tribune*, 16 February 1889, 77.

77. There is some evidence that Anthony prevented Gage from attending the National Association's annual January convention, where unification was decided, by withholding her travel expenses. Gage was broke, something well known in the movement, and needed the money for travel. Travel expenses, especially for officers, were routinely given. But in this instance, Anthony, who informally controlled the association's purse strings, offered only partial reimbursement, and may have thus ensured that Gage stayed away. See Tetrault, "Memory of a Movement."

78. Gage et al., "A Statement of Facts: Private," p. 5, in MJG Papers, 4:342. Perhaps in response to this controversy, an official version of the unification negotiations was published by Anthony's secretary and protégée, Rachel Foster Avery, who herself served on the National Association unification committee. This eleven-page pamphlet, not surprisingly, omitted any mention of controversy. Rachel Foster Avery, ed., "Negotiations between the American and National Woman Suffrage Associations in regard to Union," in the *History of Women*, microfilm, 947:8855.

79. Wagner, *Matilda Joslyn Gage*, 51.

80. Gage et al., "A Statement of Facts," 5, MJG Papers, 4:342.

81. The "Statement of Facts" never named Anthony outright, as such a direct attack was considered out of bounds, but the implication was clear. In 1888, Gage shared with her son her anger over Anthony's efforts to capture the National Association and to steer it, in Gage's view, in the wrong direction. Matilda Joslyn Gage to Thomas Clarkson Gage, 3 February 1888, in MJG Papers, 2:535, 560.

82. The *Baltimore Sun*, quoted in Harper, *Life and Work*, 2:637.

83. Corey, "Matilda Joslyn Gage"; Wagner, *Matilda Joslyn Gage*, 48–54.

84. Quoted in Wagner, *Matilda Joslyn Gage*, 53.

85. Stone to Brown Blackwell, n.d. [winter 1888], in Lasser and Merrill, *Friends and Sisters*, 255.

86. Anthony to Frances E. Willard, 6 June 1887, *Selected Papers*, 5:30, emphasis in original.

87. Minutes of the Informal Conference between Stone and Anthony, [21 December 1887], *Selected Papers*, 5:61.

88. "National Executive Session," 22 February 1890, *Woman's Tribune*, SAP, 28:43. Also partially quoted in Harper, *Life and Work*, 2:631.

89. The report appeared in the *Washington (D.C.) Star*. Quoted in *HWS*, 4:173.

90. The vote count for the president was Stanton, 131, and Anthony, 90. For the office of vice president, Anthony received 213 votes. Stone was unanimously elected. Harper, *Life and Work*, 2:632.

91. Stone's words are found in Kerr, *Lucy Stone*, 226–27. Stanton to Clara Bewick Colby, 6 March 1891, *Selected Papers*, 5:371. Anthony also expressed her frustration with the continued tensions with Blackwell. Anthony to Sarah Burger Stearns, 11 March 1890, *Selected Papers*, 5:270.

92. Bushman, *"A Good Poor Man's Wife,"* 172–76, quotation from 175.

93. *Report of the Convention for Organization*, 79; Brammer, *Excluded from Suffrage History*, 16.

94. Ibid., 76.

95. Kern, *Mrs. Stanton's Bible*, 131.

96. The *Liberal Thinker*, for example, contained a letter from Stanton supporting their bolt from NAWSA and a letter from a South Dakota woman who did not want her state society to affiliate with NAWSA. See *Liberal Thinker*, January 1890. For a discussion of Gage's increasing alienation from Anthony's course, and for the sympathy of other veteran activists with this feeling, see Parker Pillsbury to Blake, 11 April 1890, LDB Papers, box 7. For a discussion of Gage's Woman's National Liberal Union, including Stanton's interest in and Anthony's opposition to the group, see also Wagner, *Matilda Joslyn Gage*, 54–60. See also WNLU Organization and Plan of Work, 1890; Gage, "Dangers of the Hour," speech delivered at the WNLU Convention, 24 February 1890; Olympia Brown, "The Two Conventions," newspaper column, all in MJG Papers, 4:331, 334, 603.

It seems other veteran activists, including Clara Bewick Colby, editor of the *Woman's Tribune*, also departed from Anthony's new plan of work and later organized yet another suffrage society, the Federal Suffrage Association, in the early 1900s. Veteran Olympia Brown, who had signed the protest "Statement of Facts," was president of this dissenting organization. See, Olympia Brown, *Democratic Ideals*. Veteran activist Lillie Devereux Blake was also a founding member. Blake had tried to deliver a speech at the 1890 unification convention, but apparently Anthony prevented it. Anthony "dislikes me," Blake confided to her diary, "and prevents me from being on the programme when she can; but I cannot be crushed by her!!!" Blake Diary, February 1890, LDB Papers. For Blake's involvement in the Federal Suffrage Association, Stanton's apparent interest in this organization, and Anthony's attempts to suppress any appearance of Stanton's interest, see Anthony to Colby,

14 April 1901, box 1, folder 17, Clara Bewick Colby Papers, 1821–1985, Wisconsin Historical Society, Library–Archives Division, Madison. See also, Blake and Wallace, *Champion of Women*.

97. Stanton interview in the *Washington Post*, 9 February 1890.

98. Quoted in Wagner, *Matilda Joslyn Gage*, 61. Very little is known about the WNLU. For other accounts of its creation, see Votairine DeCleyre, "The Woman's National Liberal Union," *Boston Investigator*, 2 April 1890, 2; and "On Picket Duty," *Liberty*, 12 July 1890, 1.

99. Barry, *Susan B. Anthony*, 330; Ann D. Gordon, "Knowing Susan B. Anthony," 207–211.

100. Ibid., 206.

101. Kerr, *Lucy Stone*, 232, 235; Anthony to Elizabeth Boynton Harbert, 9 December 1893, *Selected Papers*, 4:307; Anthony to Elizabeth Boynton Harbert, 21 December 1884, *Selected Papers*, 4:379–81; Anthony to Elizabeth Boynton Harbert, 12 September 1885, *Selected Papers*, 4:441; Stanton to Anthony and Clara Bewick Colby, 6 June 1890, *Selected Papers*, 5:297–300.

102. On the change in how voting operated within NAWSA, see Wagner, *Matilda Joslyn Gage*, 53.

103. Brown to Colby, 10 August 1906, Clara Bewick Colby Papers, 1821–1985, Wisconsin Historical Society, Library–Archives Division, Madison.

104. Colby to Lockwood, 18 December 1915, 275704.12, Ormes Collection, National Museum of American History, Division of Politics and Reform, Smithsonian Institution, Washington, D.C.

105. On the changing face of the lyceum, see Tetrault, "The Incorporation of American Feminism."

106. Katharine Anthony, *Susan B. Anthony*, 393.

107. Stone's daughter continually tried to get her mother to record her reminiscences and the details of her life, but Stone continually declined, something for which she would pay a high price in the end. Kerr, *Lucy Stone*, 233, 237.

108. Ibid., 231.

109. "The First National Convention," *Woman's Journal*, 14 February 1891, 52, emphasis mine.

110. "The Gains of Forty Years," *Woman's Journal*, 7 February 1891, 44–45; "Reminiscences of Mrs. Abby Kelley Foster," *Woman's Journal*, 7 February 1891, 42–43; and "The First National Convention," *Woman's Journal*, 14 February 1891, 52–53.

111. Kerr, *Lucy Stone*, 238–45.

112. *Selected Papers*, 5:xxii–xxvii.

113. Kern, *Mrs. Stanton's Bible*, 51–53, 86, 96, 104.

114. Stanton to Benjamin F. Underwood, 19 October [1885], *Selected Papers*, 4:442.

115. Kern, *Mrs. Stanton's Bible*, 99.

116. Cite in Wagner, *Matilda Joslyn Gage*, 55.

117. Kern, *Mrs. Stanton's Bible,* 171; Elizabeth Cady Stanton, *The Woman's Bible*.

118. Spruill, "Race, Reform, and Reaction," 106. The classic work on expediency arguments in the turn-of-the-century movement is Kraditor, *Up from the Pedestal*.

119. Spruill, "Race, Reform, and Reaction," 106.

120. McFeely, *Frederick Douglass*; Quarles, *Frederick Douglass*.

121. Quoted in Kern, *Mrs. Stanton's Bible*, 135.

122. The list of names appeared in the *New York World*. Kern, *Mrs. Stanton's Bible*, 72, 135–71.

123. Kern, *Mrs. Stanton's Bible*, 135–71, 181.

124. Foster Avery absented herself from the executive committee and left Isabel Howland to read her report. Quoted in Stanton to Clara Berwick Colby, 24 January 1896, *Selected Papers*, 6:11–12n5.

125. Ibid.

126. Stanton to Clara Bewick Colby, 28 January [1896], *Selected Papers*, 6:13.

127. Remarks of Anthony to the National-American Woman Suffrage Association, [28 January 1896], *Selected Papers*, 6:18.

128. The vote was 53 to 41. Kern, *Mrs. Stanton's Bible*, 189; for the vote count, see Remarks of Anthony to the National-American Woman Suffrage Association, *Selected Papers*, 24n30.

129. Quoted in Kern, *Mrs. Stanton's Bible*, 180. For a fuller account of the episode, see ibid., 172–222. Stanton to Clara Bewick Colby, 28 January [1896], *Selected Papers*, 6:13.

130. For Stanton's defense of the *Woman's Bible*, see "The Woman's Bible," *Boston Investigator*, 5 December 1896, *Selected Papers*, 6:113–15. Quotation from "Women with Brains: The Opening Session of the National Council," *Washington Evening Star*, 18 February 1895, 1, 3.

131. "Woman Suffragists: Thirtieth Annual Convention of the National Association; Body to Assemble Here February 14; Miss Susan B. Anthony, Pioneer Advocate, Discusses the Issue," *Washington Evening Star*, 9 February 1898, 1.

132. "Morning Session," *Woman's Tribune*, 1 April 1888, 10; Stanton, "Two Valuable Gifts," November 1897, *Selected Papers*, 6:174–75.

133. Harper, *Life and Work*, 3:1112.

134. Rose et al., "Remembering Seneca Falls," 15; "Woman Suffragists," *Evening Star*, February 1898, *SAP*, 39:195.

135. The *Woman's Journal*'s extensive coverage of the 1898 NAWSA anniversary meeting pointedly avoided any mention of Seneca Falls, which appeared only once in their coverage, in their reprinting of the meeting's resolutions. A week before, however, they did reference the anniversary, mentioning that the Declaration of Sentiments and the Seneca Falls table were on display. "The Washington Convention," *Woman's Journal*, 19 February 1898, *SAP*, 38:202; "The Washington Convention," *Woman's Journal*, 26 February 1898, *SAP*, 38:203–4. For additional coverage of the convention in the *Woman's Journal*, see "The Washington Convention," 5 March 1898, *SAP*, 38:205; "The Washington Convention," *Woman's Journal*, 12 March 1898, *SAP*, 38:203, 205–10; and "A Congressional Evening," 12 March 1898, *SAP*, 38:211–12.

136. Utah had managed to reverse congressional moves to strip Utah women of the franchise. Janet Jennings, "Our Washington Letter," *Independent*, 24 February 1898; "Suffrage Is Their Aim," *Washington Post*, 15 February 1898, *SAP*, 38:200. For the winning of full suffrage in these four western states, see Mead, *How the Vote Was Won*; and Rebecca Edwards, "Pioneers at the Polls."

137. The names of those who had passed away in the previous year were also called. "Suffrage Is Their Aim," *Washington Post*, 15 February 1898, *SAP*, 38:200; "The Washington Convention," *Woman's Journal*, 12 March 1898, *SAP*, 38:206, 209.

138. "Death of Mrs. Matilda Joslyn Gage," *New York Times*, 19 March 1898, 2; and Wagner, *Matilda Joslyn Gage*, 65.

139. Kern, *Mrs. Stanton's Bible*, 13. A transcription of Stanton's speech is in "Our Defeats and Our triumphs," *Woman's Tribune*, 19 February 1898, *SAP*, 38:213–15, quotation from 215; and "Mrs. Stanton's Letter to the Suffrage Convention," *Boston Investigator*, 4 February 189[8], *SAP*, 38:216–18.

140. "Brought to a Close," *Evening Star*, 21 February 1898; "Mason on their Side," *Washington Post*, 20 February 1898, *SAP*, 38:199, 201.

141. It ran in seventy-two articles between the years 1889 and 1892. Ann D. Gordon, "Afterword," in Elizabeth Cady Stanton, *Eighty Years and More*, 473.

142. In 1898, Stanton also published the second and last volume of the *Woman's Bible*.

143. For an analysis about how this volume was a piece of Stanton's larger biblical critique, see Kern, *Mrs. Stanton's Bible*.

144. Stanton is quoting William Henry Channing.

145. Elizabeth Cady Stanton, *Eighty Years and More*, quotations from 155, 185.

146. Gage to Lillie Devereux Blake, 14 March 1891, LDB Papers, box 7, folder 6; Wagner, *Matilda Joslyn Gage*, 65–66.

147. Anthony to Elizabeth Smith Miller, 12 March 1897, *Selected Papers*, 6:132–33.

148. Harper and Anthony themselves acknowledge that Anthony read and approved every word of the biography. Harper, *Life and Work*, 3:1115–16; and Des Jardins, *Women and the Historical Enterprise*, 177–91.

149. *Report of the International Council of Women, 1888*, 356–57. Commenting upon Gage's 1898 death, Anthony told a reporter that Gage owned the other large repository of movement documents. "I think Mrs. Gage and myself have preserved and treasured up every scrap pertaining to the history of the woman's suffrage movement," she said. She added that when she last saw Gage, in Chicago, just before her death, Gage "said her one hope was to . . . arrange for preservation all the books and papers and documents she had accumulated" over a lifetime of activism. The fate of that large archive, to which Gage never returned, is unknown. "Woman's Work for Woman," *Post Express*, 19 March 1898.

150. Anthony to Elizabeth Smith Miller, 1 March 1897, *Selected Papers*, 6:133n1.

151. Harper, *Life and Work*, 1:vii.

152. There is a great photograph featured on a 1901 Susan B. Anthony calendar of a corner of Anthony's attic, where voluminous books and papers are loosely strewn about. The caption reads, "A corner of the famous attic, where the records of 50 years of suffrage work are stored." The Anthony Portrait Committee, "The Anthony Home Calendar," 1901. On display at "Susan B. Anthony: Celebrating 'A Heroic Life,'" an online exhibit curated by the Department of Rare Books and Special Collections, University of Rochester.

153. Barry, *Susan B. Anthony*, 324.

154. *HWS*, 1:7. For more on Harper and the *Life and Work*, including an analysis of its content, see Ann D. Gordon, "Knowing Susan B. Anthony."

155. Harper, *Life and Work*, 1:59, 63–64.

156. Ibid., 2: 643; see also 1:297, 1:321, 1:352, 2:291, 2:855.

157. "Woman Suffrage: The Growth of the National Association; Work of Susan B. Anthony: Her Name Is Synonymous with the Movement; The Results So Far," *Washington Evening Star*, 3 February 1900, 8; "Susan B. Anthony," *Deseret Evening News* (Utah), 28 February 1900, 4; "The Woman Suffragists," *Minneapolis Journal*, 27 May 1901, 4.

Epilogue

1. There are some clues about what was and what wasn't destroyed in different accounts of the burning. Quotations from Harper, *Life and Work*, 3:1296–97. See also Katharine Anthony, *Susan B. Anthony*, 474–75; Ann D. Gordon, "Knowing Susan B. Anthony, 211–19; Harper to Eliza Wright Osborne, November 30, 1897, Garrison Family Papers, 1694–2005, box 51, Sophia Smith Collection, Archives and Manuscripts Collection, Smith College, Northampton, Mass.

2. Harper, *Life and Work*, 3:1296–97. Stanton also routinely destroyed things, including much of her incoming correspondence, as did other suffragists. Anthony was interested in preservation, as well. She donated her library and scrapbooks to the Library of Congress, and she also reported plans to prepare a scrapbook on Stanton, with all her speeches and more. Gage, with intentions to preserve her papers for use by future generations (this did not happen), burned a host of newspaper columns after the *History*'s publication. And Stanton's children, Harriot and Theodore, destroyed part of their mother's papers, heavily pruning and reshaping them before donating them to archives. Several sources offer clues about what was preserved and destroyed and how the surviving portion eventually made its way into various official archives. Anthony to Helen Leslie Gage, 16 June 1903, MJG Papers, 1:532; Gage to Isabel Howland, 14 January 1892, Isabel Howland Papers, Sophia Smith Collection; Gage to Laura de Force Gordon, 31 July 1876, LdFG Papers; Des Jardins, *Women and the Historical Enterprise*, 177–213; Beck, "The Library of Susan B. Anthony"; Ann D. Gordon, introduction to *Guide and Index*, 3–7; Amy Dykeman, "'To Pour Forth from My Own Experience'" and "To Look a Gift Horse in the Mouth"; Ellen Carol DuBois, "Making Women's History"; Ann D. Gordon, introduction to *Guide and Index*, quotation from 4.

3. W. E. B. Du Bois, *Souls of Black Folk* and *Black Reconstruction in America, 1860–1880*; Hofstadter, "Conflict and Consensus in American History," 464–66. For other early female historian-activists, see Des Jardins, *Women and the Historical Enterprise*.

4. *HWS*, 4:ix–xi.

5. Blake and Wallace, *Champion of Women*, 195–205, 202–3; Barry, *Susan B. Anthony*, 330–31; Fowler and Jones, "Carrie Chapman Catt," 131–34; Anthony to Clara Bewick Colby, 23 October 1899, *Selected Papers*, 6:307–9. On Catt and Stanton, see "Remarks of Anthony to the National-American Woman Suffrage Association," 28 January 1896, *Selected Papers*, 6:16–19n2; Stanton to Clara Bewick Colby, 5 February 1896, *Selected Papers*, 43n7; and Kern, *Mrs. Stanton's Bible*.

6. Later entries, such as the account of the 1888 anniversary, did link Stanton to Seneca Falls. *HWS*, 4:xiii, 14, 4:124–25.

7. *HWS*, 4:173. Stone, who is barely visible in the fourth volume, is identified simply as the wife of Henry Blackwell, surely a conscious choice that diminished Stone and further destroyed her stature in the annals of movement memory. And Gage is reduced in the volume's opening pages to a mere assistant to Stanton and Anthony on volumes 1 through 3, drawing the ire of her children, who wrote protest letters to Anthony. Anthony to Thomas Clarkson Gage, 1903, and Anthony to Helen Leslie Gage, 16 June 1903, MJG Papers, microfilm, reel 1, images 531–32.

8. For one of her last articles, see Stanton, "How Shall We Solve the Divorce Problem?" *New York American and Journal*, [13 October 1902]; and for one of her last letters, see Stanton to Theodore Roosevelt, 22 October 1902, *Selected Papers*, 6:441–46, 448–49. For obituaries, see "Death Claims Elizabeth Cady Stanton," *Akron Daily Democrat*, 27 October 1902; "Death Summons Famous Woman," *San Francisco Call*, 27 October 1902; "Mrs. Stanton No More," *Saint Paul Globe*, 27 October 1902; "Death Comes," *Burlington Free Weekly Press*, 30 October 1902; quotation from "Famous Advocate of Woman's Rights Dead," *Washington Times*, 27 October 1902. For Anthony surviving Stanton, see "Mrs. Stanton Dies," *Kinsley Graphic*, 31 October 1902, 3; "Mrs. Stanton Dies," *Nebraska Advertiser*, 31 October 1902, 5. And see also "Susan B. Anthony Left Behind," *New York Sun*, 27 October 1902, 1. How or why Anthony's photograph ended up atop Stanton's casket is curious, given Stanton's children's growing enmity for Anthony. For a photograph of Stanton's casket, see *Selected Papers*, 6:unnumbered page before 287. For Anthony's words, see Anthony to Ida Husted Harper, 28 October 1902, *Selected Papers*, 6:455; and "Elizabeth Cady Stanton Dies at Her Home," *New York Times*, 27 October 1902.

9. "Miss Susan B. Anthony Died this Morning," *New York Times*, 13 March 1906; "Susan B. Anthony Dead," *Burlington (Vt.) Weekly Free Press*, 15 March 1906, 7; Associated Press, "Susan B. Anthony Dead," as carried in the *Daily Northwestern*, 13 March 1906, 7; "Prominent Worker Dies," *Falls City Tribune*, 16 March 1906, 1; "Susan B. Anthony Dead," *Burlington Free Press*, 15 March 1906, 7, this article includes the subheading "Only One Other Survivor"; "Where Feminine Fancy Lights: Another Miss Anthony," *Minneapolis Journal*, 5 May 1906, 14; among other appearances of this same article, see "Woman's World: Miss Mary S. Anthony, *Elkhart Daily Review*, 14 May 1906, 2; and "Another Miss Anthony," *Postville Review*, 1 June 1906, 7; "Woman Suffrage Champions," *Daily Capital Review*, 4 April 1906, 5. Howe, of course, had not attended 1848 either.

10. Ann D. Gordon, "Knowing Susan B. Anthony," 214–16, Shaw quoted on 215; Graham, *Woman Suffrage*, 47–48; Van Voris, *Carrie Chapman Catt*; Fowler, *Carrie Catt*; Anna Howard Shaw, *The Story of a Pioneer*; Linkugel and Solomon, *Anna Howard Shaw*.

11. Ford, "Alice Paul and the Triumph of Militancy"; Ford, "Alice Paul and the Politics of Nonviolent Protest"; Fowler, "Carrie Chapman Catt, Strategist," 305–9.

12. Quoted in Sims, "Armageddon in Tennessee," 347; Taylor, "Tennessee: The Thirty-Sixth State." One of the women attending the 1848 convention, Charlotte L. Woodward Pierce, lived to see the passage of the Nineteenth Amendment. Wellman, *The Road to Seneca Falls*, 231.

13. The account also erroneously elevated Seneca Falls to the first *national* convention, completely eclipsing Worcester. Other newspapers reinforced this factual error, equating Anthony and 1848. See "Only Fifty Women Have Paid Their Poll Taxes Here," *Record-Chronicle*, 17 January 1921. For examples of the United Press wire story, see "Woman's Long Fight for Ballot," *Fort Wayne News and Sentinel*, 19 August 1920; "Outline Story of Suffrage in United States," *Oelwein Daily Register*, 19 August 1920; "Nineteenth Amendment Is Living Monument to Late Susan B. Anthony," *Sandusky Star Journal*, 20 August 1920; "Ratification Assured as Tennessee Ballots," *San Antonio Evening News*, 18 August 1920; and "Vote Granted to All Women," *Des Moines News*, 18 August 1920. The *Oelwein Daily Register* carried this same story again a week later, 25 August 1920.

14. Alice Stone Blackwell to Maud Wood Park, 30 January 1945, *NAWSA Papers*, typed transcript, excerpt, NWSA file in *NAWSA Papers*, 47:322. To date, there exists only one history of the American Association, an unpublished dissertation from the 1950s: Merk, "Massachusetts in the Woman Suffrage Movement." And there exist only two scholarly biographies of Stone, and only one of those covers the post–Civil War years: Million, *Woman's Voice, Woman's Place*; and Kerr, *Lucy Stone*. See also Alice Stone Blackwell, *Lucy Stone*, 75, 99, emphasis mine. The founding myth so powerfully undergirded the suffrage movement by the early twentieth century that a suffrage opponent, Caroline Corbin, of the Illinois Association Opposed to the Extension of Suffrage to Women, tried to discredit the cause by also arguing against Seneca Falls as an origin. Corbin, "Woman's Rights in America, a Retrospect of Sixty Years, 1848–1908," handwritten manuscript copy, Research Center of the Chicago History Museum, Chicago, Ill. This was later published in pamphlet form.

15. Elizabeth Cady Stanton, *Eighty Years and More*, 149; and Theodore Stanton and Blatch, *Elizabeth Cady Stanton*, 1:146–48.

16. Elizabeth Cady Stanton, *Eighty Years and More*, 155–85; and Theodore Stanton and Blatch, *Elizabeth Cady Stanton*, 1:151–58; DuBois, *Harriot Stanton Blatch*, 242–73.

17. Paul and the NWP commissioned Adelaide Johnson to create her memorial from earlier portrait busts of Mott, Stanton, and Anthony that the artist had created, the latter two from life. First exhibited at the Columbian Exposition in 1893, these separate works had specifically "been made for the Capitol at Washington." That hope had been in vain, but now Johnson replicated the group together on a monumental scale. "A Woman's Statues of Women; Mrs. Johnson's Sculptures and What She Says about Them," *New York Sun*, 8 May 1904, sec. 2, 6. Ida Husted Harper, "An Interesting Studio," *Washington Herald Magazine*, 7 June 1914, 29. "Suffrage Statue Is Still without a Resting Place; Women's Party Plans Ready, but Question Is Where Is Sculpture Now Reposing Under Steps to Be Situated," *New York Tribune*, 10 February 1921, 4. Congress. Senate, 66th Cong., 3rd Sess., S. Con. Res 39, *Congressional Record* 60, Part 2, 2014 (27 January 1921). For the NWP depositing of the monument on the Capitol's doorstep, see Gayle Guthrie, "Susie, Lucy and Liz"; Workman, "The Woman Movement," 50. For further accounts of the monument's creation and fate, see Burton, "Adelaide Johnson," 60; "Honor Pioneer Suffragists at Nation's Capitol," *Chicago Daily Tribune*, 16 February 1921; Sutton, *The House of My Sojourn*, 53; "Portrait Monument to Lucretia Mott, Elizabeth Cady Stanton and Susan B. Anthony."

18. When the Crypt was reopened in 1963, after being renovated, the name Johnson had given her sculpture was changed by congressional authorities, who were unable to verify its name, to the much blander and empty "Portrait Monument." "Congress Gets Marble Busts of Feminists," *Washington Herald*, 16 February 1921.

19. "Adelaide Johnson's Inscription Cut on the Suffrage Memorial," *New York Evening World*, 22 January 1921, 3; "Engraved Tribute to Pioneers on Suffrage Statue; National Woman's Party Inscribes Marble Memorial at Capitol," *Washington Herald*, 25 September 1921, 1; despite these headlines, the inscription was never actually cut into the marble. William C. Allen, *History of the United States Capitol*, 170–71. "Ask Choice Site for Group," *Washington Herald Weekly Review*, 3 April 1921, 34. "Women Scrub the Statue of Suffragists," *Westville*

Indicator, 6 October 1921, 1; the article, which featured a cartoon of the women scrubbing a recognizable Susan B. Anthony, was carried by many other newspapers throughout October. "Painted a Suffrage Statue: Inscription to Three Women Leaders Mysteriously Covered Over," *Kansas City Star*, 15 October 1921, 10. Interestingly, this contemporary report specifies that the inscription was only "partly covered by cream colored paint," the exact passage naming Mott, Stanton, and Anthony and describing their separate contributions to the movement. When the remainder of the inscription was removed is unknown, but it was entirely gone by the end of the month, when Johnson returned from New York to Washington to inspect the damage. "Who Removed Legend from National Women's Memorial? Suffrage Leaders Probe Indignity to Group in Capitol; Moved from Place, Unique Marble Also Loses Inscription," *Washington Times*, 6 November 1921, sec. 2, 3. For the monument's nickname, see "3 Suffragists (in Marble) to Move Up in the Capitol," *New York Times*, 27 September 1996; and Workman, "The Woman Movement," 47.

20. "Erasing the Superlative," *Galveston Daily News*, 24 October 1921, 4. Capitol curator Charles Fairman later saw fit to preserve the missing inscription for posterity, publishing its full text in *The Woman Patriot*, 26 February 1929, 8.

21. Congress. Senate, 68th Cong., 1st Sess., S.J. 21, *Congressional Record* 65, 150 (10 December 1923). Women had earlier returned to Seneca Falls in 1908, for the sixtieth anniversary, placing a bronze plaque on the side of the old Wesleyan Chapel that read: "On this spot stood the Wesleyan Chapel where the first Women's Rights Convention in the world's history was held, July 19 and 20, 1848." Wellman, *The Road to Seneca Falls*, 229–30. For other occasions on which women returned to Seneca Falls, to honor the past, see also Rose, "Remembering Seneca Falls," 15–17, and "Seneca Falls Remembered." An elaborate historical pageant, *Into the Light*, accompanied this seventy-fifth anniversary return. Hewett, "Progressive Compromises," 180–81. Paul movingly hoped that the anniversary event would "start a revival of interest in feminist history." Quoted in Marian Hale, "Women Meet to Make Firm Stand for All Rights," *Fitchburg Sentinel*, 27 July 1923, 13. Among many examples of this photograph, caption, and headline, "Wreaths for Susan B. Anthony's Grave," see *Cedar Rapids Tribune*, 10 August 1923, 2; *Advance Hustler*, 16 August 1923, 6; *Carbondale Free Press*, 21 August 1923, 1; and *Orrville Courier Crescent*, 29 August 1923, 6. See also, "Tribute to Miss Anthony," *Washington Post*, 11 June 1923, 8. For a discussion of early twentieth-century feminism and the character of the NWP after 1920, see Cott, *Grounding of Modern Feminism*.

22. The table remains a sacred object today and is on continuous display, albeit with new copy, at the Smithsonian Institution's National Museum of American History. The caption to the calendar incorrectly claimed the call had been written on the table, when it was actually the meeting's manifesto. The Anthony Portrait Committee, "The Anthony Home Calendar," 1901, on display at "Susan B. Anthony: Celebrating 'A Heroic Life,'" an online exhibit curated by the Department of Rare Books and Special Collections, University of Rochester. Anthony's receipt of the table from Stanton can be found on an old label attached to the table. The table caption in the Smithsonian exhibit, created shortly after 1920, comes from an early surviving photograph of the display. Both the photograph and the label are in the Division of Political History, National Museum of American History, Smithsonian Institution.

23. Margaret Stanton Lawrence, one of Stanton's daughters, joined Harriot and Theodore in their crusade to set the historical record straight: "Miss Anthony was not the founder of the suffrage movement. Susan B. Anthony was not present at the original Women's Rights Convention, although she has been proclaimed as the Moses of Israel." "Susan B. Anthony's Title as Suffrage Founder Is Challenged by Waterloo," *Syracuse Herald*, 1 July 1923, 1. Theodore Stanton, "Seneca Falls and Women's Rights," *Independent*, 4 August 1923, 42, and "Miss Anthony and Suffrage," *New York Times*, 19 July 1923, 14. Stanton's portrait was eventually added to the exhibit. DuBois, *Harriot Stanton Blatch*, 250; "Portrait Presented to Museum," *New York Times*, 23 December 1924.

24. *HWS*, 5:iii; *HWS*, 6. For a general discussion of volumes 5 and 6, see DuBois, "Making Women's History"; and Buhle and Buhle, "Preface" and "Introduction," *Concise History of Woman Suffrage*, xvii–45. An important anthology about black women's suffrage activism, edited by Ann D. Gordon and Betty Collier-Thomas, periodizes that story not from 1848 to 1920, but from 1837 to 1965. Ann D. Gordon and Collier-Thomas, eds., *African American Women and the Vote*; Terborg-Penn, African American Women, 155–56; Ann D. Gordon, "Woman Suffrage (Not Universal Suffrage)," 20.

25. Ruth Rosen, *World Split Open*, 291–94; Martin and Vossen, "Sisters of '77"; and *The Spirit of Houston*.

26. Wellman, "'It's a Wide Community Indeed,'" 233–34, emphasis mine.

27. Ibid., quotation from 237. Brown, "Historic Structure Report, 73–112.

28. Wellman, "'It's a Wide Community Indeed.'"

29. Ibid.

30. The initial provision, when the 1996 relocation bill passed, was that the monument would reside in the Rotunda for no more than a year, but that did not hold, partly due to the exorbitant costs of moving it again. "Women Mark 75 Years of Voting Rights," *New York Times*, 27 August 1995; "3 Suffragists (in Marble) to Move Up in the Capitol," *New York Times*, 27 September 1996, A18; Katz, "Women Mark 75 Years of Voting Rights," *New York Times*, 27 August 1995; Guthrie, "Susie, Lucy and Liz"; *Chicago Tribune*, 27 June 1997, 3. For the current text accompanying the monument, which does now identify the women by name, and for general information about its relocation, see Workman, "The Woman Movement."

31. Senator Hillary Rodham Clinton helped introduce the legislation to have Truth carved into the Portrait Monument. Congress, Senate, 108th Cong., 2nd Sess., S.2600, *Congressional Record* 150, Part 10, 13889 (24 June 2004). For the successful legislation, see Congress, House, 109th Cong., 1st Sess., H.R. 4510, *Congressional Record* 151, Part 22, 30435–36 (18 December 2005); and "An Act to Direct the Joint Committee on the Library to Accept a Bust Depicting Sojourner Truth and to Display the Bust in a Suitable Location in the Capitol," Public Law 109-427, 109th Congress (20 December 2006). "A Vote Against Suffrage Statue; Some Black Women Now Oppose Its Move to Prominence in Capitol," *Washington Post*, 14 April 1997; "Truth of the Suffrage Movement," *Off Our Backs*, May 1997; "Celebrating Truth," *New York Times*, 28 April 2009; "Truth's Rightful Place on the Hill," *Washington Post*, 29 April 2009; "Sojourner Truth Bust Unveiled in Capitol," *Roll Call*, 29 April 2009; "Sojourner Truth Takes Her Place in the Capitol," *Philadelphia Tribune*, 3 May 2009; Workman, "The Woman Movement," 55–56; and National Congress of Black Women, Sojourner Truth Memorial Fund.

32. Ibid., quotations from "Celebrating Truth," and "Sojourner Truth Bust Unveiled in Capitol."

33. Hillary Rodham Clinton, Twitter post, 13 July 2013, 4:10 P.M.

34. The literature challenging the waves is too vast to cite here. But much of it can be found in the citations to the debates about what to do with the wave metaphor. For that debate, see Hewitt, "Feminist Frequencies" and "From Seneca Falls to Suffrage?"; Hewitt, ed., *No Permanent Waves*; Ginzberg, "Re-Viewing the First Wave"; Thompson, "Multiracial Feminism"; Evans, *Tidal Wave*; Laughlin et al., "Is It Time to Jump Ship? Historians Rethink the Waves Metaphor."

Bibliography

Newspapers and Periodicals

The Agitator (Chicago, Ill.)
Akron (Ohio) Daily Democrat
Arkansas Daily Gazette
Ballot Box (Toledo, Ohio)
Baltimore Sun
Boston Investigator
Buffalo Commercial Advertiser
Burlington (Vt.) Free Press
Burlington (Vt.) Weekly Free Press
California Evening Mercury
The Call (San Francisco, Calif.)
Carbondale (Ill.) Free Press
Cedar Rapids (Iowa) Tribune
Chicago Inter Ocean
Chicago Times
Chicago Tribune
Christian Advocate
Christian Union (New York, N.Y.)
Cincinnati Daily Gazette
Cleveland Leader
Cleveland Plain Dealer
Daily Capital Review (Salem, Ore.)
Daily Evening Bulletin (San Francisco, Calif.)
Daily Missouri Democrat (St. Louis)
Daily Missouri Republican (St. Louis)
Daily Morning Chronicle (Washington, D.C.)
Daily Northwestern (Oshkosh, Wis.)
Democrat and Chronicle (Rochester, N.Y.)
Deseret Evening News (Utah)
Des Moines News (Des Moines, Iowa)
Detroit Advertiser and Tribune
Elkhart (Ind.) Daily Review
Evening Bulletin (Philadelphia)
Evening Star (Washington, D.C.)
Fall City (Neb.) Tribune
Fitchburg (Mass.) Sentinel
Fort Wayne (Ind.) News and Sentinel
Friends' Intelligencer (Philadelphia)
Galveston (Tex.) Daily News
Galveston (Tex.) News

The Grange Advance (Red Wing, Minn.)
Harper's Bazaar (New York, N.Y.)
Harper's Weekly (New York, N.Y.)
Hartford Daily Courant
The Independent (New York, N.Y.)
Jackson (Iowa) Sentinel
Kansas City Star
Kinsley (Kans.) Graphic
The Ladies Bureau (Marshalltown, Iowa)
Leavenworth (Kans.) Daily Times
Leavenworth (Kans.) Weekly Times
Leeds Mercury (Leeds, England)
The Liberal Thinker (Syracuse, N.Y)
The Liberator (Boston, Mass.)
Liberty (Boston, Mass.)
Methodist (New York, N.Y.)
Milwaukee Daily Sentinel
Minneapolis Journal
The Nation (New York, N.Y.)
National Citizen and Ballot Box (Syracuse, N.Y.)
National Republican (Washington, D.C.)
Nebraska Advertiser (Nemaha, Nebraska)
New Northwest (Portland, Ore.)
New York American and Journal
New York Herald
New York Evening Post
New York Sun
New York Times
New York Tribune
New York World
Off Our Backs: The Feminist Newsjournal (Washington, D.C.)
Oelwein (Iowa) Daily Register
Orrsville (Ohio) Courier Crescent
Philadelphia Evening Bulletin
Philadelphia Tribune
The Pioneer (San Francisco, Calif.)
Post Express (Rochester, N.Y.)
Postville (Iowa) Review
Record-Chronicle (Denton, Tex.)

The Revolution (New York, N.Y.)
Rocky Mountain News (Denver, Colo.)
Roll Call (Washington, D.C.)
Sandusky (Ohio) Star Journal
San Antonio (Tex.) Evening News
San Francisco Call
San Francisco Chronicle
Saturday Evening Mercury
   (San Francisco, Calif.)
St. Paul Globe
St. Louis Daily Times
Syracuse (N.Y.) Herald
Toledo Blade
Tribune (Washington, D.C.)
Washington Post
Washington (D.C.) Herald

Washington Herald Magazine
Washington Herald Weekly Review
Washington (D.C.) Star
Washington (D.C.) Times
Westville (Ind.) Indicator
Woman's Advocate (Dayton, Ohio)
Woman's Advocate (New York, N.Y.)
Woman's Exponent (Salt Lake City, Utah)
Woman's Journal (Boston, Mass.)
Woman Patriot (Washington, D.C.)
Woman's Tribune (Beatrice, Neb.)
Woman's Words
Woodhull and Claflin's Weekly
   (New York, N.Y.)
Zion's Herald (Boston, Mass.)

Manuscripts

Berkeley, Calif.
   The Bancroft Library, University of California, Berkeley
      Laura [de Force] Gordon Papers, 1856–82
Boston, Mass.
   Boston Public Library, Books and Manuscripts Division
      William Lloyd Garrison Correspondence, 1823–79
Cambridge, Mass.
   Arthur and Elizabeth Schlesinger Library on the History of Women, Radcliffe College,
      Archives and Manuscripts
      Olympia Brown Papers, 1849–1963
      Papers of Harriet Jane Hanson Robinson and Harriette Lucy Robinson Shattuck,
         1833–1937
Chicago, Ill.
   Chicago History Museum, Research Center, Archives and Manuscripts
Madison, Wis.
   Wisconsin Historical Society, Library–Archives Division
      Clara Bewick Colby Papers, 1821–1985
      Fritz Anneke and Mathilde Franziska Anneke Papers, 1791–1934
Northampton, Mass.
   Sophia Smith Collection, Archives and Manuscripts Collection, Smith College
      Garrison Family Papers, 1694–2005
      Isabel Howland Papers, 1888–1903
San Marino, Calif.
   Huntington Research Library, Manuscripts Division
      Papers of Elizabeth Boynton Harbert, 1863–1925
      Papers of Ida Husted Harper, 1841–1919
St. Louis, Mo.
   Missouri History Museum Archives
      Lillie Devereux Blake Papers, 1847–1986
Washington, D.C.
   Library of Congress, Rare Books and Special Collections
      Matilda Joslyn Gage Scrapbooks
      Susan B. Anthony Collection

National Museum of American History, Division of Politics and Reform, Smithsonian
    Institution
    Krebs Collection
    Ormes Collection
Worcester, Mass.
    American Antiquarian Society, Manuscripts Department
    Abby Kelley Foster Papers, 1836–1975

Microfilm Collections

The Gerritsen Collection of Women's History. Glen Rock, N.J.: Microfilming Corp. of America,
    1975.
The History of Women. New Haven: Research Publications, Inc. 1977.
Matilda Joslyn Gage Papers. *Women's Studies Manuscript Collections from the Schlesinger
    Library, Series 1: Woman Suffrage.* Edited by Anne Firor Scott. Bethesda, Md.: University
    Publications of America, 1990.
Papers of the Blackwell Family. Washington, D.C.: Library of Congress Photo Duplication
    Service, 1979.
The Papers of Elizabeth Cady Stanton and Susan B. Anthony: Microfilm Edition. Edited by
    Patricia G. Holland and Ann D. Gordon. Wilmington, Del.: Scholarly Resources, 1992.
The Records of the National American Woman Suffrage Association. Washington, D.C.: Library
    of Congress, 1981.

Published Primary Sources

American Cyclopaedia. Vol. 16. New York: D. Appleton and Company, 1876.
"American State Papers." From Library of Congress, *A Century of Lawmaking for a New
    Nation: U.S. Congressional Documents and Debates, 1774–1875.* http://memory.loc.gov/
    ammem/amlaw/lwsp.html. Accessed 4 February 2013.
"An Act to Direct the Joint Committee on the Library to Accept the Donation of a Bust
    Depicting Sojourner Truth and to Display the Bust in a Suitable Location in the Capitol."
    Public Law 109-427. 109th Congress, 20 December 2006.
Anthony, Susan B. *An Account of the Trial of Susan B. Anthony on the Charge of Illegal Voting,
    at the Presidential Election in Nov., 1872, and on the Trial of Beverley W. Jones, Edwin T.
    Marsh and William B. Hall, The Inspectors of Election by whom Her Vote was Received.*
    Rochester, N.Y.: Daily Democrat and Chronicle Book Print, 1874.
———. "Elizabeth Cady Stanton." In vol. 4 of *Johnson's New Universal Cyclopaedia.*
    New York: Alvin J. Johnson & Son, 1878.
———. "Woman's Rights." In vol. 4 of *Johnson's New Universal Cyclopaedia.* New York:
    Alvin J. Johnson & Son, 1878.
Anthony, Susan B., and Ida Husted Harper, eds. *The History of Woman Suffrage.* Vol. 4,
    1883–1900. Rochester, N.Y.: Susan B. Anthony, 1902; reprint, New York: Arno Press, 1969.
*Arguments before the Committee on Privileges and Elections of the United States Senate on
    behalf of a Sixteenth Amendment to the Constitution of the United States.* 11–12 January
    1878. Washington, D.C.: Government Printing Office, 1878.
Blatch, Harriot Stanton, and Alma Lutz. *Challenging Years: The Memoirs of Harriot Stanton
    Blatch.* New York: G. P. Putnam's Sons, 1940.
Bloomer, Dexter C. *Life and Writings of Amelia Bloomer.* Boston: Arena, 1895.
Bowditch, William I. *Taxation of Women in Massachusetts.* Rev. ed. Cambridge, Mass.: John
    Wilson & Son, 1875.
Brown, Olympia. *Acquaintances, Old and New, Among Reformers.* Milwaukee, Wis.: S. E.
    Tate, 1911.

————, ed. *Democratic Ideals: A Memorial Sketch of Clara B. Colby*. The Federal Suffrage Association, 1917.

Buhle, Mari Jo, and Paul Buhle, eds. *The Concise History of Woman Suffrage: Selections from History of Woman Suffrage, by Elizabeth Cady Stanton, Susan B. Anthony, Matilda Joslyn Gage, and the National American Woman Suffrage Association*. Urbana: University of Illinois Press, 1978.

Catt, Carrie Chapman, and Nettie Rogers Shuler. *Woman Suffrage and Politics: The Inner Story of the Suffrage Movement*. New York: C. Scribner's Sons, 1926.

Constitution of the American Woman Suffrage Association and the History of Its Formation. With the Times and Places in which the Association has Held Meetings up to 1880. Boston: George H. Ellis, 1881.

Davis, Paulina Wright. *A History of the National Woman's Rights Movement, for Twenty Years, with the Proceedings of the Decade Meeting held at Apollo Hall, October 20, 1870, From 1850 to 1870, with an Appendix Containing the History of the Movement during the Winter of 1871, in the National Capitol*. New York: Journeymen Printers' Co-operative Association, 1871.

The Debates and Proceedings of the Constitutional Convention of the State of Michigan, Convened at the City of Lansing, Wednesday, May 15, 1867. 2 vols. Officially reported by Wm. Blair Lord and David Wolfe Brown. Lansing, Mich.: John A. Kerr & Co., 1867.

Debates and Proceedings of the Convention Which Assembled at Little Rock January 7 1868 Under the Provisions of the Act of Congress of March 2nd 1867 and the Acts of March 23d and July 19th 1867 Supplementary Thereto to Form a Constitution for the State of Arkansas. Little Rock: John G. Price, 1868.

Douglass, Frederick. *The Life and Times of Frederick Douglass from 1817 to 1882. Written by Himself. Illustrated. With an Introduction by The Right Hon. John Bright, M.P. Edited by John Lobb, F.R.G.S.* London, U.K.: Christian Age Office, 1882.

Fuller, Sarah Margaret. *Woman in the Nineteenth Century*. New York: Greeley & McElrath, 1845.

Gage, Frances Dana. *Report of the Eighth National Woman's Rights Convention*. Richmond, Ind.: 1858. Women and Social Movements in the United States, 1600–2000. http://asp6new.alexanderstreet.com/wam2/wam2.object.details.aspx?dorpid=1000676880. Accessed 7 August 2013.

Gordon, Ann D., Tamara Gaskell Miller, Stacy Kinlock Sewell, Ann Pfau, and Arlene Kriv, eds. *In the School of Anti-Slavery, 1840 to 1866*. Vol. 1 of *The Selected Papers of Elizabeth Cady Stanton and Susan B. Anthony*. New Brunswick, N.J.: Rutgers University Press, 1997.

Gordon, Ann D., Tamara Gaskell Miller, Susan I. Johns, Oona Schmid, Mary Poole, Veronica A. Wilson, and Stacy Kinlock Sewell, eds. *Against an Aristocracy of Sex, 1866 to 1873*. Vol. 2 of *The Selected Papers of Elizabeth Cady Stanton and Susan B. Anthony*. New Brunswick, N.J.: Rutgers University Press, 2000.

Gordon, Ann D., Allison L. Sneider, Ann Elizabeth Pfau, Kimberly J. Banks, Lesley L. Doig, Meg Meneghel MacDonald, and Margaret Sumner, eds. *National Protection for National Citizens, 1873 to 1880*. Vol. 3 of *The Selected Papers of Elizabeth Cady Stanton and Susan B. Anthony*. New Brunswick, N.J.: Rutgers University Press, 2003.

Gordon, Ann D., Krystal Frazier, Lesley L. Doig, Emily Westkaemper, and Robin Chapdelaine, eds. *When Clowns Make Laws for Queens, 1880 to 1887*. Vol. 4 of *The Selected Papers of Elizabeth Cady Stanton and Susan B. Anthony*. New Brunswick, N.J.: Rutgers University Press, 2006.

Gordon, Ann D., Lesley L. Doig, Patricia Hampson, Kathleen Manning, and Shannen Dee Williams, eds. *Their Place inside the Body-Politic, 1887 to 1895*. Vol. 5 of *The Selected Papers of Elizabeth Cady Stanton and Susan B. Anthony*. New Brunswick, N.J.: Rutgers University Press, 2009.

Gordon, Ann D., Michael David Cohen, Sara Rzeszutek Haviland, Andy Duane Bowers, and Katherine D. Lee, eds. *An Awful Hush, 1895 to 1906*. Vol. 6 of *The Selected Papers of Elizabeth Cady Stanton and Susan B. Anthony*. New Brunswick, N.J.: Rutgers University Press, 2013.

Grimké, Angelina. *An Appeal to Women of the Nominally Free States*. New York: William S. Dorr, 1837.

Grimké, Sarah M. *Letters on the Equality of the Sexes, and the Condition of Woman. Addressed to Mary S. Parker, President of the Boston Female Anti-Slavery Society*. Boston: Isaac Knapp, 1838.

Hanaford, Phebe. *Daughters of America; or Women of the Century*. Boston: B. B. Russell, 1883.

Harper, Ida Husted, ed. *The History of Woman Suffrage. Vol. 5, 1900–1920*. New York: National American Woman Suffrage Association, 1922.

———. *The Life and Work of Susan B. Anthony Including Public Addresses, Her Own Letters and Many from Her Contemporaries during Fifty Years*. 3 vols. Indianapolis and Kansas City: The Bowen-Merrill Company, 1898–1908; reprint, North Stratford, N.H.: Ayer Press, 1998.

Hurlbut, Elisha P. *Essays of Human Rights and Their Political Guaranties*. New York: Greeley & McElrath, 1845.

Jacobs, Harriet. *Incidents in the Life of a Slave Girl: Written by Herself*. Boston: For the Author, 1861; reprint, Cambridge, Mass.: Harvard University Press, 1987.

Lasser, Carol, and Marlene Deahl Merrill, eds. *Friends and Sisters: Letters between Lucy Stone and Antoinette Brown Blackwell, 1846–1893*. Urbana: University of Illinois Press, 1987.

Lewis, Dio. "A Brief History of the Woman's Crusade." In *Prohibition a Failure: or The True Solution of the Temperance Question*. Boston: James R. Osgood & Co., 1875.

Lincoln, Abraham. "Gettysburg Address," 19 November 1863. From the Library of Congress, *The Abraham Lincoln Papers at the Library of Congress*. http://memory.loc.gov/ammem/alhtml/malhome.html. Accessed 4 February 2013.

Livermore, Mary. *The Story of My Life*. Hartford, Conn: A. D. Worthington and Company, 1899; reprint, New York: Arno Press, 1974.

Minor v. Happersett, 88 U.S. 162. In *Cases Argued and Adjudged in the Supreme Court of the United States, October Term, 1874. Reported by John William Wallace*. Vol. 21. Washington, D.C.: William H. Morrison, 1875.

Palmer, Beverly Wilson, ed. *Selected Letters of Lucretia Coffin Mott*. Urbana: University of Illinois Press, 2002.

Papers and Letters Presented at the First Woman's Congress of the Association for the Advancement of Woman. Held in the Union League Theatre, Corner of 20th Street and Madison Avenue, New York, October 1873. New York: Mrs. Wm. Ballard, 1874.

Parton, James, ed. *Eminent Women of the Age; Being Narratives of the Lives and Deeds of the Most Prominent Women of the Present Generation*. Hartford, Conn.: S. M. Betts & Company, 1869; reprint, New York: Arno Press, 1974.

Proceedings of the Eleventh National Woman's Rights Convention, Held at the Church of the Puritans, New York, May 10, 1866. New York: Robert J. Johnston, 1866.

Proceedings of the General Anti-Slavery Convention, Called by the Committee of the British and Foreign Anti-Slavery Society and Held in London, from Friday, June 12th, to Tuesday, June 23rd, 1840. London: British and Foreign Anti-Slavery Society, 1841.

Proceedings of the National Women's Rights Convention, held at Cleveland, Ohio, on Wednesday, Thursday, and Friday, October 5th, 6th, and 7th, 1853. Cleveland: Gray, Beardsley, Spear, & Co., Printers, 1854.

Proceedings of the Ninth National Woman's Rights Convention Held in New York City, Thursday May 12, 1859 with a Phonographic Report of the Speech of Wendell Phillips by J. M. W. Yerrinton. Rochester, N.Y.: A. Strong & Co., 1859.

Proceedings of the Seventh National Woman's Rights Convention, Held in New York City at the Broadway Tabernacle, on Tuesday and Wednesday, Nov. 25 & 26, 1856. New York: Edward O. Jenkins, Printer.

Proceedings of the Tenth National Woman's Rights Convention Held at the Cooper Union Institute, New York City, May 10th and 11th, 1860. Phonographic Report by J. M. W. Yerrinton. Boston: Yerrinton & Garrison, 1860.

Proceedings of the Woman's Rights Conventions at Seneca Falls and Rochester, N.Y., July and August, 1848. New York: Robert J. Johnston, 1870.

Proceedings of the Woman's Rights Convention Held at Syracuse, September 8th, 9th, & 10th, 1852. Syracuse, N.Y.: J. E. Masters, 1852.

Proceedings of the Woman's Rights Convention Held at Worcester, October 23d & 24th, 1850. Boston: Prentiss & Sawyer, 1851.

Proceedings of the Woman's Rights Convention Held at Worcester, October 15th and 16th, 1851. New York: Fowlers and Wells, 1852.

Report of the Convention for Organization, Feb. 24–25, 1890, Willard Hall, Washington, D.C. Syracuse, N.Y.: Masters and Stone, 1890.

Report of the International Council of Women, Assembled by the National Woman Suffrage Association, Washington, D.C., U.S. of America, March 25 to April 1, 1888. Washington, D.C.: Rufus H. Darby Printer, for the National Woman Suffrage Association, 1888.

Report of the Woman's Rights Convention, Held at Seneca Falls, N. Y., July 19th and 20th, 1848. Rochester, N.Y.: John Dick, 1848. http://hdl.loc.gov/loc.rbc/rbcmil.scrp4006702. Accessed 22 February 2013.

Report of the Woman's Rights Convention, Held at Seneca Falls, N. Y., July 19th and 20th, 1848. Rochester, N.Y.: John Dick. *American Women's History Online.* Facts on File, Inc. http://www.fofweb.com/activelink2.asp?ItemID=WE42&iPin=3111&SingleRecord=True. Accessed 12 November 2013.

Republican Party Platform of 1872. American Presidency Project. http://www.presidency.ucsb.edu/ws/index.php?pid=29623. Accessed 31 May 2013.

Richardson, Marilyn, ed. *Maria W. Stewart: America's First Black Woman Political Writer, Essays and Speeches.* Bloomington, Ind.: Indiana University Press, 1987.

Robinson, Harriet Hanson. *Massachusetts in the Woman Suffrage Movement.* 2nd ed. Boston: Roberts Brothers, 1883.

Shaw, Anna Howard. With collaboration of Elizabeth Jordon. *The Story of a Pioneer.* New York: Harper & Brothers, 1915.

Smith, Julia E. *Abby Smith and Her Cows, With a Report of the Law Case Decided Contrary to Law.* 1877; reprint, New York: Arno Press, 1972.

The Spirit of Houston: The First National Women's Congress, An Official Report to the President, the Congress and the People of the United States. Washington, D.C.: National Commission on the Observation of International Women's Year, 1978.

Stanton, Elizabeth Cady. *Eighty Years & More: Reminiscences, 1815–1897.* New York: T. Fisher Unwin, 1898; reprint, with introduction by Ellen DuBois and afterword by Ann D. Gordon. Boston: Northeastern University Press, 1993.

———. *The Woman's Bible.* 1895; reprint, with forward by Maureen Fitzgerald. Boston: Northeastern University Press, 1993.

———. "The Woman's Rights Movement and its Champions in the United States." In *Eminent Women of the Age, being narratives of the lives and deeds of the most eminent women of the present generation*, edited by James Parton et al. Hartford, Conn.: S. M. Betts, 1869; reprint, New York: Arno Press, 1974.

Stanton, Elizabeth Cady, and Susan B. Anthony, eds. *Report of the Sixteenth Annual Washington Convention, March 4th, 5th, 6th, and 7th, 1884 with Reports of the Forty-Eight Congress.* Rochester, N.Y.: Charles Mann, 1884.

Stanton, Elizabeth Cady, Susan B. Anthony, and Matilda Joslyn Gage, eds. *History of Woman*

Suffrage. Vol. 1, 1848–1861. New York: Fowler & Wells, 1881; reprint, New York: Arno Press & New York Times, 1969.

———. *History of Woman Suffrage. Vol. 1, 1848–1861*. 2nd ed. Rochester, N.Y.: Charles Mann, 1889; reprint, New York: Source Book Press, 1970.

———. *History of Woman Suffrage. Vol. 2, 1861–1876*. New York: Fowler & Wells, 1882; reprint, New York: Arno Press & New York Times, 1969.

———. *History of Woman Suffrage. Vol. 3, 1876–1885*. Rochester, N.Y.: Susan B. Anthony, 1886; reprint, New York: Arno Press & New York Times, 1969.

Stanton, Theodore, and Harriot Stanton Blatch, eds. *Elizabeth Cady Stanton: As Revealed in Her Letters, Diary, and Reminiscences*. 2 vols. New York: Harper & Brothers, 1922.

Stapler, Martha G., ed. *The Woman Suffrage Year Book*. New York: National Woman Suffrage Publishing Company, Inc., 1917.

Stebbins, Jane E. *Fifty Years History of the Temperance Cause*. Hartford, Conn.: J. P. Fitch, 1876.

Steel, W. C. *The Woman's Temperance Movement: A Concise History of Woman's War on Alcohol*. New York: National Temperance Society and Publication House, 1874.

Stewart, Eliza Daniel "Mother Stewart." *Memories of the Crusade*. Chicago: H. J. Smith and Company, 1890.

Tilton, Theodore. "Mrs. Elizabeth Cady Stanton." In *Eminent Women of the Age, being narratives of the lives and deeds of the most eminent women of the present generation*, edited by James Parton et al. Hartford, Conn.: S. M. Betts & Co., 1869; reprint, New York: Arno Press, 1974.

Train, George Francis. *The Great Epigram Campaign of Kansas: Champion of Woman*. Leavenworth, Kans.: Prescott & Hume, 1867.

U.S. Bureau of Census. *The Seventh Census of the United States, 1850: Embracing a Statistical View of Each of the States and Territories, Arranged by Counties, Towns, Etc.* . . . Washington, D.C.: Robert Armstrong, 1853.

U.S. Centennial Commission. *International Exhibition, 1876: Reports of the President, Secretary, and Executive Committee, Together with the Journal of the Final Session of the Commission*. Vol. 2. Washington, D.C.: Government Printing Office, 1880.

U.S. Congress. House. 109th Cong., 1st sess., *Congressional Record*, vol. 151, part 22, Washington, D.C.: United States Government Printing Office, 2005.

U.S. Congress. Senate. 45th Cong., 1st sess., *Congressional Record*, vol. 7. Washington, D.C.: Government Printing Office, 1878.

U.S. Congress. Senate. 46th Cong., 2nd sess., *Congressional Record*, vol. 10, Washington, D.C.: Government Printing Office, 1880.

U.S. Congress. Senate. 66th Cong., 3rd sess., *Congressional Record*, vol. 60, part 2, Washington, D.C.: Government Printing Office, 1921.

U.S. Congress. Senate. 68th Cong., 1st sess., *Congressional Record*, vol. 65, Washington, D.C.: Government Printing Office, 1924.

U.S. Congress. Senate. 108th Cong., 2nd sess., *Congressional Record*, vol. 150, part 10, Washington, D.C.: United States Government Printing Office, 2004.

U.S. Congress. Senate. Committee on Privileges and Elections. *Arguments before the Committee on Privileges and Elections of the United States Senate on behalf of a Sixteenth Amendment to the Constitution of the United States*. 45th Cong., 1st sess., 11–12 January 1878. Washington, D.C.: Government Printing Office, 1878.

U.S. Congress. Senate. Committee on Privileges and Elections. *Report No. 523*. 45th Cong., 2nd sess., 14 June 1878. Washington, D.C.: Government Printing Office, 1878.

U.S. Department of the Interior. *Compendium of the Tenth Census (June 1, 1880), Compiled Pursuant to an Act of Congress Approved August 7, 1882. Part I*. Washington, D.C.: Government Printing Office, 1883.

Willard, Frances E. *Home Protection Manual: Containing an Argument for the Temperance*

Ballot for Woman, and How to Obtain it, as a Means of Home Protection; Also Constitution and Plan of Work for State and Local W.C.T. Unions. New York: The Independent, 1879.

———. *Let Something Good Be Said: The Speeches and Writings of Frances E. Willard.* Edited by Carolyn DeSwarte Gifford and Amy R. Slagell. Urbana: University of Illinois Press, 2007.

Willard, Frances, and Mary A. Livermore. *A Woman of the Century.* Buffalo, N.Y.: C. W. Moulton, 1893.

Wittenmyer, Annie. *History of the Woman's Temperance Crusade.* Philadelphia: Office of the Christian Woman, 1878.

Secondary Sources

Allen, William C. *History of the United States Capitol: A Chronicle of Design, Construction, and Politics.* Washington, D.C.: Government Printing Office, 1990.

Anderson, Bonnie. *Joyous Greetings: The First International Women's Movement, 1830–1860.* New York: Oxford University Press, 2000.

Anthony, Katharine. *Susan B. Anthony: Her Personal History and Her Era.* Garden City, N.Y.: Doubleday, 1954.

The Anthony Portrait Committee. "The Anthony Home Calendar," 1901. On display at "Susan B. Anthony: Celebrating 'A Heroic Life,'" an online exhibit curated by the Department of Rare Books & Special Collections, University of Rochester, http://www.lib.rochester.edu/index.cfm?page=4118. Accessed 8 August 2013.

Appleby, Joyce, Lynn Hunt, and Margaret Jacob. *Telling the Truth about History.* New York: W. W. Norton & Company, 1995.

Attie, Jeanie. *Patriotic Toil: Northern Women and the American Civil War.* Ithaca, N.Y.: Cornell University Press, 1998.

Baker, Jean H. "Getting Right with Women's Suffrage." *Journal of the Gilded Age and Progressive Era* 5, no. 1 (January 2006): 7–17.

Balser, Diane. *Sisterhood and Solidarity: Feminism and Labor in the Modern Times.* Boston: South End Press, 1987.

Barry, Kathleen. *Susan B. Anthony: A Biography of a Singular Feminist.* New York: New York University Press, 1988.

Basch, Norma. *In the Eyes of the Law: Women, Marriage, and Property in Nineteenth-Century New York.* Ithaca, N.Y.: Cornell University Press, 1982.

———. "Invisible Women: The Legal Fiction of Marital Unity in Nineteenth-Century America." *Feminist Studies* 5, no. 2 (Summer 1979): 346–66.

———. "Reconstructing Female Citizenship: *Minor v. Happersett.* In *The Constitution, Law, and American Life: Critical Aspects of the Nineteenth-Century Experience,* edited by Donald G. Neiman. Athens: University of Georgia Press, 1992.

Baym, Nina. *American Women Writers and the Work of History, 1790–1860.* New Brunswick, N.J.: Rutgers University Press, 1995.

Beck, Leonard N. "The Library of Susan B. Anthony." *Quarterly Journal of the Library of Congress* 32 (October 1975): 324–35.

Beeton, Beverly. *Women Vote in the West: The Woman Suffrage Movement, 1869–1896.* New York: Garland, 1986.

Beisel, Nicola. *Imperiled Innocents: Anthony Comstock and Family Reproduction in Victorian America.* Princeton, N.J.: Princeton University Press, 1998.

Bennion, Sherilyn Cox. *Equal to the Occasion: Women Editors of the Nineteenth-Century West.* Reno, Nev.: University of Nevada Press, 1990.

Berlin, Ira. "Who Freed the Slaves? Emancipation and Its Meaning." In *Major Problems in the Civil War and Reconstruction: Documents and Essay,* 2nd ed., edited by Michael Perman. Boston: Wadsworth, 1998.

Berthoff, Rowland. "Conventional Mentality: Free Blacks, Women, and Business

Corporations as Unequal Persons, 1820–1870." *Journal of American History* 76, no. 3 (December 1989): 753–84.

Birney, Catherine H. *The Grimké Sisters: Sarah and Angelina Grimké, the First American Women Advocates of Abolition and Woman's Rights*. Boston: Lee & Sheppard, 1885.

Blackwell, Alice Stone. *Lucy Stone: Pioneer of Women's Rights*. Boston: Little, Brown & Company, 1930.

Blackwell, Marilyn Schultz. "The Politics of Motherhood: Clarina Howard Nichols and School Suffrage." *New England Quarterly* 78, no. 4 (December 2005): 570–98.

Blair, Karen J. *The Clubwoman as Feminist: True Womanhood Redefined, 1868–1914*. New York: Holmes & Meier Publishers, Inc., 1980.

———. "Women's Club Movement." In *The Oxford Companion to United States History*, edited by Paul S. Boyer. New York: Oxford University Press, 2001.

Blake, Katherine Devereux, and Margaret Louise Wallace. *Champion of Women: The Life of Lillie Devereux Blake*. New York: Fleming H. Revell Company, 1943.

Blewett, Mary. *Men, Women, and Work: Class, Gender, & Protest in the New England Show Industry, 1780–1910*. Urbana: University of Illinois Press, 1988.

Blight, David W. *Race and Reunion: The Civil War in American Memory*. Cambridge, Mass.: The Belknap Press of Harvard University Press, 2001.

Blocker, Jack S., Jr., "Separate Paths: Suffragists and the Women's Temperance Crusade." *Signs* 10, no. 3 (Spring 1985): 460–76.

Bloomberg, Kristin Mapel. "'Striving for Equal Rights for All': Woman Suffrage in Nebraska, 1855–1882." *Nebraska History* 90 (Summer 2009): 84–103.

Blouin, Francis X., Jr., and William G. Rosenberg. *Processing the Past: Contesting Authority in History and the Archives*. New York: Oxford University Press, 2011.

———, eds. *Archives, Documentation and Institutions of Social Memory: Essays from the Sawyer Seminar*. Ann Arbor: University of Michigan Press, 2006.

Bogle, Lori. "Paradox of Opportunities: Lucy Stone, Alice Stone Blackwell, and the Tragedy of Reform." *Historical Journal of Massachusetts* 23 (Winter 1994): 17–33.

Bordin, Ruth. *Woman and Temperance: The Quest for Power and Liberty, 1873–1900*. Philadelphia: Temple University Press, 1981; reprint, New Brunswick, N.J.: Rutgers University Press, 1990.

Boydston, Jeanne, Mary Kelly, and Anne Margolis. *The Limits of Sisterhood: The Beecher Sisters on Women's Rights and Woman's Sphere*. Chapel Hill: University of North Carolina Press, 1988.

Boylan, Anne M. *Origins of Women's Activism: New York and Boston, 1797–1840*. Chapel Hill: University of North Carolina Press, 2001.

Brammer, Leila R. *Excluded from Suffrage History: Matilda Joslyn Gage, Nineteenth-Century American Feminist*. Westport, Conn.: Greenwood Press, 2000.

Braude, Ann. *Radical Spirits: Spiritualism and Women's Rights in Nineteenth-Century America*. 2nd ed. Bloomington: Indiana University Press, 2001.

Brodie, Janet Farrell. *Contraception and Abortion in 19th Century America*. Ithaca, N.Y.: Cornell University Press, 1994.

———. "Reproductive Control and Conflict in the Nineteenth Century." In vol. 1 of *Women and Power in American History: A Reader*, 2nd ed., edited by Thomas Dublin and Katherine Kish Sklar. Englewood Cliffs, N.J.: Prentice Hall, 2002.

Brown, Elsa Barkley. "Negotiating and Transforming the Public Sphere: African American Political Life in the Transition from Slavery to Freedom." *Public Culture* 7, no. 1 (Fall 1994): 107–46.

———. "To Catch the Vision of Freedom: Reconstructing Southern Black Women's Political History, 1865–1880." In *African American Women and the Vote, 1837–1965*, edited by Ann D. Gordon and Bettye Collier-Thomas. Amherst: University of Massachusetts Press, 1997.

———. "'What Has Happened Here': The Politics of Difference in Women's History and Feminist Politics." *Feminist Studies* 18, no. 2 (Summer 1992): 295–312.

————. "Womanist Consciousness: Maggie Lena Walker and the Independent Order of Saint Luke." *Signs* 14, no. 3 (Spring 1989): 610–33.

Brown, Sharon A. "Historic Structure Report, Historical Data Section, Wesleyan Chapel, Women's Rights National Historical Park." Washington, D.C.: U.S. Department of the Interior, National Park Service, 1987.

Brundage, Fitzhugh, ed. *Where These Memories Grow: History, Memory, and Southern Identity.* Chapel Hill: University of North Carolina Press, 2000.

Bruner, Jerome. *Making Stories: Law, Literature, Life.* Cambridge, Mass.: Harvard University Press, 2003.

Buechler, Steven M. *The Transformation of the Woman Suffrage Movement: The Case of Illinois.* New Brunswick, N.J.: Rutgers University Press, 1986.

Buhle, Mari Jo, and Paul Buhle. "Introduction." In *The Concise History of Woman Suffrage: Selections from the Classic Work of Stanton, Anthony, Gage, and Harper.* Urbana: University of Illinois Press, 1978.

————. "Preface." In *The Concise History of Woman Suffrage: Selections from the Classic Work of Stanton, Anthony, Gage, and Harper.* Urbana: University of Illinois Press, 1978.

Burton, Shirley J. "Adelaide Johnson: To Make Immortal Their Adventurous Will." *Western Illinois Monograph Series,* no. 7. Macomb: Western Illinois University, 1986.

Bushman, Claudia. *"A Good Poor Man's Wife": Being a Chronicle of Harriet Hanson Robinson & Her Family in 19th-Century New England.* Hanover, N.H.: University Press of New England, 1981.

Buss, Helen M., and Marlene Kadar, eds. *Working in Women's Archives: Researching Women's Private Literature and Archival Documents.* Waterloo, Ont.: Wilfrid Laurier University Press, 2001.

Carpenter, Matilda Gilruth. *The Crusade: Its Origins and Development.* Columbus, Ohio: W. G. Hubbard & Co., 1893.

Cartledge, Pamela. "Seven Cows on the Auction Block: Abby and Julia Smith's Fight for the Enfranchisement of Women." *Connecticut Historical Society Bulletin* 52, no. 1 (Winter 1987): 15–43.

Caruso, Virginia Ann Pagenelli. "A History of Woman Suffrage in Michigan." Ph.D. thesis, University of Michigan, 1986.

Child, Lydia Maria Francis. *The History of the Condition of Women, in Various Ages and Nations.* Boston: John Allen & Company, 1835.

Clark, Elizabeth B. "Self-Ownership and the Political Theory of Elizabeth Cady Stanton." *Connecticut Law Review* 21, no. 4 (Summer 1989): 905–41.

Clark, Kathleen. *Defining Moments: African American Commemoration and Political Culture in the American South, 1863–1913.* Chapel Hill: University of North Carolina Press, 2006.

Clinton, Hillary R. "Seneca Falls, 165 years ago today, began a movement that remains the unfinished business of the 21st century." Twitter post, 19 July 2013, 4:10 P.M. https://twitter.com/HillaryClinton/status/358363269603409920.

Cobble, Dorothy Sue. *The Other Women's Movement: Workplace Justice and Social Rights in Modern America.* Princeton, N.J.: Princeton University Press, 2004.

Cogan, Jacob Katz, and Lori D. Ginzberg. "1846 Petition for Woman's Suffrage, New York State Constitutional Convention." *Signs* 22 (Winter 1997): 427–39.

Cohen, Nancy. *The Reconstruction of American Liberalism, 1865–1914.* Chapel Hill: University of North Carolina Press, 2002.

Coleman, Willi. "'. . . Like Hot Lead to Pour on the Americans': Sarah Parker Remond and the International Fight against Slavery." In *Sisterhood and Slavery: International Antislavery and Women's Rights,* edited by James Brewer Stewart and Kathryn Kish Sklar. New Haven, Conn.: Yale University Press, 2006.

Collier-Thomas, Bettye. "Frances Ellen Watkins Harper: Abolitionist and Feminist Reformer, 1825–1922." In *African-American Women and the Vote, 1837–1965,* edited by Ann D. Gordon and Bettye Collier-Thomas. Amherst: University of Massachusetts Press, 1997.

Connerton, Paul. *How Societies Remember*. Cambridge: Cambridge University Press, 1989.

Cooper, Anna Julia. *A Voice from the South*. Xenia, Ohio.: Aldine Printing, 1892; reprint, New York: Oxford University Press, 1988.

Cordato, Mary Frances. "Toward a New Century: Women and the Philadelphia Centennial Exhibition, 1876." *Pennsylvania Magazine of History and Biography* 107 (January 1983): 113–35.

Corey, Mary E. Paddock. "Matilda Joslyn Gage: Woman Suffrage Historian, 1852–1898." Ph.D. diss., University of Rochester, 1995.

Cott, Nancy. "Feminist Politics in the 1920s: The National Woman's Party." *Journal of American History* 71, no. 1 (June 1984): 43–68.

———. *The Grounding of Modern Feminism*. New Haven, Conn.: Yale University Press, 1989.

———. "Passionlessness: An Interpretation of Victorian Sexual Ideology, 1790–1850." *Signs* 4, no. 2 (Winter 1978): 219–36.

———. *Public Vows: A History of Marriage and Nation*. Cambridge, Mass.: Harvard University Press, 2000.

Coulter, Thomas Chalmer. "History of Woman Suffrage in Nebraska, 1856–1920." Unpublished Ph.D. thesis, Ohio State University, 1967.

Davis, Angela. "Racism in the Woman Suffrage Movement." In *Women, Race, and Class*. New York: Vintage Books, 1983.

Davis, Joseph E., ed. *Stories of Change: Narrative and Social Movements*. Albany: State University of New York Press, 2002.

Davis, Sue. *The Political Thought of Elizabeth Cady Stanton: Women's Rights and the American Political Traditions*. New York: New York University Press, 2008.

Des Jardins, Julie. *Women and the Historical Enterprise in America: Gender, Race, and the Politics of Memory, 1880–1945*. Chapel Hill: University of North Carolina Press, 2003.

Dittmer, John. *Local People: The Struggle for Civil Rights in Mississippi*. Urbana: University of Illinois Press, 1995.

Doress-Worters, Paula. *Mistress of Herself: Speeches and Letters of Ernestine Rose, Early Women's Rights Leader*. New York: Feminist Press at CUNY, 2008.

Dorr, Rheta Childe. *Susan B. Anthony, The Woman Who Changed the Mind of a Nation*. New York: Frederick A. Stokes, 1928.

Dow, Bonnie. "The *Revolution*, 1868–1870: Expanding the Woman Suffrage Agenda." In *A Voice of Their Own: The Woman Suffrage Press, 1849–1914*, edited by Martha Solomon. Tuscaloosa: University of Alabama Press, 1991.

Dublin, Thomas. *Women at Work*. 2nd ed. New York: Columbia University Press, 1981.

DuBois, Ellen Carol. "Feminism and Free Love." H-Net Women, 2001. http://www.h-net .org/~women/papers/freeloveintro.html. Accessed 11 August 2013.

———. *Feminism and Suffrage: The Emergence of an Independent Women's Movement in America, 1848–1869*. Ithaca: Cornell University Press, 1978.

———. *Harriot Stanton Blatch and the Winning of Woman Suffrage*. New Haven: Yale University Press, 1997.

———. "Making Women's History: Historian-Activists of Women's Rights, 1880–1940." In *Woman Suffrage and Women's Rights*. New York: New York University Press, 1998.

———. "On Labor and Free Love: Two Unpublished Speeches of Elizabeth Cady Stanton." *Signs* 1, no. 1 (Autumn 1975): 257–68.

———. "Outgrowing the Compact of the Fathers: Equal Rights, Woman Suffrage, and the United States Constitution." *Journal of American History* 74, no. 3 (December 1987): 836–62.

———. "Taking the Law into Our Own Hands: Bradwell, Minor and Suffrage Militance in the 1870s." In *One Woman, One Vote: Rediscovering the Woman Suffrage Movement*, edited by Marjorie Spruill Wheeler. Troutdale, Ore.: NewSage Press, 1995.

———. *Woman Suffrage and Women's Rights*. New York: New York University Press, 1998.

DuBois, Ellen Carol, and Linda Gordon. "Seeking Ecstasy on the Battlefield: Danger and Pleasure in Nineteenth-Century Feminist Sexual Thought." *Feminist Studies* 9, no. 1 (Spring 1983): 7–25.

Dubois, Ellen Carol, and Richard Cándida Smith, eds. *Elizabeth Cady Stanton, Feminist as Thinker: A Reader with Documents and Essays.* New York: New York University Press, 2007.

Du Bois, W. E. B. *Black Reconstruction in America, 1860–1880.* New York: Harcourt, Brace, 1935; reprint, New York: Free Press, 1990.

———. *Souls of Black Folk.* Chicago: A. C. McClurg & Co., 1903; reprint New York: Vintage Books/Library of America, 1990.

Dudden, Faye. *Fighting Chance: The Struggle over Woman Suffrage and Black Suffrage in Reconstruction America.* New York: Oxford University Press, 2011.

Dykeman, Amy. "To Look a Gift Horse in the Mouth: The History of the Theodore Stanton Collection." *Journal of Library History* 17 (Fall 1982): 468–73.

———. "'To Pour Forth From My Own Experience': Two Versions of Elizabeth Cady Stanton." *Journal of the Rutgers University Libraries* 44 (June 1983): 1–16.

Edwards, Laura F. *Gendered Strife and Confusion: The Political Culture of Reconstruction.* Urbana: University of Illinois Press, 1997.

Edwards, Rebecca. *Angels in the Machinery: Gender in American Party Politics from the Civil War to the Progressive Era.* New York: Oxford University Press, 1997.

———. "Pioneers at the Polls: Woman Suffrage in the West." In *Votes for Women: The Struggle for Suffrage Revisited,* edited by Jean H. Baker. New York: Oxford University Press, 2002.

Eiss, Paul K. "Redemption's Archive: Remembering the Future in a Revolutionary Past." In *Archives, Documentation and Institutions of Social Memory: Essays from the Sawyer Seminar,* edited by Francis X. Blouin Jr. and William G. Rosenberg. Ann Arbor: University of Michigan Press, 2006.

Ellet, Elizabeth F. *Pioneer Women of the West.* New York: Charles Scribner, 1852.

———. *The Women of the American Revolution. In two Volumes.* New York: Baker and Scribner, 1849.

Endres, Kathleen L., and Therese L. Lueck, eds. *Women's Periodicals in the United States: Social and Political Issues.* Westport, Conn.: Greenwood Press, 1996.

Epps, Garrett. *Democracy Reborn: The Fourteenth Amendment and the Fight for Equal Rights in Post–Civil War America.* New York: Henry Holt and Company, 2006.

Evans, Sara M. "Reviewing the Second Wave." *Feminist Studies* 28, no. 2 (Summer 2002): 259–67.

———. *Tidal Wave: How Women Changed America at Century's End.* New York: Free Press, 2003.

Fabian, Ann. *The Unvarnished Truth: Personal Narratives in Nineteenth-Century America.* Berkeley: University of California Press, 2000.

Fahs, Alice. "The Feminized Civil War: Gender, Northern Popular Literature, and the Memory of the War, 1861–1900." *Journal of American History* 85, no. 4 (March 1999): 1461–94.

Fahs, Alice, and Joan Waugh, eds. *The Memory of the Civil War in American Culture.* Chapel Hill: University of North Carolina Press, 2004.

Faulkner, Carol. *Lucretia Mott's Heresy: Abolition and Women's Rights in Nineteenth-Century America.* Philadelphia: University of Pennsylvania Press, 2011.

———. "The Root of the Evil: Free Produce and Radical Antislavery, 1820–1860." *Journal of the Early Republic* 27, no. 3 (Fall 2007): 377–405.

———. *Women's Radical Reconstruction: The Freedmen's Aid Movement.* Philadelphia: University of Pennsylvania Press, 2004.

Fischer, Gayle V. *Pantaloons and Power: A Nineteenth-Century Dress Reform in the United States.* Kent, Ohio: Kent State University Press, 2001.

Flexner, Eleanor. *Century of Struggle: The Woman's Rights Movement in the United States.* Cambridge, Mass.: Harvard University Press, 1959.

Flexner, Eleanor, and Ellen Fitzpatrick. *Century of Struggle: The Woman's Rights Movement in the United States.* Enlarged ed. Cambridge, Mass.: The Belknap Press of Harvard University Press, 1996.

Foner, Eric. "The Meaning of Freedom in the Age of Emancipation." *Journal of American History* 81, no. 2 (September 1994): 435–60.

———. *Reconstruction: America's Unfinished Revolution, 1863–1877.* New York: Harper & Row, 1988.

———. *The Story of American Freedom.* New York: W. W. Norton & Company, 1998.

Foner, Philip S., ed. *Frederick Douglass on Women's Rights.* New York: Greenwood Press, 1976.

Ford, Linda G. "Alice Paul and the Politics of Nonviolent Protest." In *Votes for Women: The Struggle for Suffrage Revisited,* edited by Jean H. Baker. New York: Oxford University Press, 2002.

———. "Alice Paul and the Triumph of Militancy." *One Woman, One Vote: Rediscovering the Woman Suffrage Movement,* edited by Marjorie Spruill Wheeler. Troutdale, Ore.: NewSage Press, 1995.

Fowler, Robert Booth. *Carrie Catt: Feminist Politician.* Boston: Northeastern University Press, 1986.

———. "Carrie Chapman Catt, Strategist." *One Woman, One Vote: Rediscovering the Woman Suffrage Movement,* edited by Marjorie Spruill Wheeler. Troutdale, Ore.: NewSage Press, 1995.

Fowler, Robert Booth, and Spencer Jones. "Carrie Chapman Catt and the Last Years of the Struggle for Woman Suffrage: 'The Winning Plan.'" In *Votes for Women: The Struggle for Suffrage Revisited,* edited by Jean H. Baker. New York: Oxford University Press, 2002.

Fox, Richard Wightman. *Trials of Intimacy: Love and Loss in the Beecher-Tilton Scandal.* Chicago: University of Chicago Press, 1999.

Frisken, Amanda. *Victoria Woodhull's Sexual Revolution: Political Theater and the Popular Press in Nineteenth-Century America.* Philadelphia: University of Pennsylvania Press, 2004.

Fuller, Paul E. *Laura Clay and the Woman's Rights Movement.* Lexington: University Press of Kentucky, 1992.

Gabriel, Mary. *Notorious Victoria: The Life of Victoria Woodhull, Uncensored.* Chapel Hill, N.C.: Algonquin Books of Chapel Hill, 1998.

Gallaher, Ruth A. *Legal and Political Status of Women in Iowa: An Historical Account of the Rights of Women in Iowa from 1838–1918.* Iowa City: The State Historical Society of Iowa, 1918.

Gallman, J. Matthew. *America's Joan of Arc: The Life of Anna Elizabeth Dickinson.* New York: Oxford University Press, 2006.

Garrison, Wendell Phillips, and Francis Jackson Garrison. *William Lloyd Garrison, 1805–1879: The Story of His Life Told by His Children.* 4 vols. New York: The Century Co., 1885–89.

Gatewood, Willard, Jr. "'The Remarkable Misses Rollin': Black Women in Reconstruction South Carolina." *South Carolina Historical Magazine* 92, no. 3 (July 1991): 172–88.

Geary, Patrick, "Medieval Archivists as Authors: Social Memory and Archival Memory." In *Archives, Documentation and Institutions of Social Memory: Essays from the Sawyer Seminar,* edited by Francis X. Blouin Jr. and William G. Rosenberg. Ann Arbor: University of Michigan Press, 2006.

Giele, Janet Zollinger. *Two Paths to Women's Equality: Temperance, Suffrage, and the Origins of Modern Feminism.* New York: Twayne Publishers, 1995.

Gillette, William. *The Right to Vote: Politics and the Passage of the Fifteenth Amendment.* Baltimore, Md.: Johns Hopkins University Press, 1965.

Gilmore, Glenda Elizabeth. *Gender and Jim Crow: Women and the Politics of White Suprema-cy in North Carolina, 1896–1920*. Chapel Hill: University of North Carolina Press, 1996.

Ginzberg, Lori D. *Elizabeth Cady Stanton: An American Life*. New York: Hill and Wang, 2009.

———. "Re-Viewing the First Wave." *Feminist Studies* 28, no. 2 (Summer 2002): 419–34.

———. *Untidy Origins: A Story of Women's Rights in Antebellum New York*. Chapel Hill: University of North Carolina Press, 2005.

———. *Women and the Work of Benevolence: Morality, Politics, and Class in the 19th Century United States*. New Haven: Yale University Press, 1990.

Goldsmith, Barbara. *Other Powers: The Age of Suffrage, Spiritualism, and the Scandalous Victoria Woodhull*. New York: Alfred A. Knopf, 1998.

Gordon, Ann D. "Afterword." In Elizabeth Cady Stanton, *Eighty Years and More: Reminiscences, 1815–1897*. New York: T. Fisher Unwin, 1898; reprint, with introduction by Ellen DuBois and afterword by Ann D. Gordon. Boston: Northeastern University Press, 1993.

———. "Conversation: Votes for Women, Recent and Future Scholarship on Woman Suffrage." Unpublished comments, Organization of American Historians Annual Convention, Toronto, Canada, April 1999.

———. "Introduction." In *Guide and Index to the Microfilm Edition of the Papers of Elizabeth Cady Stanton and Susan B. Anthony*, edited by Patricia G. Holland and Ann D. Gordon; associate editors, Kathleen A. McDonough and Gail K. Malmgreen. Wilmington, Del.: Scholarly Resources, Inc., 1992.

———. "Knowing Susan B. Anthony: The Stories We Tell of a Life." In *Susan B. Anthony and the Struggle for Equal Rights*, edited by Christine L. Ridarsky and Mary Huths. Rochester, N.Y.: Rochester University Press, 2012.

———. "Stanton and the Right to Vote: On Account of Race or Sex." In *Elizabeth Cady Stanton, Feminist as Thinker: A Reader in Documents and Essays*, edited by Ellen Carol DuBois and Richard Cándida Smith. New York: New York University Press, 2007.

———. "Woman Suffrage (Not Universal Suffrage) by Federal Amendment." In *Votes for Women! The Woman Suffrage Movement in Tennessee, the South, and the Nation*, edited by Marjorie Spruill Wheeler. Knoxville: University of Tennessee Press, 1995.

Gordon, Ann D., and Bettye Collier-Thomas, eds. *African-American Women and the Vote, 1837–1965*. Amherst: University of Massachusetts Press, 1997.

Gordon, Sarah Barringer. *The Mormon Question: Polygamy and Constitutional Conflict in Nineteenth-Century America*. Chapel Hill: University of North Carolina Press, 2002.

Gornick, Vivian. *The Solitude of Self: Thinking about Elizabeth Cady Stanton*. New York: Farrar, Straus and Giroux, 2006.

Graham, Sara Hunter. *Woman Suffrage and the New Democracy*. New Haven: Yale University Press, 1996.

Greef, Robert J. *Public Lectures in New York, 1851–1878: A Cultural Index of the Times*. Chicago: University of Chicago, 1945.

Green, James. *Taking History to Heart: The Power of the Past in Building Social Movements*. Amherst: University of Massachusetts Press, 2000.

Griffith, Elisabeth. *In Her Own Right: The Life of Elizabeth Cady Stanton*. New York: Oxford University Press, 1984.

Gurko, Miriam. *The Ladies of Seneca Falls: The Birth of the Woman's Rights Movement*. New York: Macmillan Publishing Co., 1974.

Gusfield, Joseph R. "Social Structure and Moral Reform: A Study of the Woman's Christian Temperance Union." *American Journal of Sociology* 61, no. 3 (November 1955): 221–32.

Gustafson, Melanie Susan. *Women and the Republican Party, 1854–1924*. Urbana: University of Illinois Press, 2001.

Guthrie, Gayle E. "Susie, Lucy, and Liz: Susan B. Anthony, Lucretia Mott, and Elizabeth Cady Stanton—Women of Vision, Women of Courage." 19 January 1998, unpublished paper on file at National Museum of Women's History, Alexandria, Va.

Hall, Jacquelyn Dowd. "The Long Civil Rights Movement and the Political Uses of the Past." *Journal of American History* 91, no. 4 (March 2005): 1233–63.

Hansen, Debra Gold. *Strained Sisterhood: Gender and Class in the Boston Female Anti-Slavery Society*. Amherst: University of Massachusetts Press, 2009.

Hattam, Victoria C. "Economic Visions and Political Strategies: American Labor and the State, 1865–1896." *Studies in American Political Development* 4 (March 1990): 82–129.

———. *Labor Visions and State Power: The Origins of Business Unionism in the United States*. Princeton, N.J.: Princeton University Press, 1993.

Hersh, Blanche Glassman. *The Slavery of Sex: Feminist-Abolitionists in America*. Urbana: University of Illinois Press, 1978.

Hewett, Rebecca Coleman. "Progressive Compromises: Performing Gender, Race, and Class in Historical Pageants of 1913." Ph.D. diss., University of Texas at Austin, 2010.

Hewitt, Nancy A. "Feminist Frequencies: Regenerating the Wave Metaphor." *Feminist Studies* 38, no. 3 (Fall 2012): 658–80.

———. "From Seneca Falls to Suffrage? Re-imagining a 'Master' Narrative in U.S. Women's History," In *No Permanent Waves: Recasting Histories of U.S. Feminism*, edited by Nancy A. Hewitt. New Brunswick, N.J.: Rutgers University Press, 2010.

———. "'Seeking a Larger Liberty': The U.S. Woman's Rights Movement in Transatlantic Perspective." In *Woman's Rights and Abolition in the Atlantic World*, edited by Kathryn Kish Sklar and James Brewer Stewart. New Haven: Yale University Press, 2007.

———. *Women's Activism and Social Change: Rochester, New York, 1822–1872*. Ithaca, N.Y.: Cornell University Press, 1984.

———, ed. *No Permanent Waves: Recasting Histories of U.S. Feminism*. New Brunswick, N.J.: Rutgers University Press, 2010.

Higginbotham, Evelyn Brooks. "African-American Women's History and the Metalanguage of Race." *Signs* 17, no. 21 (Winter 1992): 251–74.

———. *Righteous Discontent: The Women's Movement in the Black Baptist Church, 1880–1920*. Cambridge, Mass.: Harvard University Press, 1993.

Hine, Darlene Clark. "Rape and the Inner Lives of Black Women in the Middle West: Preliminary Thoughts on the Culture of Dissemblance." *Signs* 14, no. 4 (Summer 1989): 912–20.

Hoffert, Sylvia D. *When Hens Crow: The Women's Rights Movement in Antebellum America*. Bloomington: Indiana University Press, 1995.

Hofstadter, Richard. "Conflict and Consensus in American History." In *The Progressive Historians: Turner, Beard, Parrington*, by Richard Hofstadter. Chicago: University of Chicago Press, 1968.

Horowitz, Daniel. *Betty Friedan and the Making of "The Feminine Mystique": The American Left, the Cold War, and Modern Feminism*. Amherst: University of Massachusetts Press, 1998.

Horowitz, Helen Lefkowitz. *Rereading Sex: Battles over Sexual Knowledge and Suppression in Nineteenth-Century America*. New York: Knopf, 2002.

———. "Victoria Woodhull, Anthony Comstock, and Conflict over Sex in the United States in the 1870s." *Journal of American History* 87, no. 2 (September 2000): 403–34.

Hunter, Tera W. *To 'Joy My Freedom: Southern Black Women's Lives and Labors after the Civil War*. Cambridge, Mass.: Harvard University Press, 1997.

Huxman, Susan Shultz. "The Woman's Journal, 1870–1890: The Torch Bearer for Suffrage." In *A Voice of Their Own: The Woman Suffrage Press. 1849–1914*, edited by Martha Solomon. Tuscaloosa: University of Alabama Press, 1991.

Isenberg, Nancy. *Sex and Citizenship in Antebellum America*. Chapel Hill: University of North Carolina Press, 1998.

Jacobs, Ronald. "The Narrative Integration of the Personal and Collective Identity in Social Movements." In *Narrative Impact: Social and Cognitive Foundations*, edited by Melanie C. Green, Jeffrey Strange, and Timothy Brock, 205–28. Mahwah, N.J.: Erlbaum, 2002.

Janney, Caroline. *Remembering the Civil War: Reunion and the Limits of Reconciliation.* Chapel Hill: University of North Carolina Press, 2013.

Jeffrey, Julie Roy. *Abolitionists Remember: Antislavery Autobiographies and the Unfinished Work of Emancipation.* Chapel Hill: University of North Carolina Press, 2008.

———. *The Great Silent Army of Abolitionism: Ordinary Women in the Antislavery Movement.* Chapel Hill: University of North Carolina Press, 1998.

Jensen, Billie Barnes. "Colorado Woman Suffrage Campaigns of the 1870s." *Journal of the West* 12 (April 1973): 254–71.

Jones, Carolyn C. "Dollars and Selves: Women's Tax Criticism and Resistance in the 1870s." *University of Illinois Law Review* (1994): 265–309.

Jones, Martha S. *All Bound Up Together: The Woman Question in African American Public Culture, 1830–1900.* Chapel Hill: University of North Carolina Press, 2007.

Kachun, Mitch. *Festivals of Freedom: Memory and Meaning in African American Emancipation Celebrations, 1808–1915.* Amherst: University of Massachusetts Press, 2003.

Keller, Morton. *Affairs of State: Public Life in Late Nineteenth Century America.* Cambridge, Mass.: Harvard University Press, 1977.

Kerber, Linda. *No Constitutional Right to Be Ladies: Women and the Obligations of Citizenship.* New York: Hill and Wang, 1998.

Kern, Kathi. *Mrs. Stanton's Bible.* Ithaca, N.Y.: Cornell University Press, 2002.

Kerr, Andrea Moore. *Lucy Stone: Speaking Out for Equality.* New Brunswick, N.J.: Rutgers University Press, 1992.

Keyssar, Alexander. *The Right to Vote: The Contested History of Democracy in the United States.* New York: Basic Books, 2000.

Klinghoffer, Judith Apter, and Lois Elkis, "'The Petticoat Electors': Women's Suffrage in New Jersey, 1776–1807." *Journal of the Early Republic* 12, no. 2 (Summer 1992): 159–93.

Kogan, Jacob Katz, and Lori D. Ginzberg. "1846 Petition for Woman's Suffrage, New York State Constitutional Convention." *Signs* 22, no. 2 (Winter 1997): 427–39.

Kolmerten, Carol A. *The American Life of Ernestine L. Rose.* Syracuse, N.Y.: Syracuse University Press, 1999.

Kraditor, Aileen S., ed. *Up from the Pedestal: Selected Writings in the History of American Feminism.* Chicago: Quadrangle Books, 1968.

Kugler, Israel. *From Ladies to Women: The Organized Struggle for Woman's Rights in the Reconstruction Era.* New York: Greenwood Press, 1987.

Laughlin, Kathleen A., and Jacqueline L. Castledine, eds. *Breaking the Wave: Women, Their Organizations, and Feminism, 1945–1985.* New York: Routledge, 2011.

Laughlin, Kathleen A., Julie Gallagher, Dorothy Sue Cobble, Ellen Boris, Premilla Nadasen, Stephanie Gilmore, and Leandra Zarnow. "Is It Time to Jump Ship? Historians Rethink the Waves Metaphor." *Feminist Formations* 22, no. 1 (Spring 2010): 76–135.

Lederman, Sarah Henry. "Davis, Paulina Kellogg Wright." In *American National Biography Online.* http://www.anb.org/articles/15/15-00166.html. Accessed 21 December 2012.

Lerner, Gerda. *The Feminist Thought of Sarah Grimké.* New York: Oxford University Press, 1998.

———. *The Grimké Sisters from South Carolina: Pioneers for Woman's Rights and Abolition.* Boston: Houghton Mifflin, 1967; reprint, New York: Oxford University Press, 1998.

Levenson, Roger. *Women in Printing, Northern California, 1857–1890.* Santa Barbara, Calif.: Capra Press, 1994.

Linkugel, Wil, and Martha Solomon. *Anna Howard Shaw: Suffrage Orator and Social Reformer.* New York: Greenwood Press, 1991.

Loewen, James W. *Lies My Teacher Told Me: Everything Your American History Textbook Got Wrong.* New York: Simon & Schuster, 1997.

Lutz, Alma. *Created Equal: A Biography of Elizabeth Cady Stanton, 1815–1902.* New York: The John Day Company, 1940; reprint, New York: Octagon Books, 1974.

———. *Susan B. Anthony: Rebel, Crusader, Humanitarian.* Boston: Beacon Press, 1959.

Marilley, Suzanne M. *Woman Suffrage and the Origins of Liberal Feminism in the United States, 1820–1920*. Cambridge, Mass.: Harvard University Press, 1996.

Martin, Eric, and Lois Vossen. *Sisters of '77*. Directed by Allen Mondell and Cynthia Salzman Mondell. Independent Lens, season 6, episode 15, 3 March 2005.

Masur, Kate. *An Example for All the Land: Emancipation and the Struggle over Equality in Washington, D.C.* Chapel Hill: University of North Carolina Press, 2012.

———. "'A Rare Phenomenon of Philological Vegetation': The Word 'Contraband' and the Meanings of Emancipation in the United States." *Journal of American History* 93, no. 4 (March 2007): 1050–84.

Mayhall, Laura. "Creating the 'Suffragette Spirit': British Feminism and the Historical Imagination." In *Archive Stories: Fact, Fictions, and the Writing of History*, edited by Antoinette Burton. Durham, N.C.: Duke University Press, 2006.

McAdams, Dan P. *The Redemptive Self: Stories Americans Live By*. New York: Oxford University Press, 2006.

McCammon, Holly J., and Karen E. Campbell, "Winning the Vote in the West: The Political Successes of the Women's Suffrage Movements, 1866–1919," *Gender and Society* 15, no. 1 (February 2001): 55–82.

McClymer, John. *This High and Holy Moment: The First National Women's Rights Convention, Worcester, 1850*. Forth Worth: Harcourt Brace College Publishers, 1999.

McFadden, Margaret H. *Golden Cables of Sympathy: The Transatlantic Sources of Nineteenth-Century Feminism*. Lexington, K.Y: University Press of Kentucky, 1999.

McFeely, William S. *Frederick Douglass*. New York: W. W. Norton, 1991.

McGuire, Danielle. *At the Dark End of the Street: Black Women, Rape, and Resistance— A New History of the Civil Rights Movement from Rosa Parks to the Rise of Black Power*. New York: Alfred A. Knopf, 2010.

McMillen, Sally G. *Seneca Falls and the Origins of the Women's Rights Movement*. New York: Oxford University Press, 2008.

McPherson, James M. *What They Fought For, 1861–1865*. Baton Rouge: Louisiana State University Press, 1994; reprint, New York: Anchor Books, 1995.

Mead, Rebecca J. *How the Vote Was Won: Woman Suffrage in the Western United States, 1868–1914*. New York: New York University Press, 2004.

Melman, Billie. "Gender, History and Memory: The Invention of Women's Past in the Nineteenth and Early Twentieth Centuries." *History and Memory* 5 (Spring 1993): 5–41.

Merk, Lois Bannister. "Massachusetts and the Woman-Suffrage Movement." Ph.D. thesis, Radcliffe College, 1956.

Messer-Kruse, Timothy. *The Yankee International: Marxism and the American Reform Tradition, 1848–1876*. Chapel Hill: University of North Carolina Press, 1998.

Million, Joelle. *Woman's Voice, Woman's Place: Lucy Stone and the Birth of the Woman's Rights Movement*. Westport, Conn.: Praeger Publishers, 2003.

Mires, Charlene. *Independence Hall in American Memory*. Philadelphia: University of Pennsylvania Press, 2002.

Mitchell, Michele. "'Lower Orders,' Racial Hierarchies, and Rights Rhetoric: Evolutionary Echoes in Elizabeth Cady Stanton's Thought during the late 1860s." In *Elizabeth Cady Stanton, Feminist as Thinker: A Reader in Documents and Essays*, edited by Ellen Carol DuBois and Richard Cándida Smith. New York: New York University Press, 2007.

Montgomery, David. *Beyond Equality: Labor and the Radical Republicans, 1862–1872*. New York: Knopf, 1967.

Morris, Monia Cook. "The History of Woman Suffrage in Missouri, 1867–1901." Unpublished M.A. thesis, University of Missouri, 1928.

Morris, Roy, Jr., *Fraud of the Century: Rutherford B. Hayes, Samuel Tilden, and the Stolen Election of 1876*. New York: Simon & Schuster, 2004.

Nash, Gary B. *The Liberty Bell*. New Haven, Conn.: Yale University Press, 2010.

National Congress of Black Women. "Sojourner Truth Memorial Fund." http:// nationalcongressbw.org/sojournertruthsupporters.aspx. Accessed 10 October 2013.

Newell, Clayton R., and Charles R. Shrader. *Of Duty Well and Faithfully Done: A History of the Regular Army in the Civil War.* Lincoln: University of Nebraska Press, 2011.

Newman, Louise Michele. *White Women's Rights: The Racial Origins of Feminism in the United States.* New York: Oxford University Press, 1999.

Nicholson, Linda. "Feminism in 'Waves': Useful Metaphor or Not?" *New Politics* 12, no. 4, whole number 48 (Winter 2010). http://newpol.org/content/feminism-waves-useful -metaphor-or-not. Accessed 12 August 2013.

Norgren, Jill. *Belva Lockwood: The Woman Who Would Be President.* New York: New York University Press, 2008.

Noun, Louise. *Leader and Pariah: Annie Savery and the Campaign for Women's Rights in Iowa, 1868–1891.* Iowa City: Iowa Women's Archives, 2002.

———. *Strong-Minded Women: The Emergence of the Woman-Suffrage Movement in Iowa.* Ames: Iowa State University Press, 1986.

Novick, Peter. *That Noble Dream: The 'Objectivity Question' and the American Historical Profession.* New York: Cambridge University Press, 1988.

Paine, Judith. "The Woman's Pavilion of 1876." *The Feminist Art Journal* 4 (Winter, 1875–76): 5–12.

Painter, Nell Irvin. "Representing Truth: Sojourner Truth's Knowing and Becoming Known," *Journal of American History* 81, no. 2 (September 1994): 461–92.

———. *Sojourner Truth: A Life, a Symbol.* New York: W. W. Norton & Company, 1996.

———. "Voices of Suffrage: Sojourner Truth, Frances Watkins Harper, and the Struggle for Woman Suffrage." In *Votes for Women: The Struggle for Suffrage Revisited,* edited by Jean H. Baker. New York: Oxford University Press, 2002.

Parsons, Elaine Frantz. "Elizabeth Avery Meriwether and the Gender Politics of the Memphis Ku Klux Klan." Conference paper delivered at the Organization of American Historians Annual Meeting, Washington, D.C., 11–14 April 2002.

Passet, Joanne E. *Sex Radicals and the Quest for Women's Equality.* Urbana: University of Illinois Press, 2003.

Payne, Charles. *I've Got the Light of Freedom: The Organizing Tradition and the Mississippi Freedom Struggle.* Berkeley: University of California Press, 1995.

Penney, Sherry H., and James D. Livingston. *A Very Dangerous Woman: Martha Wright and Women's Rights.* Amherst: University of Massachusetts Press, 2004.

Perman, Michael. *Struggle for Mastery: Disfranchisement in the South, 1888–1908.* Chapel Hill: University of North Carolina Press, 2001.

Pierson, Michael D. *Free Hearts and Free Homes: Gender and American Anti-Slavery Politics.* Chapel Hill: University of North Carolina Press, 2003.

Polletta, Francesca. *It Was Like a Fever: Storytelling in Protest and Politics.* Chicago: University of Chicago Press, 2006.

Porter, Dorothy Burnett. "The Remonds of Salem, Massachusetts: A Nineteenth-Century Family Revisited." *Proceedings of the American Antiquarian Society* 95 (October 1985): 259–95.

"Portrait Monument to Lucretia Mott, Elizabeth Cady Stanton and Susan B. Anthony." *Architect of the Capitol.* http://www.aoc.gov/capitol-hill/other-statues/portrait- monument. Accessed 16 June 2013.

Pounds, Diana. "Suffragists, Free Love, and the Woman Question." *The Palimpsest* 72 (Spring 1991): 2–15.

Quarles, Benjamin. *Frederick Douglass.* Washington, D.C.: Associated Publishers, 1948.

———. "Frederick Douglass and the Woman's Rights Movement." *Journal of Negro History* 25 (June 1940): 35–44.

Ray, Angela G. "Representing Working Class in Early U.S. Feminist Media: The Case of Hester Vaughn." *Women's Studies in Communication* 26, no. 1 (Spring 2003): 1–26.

Rhodes, Jane. *Mary Ann Shadd Cary*. Bloomington: Indiana University Press, 1998.

Richardson, Heather Cox. *West from Appomattox: The Reconstruction of America after the Civil War*. New Haven: Yale University Press, 2008.

Richardson, James D. *A Compilation of the Messages and Papers of the Presidents, 1787–1897, Published by Authority of Congress*. 10 vols. Washington, D.C.: Government Printing Office, 1896–99.

Riegel, Robert E., ed. "'Woman's Rights and Other "Reforms" in Seneca Falls': A Contemporary View." *New York History* 46, no. 1 (1965): 41–59.

Robertson, Stacy M. *Hearts Beating for Liberty: Women Abolitionists in the Old Northwest*. Chapel Hill: University of North Carolina Press, 2010.

Romano, Renee C., and Leigh Raiford, eds. *The Civil Rights Movement in American Memory*. Athens: University of Georgia Press, 2006.

Rose, Vivien Ellen. "Seneca Falls Remembered: Celebrations of the 1848 First Women's Rights Convention." *Cultural Resource Management* 21, no. 11 (1998): 9–15.

Rose, Vivien Ellen, Paul Barnes, Ellen Carol DuBois, Ann D. Gordon, and Molly Murphy MacGregor. "Remembering Seneca Falls: A Roundtable on Commemorating the Sesquicentennial of the 1848 Seneca Falls Women's Rights Convention." *Public Historian* 21, no. 2 (Spring 1999): 11–47.

Rosen, Hannah. *Terror in the Heart of Freedom: Citizenship, Sexual Violence, and the Meaning of Race in the Postemancipation South*. Chapel Hill: University of North Carolina Press, 2009.

Rosen, Ruth. *World Split Open: How the Modern Women's Movement Changed America*. Rev. ed. New York: Penguin, 2006.

Rossi, Alice. "A Feminist Friendship: Elizabeth Cady Stanton (1815–1902) and Susan B. Anthony (1820–1906)." In *The Feminist Papers: From Adams to de Beauvoir*, edited by Alice S. Rossi. Lebanon, N.H.: University Press of New England, 1973.

Rupp, Leila J. "Constructing Internationalism: The Case of Transnational Women's Organizations, 1888–1945. *American Historical Review* 99, no. 5 (December 1994): 1571–1600.

———. *Worlds of Women: The Making of an International Women's Movement*. Princeton, N.J.: Princeton University Press, 1997.

Russo, Ann, and Cherise Kramarae. *The Radical Women's Press of the 1850s*. New York: Routledge, 1991.

Said, Edward. *Beginnings: Intention and Method*. New York: Basic Books, 1975.

Salerno, Beth Ann. *Sister Societies: Women's Antislavery Organizations in Antebellum America*. DeKalb: Northern Illinois University Press, 2005.

Sandage, Scott A. *Born Losers: A History of Failure in America*. Cambridge, Mass.: Harvard University Press, 2005.

Savage, Kirk. *Standing Soldiers, Kneeling Slaves: Race, War, and Monument in Nineteenth-Century America*. Princeton, N.J.: Princeton University Press, 1997.

Saville, Julie. *The Work of Reconstruction: From Slave to Wage Laborer in South Carolina, 1860–1870*. New York: Cambridge University Press, 1996.

Schuele, Donna C. "'None Could Deny the Eloquence of This Lady': Women, Law, and Government in California, 1850–1890." *California History* 81, no. 3/4 (2003): 169–98.

Schwalm, Leslie A. *A Hard Fight for We: Women's Transition from Slavery to Freedom in South Carolina*. Urbana: University of Illinois Press, 1997.

Scott, Anne Firor. *The Southern Lady: From Pedestal to Politics, 1830–1930*. Chicago: University of Chicago Press, 1970; reprint, Charlottesville: University Press of Virginia, 1995.

Sewall, Mary Wright, compiler. *Genesis of the International Council of Women and the Story of Its Growth, 1888–1893*. Indianapolis: n.p., 1914.

Shaw, Stephanie. "Black Club Women and the Creation of the National Association of Colored Women." *Journal of Women's History* 3, no. 2 (Fall 1991): 11–25.

———. *What a Woman Ought to Be and to Do: Black Professional Women Workers during the Jim Crow Era*. Chicago: University of Chicago Press, 1996.

Silver-Isenstadt, Jean L. *Shameless: The Visionary Life of Mary Grove Nichols.* Baltimore, Md.: Johns Hopkins University Press, 2002.

Sims, Anastasia. "Armageddon in Tennessee: The Final Battle over the Nineteenth Amendment." *One Woman, One Vote: Rediscovering the Woman Suffrage Movement,* edited by Marjorie Spruill Wheeler. Troutdale, Ore.: NewSage Press, 1995.

Sklar, Katherine Kish. "American Female Historians in Context, 1770–1930." *Feminist Studies* 3, no. 1/2 (Autumn 1975): 171–84.

———. "Women's Rights Emerges within the Anti-slavery Movement: Angelina and Sarah Grimké in 1837." In vol. 1 of *Women and Power in American History: A Reader,* 2nd ed., edited by Thomas Dublin and Katherine Kish Sklar. Englewood Cliffs, N.J.: Prentice Hall, 2002.

Smedley, Katherine. "Martha Schofield and the Rights of Women." *South Carolina Historical Magazine* 85 (July 1984): 195–210.

Smith, Ann. "Ann Martin and a History of Woman Suffrage in Nevada, 1869–1914." Ph.D. diss., University of Nevada–Reno, 1976.

Smith, Bonnie G. "The Contribution of Women to Modern Historiography in Great Britain, France, and the United States, 1750–1940." *American Historical Review* 89, no. 3 (June 1984): 709–32.

———. *The Gender of History: Men, Women, and Historical Practice.* Cambridge, Mass.: Harvard University Press, 2000.

———. "Women's History: A Retrospective from the United States." *Signs* 35, no. 3 (Spring 2010): 723–47.

Sneider, Allison L. *Suffragists in an Imperial Age: U.S. Expansion and the Woman Question, 1870–1929.* New York: Oxford University Press, 2008.

Spruill, Marjorie Julian. "Race, Reform, and Reaction at the Turn of the Century: Southern Suffragists, the NAWSA, and the 'Southern Strategy' in Context." In *Votes for Women: The Struggle for Suffrage Revisited,* edited by Jean H. Baker. New York: Oxford University Press, 2002.

Stanley, Amy Dru. *From Bondage to Contract: Wage Labor, Marriage, and the Market in the Age of Slave Emancipation.* New York: Cambridge University Press, 1998.

Stapler, Martha G., ed. *The Woman Suffrage Year Book.* New York: National Woman Suffrage Publishing Company, Inc., 1917.

Steedman, Carolyn. *Dust: The Archive and Cultural History.* New Brunswick, N.J.: Rutgers University Press, 2002.

Stowell, David O., ed. *The Great Strikes of 1877.* Urbana: University of Illinois Press, 2008.

Sumler-Edmond, Janice. "The Quest for Justice: African American Women Litigants, 1867–1890. In *African-American Women and the Vote, 1837–1965,* edited by Ann D. Gordon and Bettye Collier-Thomas. Amherst: University of Massachusetts Press, 1997.

Sutton, Jane S. *The House of My Sojourn: Rhetoric, Women, and the Question of Authority.* Tuscaloosa: University of Alabama Press, 2010.

Taylor, A. Elizabeth. "Tennessee: The Thirty-Sixth State." In *Votes for Women! The Woman Suffrage Movement in Tennessee, the South, and the Nation,* edited by Marjorie Spruill Wheeler. Knoxville: University of Tennessee Press, 1995.

Terborg-Penn, Rosalyn. "African American Women and the Vote: An Overview." In *African American Women and the Vote, 1837–1965,* edited by Ann D. Gordon and Bettye Collier-Thomas. Amherst: University of Massachusetts Press, 1997.

———. *African American Women in the Struggle for the Vote, 1850–1920.* Bloomington: Indiana University Press, 1998.

Tetrault, Lisa. "The Incorporation of American Feminism: Suffragists and the Postbellum Lyceum." *Journal of American History* 96, no. 4 (March 2010): 1027–56.

———. "Memory of a Movement: Woman Suffrage and Reconstruction America, 1865–1890." Ph.D. diss., University of Wisconsin–Madison, 2004.

———. "We Shall Be Remembered: Susan B. Anthony and the Politics of Writing History."

In *Susan B. Anthony and the Struggle for Equal Rights*, edited by Christine L. Ridarsky and Mary M. Huth. Rochester, N.Y.: University of Rochester Press, 2012.

Theoharis, Jeanne. *The Rebellious Life of Mrs. Rosa Parks*. Boston: Beacon Press, 2013.

Thomas, Edmund B., Jr., "School Suffrage and the Campaign for Women's Suffrage in Massachusetts, 1879–1920." *Historical Journal of Massachusetts* 25, no. 1 (1997): 1–17.

Thompson, Becky. "Multiracial Feminism: Recasting the Chronology of Second Wave Feminism." *Feminist Studies* 28, no. 2 (Summer 2002): 337–60.

Tolles, Frederick B., ed. "Slavery and 'The Woman Question': Lucretia Mott's Diary of Her Visit to Great Britain to Attend the World's Anti-Slavery Convention of 1840." Supplement No. 23 to the *Journal of the Friends' Historical Society*. Haverford, Pa.: Friends' Historical Association and Friends Historical Society, 1952.

Tutt, Juliana. "'No Taxation without Representation' in the American Woman Suffrage Movement." *Stanford Law Review* 62, no. 5 (2010): 1473–1512.

Tyler, Alice Felt. "Davis, Paulina Kellogg Wright." In *Notable American Women: 1607–1950*. Cambridge, Mass.: Harvard University Press, 1971. http://www.credoreference.com/entry/hupnawi/davis_paulina_kellogg_wright_aug_7_1813_aug_24_1876. Accessed 13 February 2013.

Underhill, Lois Beachy. *The Woman Who Ran for President: The Many Lives of Victoria Woodhull*. New York: Penguin Books, 1995.

Van Tyne, Claude Halstead, and Waldo Gifford Leland. *Guide to the Archives of the Government of the United States in Washington*. Washington, D.C.: Published by the Carnegie Institution of Washington, 1904.

Van Voris, Jacqueline. *Carrie Chapman Catt: A Public Life*. New York: Feminist Press at CUNY, 1996.

Vapnek, Laura. *Breadwinners: Working Women and Economic Independence*. Urbana: University of Illinois Press, 2009.

Venet, Wendy Hamand. *A Strong-Minded Woman: The Life of Mary Livermore*. Amherst: University of Massachusetts Press, 2005.

Wagner, Sally Roesch. *Matilda Joslyn Gage: She Who Holds the Sky*. Aberdeen, S.D.: Sky Carrier Press, 1998.

———. *A Time of Protest: Suffragists Challenge the Republic, 1870–1887*. Aberdeen, S.D.: Sky Carrier Press, 1992.

Walker, Alice. "Women." In *All the Women Are White, and All the Blacks Are Men, but Some of Us Are Brave*, edited by Gloria T. Hull, Patricia Bell Scott, and Barbara Smith. Old Westbury, N.Y.: Feminist Press, 1982.

Walter, Loretta Mae. "Woman Suffrage in Missouri, 1866–1880." Unpublished M.A. thesis, Washington University, 1963.

Walters, Lynne Masel. "A Burning Cloud by Day: The History and Content of the *Woman's Journal*." *Journalism History* (Winter 1977): 103–10.

———. "Their Rights and Nothing Less: A History of the Revolution." *Journalism Quarterly* (Summer 1976): 242–51.

———. "To Hustle with the Rowdies: The Organization and Function of the American Woman Suffrage Press." *Journal of American Culture* (Spring 1980): 167–84.

Wang, Xi. *The Trial of Democracy: Black Suffrage and Northern Republicans, 1860–1910*. Athens: University of Georgia Press, 1997.

Waugh, Joan. "Ulysses S. Grant: Historian." In *The Memory of the Civil War in American Culture*. Chapel Hill: University of North Carolina Press, 2004.

Weatherford, Doris. "Postwar Politics and the Fourteenth and Fifteenth Amendments." In vol. 1 of *Women in American Politics: History and Milestones*. Thousand Oaks, Calif.: CQ Press, 2012.

Welch, Gaylynn. "Local and National Forces Shaping the American Woman Suffrage Movement, 1870–1890." Ph.D. diss., Binghamton University, 2009.

Wellman, Judith. "'It's a Wide Community Indeed': Alliances and Issues in Creating

Woman's Rights National Historic Park, Seneca Falls, New York." In *Restoring Women's History through Historic Preservation*, edited by Gail Lee Dubrow and Jennifer B. Goodman. Baltimore, Md.: Johns Hopkins University Press, 2003.

———. *The Road to Seneca Falls: Elizabeth Cady Stanton and the First Woman's Rights Convention*. Urbana: University of Illinois Press, 2004.

———. "The Seneca Falls Women's Rights Convention: A Study of Social Networks." *Journal of Women's History* 3, no. 1 (Spring 1991): 9–37.

Welter, Barbara. "The Cult of True Womanhood: 1820–1860." *American Quarterly* 18, no. 2, part 1 (Summer 1966): 151–74.

Wilhite, Ann L. Wiegman. "Sixty-Five Years till Victory: A History of Woman Suffrage in Nebraska." *Nebraska History* 49 (Summer 1968): 149–63.

Workman, Courtney. "The Woman Movement: Memorial to Women's Rights Leaders and the Perceived Images of the Woman Movement." In *Myth, Memory, and the Making of the American Landscape*, edited by Paul A. Shackel. Gainesville: University Press of Florida, 2001.

Wright, Joanne H. *Origin Stories in Political Thought: Discourses on Gender, Power, and Citizenship*. Toronto: University of Toronto Press, 2004.

Yee, Shirley J. *Black Women Abolitionists: A Study in Activism, 1828–1860*. Knoxville: University of Tennessee Press, 1992.

Yellin, Jean Fagan. *Women and Sisters: The Antislavery Feminists in American Culture*. New Haven: Yale University Press, 1989.

Yellin, Jean Fagan, and John C. Van Horne, eds. *The Abolitionist Sisterhood: Women's Political Culture in Antebellum America*. Ithaca: Cornell University Press, 1994.

Young, Alfred F. *The Shoemaker and the Tea Party: Memory and the American Revolution*. Boston: Beacon Press, 1999.

Zaeske, Susan. *Signatures of Citizenship: Petitioning, Antislavery, and Women's Political Identity*. Chapel Hill: University of North Carolina Press, 2003.

Index

Abolitionists: Civil War end and, 8, 20; woman suffrage lack of support and, 21, 39–40, 122, 229 (n. 45); woman suffrage support and, 11, 12, 13, 21, 34, 35, 42, 139, 232–33 (n. 107); woman vs. African American suffrage support and, 21–22, 24, 27, 29, 38, 42; women as, 10, 11–12, 14, 15, 20, 21, 39–40, 121–22, 135. *See also* World's Anti-Slavery Convention

Abortion, 91, 222 (n. 100)

Abzug, Bella, 194

Adams, Abigail, 121

Adams, Herbert Baxter, 118

Adams, John, 121

Addams, Jane, 188

African Americans: civil rights after Civil War and, 20, 21, 24, 77, 135; Civil War memory and, 7–8, 38–39, 40, 229 (n. 36); support for woman suffrage and, 13, 21

African American suffrage: citizenship and, 20, 39; Fifteenth Amendment and, 27–28, 37, 153, 154; partial, 85; whittling away of, 1870s, 74, 98. *See also* Women's voting rights

African American women: *History of Woman Suffrage* and, 133–35; voting rights and, 21, 22, 29, 48–49, 84, 193, 206 (nn. 9, 13); woman suffrage movement and, 133–34, 193, 212 (nn. 20–21), 215 (n. 68), 246 (n. 24); women's rights and, 5, 14, 95–96, 197–98, 232 (n. 98)

Albany Times, 82

Alcohol, 76, 80, 85, 87–89

Alda, Alan, 195

American Anti-Slavery Society: disbandment, 37, 40; woman vs. African American suffrage support and, 21, 22, 206 (n. 9); women in, 11, 15

American Equal Rights Association (AERA): Fifteenth Amendment and, 28, 29, 30, 33, 39, 131; Kansas and, 22–24; Stanton and Anthony and, 19, 21, 23–27, 28–30, 31, 37, 131, 134, 136, 207 (n. 35), 209 (n. 74); woman vs. African American suffrage support and, 19, 22, 24, 25, 27, 28–30, 35, 134

American Historical Association, 118

American Revolution, 82, 121

American State Papers, 114

American Woman Suffrage Association, 63, 64, 72, 78, 83, 88, 95, 186, 244 (n. 14); calls for unification and, 35–37, 55, 155–56, 157–61, 237 (nn. 59, 61), 238 (nn. 71, 73–74); establishment of, 33–34, 214 (n. 48); Fifteenth Amendment and, 33, 34; *History of Woman Suffrage* and, 135–36, 137–38, 232 (n. 104); International Council of Women of 1888 and, 146, 151, 152, 153, 158–59; National Woman Suffrage Association and, 35–36, 37, 41, 44, 45, 137, 146, 155, 216 (n. 100); partial suffrage and, 84, 85, 86, 103, 158; Republican Party and, 67, 84, 216 (n. 100); Seneca Falls thirtieth anniversary and, 106–7; state associations and, 53, 54, 55, 214 (n. 48); state vs. federal approach and, 34, 60, 73, 74, 75, 102, 103, 136, 158, 208 (n. 52); unification and dissolution and, 162–64, 239 (n. 91). *See also* Stone, Lucy; *Woman's Journal*

Angelou, Maya, 193

Anniversaries for woman suffrage. *See* International Council of Women (ICW) of 1888; National Woman Suffrage Association; Nineteenth Amendment; Second Decade Convention of 1870; Seneca Falls convention of 1848; Worcester, Mass., national convention of 1850

Anthony, Mary, 179, 181

Anthony, Susan B.: archive for woman suffrage history and, 178, 181, 199, 242 (nn. 149, 152, 1–2); arrest for voting and, 67–68, 72, 73, 74, 97, 106, 237 (n. 50); autobiography of, 173, 177–80, 182, 242 (n. 148); biographies of, 10, 204 (n. 22);

7, 8, 17, 38–40, 130, 131–32, 229 (n. 36),
231 (n. 80); reform movement after, 6,
19–20, 61; women's work and, 47, 129
Claflin, Tennessee, 57
Clinton, Hillary Rodham, 198, 246 (n. 31)
Colby, Clara Bewick, 148, 151, 153, 161, 167,
171, 172, 176, 236 (n. 45), 237 (n. 50),
239–40 (n. 96)
Collins, Emily, 124
Collins, Jeannie, 93–94, 97
Colorado, 103, 175
Colored National Labor Convention of 1869,
49, 212 (n. 21)
Communist Manifesto (Marx), 57
Comstock, Anthony, 91
Comstock Law, 91, 222 (nn. 99–100)
Connecticut, 83
Contraception, 91
Couzins, Phoebe, 55, 100
Curtis, George William, 36

Daley, Charlotte F., 160
Davis, Paulina Wright, 5, 49, 211 (n. 3),
230 (n. 68); African American woman
suffrage and, 29, 133, 212 (nn. 19–20);
creating origin story, 43–44, 69; Second
Decade Convention of 1870 and, 37–38,
40–41, 42–43, 44–45, 69; Seneca Falls
mythology and, 44–45, 69, 179; Worcester, Mass., national convention and, 14,
69
Declaration of Independence, 12, 99, 100
Declaration of Rights for Women. *See*
Woman's Declaration of Rights
"Declaration of Sentiments," 179, 187;
demands of, 12–14; nonpreservation of,
69, 70; reprinting of, 70–71, 175; Seneca
Falls mythology and, 2, 16, 106, 111, 123,
193–94, 227 (n. 199); table written on,
12, 123, 174–75, 191–92, 241 (n. 135), 245
(n. 22)
Dickinson, Anna, 52
Divorce, 26, 45, 57, 207 (n. 23)
Douglass, Frederick, 21, 35, 63–64, 182;
African American suffrage and, 131, 154;
Seneca Falls convention of 1848 and, 13,
70, 110, 111, 150, 151–52, 186; support for
woman suffrage and, 13, 107, 151–52, 170,
236 (n. 40); woman vs. African American
suffrage support and, 28–29, 30
Downing, George T., 19
Dred Scott decision, 23
Du Bois, W. E. B., 182

Eighty Years and More (Stanton), 176, 178,
227 (n. 199), 241 (n. 141)
Elizabeth Cady Stanton Foundation, 195
Emancipation, 8, 17, 27, 38–39, 40, 60, 132
Eminent Women of the Age (Parton), 45
Equal Rights Amendment (ERA), 190, 196
Equal Rights Party, 63, 64
European immigrants, 92

Feminine Mystique, The (Friedan), 4
Feminism, 2, 3; first- and second-waves and,
198–99, 246 (n. 34); myth of Seneca Falls
convention as beginning of, 4, 193, 203–4
(n. 20). *See also* Woman suffrage movement; Women's rights movement
Ferry, Thomas W., 100
Fifteenth Amendment: African Ameri-
can suffrage and, 27–28, 37, 153, 154;
American Equal Rights Association and,
28, 29, 30, 33, 39, 131; American Woman
Suffrage Association and, 33, 34; New
Departure and, 58–59, 60; ratification of,
38; Stanton and Anthony and, 28, 29–30,
31–33, 103, 122, 131, 153–54, 193, 232–33
(n. 107); U.S. Congress and, 27–28; voting
rights and, 31–32, 75, 130
Fifth Avenue Convention, 35
Flagg, Marietta, 83
Foltz, Clara, 165
Ford, Betty, 194
Foster, Abby Kelley. *See* Kelley Foster, Abby
Foster, Rachel, 147, 148, 155, 159, 172, 238
(n. 78), 240 (n. 124)
Foster, Stephen, 22, 27, 28, 83
Fourteenth Amendment, 23, 37, 39, 58, 130
Fowler and Wells, 141
Free love, 57, 60, 64, 67, 75–76, 80, 89–91,
94
Friedan, Betty, 4, 194

Gage, Frances Dana, 105, 133, 226 (n. 172)
Gage, Matilda Joslyn, 68, 170, 171, 176, 177,
182; archive for woman suffrage history
and, 115–16, 242 (nn. 149, 2); calls for
unification in movement and, 156, 157,
160–61, 238 (n. 77), 239 (n. 81); centennial celebration of United States and, 98,
99, 100, 114, 223 (n. 143), 224 (n. 151);
history of woman suffrage movement
and, 101, 203 (n. 17); National American
Woman Suffrage Association leadership
and, 164–65, 166, 167, 239–40 (n. 96);
National Citizen and Ballot Box and,

Anthony leadership and, 63, 64, 66, 68–69, 74, 89; calls for unification and, 35–37, 55, 155–56, 157–61, 237 (n. 61), 238 (nn. 69, 71, 73, 76–78), 239 (n. 81); centennial celebration of United States and, 98–102, 112, 114, 223 (nn. 142–43), 223–24 (n. 149), 224 (nn. 151–52, 154); establishment of, 31, 33, 207 (n. 35); *History of Woman Suffrage* and, 136, 137, 140, 155; International Council of Women of 1888 and, 145–47, 151, 153, 158–59, 236 (n. 45); newspaper and, 31, 34, 35, 36, 108, 128; Second Decade Convention of 1870 and, 41, 43–45; Seneca Falls thirtieth anniversary and, 104–8, 109, 225 (n. 166), 226 (nn. 169, 175, 185); Seneca Falls twenty-fifth anniversary and, 46, 69–73, 74, 87, 217 (n. 134); Sixteenth Amendment proposal and, 33, 74, 97–98, 102–3, 114; Stanton and Anthony and, 31, 33, 35, 46, 52–53, 55, 56, 64, 104, 211 (nn. 5–6); state associations and, 53, 54, 55, 85; state vs. federal approach and, 43, 53, 68, 74, 84, 86, 97–99, 102–4, 136, 158, 208 (n. 52), 228 (n. 34); unification and dissolution and, 162–64, 239 (n. 91); women's rights history and, 101–2; Woodhull and, 60, 64, 66, 89, 90
National Woman Suffrage Association of Massachusetts. *See* Massachusetts Woman Suffrage Association
National Women's Conference of 1977, 193
National Women's Rights Convention of 1853, 16
Nebraska, 77–78, 141, 148, 233 (n. 121)
Nevada, 48, 81
New Departure, 56, 57–60, 67–68, 73–74, 76, 79, 82, 84, 219 (n. 51)
New England Anti-Slavery Society, 27
New England Free Love League, 91
New England Woman's Club, 94
New England Woman Suffrage Association (NEWSA), 27, 33, 78, 85
New England Women's Club, 93
New Jersey, 59, 77, 99, 124
New Mexico, 81
New York City, 1, 33, 49–50, 65, 69, 93, 94
New York Herald, 139
New York State, 5, 14, 40, 77, 83, 84, 142, 185, 194, 220 (nn. 61, 67); *History of Woman Suffrage* and, 124, 125, 127
New York Sun, 119
New York Times, 47, 192
Nichols, Mary Gove, 5

Nineteenth Amendment, 187, 192, 225 (n. 164); ratification of, 185–86; Seneca Falls mythology and, 186, 198, 243 (n. 12); seventy-fifth anniversary and, 196
North Dakota, 81, 219 (n. 38)
Northern Iowa Woman Suffrage Association, 48
"Northern Reconstruction," 92
North Star, 70
Northwestern Woman Suffrage Association, 55, 78, 214 (n. 54)

Obama, Michelle, 197–98
Oberlin College, 15, 152–53
Ohio, 77, 78, 87, 91, 105, 124, 133
Oregon, 81
Organization of American Historians, 196

Pacific Slope Convention, 55, 214 (n. 56)
Parks, Rosa, 4, 198
Partial suffrage, 84–86, 103, 158, 169, 175, 220–21 (n. 74), 233 (n. 121), 238 (n. 69)
Parton, James, 45
Paul, Alice, 185, 188, 190, 196, 244 (n. 17), 245 (n. 21)
Peckham, Lillie, 54, 214 (n. 48)
"People's Convention" (Chicago), 55–56, 214 (n. 61)
"People's Convention" (Union Association), 62, 215 (n. 81)
"People's Party," 61, 227 (n. 198)
Philips, Wendell, 21, 22, 206 (n. 9)
Pillsbury, Parker, 22, 36
Pioneer, 88
Portrait Monument, 188, 189–90, 191, 192, 196–98, 244 (n. 18), 246 (nn. 30–31)
Post, Amy, 70, 106, 217 (n. 128), 226 (n. 175)
Presidential election of 1872, 60, 64, 65, 66–68, 72, 216 (nn. 100–101)
Presidential election of 1876, 98, 102
Presidential suffrage, 84–85, 220–21 (n. 74)
Purvis, Harriet, 21, 22
Purvis, Robert, 21, 153

Quakers, 12, 70

Racism, 28–29, 130–32, 153–54, 231 (n. 87), 236 (n. 46)
Reagan, Ronald, 195
Reconstruction: African American civil rights and, 20, 21, 24, 77, 135; "Northern Reconstruction," 92; women's voting rights and, 48, 49, 77, 135, 212 (n. 19)

Republican Party and, 26–27, 67–68, 79; Seneca Falls convention of 1848 event and, 13, 69, 105, 186, 187, 192, 194, 209 (n. 74), 226 (n. 174), 245 (n. 23); Seneca Falls mythology and, 2, 12, 44–45, 176, 177, 185, 190, 217 (n. 130), 227 (n. 199); Seneca Falls woman suffrage resolution and, 13, 44, 107, 110, 150, 151–52, 153–54, 187, 202 (n. 2); *Woman's Bible* and, 170, 171–73, 241 (n. 142); Woman's National Liberation Union and, 165–66, 239–40 (n. 96); woman suffrage history and, 109, 227 (n. 193), 227 (nn. 2, 4); women's rights history and, 15–16, 73, 205 (n. 42); World's Anti-Slavery Convention and, 10–11, 121–22, 184, 229 (n. 45). See also *History of Woman Suffrage*; Stanton and Anthony and women's rights

Stanton, Harriot, 187, 233 (n. 124), 245 (n. 23)

Stanton, Henry, 10, 12

Stanton, Theodore, 187, 192, 245 (n. 23)

Stanton and Anthony and women's rights: alliance with Train and, 24–26, 27, 28, 216 (n. 100); American Equal Rights Association and, 21, 23–27, 28–30, 31, 37, 131, 134, 136, 207 (n. 35), 209 (n. 74); Beecher affair and, 64, 65–66, 68, 79–80, 94; beginnings and, 6–7, 14; calls for unification of woman suffrage movement and, 35–36, 155–56, 157–60; centennial celebration of United States and, 99–102, 114, 223 (n. 147), 223–24 (n. 149), 224 (nn. 151–52); after Civil War, 7, 15, 47; creating histories and, 8–9, 76–77; Fifteenth Amendment and, 28, 29–30, 31–33, 103, 122, 131, 153–54, 193, 232–33 (n. 107); history of woman suffrage movement and, 72–73, 101–2, 108–11, 112–13, 196, 204 (n. 22), 224 (n. 152); International Council of Women of 1888 and, 145–46, 147, 148, 149–51, 178, 235–36 (n. 28); leadership of movement and, 33, 50–51, 55, 56, 71, 72–73, 125, 152, 154–55, 162–66, 211 (n. 8), 217 (n. 123); National Woman Suffrage Association and, 31, 33, 35, 46, 52–53, 55, 56, 64, 104, 211 (nn. 5–6); newcomers to women's rights and, 47, 48, 50, 52, 72, 211 (nn. 5–6); *Revolution* and, 25, 27, 28, 31, 35, 93; Second Decade Convention of 1870 and, 41–42, 43, 69, 210 (n. 110); Seneca Falls fiftieth anniversary and, 173,

174–80; Seneca Falls fortieth anniversary and, 145–55; Seneca Falls origin myth and, 7, 9–10, 16, 47, 76, 105–6, 109–10, 111, 145–46, 147, 149, 150–52, 168, 173, 175, 180, 198; Seneca Falls thirtieth anniversary and, 104–8; Seneca Falls twenty-fifth anniversary and, 46, 69–70, 71–73, 217 (nn. 121, 128, 130); Sixteenth Amendment proposal and, 32–33, 34, 43, 59–60, 74, 97–98, 102–4, 109, 114, 128, 225 (nn. 164–65); state associations and, 48, 50, 75, 78–80, 81, 82, 141, 214 (n. 54); Lucy Stone and, 65, 78, 136, 137, 138; tax revolts and, 84, 220 (nn. 54, 61); Woodhull and, 60, 61, 62–63, 64, 65, 79, 89, 136, 216 (n. 100), 227 (n. 198); Worcester, Mass., national convention and, 44. See also *History of Woman Suffrage*; National Woman Suffrage Association; Woman suffrage movement

State constitutions after Civil War, 77–78, 80, 218 (n. 9), 219 (n. 26)

"Statement of Facts, A: Private," 160–61, 239 (n. 81), 239–40 (n. 96)

Stevens, Emily Pitts, 88

Stewart, Maria, 14

Stone, Lucy, 32, 86, 94, 102, 122; American Equal Rights Association and, 21, 22, 24, 25, 29, 30, 37; American Woman Suffrage Association and, 33–34, 35, 36, 41, 44, 54, 60, 78; calls for unification in movement and, 155–56, 162; *History of Woman Suffrage* and, 116, 119–20, 126, 135–37, 138, 145, 186, 243 (n. 7); importance of, in early women's rights, 5, 15, 45, 153, 186, 244 (n. 14); International Council of Women of 1888 and, 147, 148, 150, 151, 152, 236 (n. 45); leadership of movement and, 55, 56, 71; National American Woman Suffrage Association leadership and, 162, 163–64, 166, 239 (n. 90); National Woman Suffrage Association and, 31, 33, 207 (n. 35); Second Decade Convention of 1870 and, 43, 44; Seneca Falls mythology and, 70, 76, 108, 145–46, 147, 152, 153, 168, 180, 186; Stanton and Anthony and, 65, 78, 136, 137, 138; tax revolts and, 83, 99; Worcester, Mass., national convention and, 15, 44, 108, 168–69; on wrong side of history and, 43, 71, 111, 179, 186, 240 (n. 107), 243 (n. 7)

Stone Blackwell, Alice, 155, 175, 186

Stowe, Harriet Beecher, 50, 133
Sumner, Charles, 20
Susan B. Anthony Calendar, 192, 242 (n. 152)

Tax revolts, 82–84, 219 (n. 51), 220 (nn. 54, 58, 61, 67)
Tennessee, 186
Terborg-Penn, Rosalyn, 49
Tilton, Elizabeth, 64, 65–66
Tilton, Theodore, 35, 36, 45, 65, 70–71, 209 (n. 65)
Train, George Francis, 24, 27, 28, 136, 216 (n. 100)
Truth, Sojourner, 21, 22, 107, 133–34, 197–98, 246 (n. 31)
Tucker, C. DeLores, 197
Tyson, Cicely, 197

Una, 41, 230 (n. 68)
Uncle Tom's Cabin (Stowe), 133
Union Woman Suffrage Association, 53, 65; convention of 1870, 41, 212 (n. 27); convention of 1871, 50, 56, 59–60; convention of 1872, 61–63, 64; establishment of, 36–37; Second Decade Convention of 1870 and, 41, 43
United Nations, 193
U.S. Congress: Comstock Law, 91, 222 (nn. 99–100); declaratory act for woman suffrage and, 59, 60; federal amendment for woman suffrage and, 155, 185–86, 237 (n. 54); federal interference in states' rights and, 59, 97–99, 223 (n. 133); Fifteenth Amendment and, 27–28, 59, 131; Fourteenth Amendment and, 23; House Judiciary Committee advocating women's enfranchisement, 56, 57–59, 74, 215 (nn. 66, 74); monument of women in suffrage movement and, 188–89, 191, 192, 196–98, 244 (nn. 17–18), 244–45 (n. 19), 245 (n. 20), 246 (nn. 30–31); Senate Committee on Woman Suffrage and, 119, 228 (n. 34); Sixteenth Amendment proposal and, 32–33, 97–98, 102–4, 225 (nn. 164–65); taxation and women's voting rights and, 84
U.S. Constitution, 180; Fifteenth Amendment and, 31–32, 37; Fourteenth Amendment and, 23, 37; Nineteenth Amendment and, 186
U.S. Supreme Court, 136, 222 (n. 100); Dred Scott decision, 23; *Minor v. Happersett*, 73–74, 77, 81, 97, 98, 220 (n. 67)

United Suffrage Associations, 155
Universal Franchise Association, 85
Utah, 34, 48, 77, 155, 175, 223 (n. 133), 241 (n. 136)

Vanderbilt, Cornelius, 57
Vaughn, Hester, 26
Vermont, 81
Vindication of the Rights of Woman, A (Wollstonecraft), 3
Voting rights: citizenship and, 20, 73–74, 220 (n. 67); Fifteenth Amendment and, 31–32, 75, 130; property rights and, 77, 82, 86; universal suffrage and, 21–22, 25, 28, 65, 129, 130, 132–33, 214 (n. 61). *See also* African American suffrage; Woman suffrage movement; Women's voting rights
Voting Rights Act of 1965, 193

Waisbrooker, Lois, 90
Wall, Sarah, 83
Wall Street, 57
War of the Rebellion, The: A Compilation of the Official Records of the Union and Confederate Armies, 113
Warren, Mercy Otis, 121
Washington D.C., 49, 84, 85, 131, 148
Washington Star, 154, 174, 180
Washington Territory, 59, 77, 155
Washington Times, 184, 190
Watt, James, 195
Western Woman Suffrage Association, 54
Western Women's Emancipation Society, 91
White supremacy, 8, 17, 38, 39, 98; women's voting rights and, 24, 49, 135
Whittier, John Greenleaf, 38
Wilbour, Charlotte Beebe, 36, 94, 95
Willard, Frances, 89, 162, 165, 176
Williams, E. Faye, 197
Wilson, Woodrow, 185
Wisconsin, 54
Wollstonecraft, Mary, 3, 109
Woman's Anti-Tax Paying League of San Francisco, 83
Woman's Bible, 170, 171–73, 241 (n. 142)
Woman's Christian Temperance Union (WCTU): African American women and, 96; creation and success of, 87–89, 162; partial suffrage and, 85, 158, 238 (n. 69); religious conservatism and, 156–57, 165; woman suffrage and, 76, 89, 91, 102–3, 156–57, 165, 176, 183

Convention of 1866, 1, 2–3; newspapers and, 24–26, 28, 29, 31, 34, 35, 41, 57, 105; property rights and, 14, 40–41, 123, 127, 230 (n. 66); sexuality and, 26, 41, 57, 64–65, 66, 76, 80, 90, 91; speaking publicly and, 11, 15, 51–53, 213 (n. 34); suffrage as main right and, 109–11, 156–57; temperance and, 87–89, 127, 149, 176, 221 (n. 90), 230 (n. 68); women abolitionists and, 11–12, 14, 15; working-class women and, 91–95. *See also* Seneca Falls convention of 1848; Stanton and Anthony and women's rights; Woman suffrage movement; Worcester, Mass., national convention of 1850

Women's Rights National Historical Park, 4, 195–96

Women's sexuality, 57; controlling own bodies and, 26, 41, 76, 90, 91; double standard regarding, 64–65, 66, 80, 90. *See also* Free love

Women's Tea Parties, 83

Women's voting rights: vs. African American suffrage and, 7, 19–20, 21–22, 24–26, 35, 38, 42, 49, 107, 129, 131, 132, 153, 206 (nn. 9, 13), 212 (n. 19); citizenship and, 23, 58, 59, 60; disagreement on goal of, after Civil War, 6, 8, 19–20, 21, 43, 205 (n. 1); educated women and, 19, 22, 24, 25, 28, 29, 130–32, 133, 134–35, 153–54, 231 (n. 87), 232 (n. 98), 236 (n. 46); federal amendment for woman suffrage and, 155, 185–86, 237 (n. 54); federal interference in states' rights and, 59, 97–99, 223 (n. 133); Nineteenth Amendment and, 185–86, 187, 192, 196, 198, 225 (n. 164), 243 (n. 12); public opinion and, 51–52, 53, 65, 68, 81, 97; Reconstruction in South and, 48, 49, 77, 212 (n. 19); state constitutions after Civil War and, 77–78, 218 (n. 9); women's direct action voting and, 59, 60, 66–68, 139–40, 142, 215 (n. 68), 218 (n. 139), 233 (n. 112); Wyoming and Utah and, 34, 48, 77, 155, 175, 223 (n. 133), 241 (n. 136). *See also* African

American suffrage; Seneca Falls convention of 1848; Woman suffrage movement

Woodhull, Canning, 57

Woodhull, Victoria Claflin, 56–59, 136; addressing Congress and, 56, 57–59, 74, 215 (nn. 66, 74); arrest for obscenity and, 65, 91; Beecher affair and, 64–66, 216 (n. 96); free love and, 57, 60, 64, 67, 89–90, 94; National Woman Suffrage Association and, 60, 64, 66, 89, 90; New Departure and, 56, 57–59, 219 (n. 51); "People's Convention" and, 62–63; "People's Party" and, 61, 227 (n. 198); as presidential candidate and, 63–64; as scandalous for conservative suffragists, 78, 79, 80, 82, 90, 94, 216 (n. 100)

Woodhull & Claflin's Weekly, 57, 64, 89, 90, 91, 216 (n. 96)

Worcester, Mass., Anti-Tax Convention, 83

Worcester, Mass., national convention of 1850, 5, 14; commemorative events and, 37–38, 41, 69, 108, 168–69, 210 (n. 110); origin myth of women's rights movement and, 17, 37, 41, 42, 45, 46, 69, 71, 152, 168, 243–44 (n. 13); Stanton and Anthony and, 44; Lucy Stone and, 15, 44, 108, 168–69

Working Women's Association (WWA), 93

World's Anti-Slavery Convention: exclusion of women and, 2, 3, 10–11, 12, 45, 121, 229 (n. 45); nonrelationship to Seneca Falls, 3, 12, 16, 45, 121–22, 139; origin myth of women's rights movement and, 2, 3, 16, 121–22, 150, 184

World's Congress of Representative Women of 1893, 169

Wright, Frances, 121

Wright, Martha Coffin, 12, 46, 50, 68, 69, 72, 109, 122, 217 (n. 134)

Wright, Paulina. *See* Davis, Paulina Wright

Wyoming, 34, 175

Young Men's Suffrage League, 49–50, 212 (n. 25)